VISUAL QUICKSTART GUIDE

MACROMEDIA
DIRECTOR MX

FOR WINDOWS AND MACINTOSH

Andre Persidsky and Mark Schaeffer

 **Peachpit Press**

Visual QuickStart Guide
Macromedia Director MX for Windows and Macintosh: Visual QuickStart Guide
Andre Persidsky and Mark Schaeffer

Peachpit Press
1249 Eighth Street
Berkeley, CA 94710
510/524-2178
800/283-9444
510/524-2221 (fax)

Find us on the World Wide Web at: http://www.peachpit.com
To report errors, please send a note to errata@peachpit.com
Peachpit Press is a division of Pearson Education

Editor: Karen Reichstein
Production Coordinator: Gloria Márquez
Copyeditor: Sally Zahner
Compositor: Owen Wolfson
Indexer: Joy Dean Lee
Cover design: The Visual Group

ISBN 0-321-19399-7

9 8 7 6 5 4 3 2 1

Printed and bound in the United States of America

Thank You

Debra Goldentyer, my wife, for her love, patience, and support in this and in all things.

Brad Hartfield, my good friend, for his unstinting encouragement, and for inadvertently introducing me to Director many years ago.

Karen Reichstein, my editor; Marjorie Baer, Sally Zahner, Gloria Márquez and the other dedicated people at Peachpit Press whose skill, high standards, professionalism, and good sense have made this project much better than I'd imagined it could be.

Andre Persidsky, who wrote all the previous editions of this book, for providing a solid foundation to build upon in expanding this book for Director MX.

— Mark Schaeffer

Special thanks to the following organizations for making artwork available for Chapter 6 of this book: the CD-ROM title *People in the Past, The Ancient Puebloan Farmers of Southwest Colorado*

Public Land Interpretive Association
6501 4th Street NW, Suite 1
Albuquerque, NM 87107

Produced for:
Anasazi Heritage Center Bureau of Land Management
27501 Highway 184
Dolores, CO 81323
970-882-4811 (to order the CD-ROM, call)

Produced by:
Paradox Productions
PO Box 331
Bluff, Utah 84512
435-672-2205

and
Living Earth Studios, Inc.
PO Box 317 Bluff, UT 84512
435-672-2277

TABLE OF CONTENTS

INTRODUCTION

When a simple animation program called VideoWorks first appeared on Macintosh desktops in 1985, no one expected that—under the name of Macromedia Director—it would evolve into the leading tool for creating interactive multimedia. Over the years, Director has been a pioneer in giving creative people the tools and the framework they needed to bring their ideas to life and distribute them in an increasing variety of formats, from floppy disks to CD-ROMs, DVD-ROMs, and Web pages.

Director MX, the latest version of Macromedia's all-purpose authoring program, allows you to combine images, text, sounds, music, video, and even 3D objects into fully interactive "movies" that put the user in control. Its capability to handle all sorts of media allows you to repurpose content—for example, to distribute an interactive presentation as a stand-alone CD-ROM and also as a streaming Shockwave movie—with a minimum of effort.

Who Uses Director?

Director is one of those rare pieces of software that has something to offer to almost everyone. Its intuitive, time-based interface allows new users to begin creating simple animations almost immediately. But Director's feature set is broad and flexible enough for professional developers to use it to create content for nearly every imaginable distribution channel. Director's scripting language, Lingo, allows nonprogrammers to add interactivity to movies using basic English commands. Yet Lingo is sophisticated enough to allow experienced programmers to do almost anything that can be done in more mainstream programming languages.

In short, the possible uses for Director are limited only by your imagination. Here are just a few of the kinds of people who typically work with Director:

◆ **Animators** use it to create animation for output to videotape or streaming Web movies.

◆ **Web developers** use it to add motion, sound, interactivity, and data-processing capability to their Web pages.

◆ **Game and entertainment developers** use it to create single-user games for distribution on CD- or DVD-ROM, or multiuser online games.

◆ **Educators** use it to create interactive learning and testing materials for distribution over the Web or on CD.

◆ **Software developers** use it to create working models of applications, allowing them to demonstrate and fine-tune the interface or the "look and feel" of products that are still in development.

◆ **Software publishers** use it to create tutorials for their products, or to guide users through the installation process.

◆ **Business people** use it to create presentations and training materials.

◆ **Artists** use it to create multimedia artwork.

◆ **Exhibit designers** use it to create touchscreen kiosks that provide instant information for tourists, museum visitors, or conference attendees.

◆ **Consultants** use it for just about anything. Does a rug store need an interactive catalog that will help buyers choose colors and patterns? Does an acupuncturist need a way to illustrate the flow of *qi* through various parts of the body? If a particular application can't be bought "off the shelf," a good consultant can always find a way to build it in Director.

Director's Place in the MX Family

In 2002, Macromedia began to release new versions of its products with the designation MX in place of a version number. (In case you're wondering, the initials don't stand for anything; Macromedia's marketing department just thought "MX" sounded cool.) Macromedia Flash MX came first, followed by Dreamweaver MX, ColdFusion MX, and Fireworks MX. Macromedia bundled all four MX products (along with FreeHand, not yet upgraded to MX status) into a single package called Macromedia Studio MX, intended to serve as a tightly integrated set of tools for the creation of media-rich, data-driven Web sites and Web applications.

Director's conspicuous absence from the package didn't come as much of a shock, given that much of the role previously played by Director in the development of interactive, multimedia Web sites had gradually been taken over by Flash. With Flash offering multimedia authoring and interactive scripting capability, Dreamweaver providing the HTML and JavaScript framework, Fireworks doing the image processing, and ColdFusion providing integration with databases, the MX family seemed to be complete without Director.

It therefore surprised many observers when, months after the release of Studio MX, Macromedia unveiled an MX version of Director. Though largely unchanged from the previous version, Director MX does sport the hallmarks of an MX product: a new, screen-friendly interface and integration with other MX products. If nothing else, the release of Director MX reaffirmed Macromedia's commitment to Director. It also reflected Macromedia's acknowledgment—despite its having positioned itself as the prophet of "what the Web can be"—that not all multimedia development is intended exclusively for the Internet.

Director has not been bundled into Studio MX, and it's unlikely that it will be. The Studio MX applications are designed to work together seamlessly, almost as though they're a single application. Director has close operational ties to Flash, and it offers round-trip editing capability with Fireworks as well, but its relationships with Dreamweaver and ColdFusion are strictly arm's-length. For the most part, Director remains what it always was: a stand-alone application that works well with all kinds of media and all kinds of hardware. Though officially a member of the MX family, Director might best be considered a distant cousin, continuing to do its own thing in its own way.

WHO USES DIRECTOR?

Director Compared with Flash

In the mid-1990s, when the Web replaced CD-ROMs as the primary means for delivering multimedia content, Macromedia saw both a problem and an opportunity. The problem was that the Web demanded quickly downloadable, low-overhead files, which Director movies certainly were not. The opportunity was that the Web at that time was a basically static environment that cried out for the kinds of movement, richness, and interactivity that were Macromedia's specialty.

Macromedia responded by developing Shockwave technology, which allowed Director movies to be compressed, streamed over the Internet, and played back transparently by means of a plug-in in the user's Web browser. At the same time, Macromedia hedged its bet by acquiring a simple, third-party product that came to be named Macromedia Flash. Flash could do some of the same things Director could do, but had been designed from the beginning to meet the demands of the Web.

Flash rose quickly in popularity. For developers, it offered a streamlined interface and the ability to create amazingly tiny files. For Web users, it offered a browser plug-in that was much smaller and faster to download than the Shockwave player required by Director. As Flash became more and more popular, Macromedia added more and more features to it—most significantly ActionScript, a scripting language that eventually acquired many of the same capabilities as Director's Lingo. The unfortunate result was that Macromedia now had two products with a largely overlapping feature set, and developers had no clear-cut way to decide whether to develop a project in Director or Flash.

In many ways, Flash has won out, and for good reasons: Flash is designed to use vector graphics, which are often much faster to download than the bit-mapped graphics that Director prefers to use. Flash's scripting language, ActionScript, is closely related to JavaScript and is therefore more comfortable than Lingo for many Web developers. Flash has a much larger installed base (98% of U.S. Web users have the Flash plug-in, as opposed to only 63% who have Shockwave). Flash's retail price is significantly lower than Director's. And on top of everything else, there is the intangible but very real "coolness" factor: At least for the time being, Flash is, Director isn't.

Why would anyone want to use Director?

If you're developing exclusively for the Web, it probably makes sense to use Flash and the other MX Studio applications. But if you plan to use other distribution channels—either instead of or in addition to the Web—Director can still do a lot of things that Flash can't:

◆ **For many people, Director is easier to use.** While Director's interface is similar to Flash's, it is in many ways more flexible and more forgiving. And for people who have no scripting or programming experience, Lingo—with its ability to use plain-English syntax—is often easier to learn than ActionScript.

◆ **Director offers superior bitmap handling.** Vector graphics may be faster to download, but many kinds of visual material—particularly photographs—still require the kinds of subtlety and fluidity offered only by bitmaps. Director is significantly more bitmap-friendly than Flash, particularly in its ability to use alpha channels for smooth compositing.

◆ **Director works better with digital video.** The ability to use digital video was added to Flash only recently, with the release of Flash MX. Flash is comfortable with only small bits of video, using only a single compression method. Director can handle big or long video files in a variety of formats.

◆ **Director accepts more types of media.** If your multimedia content exists in a digital format, chances are that Director can import it and work with it. The most noteworthy example is the ability to import 3D models, added in Director 8.5. But there are many other data types that are at least as useful. (Try importing a PowerPoint presentation into Flash!)

◆ **Director movies are more accessible.** Both Flash MX and Director MX have new features that make their movies accessible to visually impaired users. But unlike Flash, whose accessibility features are designed to work only with third-party screen-reader software, Director has text-to-speech and keyboard navigation features that require no special software on the user's computer.

◆ **Director remains the tool of choice for CD- and DVD-ROM development.** While the Web gets all the attention these days, much multimedia development is still aimed at "fixed media" such as CD-ROM, DVD-ROM, and the hard drives of computer-based kiosks. For these applications, Director still offers a wide array of features—such as advanced memory management and the ability to interact directly with external hardware and software—that are not even dreamed of in Flash.

◆ **Director is infinitely extensible.** If there are features you need that aren't built into Director, chances are you can add them by means of an Xtra. Xtras are Photoshop-style plug-ins that expand the capabilities of Director. If the Xtra you need isn't available off the shelf, you can find third-party developers who can create custom Xtras to meet your needs.

DIRECTOR COMPARED WITH FLASH

What's New in Director MX

Director MX is a relatively minor update from the previous version, Director 8.5. Instead of adding significant new features, Director MX focuses on making Director compatible with the latest standards in hardware and software, and in helping it work more closely with other members of the MX family of products. Here are the most noteworthy improvements:

◆ Director is now more tightly integrated with Flash. Director MX can import Flash MX files and control them with Lingo. In addition, Flash MX can be launched from within Director MX to allow seamless editing of imported Flash cast members.

◆ Director now shares common interface elements (such as dockable panels and an online "Answers" window) with Macromedia's other MX products, allowing users to keep the same work habits when moving from application to application.

◆ The Macintosh version of Director is now Mac OS X–native. (Although Director MX will run only under OS X, Director movies created in OS X can still be played on Macs that use the Classic OS.)

◆ Director's new text-to-speech, keyboard navigation, and captioning features allow movies to meet accessibility guidelines for sight- and hearing-impaired users.

◆ Several tools within Director, such as the message window and the debugger, have been improved, and a new object inspector has been added.

◆ Director now works with Macromedia's advanced server technologies to allow the creation of multiuser games and collaborative environments; and Director can now use the Flash Remoting Service to create data-driven Web sites in collaboration with ColdFusion MX. (These features are noted here for the sake of completeness, but they are beyond the scope of this book.)

Director's interface remains easy to use, allowing beginners to create exciting, media-rich projects without a steep learning curve. Using Director MX and this book, you'll soon be able to:

◆ Create, import, and manage the collection of multimedia elements—images, music, and so on—that form the heart of your multimedia project.

◆ Animate your drawings, photos, text, and other visual elements, and synchronize your animation with sound, music, and video.

◆ Use Director's library of behaviors to add interactivity to your movie.

◆ Create extruded text and other 3D elements, and import 3D models from other programs.

◆ Create a standalone "projector" file, suitable for CD- or DVD-ROM.

◆ Produce a Shockwave-format file for distributing over the Internet.

◆ Use new features in Director MX to make your movie accessible to users with visual or hearing impairments.

◆ Use Xtras, add-on modules that provide extra features.

◆ Introduce yourself to Lingo, Director's scripting language.

Using This Book

The Visual QuickStart Guide format is intended to get you working with the software immediately, without having to read long-winded explanations.

This book assumes that you've already mastered the basic skills for using your computer: clicking and dragging with the mouse, choosing items from menus, and so forth. Given that Director is a multimedia authoring program, it's also assumed that you have at least minimal experience working with basic media formats, such as image, sound, and text files. From that starting point, how you can make the best use of this book will depend on your level of experience and on your preferred style of working.

If You're a Beginner

If you're new to the process of multimedia authoring, or if you're the kind of person who likes to approach things in logical, linear fashion, your best bet is to start at the beginning of the book, learning the most basic Director techniques, and work your way to the end, by which time you'll have acquired the skills to create a full-featured, interactive movie. The book is structured to support this type of learning: Each chapter builds on the skills and concepts that were introduced previously, and no chapter assumes that you have knowledge of anything in a later chapter.

If You Have Some Experience

If you've used earlier versions of Director, or if you have experience with similar multimedia authoring programs (such as Flash), you might prefer to treat this book as a task-based reference. Use the table of contents, thumb tabs, or index to find the topic you're interested in, and then go directly to the applicable pages. Although learning a particular skill or completing a particular task

may require that you understand the relevant concepts and vocabulary, no set of instructions directly depends on your having completed any previous set of instructions. In many cases, the illustrations alone may give you the information you need to accomplish what you're trying to do.

If You're a Flash User

Many new Director users these days are people who already have some experience with Flash but are moving over to Director for some of the reasons listed earlier. If you're in that category, you may be confused by a number of Director features that seem similar to those in Flash but in fact operate differently.

To help you make the transition from Flash to Director, this book contains a number of sidebars just for you. These shaded boxes with the heading "Flash Talk" will succinctly compare the functionality of corresponding features in Director and Flash—explaining, for example, the differences between the Score and the Timeline, or between the Cast Window and the Library.

Cross-Platform Issues and System Requirements

Director MX for Windows and Director MX for Macintosh differ very little. In the few cases that some techniques are performed slightly differently in Windows and on the Mac, a step has one method for Mac and one for Windows.

Even rarer are tasks that differ completely on the two types of computers. In those cases, the platform to which a particular set of instructions applies will appear in parentheses in the heading for the task. For example, only the Macintosh can record sounds into Director, so there is a task called "To record a sound in Director (Mac)."

WHAT'S NEW IN DIRECTOR MX

Illustrations

The screen shots that illustrate the tasks in this book come from both Mac and Windows versions of Director MX. If a task is performed differently on the Mac and in Windows, there will usually be two screen shots, one for each platform. If a task is performed the same way on both platforms, the accompanying screen shot will be taken arbitrarily from one version or the other.

Modifier Keys

Modifier keys for keyboard shortcut commands differ on the Mac and in Windows. In Windows, the keys used are Shift, Ctrl, and Alt. These correspond to the Shift, Command, and Option keys on Mac. Instructions for each task will include the modifier keys for both platforms, as in "Hold the Alt key (Windows) or Option key (Mac) while dragging the Lasso."

Menus

Mac OS X, the required operating system for the Macintosh version of Director MX, has a new menu structure that is slightly different from that of Windows (and, for that matter, from that of previous versions of the Mac OS). In cases where the location of a menu item is different on the two platforms, the instructions will include both menu paths—for example, "Choose Edit > Preferences > General (Windows) or Director > Preferences > General (Mac) to open the General Preferences dialog box."

System Requirements

To run Director MX, your system must meet these requirements:

Windows requirements

◆ Intel Pentium II processor or higher

◆ Windows 98 SE, Windows 2000, or Windows XP

◆ 128 MB or more of free system RAM

◆ 1024 x 768, 16-bit (or better) color display

◆ 100 MB of available disk space

◆ CD-ROM drive

Recommended:

◆ Microsoft DirectX 5.2 or OpenGL

◆ 3D accelerator

Macintosh requirements

◆ Power Macintosh with PowerPC processor

◆ Mac OS 10.1.2 or later

◆ 128 MB or more of free system RAM

◆ 1024 x 768, 16-bit (or better) color display

◆ 100 MB of available disk space

◆ CD-ROM drive

Recommended:

◆ G3 processor or better

◆ Mac OS 10.2 or later

◆ OpenGL 1.1.2

◆ 3D accelerator

DIRECTOR BASICS

Imagine you're moving into a new office or workshop that's fully stocked with furniture, supplies, and equipment. Would you just walk in and start working?

No, of course not—you'd want to get settled in first. You'd look through the drawers and supply cabinets to see what's there. You'd find out where the electrical outlets are. You'd try out the high-tech equipment to see how it works. You'd arrange the furniture and decorate the walls in a way that made you comfortable.

Well, Director is an environment where you're going to be spending a lot of time, so it's worth spending a few minutes to set it up the way you like it. This chapter will show you some of the tools you'll be using and introduce a few basic concepts. It will also show you how you can customize Director's interface to suit your working style.

Getting Started

The instructions in this chapter assume that Director is already installed on your computer. If it isn't, you'll have to install it according to the instructions that come with the program. (Make sure that you have enough room on your disk before installation.) The installation CD leads you through the process.

Before you do anything else, it's helpful to be familiar with a few basic file operations. A *movie* is the general term for a project created in Director. A new, empty movie opens automatically whenever you start Director, unless you start the program by double-clicking an existing movie file. If Director is already running, you can open an existing movie file, or open a brand new movie file.

To start Director:

◆ From the Start menu, choose Programs > Macromedia > Macromedia Director MX (Windows).

or

Click the Director icon in the Dock (Mac).

or

Find and double-click the Director application icon (**Figure 1.1**).

or

Double-click a Director movie file (**Figure 1.2**).

To open a new movie:

◆ With Director running, choose File > New > Movie.

If a movie is already open, Director prompts you to save it before proceeding.

Director MX

Figure 1.1 This icon identifies the Director MX application. You can double-click it in the Director application folder, or single-click it in the Dock in Mac OS X.

moviefile.dir

Figure 1.2 You can open both the Director program and an existing movie in one step by double-clicking a Director movie file.

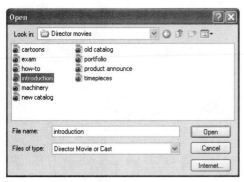

Figure 1.3 The Open dialog box.

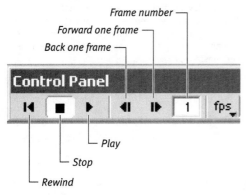

Figure 1.4 The control panel has buttons similar to those on a VCR or tape player.

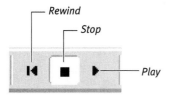

Figure 1.5 A portion of Director's toolbar.

To open an existing movie:

1. Choose File > Open to display the Open dialog box.

2. Select a movie file (**Figure 1.3**).

3. Click Open (Windows) or Choose (Mac).

To play a movie:

1. Choose Window > Control Panel to display the control panel (**Figure 1.4**).

2. Click Rewind to move the playback head to frame 1.

   or

   Click the frame box and type a frame number from which the movie should begin playing.

3. Click Play.

✔ Tip

■ An abbreviated control panel (without the frame-entry box) is attached to the bottom of the Stage. There are also Rewind, Stop, and Play buttons on the main toolbar (**Figure 1.5**).

To save a movie:

◆ Choose File > Save to save the current version of your movie to disk, writing over the movie's previous saved version.

When you save a movie for the first time, Director opens the Save As dialog box, where you can name your movie and choose the folder to which the movie will be saved. Director automatically adds a .dir extension to the filename (although the extension may be hidden on your computer).

✔ Tips

■ As you work on a project, instead of repeatedly using File > Save to overwrite the existing file, it's a good idea occasionally to use File > Save As to save the movie with incrementing numbers at the end of the file name (**Figure 1.6**). This allows you to return to previous versions of your movie if something goes wrong with the current version.

■ When you're ready to test your movie's performance, choose File > Save and Compact to save an optimized version of your movie under its original file name. Director reorders the Cast, reduces the movie to its minimum size, and eliminates any unused space that might have accumulated in the original file.

To revert to the last saved version of your movie:

◆ Choose File > Revert to open the last saved version of your current movie.

✔ Tip

■ The Revert command is particularly useful when you want to undo something you've changed that can't be corrected with the Undo command. The Revert command works best when you want to go back to the previous saved version quickly.

Figure 1.6 Since Director has no history palette (and only one level of Undo), it's a good idea to use Save As rather than Save when you're working on a movie. By adding an incrementing number to the end of the filename, you can easily keep track of your previous versions.

Figure 1.7 The Update Movies dialog box. Besides updating movies from older versions of Director, you can use this dialog box to protect movies from editing or to convert them to Shockwave format. (These topics will be covered in chapters 15 and 16.)

Converting Older Movies to MX Format

Director MX can open movie files created in Director 7 or later. If you wish to update a batch of such files without opening and saving them individually, Director provides an automated method for doing so.

To update an individual movie from a previous version of Director:

1. Open the movie in Director MX.

2. Choose File > Save As.

   The ordinary Save option will not be available.

3. *(optional)* Enter a new file name (to avoid overwriting the original file).

4. Click Save.

To update multiple movies:

1. Choose Xtras> Update Movies to display the Update Movies dialog box.

2. Choose the Update option (**Figure 1.7**).

3. Choose the Back Up into Folder option.

4. Click Browse to select a storage folder for the original files.

5. Click Open.

6. Click OK.

   The Choose Files to Update dialog box opens.

   continues on next page

7. Select a movie file that you want to update (**Figure 1.8**).

8. Click Add.

9. Repeat steps 7 and 8 to add all the files to update to the list at the bottom of the dialog box, or click Add All to add all the files in the current folder.

10. Click Update.

An alert box confirms that the selected files will be updated.

11. Click Continue.

A progress bar shows you the file names as they are updated.

✔ Tip

■ If you're sure that you no longer need the original outdated Director files, or if you have secure backups on another disk, you can choose Delete in step 3. You can't undo and recover the deleted originals, though, so make sure that you don't need the files before you click OK.

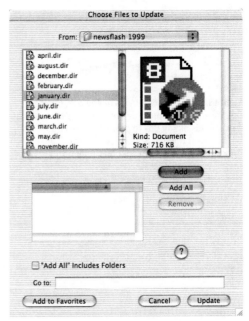

Figure 1.8 In the Choose Files to Update dialog box, you can select one or more older Director movies (version 7 or later) to convert to Director MX format.

Setting General Preferences

General Preferences are settings that relate to Stage appearance and Director's user interface. They affect every new movie you work on.

If you're new to Director, you'll probably want to leave these settings at their default values. As you become more familiar with how the program works, you may want to come back and adjust some of these settings to suit your own work style.

To set General Preferences:

1. Choose Edit > Preferences > General (Windows) or Director > Preferences > General (Mac) to open the General Preferences dialog box (**Figure 1.9**).

2. Change settings as necessary.

3. Click OK to close the dialog box.

STAGE SIZE

Use Movie Settings *makes the Stage resize to the dimensions of any new movie that opens.*

Match Current Movie *makes the Stage dimensions of any movie that is opened match the current movie.*

Center *centers the Stage on the screen automatically. If this option is not checked, the movie's settings determine where on the Stage it opens.*

Reset Monitor to Movie's Color Depth (Mac only) *makes your monitor's color depth change to match the color depth of any movie.*

Animate in Background *makes your movie capable of running in the background. You can work in other applications while a movie plays on the Stage behind other program windows.*

USER INTERFACE

Dialogs Appear at Mouse Position *makes dialog boxes pop open at the position of the mouse pointer. If this option is not selected, the dialog boxes appear in the center of the screen.*

Save Window Positions on Quit *makes the program remembers where your Director windows are when you quit and reopens them in the same position the next time.*

Message Window Recompiles Scripts *is checked by default. If this option is not checked, you need to recompile Lingo scripts manually before entering any Lingo in the Message window.*

Show Tooltips *makes definitions appear when the mouse pointer is positioned over tools. This option is checked by default.*

Enable Inline IME *allows users to type double-byte Japanese characters into text fields.*

Show Stage Scrollbars *displays scrollbars in the Stage window.*

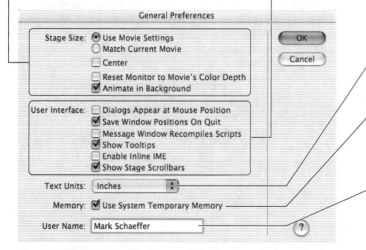

Text Units *Select the unit of measure for the Text and Field windows' rulers.*

Memory (Mac only) *When this option is checked, Director uses available system memory when it exceeds its own memory allocation.*

User Name *assigns a user name to the movie.*

Figure 1.9 Use the General Preferences dialog box to control aspects of Director's Stage and user interface.

Setting Movie Properties

Movie properties are settings that affect an entire movie. Unlike General Preferences, they affect only the movie that's currently being worked on. When you save a movie, its properties are saved with it.

As with General Preferences, it's a good idea to leave these settings at their default values until you get more experience with the program.

To set movie properties:

1. Open an existing movie or create a new movie.

2. Choose Modify > Movie > Properties to display the Movie tab of the Property Inspector (**Figure 1.10**).

3. Adjust settings as necessary.

Stage Size allows you to change the size of the Stage by choosing an option from the pop-up menu or by typing values in the Width and Height fields.

Location allows you to specify whether the Stage is placed in the center of the screen, in the top-left corner, or in another location of your choosing.

Channels sets the number of channels available for sprites in the Score.

RGB represents colors in the movie as RGB values.

Preferred 3D Renderer allows you to specify a 3D rendering method that best suits your hardware. "Auto" allows Director to determine the best method.

About and Copyright are fields where you can enter About and Copyright info for your current movie. Filling in this info could be particularly important if your movie will be distributed over the Internet.

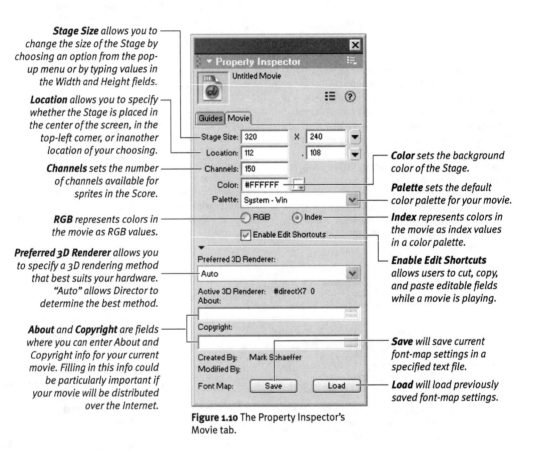

Color sets the background color of the Stage.

Palette sets the default color palette for your movie.

Index represents colors in the movie as index values in a color palette.

Enable Edit Shortcuts allows users to cut, copy, and paste editable fields while a movie is playing.

Save will save current font-map settings in a specified text file.

Load will load previously saved font-map settings.

Figure 1.10 The Property Inspector's Movie tab.

Figure 1.11 A contextual menu offers you access to the most common commands with one click of the mouse button.

Join Sprites	Ctrl+J
Split Sprite	Ctrl+Shift+J
Extend Sprite	Ctrl+B

Figure 1.12 Menus display keyboard shortcuts alongside commands.

Working Faster

For the sake of brevity and uniformity, instructions in this book usually refer to commands only from Director's main menus (File, Edit, View, and so on). In many cases, however, you may find it faster to access these commands by using a contextual menu or a keyboard shortcut.

To display a contextual menu:

◆ Right-click (Windows) or Control-click (Mac) a movie element, such as a cast member (**Figure 1.11**), or an interface element, such as a Director window.

You'll get a menu containing the most relevant commands for that element.

To find the keyboard shortcut for a command:

◆ Open the main menu that contains the command. The keyboard equivalent is listed on the menu to the right of the command (**Figure 1.12**).

✔ Tip

■ You'll find a complete list of keyboard shortcuts in an appendix at the end of this book.

To perform a keyboard shortcut:

1. Hold down the specified modifier key or keys.

   The usual modifier keys are Shift, Control, and Alt in Windows. On the Mac, they're Shift, Command, and Option (**Table 1.1**). Ignore the plus signs that are included in the keyboard shortcuts in Windows menus; they're punctuation, not keys that you need to hold down.

2. Press and release the activator key or keys.

   Press and hold Control/Command and then press and release O to open a new file, for example. To save a file, press and hold Control/Command and then press and release S.

3. Release the modifier key.

   Director executes the command.

Table 1.1

Mac menu shortcut symbols	
MAC MENU	KEY SYMBOLS
⇧	Shift
⌘	Command
⌐	Option

Looking at Director's Interface

Before you start working in Director (or in any piece of software, for that matter), it's useful to get acquainted with your working environment. We'll look very briefly at the primary parts of Director's interface and how they relate to each other. You'll have a chance to explore these interface elements in greater depth in later chapters.

Restoring Director's default interface

When you start Director for the first time, the major interface elements are laid out in their default positions on your computer screen. If you've moved or closed any of them, you may want to restore them for this brief introduction.

To restore the default screen layout:

◆ Choose Window > Panel Sets > Default.

LOOKING AT DIRECTOR'S INTERFACE

Director's Theater/Film Metaphor

Director began as an animation tool, and its interface reflects that history. Since animation usually involves characters moving around and doing things, Director's central metaphor is that of a film or a play. For example, a Director project is called a *movie;* the elements that make up the movie are called the *Cast;* the place where the action takes place is called the *Stage;* and the window that controls all the action is called the *Score.*

At the time, these names were a fun, clever way to make a powerful piece of software seem less intimidating. Nowadays, when other multimedia programs tend to use more generic terms, people sometimes get confused or annoyed: "Every other program calls it a 'Timeline'; why does Director have to call it a 'Score'?" The answer: Director was here first, and therefore has naming rights. If you want consistency, talk to the developers of the *other* programs.

The Cast window

All the elements that play a part in your movie—images, sounds, Lingo scripts, Flash animations, and so on—are considered members of the movie's *Cast*. The Cast window is where you store and manage cast members. It appears by default in list view (**Figure 1.13**), but many people prefer to use it in thumbnail view (**Figure 1.14**).

The Score

The Score (**Figure 1.15**) is the "brain" behind the movie: it controls all the elements of your movie and tells them what to do. Just as the notes in a musical score represent sounds played by an orchestra, markings in Director's Score represent activities on the Stage.

The Stage

The Stage (**Figure 1.16**) is where images, video clips, and other visual elements of your movie will appear. The Stage is empty when you first open the program; it's your blank slate, awaiting your decisions about what to include in the movie.

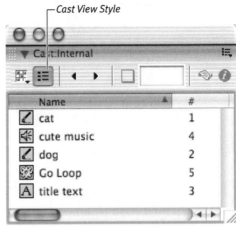

Cast View Style

Figure 1.13 The images, sounds, scripts, and other multimedia elements that make up your movie are stored in the Cast window. Click the list icon to toggle between list view (shown here) and thumbnail view.

Stage = Space; Score = Time

A Director movie takes place in *space* and *time*. The *Stage* shows how the visual images in your movie relate to each other in two-dimensional space. The *Score* shows how those relationships on the Stage change over time.

You can bring a visual cast member into your movie by dragging it into the Score or onto the Stage. Either way, the cast member will appear in both the Score and the Stage, since a visual image exists in both space and time.

Non-visual cast members, such as sounds, can't appear on the Stage—they exist in time, but not in space. These cast members can be dragged only to the Score.

Figure 1.14 To put a cast member into your movie, you drag it from the Cast window (shown here in thumbnail view) to the Score or to the Stage.

Playhead

Figure 1.15 The Score is a grid that shows how the elements in your movie change over time. Each row of the grid holds a different cast member, and each column represents a slice of time called a *frame*. As the playhead moves from left to right, it plays the frames sequentially.

Time passing

Figure 1.16 You create animation by repositioning visual cast members on the Stage. A technique called *tweening*, which you'll learn about in Chapter 4, makes it easy to change the cast members' location (or other properties, such as size or color) bit by bit and frame by frame.

The inspectors

Director relies on a group of *inspectors* to manage the details of your movie. The inspectors are context-sensitive: that is, they display different kinds of information depending on what you're doing in Director. They are also interactive: apart from getting information about a selected object; you can change aspects of the selected object by editing the information in the inspector.

There are five inspectors available:

- The *Property Inspector* (**Figure 1.17**) is the most-used inspector, and the most prominent in Director's default layout. It gives you information about the size, color, position, and other properties of any selected element of your movie (or of your movie as a whole). There are multiple tabs in the property inspector, which vary according to which object you've selected.

- The *Behavior Inspector* (**Figure 1.18**) allows you to view and edit the scripts that add interactivity to your movie.

- The *Object Inspector* (**Figure 1.19**) is new in Director MX. Unlike the Property Inspector, which deals with the properties of "real" objects such as images and sounds, the object inspector lets you view or change the properties of variables, lists, and other programming objects that exist only in Lingo. It also allows you to adjust the advanced properties of 3D cast members.

— *List View Mode icon*

Figure 1.17 Like the Cast window, the Property Inspector can be toggled between Graphical view and List view by clicking the List View Mode icon.

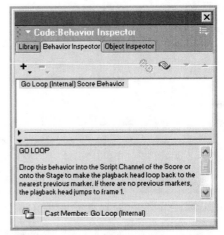

Figure 1.18 The Behavior Inspector contains controls for creating and customizing behaviors, which you'll learn about in Chapter 18.

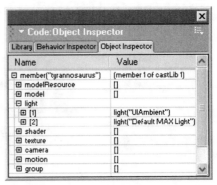

Figure 1.19 The Object Inspector is particularly useful for analyzing the structure of 3D models imported from other programs.

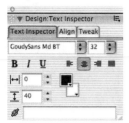

Figure 1.20 In addition to adjusting the font, size and style, the Text Inspector can be used to create a hyperlink. (See Chapter 12, "Adding Text.")

◆ The *Text Inspector* (**Figure 1.20**) allows you to view and change the font, size, style, and other properties of a block of text.

◆ The *Memory Inspector* (Windows only) (**Figure 1.21**) allows you to remove stored data from RAM when you need to perform a memory-intensive operation.

The toolbar

The toolbar (**Figure 1.22**), which is nearly always visible while you work with Director, provides quick access to the most important Director commands.

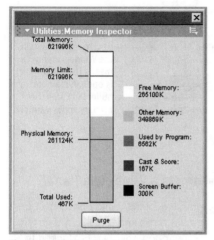

Figure 1.21 The Memory Inspector helps you monitor the memory use of a movie in progress. Knowing how much memory your Cast and Score take up helps you track whether the movie meets the target size for your finished project.

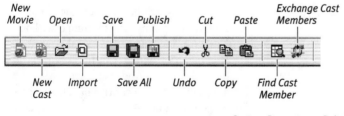

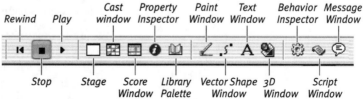

Figure 1.22 The toolbar's buttons serve as handy shortcuts to Director features.

Using Windows and Panels

In addition to the major interface elements described earlier, Director provides other windows and panels that let you accomplish specific tasks. These operate similarly to the windows and panels in other MX applications, so if you're experienced with the latest versions of Flash, Fireworks, or Dreamweaver, you can skip this section.

Windows and panels are infinitely customizable. Panels can be collapsed so that only their title bars are visible, freeing up space on the desktop. You can dock panels to other panels, group them together, or ungroup them. And once you arrange your panels and windows to your liking, you can save and retrieve that layout by name.

To open a window or panel:

◆ Choose Window > *Name of window or panel* (**Figure 1.23**).

To close a window or undocked panel:

◆ Choose Window > *Name of Window or Panel.*

or

Click the close button in the upper right corner of the window or panel (Windows), or click the red close button in the upper left corner (Mac).

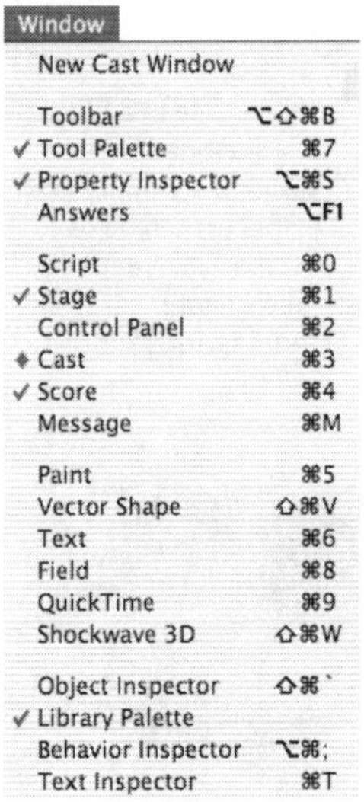

Figure 1.23 A check next to a command in the Window menu means that its window is open. A diamond or bullet indicates the primary active window.

When is a Window a Panel?

Director makes no hard-and-fast distinction between windows and panels. In theory, a *panel* is a window that can be docked to, or grouped with, other panels. (Director's documentation also refers to these as *tool windows.*) Anything that can't is a plain old *window* (sometimes referred to as a *document window*).

But the line is sometimes blurry. The Score and the Cast window can be docked to each other, but not to anything else. The paint window and the vector shape window can be grouped with other panels, but not docked. And then there are anomalies like the control panel, which—despite its name—is technically neither a window nor a panel, but a *palette*.

So don't worry about what's called what; just arrange your workspace the way you like it. If you want to dock or group something, try it. If it works, great; if not, there are plenty of other arrangements to try.

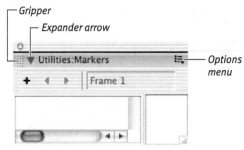

Gripper
Expander arrow
Options menu

Figure 1.24 Anatomy of a panel.

Figure 1.25 This collapsed panel (temporarily transparent, because it's being dragged) is midway through the docking process. The heavy black line indicates that this panel will end up docked between the Property Inspector and the library.

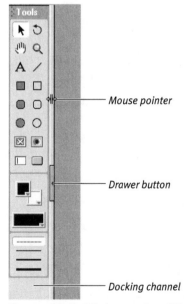

Mouse pointer
Drawer button
Docking channel

Figure 1.26 In the Windows version of Director, panels (such as the Tool palette, shown here) can be docked to docking channels on either side of the screen. If you position the mouse pointer over the border of a docking channel, it turns into a double-arrow cursor that allows you to expand or contract the channel. You can also close the docking channel by clicking the drawer button.

To expand or collapse a panel:

◆ Click the expander arrow (**Figure 1.24**).

Panels can be collapsed so that only their title bars are visible, freeing up space on the desktop. When you need to use a collapsed panel, it can be expanded with a single click.

To dock a panel:

1. Drag the panel by its gripper (**Figure 1.25**).

Panels can be docked to other panels, or (in Windows only) to the docking channels at either side of the application window (**Figure 1.26**).

As you drag the gripper over the panel or docking channel that you want to dock it to, watch for a black, rectangular outline to appear. This indicates where the docked panel will go.

2. Release the mouse button.

The panel will snap to the area indicated by the black outline.

To undock a panel:

◆ Drag the panel by its gripper until it's clear of the docking area.

Working with panel groups

Panels can be *grouped*—that is, turned into a series of tabs within a single collapsible, dockable frame. A panel group may be given a name. Some panels are already in named groups by default (**Figure 1.27**).

To add a panel to a panel group:

1. Click the panel's Options menu (**Figure 1.28**).

2. Choose Group *Panel Name* With > *Name of Panel Group*.

To remove a panel from a panel group:

1. Select the tab for the panel you want to remove.

2. Click the panel group's Options menu.

3. Choose Group *Panel Name* With > New Panel Group.

To close a panel group:

1. Click the panel's Options menu.

2. Choose Close Panel Group.

To save a screen layout:

◆ Choose Window > Panel Sets > Save Panel Layout.

Once you've found an arrangement of windows and panels that you like, use the Save Panel Layout command to save it and retrieve it by name.

To retrieve a screen layout:

◆ Choose Window > Panel Sets > *Name of Layout*.

✔ Tips

■ You can hide all panels, palettes, and toolbars—basically, everything except the Stage, Cast window, and Score—by choosing Window > Hide Panels. To show them again, choose Window > Show Panels.

■ You may want to save several different screen layouts that are suitable for doing different tasks in Director—for example, one for animation, one for Cast management, and so on.

Figure 1.27 One of Director's default panel groups.

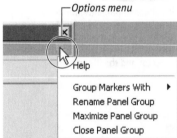

Figure 1.28 A panel's Options menu allows you to group or ungroup the panel, or to rename or resize the panel group. Unlike in other MX applications, the Options menus in Director do not give you access to any functional aspects of the program.

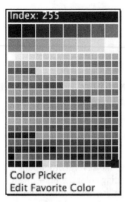

Figure 1.29 This menu pops up whenever you click on a square color chip in Director.

Selecting Colors

Many different tasks in Director will require you to select a color. (For example, when you set up your Stage for a movie, you'll need to choose a background color; when you add text to a movie, you'll need to choose a text color.) To simplify this process, Director's standard color menu (**Figure 1.29**), which you'll find throughout Director, offers a selection of 256 colors for you to choose from.

A given set of 256 colors is called a *color palette*. Which set of colors will be available on the color menu depends on which color palette is currently active in Director. (Only one color palette can be active at a time.) There are several standard color palettes from which you can select; in addition, it's possible to create custom color palettes made up of colors of your own choosing.

To change the current color palette:

◆ Choose Window > Color Palettes.

The Color Palettes window opens, with the name of the currently active color palette visible on the pop-up menu. The colors in the current palette are displayed below the menu (**Figure 1.30**).

Choose a palette name from the pop-up menu.

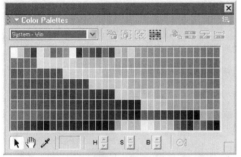

Figure 1.30 The Color Palettes window allows you to select and edit color palettes. Some people never use this window; they prefer to select their colors from the color picker.

To choose a color from a color menu:

1. Find a window or tool that contains a color menu.

   For now, the easiest place to look for a color menu is the tool palette at the very left edge of the screen. It has two overlapping color menus—one for foreground color, one for background color (**Figure 1.31**).

2. Click the square to open the menu.

   You'll see the 256 colors from the current color palette.

3. Click a color.

   The menu will snap closed, and the square will display the color you've chosen.

To choose a color that's not in the current palette:

1. Open a color menu.

2. Click Color Picker to display the color picker.

3. Choose a color.

   In Windows, enter Hue, Saturation, and Luminosity values or RGB values to specify the color. Alternatively, click a color in the color spectrum box (**Figure 1.32**).

   On the Mac, first select one of the color models and then select a new color, using its controls (**Figure 1.33**).

4. Click OK.

   The color picker will close, and the square will display the color you've chosen.

✔ Tip

■ The color picker is not actually part of Director, but part of your computer's operating system. That's why it's different in Windows and Mac, and that's why you won't find much information about it in Director's documentation.

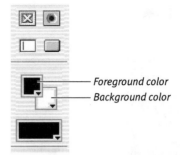

Foreground color
Background color

Figure 1.31 The Tool palette, like several other panels in Director, has two overlapping color menus—one for the foreground color, one for the background color. You'll learn what the Tool palette is used for in Chapter 9, but for now you can just treat it as a handy place to find pop-up color menus to practice with.

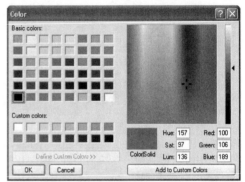

Figure 1.32 The Windows color picker allows you to select a color either by clicking in a color field or by entering specific numerical values.

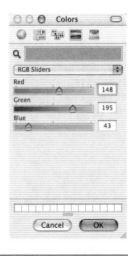

Figure 1.33 The Mac color picker offers many different methods for selecting colors, including a color wheel, RGB (red, green, blue) and CMYK (cyan, magenta, yellow, black) sliders, and even an easy-to-use crayon box.

SELECTING COLORS

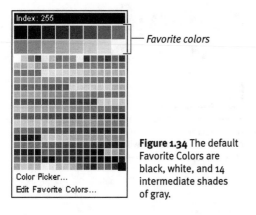

Favorite colors

Figure 1.34 The default Favorite Colors are black, white, and 14 intermediate shades of gray.

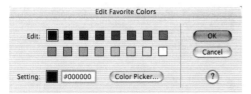

Figure 1.35 The Edit Favorite Colors dialog box.

Editing and creating custom colors

At the top of the color menu are two rows of colors—in slightly larger boxes than those in the rest of the menu —that remain constant no matter which color palette you've chosen. These 16 boxes are referred to as *favorite colors* (**Figure 1.34**). By default, they hold black, white, and 14 shades of gray (which are probably not *your* favorite colors), but you can replace their contents with any colors you choose: the thematic colors of the interface you're designing, the colors of a corporate logo, or whatever. Consider these colors your private little custom palette.

If you want to be able to choose from more than 16 custom colors, you can create additional custom color palettes. You do this by editing an existing color palette and saving it under a new name.

To edit favorite colors:

1. Open a color menu.

2. Choose Edit Favorite Colors.
   The Edit Favorite Colors dialog box appears (**Figure 1.35**), displaying 16 color boxes.

3. Select a color you want to change.

4. Enter an RGB value for the new color in hexadecimal format.
   or
   Click Color Picker to use the color picker.

5. Click OK to close either the Edit Favorite Colors dialog box or the color picker, depending on which method you used.

6. Click OK to close the Edit Favorite Colors dialog box.
   From now on, the appropriate box on the color menu will display your new color.

✔ Tip

■ Changes made to favorite colors apply only within a single Director movie, and are saved with that movie.

SELECTING COLORS

To create a custom color palette:

1. Choose Window > Color Palettes.

   The Color Palettes window opens.

2. From the pop-up menu, choose the name of the palette that's most similar to the palette you want to create.

   You'll create a new palette by changing colors, one by one, in this base palette.

3. Double-click on a color that you want to change.

   A Create Palette dialog box appears (**Figure 1.36**).

4. Enter a name for the new palette.

5. Click OK.

   The Create Palette dialog box disappears, and the color picker opens.

6. Use the color picker to choose a new color.

7. Click OK to close the color picker.

   The selected color appears in its proper position in your custom palette. At the same time, the custom palette appears as a new cast member in the Cast window (**Figure 1.37**).

8. Double-click on another color you want to change.

   The color picker opens.

9. Use the color picker to choose a new color.

Figure 1.36 The standard palettes that are supplied with Director cannot be changed. If you try to edit one of them, this dialog box will appear, allowing you to create a new, editable palette.

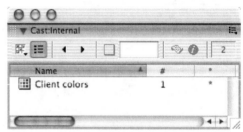

Figure 1.37 When you create a custom palette, Director considers it part of your movie's Cast, so it automatically adds the palette to the Cast window.

SELECTING COLORS

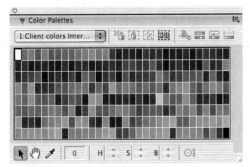

Figure 1.38 Your custom palette will appear in every menu in from which palettes are selectable. (The inter... following the palette name here means *internal*, because the palette is part of the movie's internal Cast. You'll find out more about internal vs. external Casts in Chapter 2.)

Figure 1.39 This pair of radio buttons appears on the Movie tab of the property inspector.

10. Click OK to close the color picker.

11. Repeat steps 8 through 10 until you've added the desired number of colors to your custom palette.

Your custom palette can now be selected and used like any other palette (**Figure 1.38**).

✔ **Tip**

- A custom palette is available only within the movie you created it in. To make it available in a different movie, select the custom palette in the Cast window, copy it to the Clipboard, open the other movie, and paste it into that movie's Cast window.

To change the current color mode:

1. Choose Modify > Movie > Properties to open the Movie tab of the property inspector.

2. Click the radio button for either RGB or Index (**Figure 1.39**).

✔ **Tip**

- Changing the color mode only changes how colors are specified. It has no effect on the actual colors that are used in your movie.

SELECTING COLORS

Director's Help System

Director's built-in help system is a great source of information about the program. If you need to find out how a specific tool works or how to accomplish a particular task, the Help menu is the first place you should look (after this book, of course).

To display help pages, Director uses an external help viewer that's built into the Mac or Windows operating system. Though the viewing application is different on each platform, the content is basically the same.

There are three ways to access the help information: you can browse by topic, look up specific keywords in an index, or search for words that appear in the help text.

To browse by topic:

1. Choose Help > Director Help.

   The HTML Help application (Windows) or the Help Viewer (Mac) opens and displays a list of topics.

2. Click the book icon to the left of a topic (Windows), or click the topic itself, to see a list of subtopics.

   In Windows, the subtopics appear indented beneath the selected topic (**Figure 1.40**). On the Mac, they appear in the right-hand pane of the Help Viewer (**Figure 1.41**).

3. (Windows) Drill down through further subtopics if necessary to reach the level of detail you need.

4. Click a subtopic to see the associated help page.

5. In Windows, the help text appears in the right-hand pane of the HTML Help window. On the Mac, it fills the Help Viewer window.

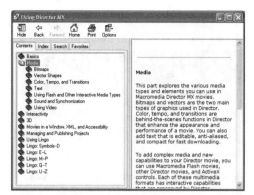

Figure 1.40 In the Windows Help application, subtopics are indented beneath major topics. There may be several levels of subtopics.

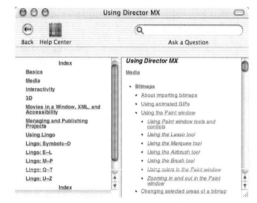

Figure 1.41 On the Mac, subtopics are listed in outline form in the right-hand pane of the Help Viewer.

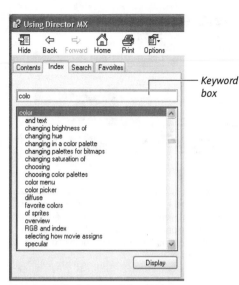

Figure 1.42 The left side of the Windows Help application with the Index tab selected. Typing the letters *col* into the keyword box makes the highlight jump to *collapse*, but adding another "o" makes it jump further down the list to "color."

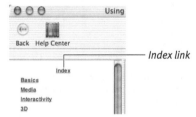

Figure 1.43 Click this link (or a similar link at the bottom of the list of topics) to jump to the alphabetical index.

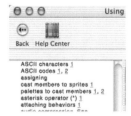

Figure 1.44
Each underlined number following a topic is a link to a help page on that topic. Some topics only have one link; others have two or more.

To use the Help index (Windows):

1. Choose Help > Director Help.

2. Click the Index tab to bring into view the alphabetical index of help contents (**Figure 1.42**).

3. Find your topic in the alphabetical list.
   or
   Type a help topic in the keyword box.

4. Click your desired topic.
   The help text will appear in the right-hand pane of the HTML Help window.

✔ Tip

- Each time you type a letter in the keyword box, the index highlight jumps to the first item in the list that matches the letters typed so far. Therefore, in most cases, you'll only have to type the first few letters of your help topic.

To use the Help index (Mac):

1. Choose Help > Director Help.

2. Click the Index link at the top or bottom of the list of topics (**Figure 1.43**).

3. Click the alphabetical index letter for your desired help topic.

4. Find your topic in the alphabetical list and click any of the numbers following the topic (**Figure 1.44**).
   The help page you've selected will fill the Help Viewer window.

To search for a help page that contains specific words (Windows):

1. Choose Help > Director Help.

2. Click the Search tab (**Figure 1.45**).

3. Type one or more words that you want to search for.

4. Click the List Topics button.

   After a few moments, a list of help pages containing the specified words appears in the bottom pane of the HTML Help window.

5. Select your desired page from the list.

6. Click the Display button.

To search for a help page that contains specific words (Mac):

1. Choose Help > Director Help.

2. In the search box at the upper right corner of the Help Viewer, type one or more words that you want to search for. (**Figure 1.46**).

3. Press the Return key.

   After a few moments, a list of help pages containing the specified words appears in the Help Viewer window. Those from Director Help will be at the top of the list. (Help pages from other programs may also appear in the list, identified by the program name and icon.)

4. Find your desired page in the list and double-click it.

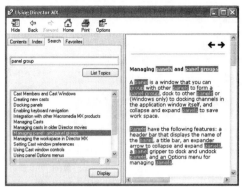

Figure 1.45 Every topic in the lower-left pane contains the words that were entered in the search field. When you select one of those topics and click Display, the search terms are highlighted in the help text in the right-hand pane.

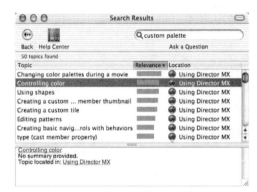

Figure 1.46 The search for *custom palette* results in a list of 50 topics. To see the help page associated with each topic, double-click the topic.

ASSEMBLING CASTS

Figure 2.1 A Cast window in List view.

Figure 2.2 A Cast window in Thumbnail view.

Director's Cast window acts as the storage bin for the cast members used in your movie. Cast members may include pictures, sounds, text, color palettes, digital videos, film loops, Lingo scripts, and other types of media. Most Director users create their cast members in external programs and import them into Director, which is what you'll be doing in this chapter. (Director also provides internal tools for creating certain kinds of cast members: The Paint, Vector Shape, and Text windows, which you'll work with in chapters 6, 8, and 12, respectively.)

You can choose to view a Cast window in either List view or Thumbnail view (**Figures 2.1, 2.2**). In List view, cast members are represented by rows and columns of text, much like the details view (Windows) or list view (Mac) of a folder on your desktop. In Thumbnail view, each cast member is represented by a thumbnail image. A small icon in the bottom-right corner of each thumbnail identifies the cast member's type (**Figure 2.3**).

continues on next page

Cast members may be divided into groups called *casts,* each of which appears on its own tab within the Cast window. A cast can contain up to 32,000 cast members. Every Director movie starts out with a single cast, but it's possible to add any number of additional casts to your movie. Each cast may be either internal (stored as part of the movie file) or external (stored as a separate file that can be shared among Director movies).

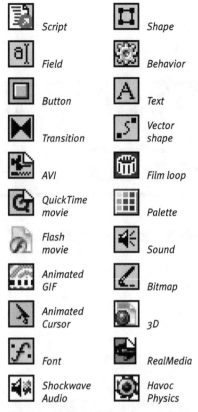

	Script		Shape
	Field		Behavior
	Button		Text
	Transition		Vector shape
	AVI		Film loop
	QuickTime movie		Palette
	Flash movie		Sound
	Animated GIF		Bitmap
	Animated Cursor		3D
	Font		RealMedia
	Shockwave Audio		Havoc Physics

Figure 2.3 The symbol in the lower-right corner of the thumbnail indicates the cast member's type.

Flash Talk: Cast vs. Library

If you've used Macromedia Flash before, you'll notice that Director's Cast window functions similarly to the Library in Flash. Nevertheless, they differ in several significant ways.

In Flash, use of the Library is optional. An object enters the Library only if you choose to convert it to a symbol; therefore, it's possible for objects to appear in the movie but not to be in the Library. In Director, *every* object becomes part of the cast from the moment it's created (or imported).

There are several different kinds of symbols in Flash, and it's possible to change the properties of an object by changing its symbol type—for example, from a graphic symbol to a button symbol. In Director, there are no such distinctions. Any visual cast member can become a button if the proper Lingo script is attached.

Finally, unlike Flash symbols, Director cast members don't have their own timelines. The Score is the only timeline in a Director movie.

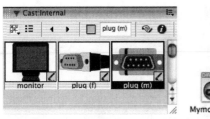

Figure 2.4 Internal casts are stored inside the Director movie file.

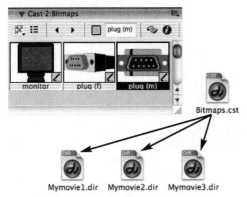

Figure 2.5 External casts are stored outside the Director movie file and can be shared by multiple Director movies.

Creating Casts

Whenever you create a cast in Director, you first must decide whether to make it internal or external. Director always saves all internal casts as part of the movie file itself. The program automatically creates one empty internal cast when you open a new movie (**Figure 2.4**). External casts (**Figure 2.5**), on the other hand, are separate files stored outside your movie and can be shared among Director movies. You must link an external cast to your movie before you can use any of its cast members. (See "To link an external cast to the current movie" later in this chapter.) Each cast, whether internal or external, appears on its own tab in the Cast window, or may be moved into its own separate Cast window.

Internal and external casts are handled differently by projector files and Shockwave movies (the two primary Director movie distribution formats, which you'll learn about in chapters 16 and 17). When you create a projector file, all internal casts are automatically stored within it, and you have the option of embedding external casts as well. A Shockwave movie file also stores all internal casts, but external casts can't be embedded. They must be distributed along with the Shockwave file or be accessible from an Internet URL.

To create a new cast:

1. Choose File > New > Cast.

   The New Cast dialog box opens (**Figure 2.6**).

2. Choose Internal or External as the cast storage type (**Figure 2.7**).

3. If the cast is external, select the Use in Current Movie check box to link the cast to the current movie (**Figure 2.8**).

4. Type a name for the cast in the text box (**Figure 2.9**).

5. Click Create.

   The new cast is created and appears as a tabbed panel in the Cast window.

✔ Tips

■ You can add as many internal or external casts to your movie as you want. If your movie involves a large number of cast members, you may find it more efficient to group related cast members into separate casts. For example, you may choose to create two casts, one for storing bitmaps and the other for sounds. Or if you're preparing a movie that will have versions in different languages, you might create different casts for each language.

■ You can also create a new cast by clicking the Choose Cast button in a Cast window and choosing New Cast from the pop-up menu (**Figure 2.10**).

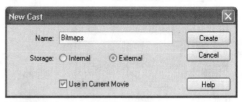

Figure 2.6 The New Cast dialog box.

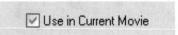

Figure 2.7 Choose Internal or External as your cast's storage type.

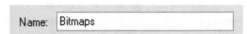

Figure 2.8 For external casts, check Use in Current Movie.

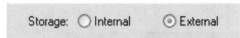

Figure 2.9 Type a name for the cast.

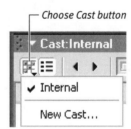

Figure 2.10 Create a new cast by clicking the Choose Cast button and choosing New Cast from the pop-up menu.

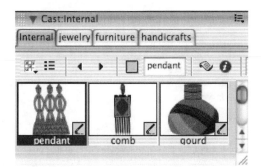

Figure 2.11 Each cast appears in its own tabbed panel in the Cast window.

Figure 2.12 Click the Choose Cast button and choose a cast from the pop-up menu.

To open a Cast window:

◆ Choose Window > Cast.

or

If multiple casts exist, choose Window > Cast > *name of cast*.

If your movie includes multiple casts, each cast has its own tab in the Cast window. You can select a cast by clicking the appropriate tab (**Figure 2.11**).

✔ Tip

■ If the tab for a particular cast has been removed from the Cast window, you can open the cast by using the Choose Cast button, described in the next task.

To open a cast that's missing from the Cast window:

1. In the Cast window, click the Choose Cast button to display a pop-up menu of available casts (**Figure 2.12**).

   The pop-up menu lists all internal casts, as well as external casts that have been linked to the current movie.

2. Choose a cast.

CREATING CASTS

Should You Create an Internal or External Cast?

When you create a new cast, you need to decide whether to make that cast internal or external. This depends largely on your own individual movie. Here are some questions to ask yourself:

◆ **Do you plan to use the cast members in more than one movie?** Internal casts belong only to the Director movie that contains them. Use an external cast for cast members that you'll want to have available for more than one movie, such as fonts, sound effects, or corporate identity items.

◆ **Is your movie likely to become unmanageably long?** Sometimes a movie gets so long and complicated that you decide, somewhere along the way, to break it down into several smaller movies. If you think that might happen with your project, it may make sense to put your cast members in an external cast. That way, if you do decide to use multiple movies later on, the cast members can easily be shared among the movie files.

◆ **Once you've finished your movie, how do you plan to distribute it?** If you plan to distribute your movie via Shockwave, and you prefer it to be contained within a single file, use internal casts, because any external casts must be supplied separately.

Opening and linking external casts

Internal and any linked external casts automatically open with the movie that contains them. If you want to access cast members from an external cast that is not currently linked to your movie, you must link it to your movie manually.

To open an external cast not linked to the current movie:

1. Choose File > Open.

   The Open dialog box appears.

2. Select an external cast file.

3. Click Open.

   The external cast opens in its own Cast window.

To link an external cast to the current movie:

1. Choose Modify > Movie > Casts.

   The Movie Casts dialog box opens (**Figure 2.13**).

2. Click the Link button.

   The Open dialog box appears.

3. Select the external cast file (**Figure 2.14**).

4. Click Open (Windows) or Choose (Mac).

   After you link an external cast to the current movie, Director automatically opens that cast whenever you open the movie. Director also automatically saves any changes made in the external cast when you save the movie.

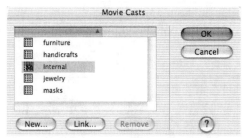

Figure 2.13 Click Link in the Movie Casts dialog box.

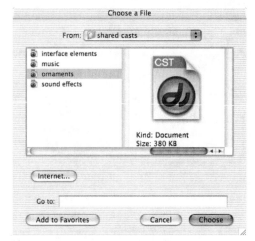

Figure 2.14 Select an external cast file.

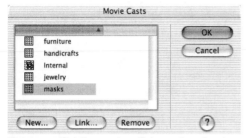

Figure 2.15 Click Remove to unlink an external cast from the current movie.

✔ Tips

- If you want to use a cast member from an external cast without linking to that cast, you can copy the cast member to either an internal cast or a linked external cast.

- Don't confuse linked external casts with linked cast members. A linked cast member can reside in any type of cast (internal, linked external, or unlinked external), but its actual media information is stored in a file outside Director. For details, see the sidebar "How to Choose Between 'Standard Import' and 'Link to External File' When Importing a File" later in this chapter.

To unlink an external cast from the current movie:

1. Choose Modify > Movie > Casts to open the Movie Casts dialog box.

2. Select the external cast you want to unlink.

3. Click Remove (**Figure 2.15**).

4. Click OK.

Saving changes to an external cast

When you make changes in an external cast that is not linked to your movie, you must explicitly save those changes, because they aren't saved when you save the Director movie. On the other hand, if you link an external cast to your current movie, any changes you make in the cast are saved automatically when you save the Director movie.

To save changes in an external cast (linked or unlinked):

1. Click the external cast that you want to save (thus making it the active window).

2. Choose File > Save As.

3. Type a filename for the external cast.

4. Click Save.

✔ Tip

- To save your movie along with all casts—internal, external linked, and external unlinked—choose File > Save All.

Table 2.1

File Formats Imported by Director	
FILE TYPE	FILE FORMATS
Animation and multimedia	Animated GIFs, Flash movies, Director movies and external casts, PowerPoint presentations
Still image	TIFF, PICT, Targa, BMP, GIF, JPEG, LRG (xRes), Photoshop 3.0 or later, MacPaint, PNG
Multiple image file formats	FLI, FLC (*Windows only*)
Multiple image file formats	Scrapbook, PICS (*Mac only*)
Sound	AIFF, WAV (compressed and uncompressed), MP3, Shockwave Audio, AU
Video	QuickTime 2 or later, AVI, RealMedia
Text	ASCII, RTF, HTML, Lingo scripts
Palette	PAL, Photoshop CLUT

Importing Cast Members

If you want your Director movie to incorporate graphics or sounds created in some other application (such as a background created in Photoshop or a set of sound effects edited in ProTools), you first have to import those elements into a Cast window. **Table 2.1** summarizes the file formats you can import into Director.

To import a cast member:

1. Choose File > Import.

The Import Files dialog box opens (**Figure 2.16**).

2. From the Files of Type menu (Windows) or Show menu (Mac), choose the kind of cast member to import (**Figure 2.17**).

Only files in the selected format are displayed in the dialog box.

continues on next page

Files of
Type menu

Media
menu

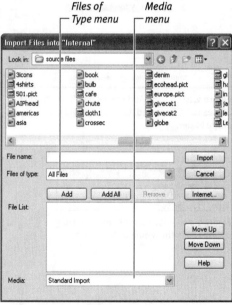

Figure 2.16 The Import Files dialog box.

Figure 2.17 Select the type of cast member to import.

3. At the top of the dialog box, find and open the folder that contains the file you want to import.

or

Click Internet and specify a URL for the file in the Open URL dialog box (**Figure 2.18**).

4. Select the file and click Add (**Figure 2.19**).

or

Click Add All to add all the folder's displayed files to the list.

5. Choose an option from the Media pop-up menu (**Figure 2.20**):

Standard Import embeds the contents of the file into your Director movie, so you won't need to provide the file when distributing your movie. (AVI and QuickTime movies are never embedded, even if you choose Standard Import.)

Link to External File creates a link to an external file, allowing you to store the cast member outside your Director movie. Director imports this cast member from its source each time you run the movie. (Text and rich text format [RTF] cast members are never linked to external files, regardless of whether you choose this option.)

Include Original Data for Editing causes Director to keep a copy of the original source file inside the movie. Use this option when you have defined an external editor for a particular media type and you want Director to pass this original data along to the editor when you edit the cast member. (You can specify an external editor via the Edit > Preferences > Editors command [Windows] or the Director > Preferences > Editors command [Mac].)

Import PICT File as PICT keeps vector PICT files from being converted to bitmaps.

6. Click Import to bring the new cast member(s) into the active Cast window.

Figure 2.18 To import a cast member from the Internet, enter a URL in the Open URL dialog box.

Files are copied from here... ⌐ *...to here*

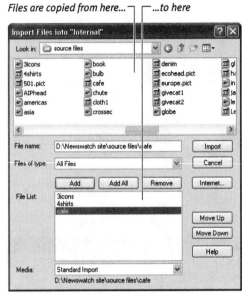

Figure 2.19 Clicking Add copies one file to the list of files to be imported. Clicking Add All copies the entire folder.

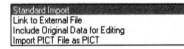

Figure 2.20 Choose one of four importing options from the Media pop-up menu.

How to Choose Between "Standard Import" and "Link to External File" When Importing a File

When you import a file into Director's cast, there are times when you may decide to link the cast member to an external file (**Figure 2.21**). In making this decision, ask yourself these questions:

1. **Is downloading time or movie file size an issue?** Importing cast members with the Standard Import option increases your movie's file size.

   When you import a file by using the linking option, Director creates a cast member that stores only the name and location of the file. This information appears in the Member tab of the Property Inspector (**Figure 2.22**). Actual linked cast-member data is downloaded only if and when your movie requires it.

2. **Does cast-member data change frequently in your movie?** If it does, linking to a cast-member file—particularly at an Internet address—provides you the greatest flexibility in being able to update components of your movie without requiring your users to download the movie again and again.

3. **Is keeping the distribution process simple and reliable more important than controlling file size?** Linking external cast members adds some complexity and risk in distributing your movies, because you must include all linked cast members. The movie can come to a halt if a file is not found.

4. **Can your target audience tolerate hiccups in movie playback?** Linked external cast members sometimes cause playback delays as they load. In the worst case, if Director can't find a linked file, it asks the viewer to locate the missing file before continuing.

Icon with bent corner

Figure 2.21 In the Cast window's Thumbnail view, an icon with a bent corner signifies that the cast member is linked to an external file.

Figure 2.22 The Property Inspector's Member tab displays information about a linked bitmap cast member.

Specifying color settings for imported cast members

When you import a bitmap cast member that uses a different palette or more colors than the current movie, the Image Options dialog box appears. This dialog box is where you specify color depth and palette attributes for the imported file.

To set image options for bitmap cast members:

1. In the Image Options dialog box (**Figure 2.23**), set the color depth option. (For more information, see the sidebar "What Is Color Depth?"):

   Choose the Image option to import the image at its original color depth.

   or

   Choose the Stage option to import the image at the movie's color depth (generally 32 bits). If you choose this option, you can skip step 2.

2. Set the Palette option:

   Click Import to keep the image's original color palette. (The color palette becomes a cast member).

   or

   Click "Remap to" and choose a palette from the pop-up menu for the imported image to adopt (**Figure 2.24**). Choosing "Remap to" causes Director to replace the image's colors with the most similar colors from the palette you choose from the pop-up menu.

3. Choose Trim White Space (**Figure 2.25**) to remove all white pixels from the borders of an image.

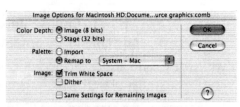

Figure 2.23 Options for importing images.

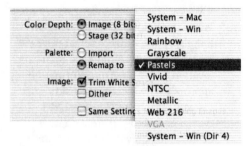

Figure 2.24 Choose a substitute palette for your imported bitmap cast member.

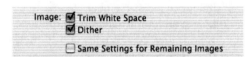

Figure 2.25 Choose the Trim White Space option to remove white pixels from the borders of an image.

Figure 2.26 An 8-bit image, remapped to the Mac System color palette, imported with Dither selected (left) and without dithering (right).

4. If you're importing an indexed color image, and if you chose to remap it to a new palette in step 2, you may wish to check the Dither box. *Dithering* is the blending of available colors to simulate a color that's not in the current palette. It's recommended for use with cast members that contain gradients (**Figure 2.26**).

If you didn't choose a palette from the "Remap to" menu, the Dither option will have no effect on your image.

5. Click OK.

✔ Tips

- If you're importing a batch of files, you can apply the options you choose to all the files at the same time. In the Image Options dialog box, check the Same Settings for Remaining Images checkbox; then click OK to import all the files.

- *Indexed-color* images (that is, images with a color depth of 8 bits or less) require less disk space than RGB images. If file size is a concern, you'll want to import indexed-color images at their original color depth, rather than having Director convert them to the movie's color depth.

What Is Color Depth?

The *color depth* of an image refers to the amount of information needed to specify the color of each pixel. A black-and-white bitmap, for example, has a 1-bit color depth, because each pixel can be described by a single bit of information: 0 (white) or 1 (black). If, instead, we use two bits of information to describe each pixel—00, 01, 10, or 11—we get a palette of four colors. Similarly, using eight bits of information for each pixel gives us a palette of 256 colors. Because 256 colors are sufficient for many purposes, you'll often encounter images with an 8-bit color depth. (All GIF images, for example, are 8-bit.)

Color of 8 bits or less is sometimes referred to as *indexed color*, because an index—or palette—is required to specify which combination of bits represents which color. Every 8-bit image file has an embedded palette, and Director offers you the option of importing this palette as a separate cast member when you import an 8-bit image.

To change a bitmap cast member's size:

1. In a Cast window, select a bitmap cast member.

2. Choose Modify > Transform Bitmap. The Transform Bitmap dialog box opens.

3. Type new values in the Width and Height boxes (**Figure 2.27**):

   Check the Maintain Proportions checkbox to maintain the cast member's original proportions.

   or

   Type a value in the Scale box to size the cast member proportionately.

✔ Tips

■ Reducing the dimensions of bitmapped images in your internal casts is a good way to reduce the file size of your Director movie. Although it's possible to change a cast member's dimensions by using the Transform Bitmap command, you'll usually get better results by resizing the cast member in an external image editor such as Photoshop.

■ You can't undo any changes made to a cast member via the Transform Bitmap command. Make sure that you have a duplicate of the original cast member before making any changes.

■ The Transform Bitmap dialog box also has controls that allow you to change the color depth, palette, color mapping, and dithering of a cast member. These buttons and menus are identical to those in the Image Options dialog box (described in the preceding section).

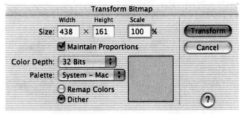

Figure 2.27 Resize a bitmap cast member by typing new values in the Width and Height boxes in the Transform Bitmap dialog box.

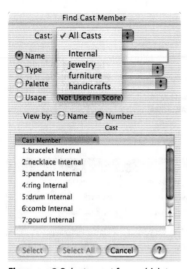

Figure 2.28 Select a cast from which to delete unused cast members.

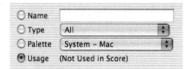

Figure 2.29 Click the Usage option.

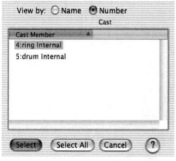

Figure 2.30 Items to be deleted appear in the file list. (If the Select and Select All buttons are dimmed, click one of the items in the list to make them active.)

Discarding unused cast members

If you've imported cast members that you haven't used in your movie, Director can find and then delete them. Deleting unused cast members makes your movie more compact, quicker to load, and more efficient in using computer memory.

To delete unused cast members:

1. Choose Edit > Find > Cast Member.
   The Find Cast Member dialog box opens.

2. From the Cast menu, choose a cast that has extraneous cast members (**Figure 2.28**).

3. Choose the Usage option (**Figure 2.29**).

4. Click Select All.
   Director finds and selects all unused cast members in the selected cast.
   You may first need to click the list to make the Select All button active (**Figure 2.30**).
   Cast members may be incorporated into your movie by way of Lingo scripts, in which case certain cast members would not necessarily appear in the Score. So before deleting the cast members that Director finds, make sure that they are not used in any scripts.

5. Choose Edit > Clear Cast Members.

✔ Tip

■ After you delete a series of cast members, save your movie by choosing File > Save and Compact. This operation reorders the cast, produces a more compact movie file, and optimizes movie playback.

Importing PowerPoint Files

Director for Windows includes an Xtras tool for importing presentations created in Microsoft PowerPoint. When you import a PowerPoint file, Director brings in the presentation in a form as true to the original as possible. Director imports the artwork, transitions, and text as cast members and converts each slide to a section in the Score. PowerPoint build effects and any tempo changes also go into the Score. You can play the presentation as imported or enhance it by adding interactivity, animations, and other Director effects.

Figure 2.31 To import a PowerPoint file, use the Xtras menu—not the File menu, as you would for other types of imports.

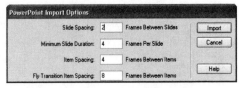

Figure 2.32 The PowerPoint Import Options dialog box.

To import a PowerPoint presentation (Windows only):

1. In Director, choose File > New > Movie.

   You must create a new movie to import a presentation.

2. Choose Xtras > Import PowerPoint File (**Figure 2.31**).

3. Choose a PowerPoint file and click Open.

   The PowerPoint Import Options dialog box appears (**Figure 2.32**).

4. Enter a value for Slide Spacing to specify the number of blank frames to allow between each pair of slides in the Score.

5. Specify the Minimum Slide Duration, which is the minimum number of frames a slide occupies in the Score.

6. If the presentation has build effects other than fly effects, enter a value for Item Spacing to specify the number of frames allocated for each item.

7. Specify Fly Transition Item Spacing, which is the number of frames between keyframes.

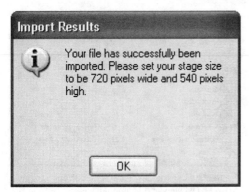

Import Results

Your file has successfully been imported. Please set your stage size to be 720 pixels wide and 540 pixels high.

OK

Figure 2.33 If the screen size of the PowerPoint presentation is different from the Stage size in your Director movie, Director will display this dialog box after you click Import. (To adjust the Stage size, see "To change the size and location of the Stage" in Chapter 9.)

8. Click Import (**Figure 2.33**).

Several progress bars indicate that the PowerPoint file is being converted to Director format. The text, images, and other elements of the PowerPoint presentation appear as individual cast members in the Cast window, and the presentation itself is mapped out in the Score.

9. Play the movie.

If necessary, import the movie again with different settings.

✔ Tip

■ If the Import PowerPoint File option doesn't appear on your Xtras menu, it's likely that the necessary Xtra wasn't installed when you installed Director. Go back to the original installation CD and look in the Goodies folder for a folder called PowerPoint Xtra. Copy that folder into the Xtras folder in the Director MX folder on your hard drive.

Managing Cast Windows

You have two different ways of viewing your Cast windows—in List view or Thumbnail view. When a Cast window is displayed in List view, cast members are represented by rows and columns of text attributes. List view is especially advantageous when you need to sort cast members by various attributes, such as name, size, or last time modified.

When a Cast window is displayed in Thumbnail view, cast members are represented by small images. When you have a large number of graphical cast members, Thumbnail view can be a more convenient way to view your cast, because you can select cast members by sight. If you want to reorder cast members within a cast by dragging and dropping, you must use Thumbnail view.

By default, cast members are labeled with a number in the Cast window. It's a good idea to give cast members descriptive names so that they're easier to recognize, find, and manage in the Cast window and throughout your movie.

To toggle the view style for an open Cast window:

1. Select a Cast window to make it the active window.

2. Click the Cast View Style button (**Figure 2.34**) to toggle between List view and Thumbnail view.

   or

   Choose View > Cast > *view style*.

Cast View Style button

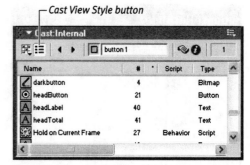

Figure 2.34 Use the Cast View Style button to toggle between List view and Thumbnail view.

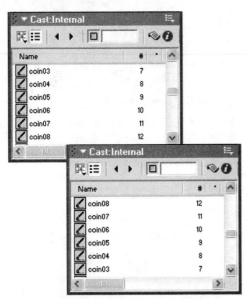

Figure 2.35 Click a column header to sort cast members, then click again to reverse the sort order.

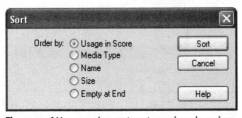

Figure 2.36 You can also sort cast members by using the Sort dialog box.

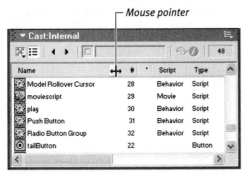

Figure 2.37 When you position your mouse pointer over a column separator, it becomes a double-headed arrow. You can then resize the column to the left by dragging the column separator.

To sort columns in a Cast window:

1. Open a Cast window and select List view:

2. Click any column header to sort the cast members by that column.

3. *(optional)* Click the column header again to reverse the sort order (**Figure 2.35**).

or

1. Activate a Cast window by clicking on it.

2. Select Edit > Select All.

3. Choose Modify > Sort and select a sort option in the Sort dialog box (**Figure 2.36**).

   The Sort command works in either cast view style.

✔ Tip

■ When you sort by any column other than name, secondary sorting is performed by name.

To resize columns in a Cast window:

1. Open a Cast window and select list view.

2. Drag the separator between column headers to resize the column to the left (**Figure 2.37**).

   Column widths can be customized for each Cast window.

To change Cast window preferences:

1. Activate a Cast window by clicking it.

2. Choose Edit > Preferences > Cast (Windows) or Director > Preferences > Cast (Mac).

   The Cast Window Preferences dialog box opens (**Figure 2.38**).

3. Make choices from the pop-up menus in the Cast Window Preferences dialog box (**Figure 2.39**) to determine thumbnail size, quantity displayed, and the way labels and icons are displayed.

4. To specify which columns you want to display in List view, select the appropriate checkboxes (**Figure 2.40**).

5. Leave the Apply to All Casts checkbox unselected if you want your column preferences to apply only to the Cast window you selected in step 1.

   or

   Select the Apply to All Casts checkbox to apply your column preferences to all Cast windows.

✔ Tip

■ Most of the column attributes are self-explanatory, but two need clarification: The Modified attribute corresponds to the column with the asterisk (*) header. An asterisk means that the cast member has been modified and not saved. The Script column indicates which cast members have a script attached.

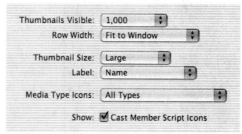

Figure 2.38 Change Thumbnail view preferences in the Cast Window Preferences dialog box.

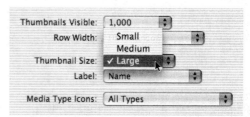

Figure 2.39 Use the pop-up menus in the Cast Window Preferences dialog box to change the way thumbnails are displayed.

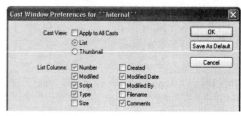

Figure 2.40 In the Cast Window Preferences dialog box, select which list columns you want to display.

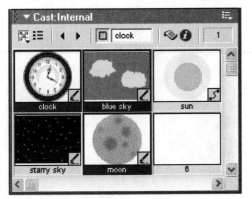

Figure 2.41 In Thumbnail view, Ctrl+click (Command+click, on the Mac) to select multiple nonadjacent cast members.

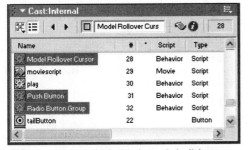

Figure 2.42 In List view in Windows, Ctrl+click to select multiple nonadjacent cast members.

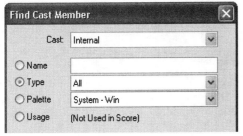

Figure 2.43 Use the Edit > Find > Cast Member command to find cast members by type, palette, or use.

Selecting, Moving, and Deleting Cast Members

Often, for "housekeeping" purposes, you'll want to name cast members, rearrange cast members in the Cast window, or delete cast members that aren't being used in your movie. These changes don't affect your movie at all, but they make it easier to find things when you come back later to make revisions.

To select a cast member:

1. If you're in Thumbnail view, click the thumbnail image to select a single cast member.

   or

   Shift+click to select a continuous range of cast members.

   or

   Ctrl+click (Windows) or Command+click (Mac) to select multi-ple nonadjacent cast members (**Figure 2.41**).

2. If you're in List view, click the name or icon (Windows) or column (Mac) to select a single cast member.

   or

   Select a continuous range of cast members by Shift+clicking (Windows) or by using the marquee selection (Mac).

   or

   Ctrl+click (Windows, **Figure 2.42**) or Command+Click (Mac) to add or remove nonadjacent cast members.

✔ Tip

- The Edit > Find > Cast Member command allows you to find and select cast members in any cast by name, type, or palette (**Figure 2.43**). (It can also be used to find cast members that are not used in the score: see "To delete unused cast members," earlier in this chapter.) This command works in either cast view style.

To name a cast member:

1. In either Thumbnail or List view, click to select a cast member in the Cast window.

2. Click the cast member Name field at the top of the Cast window.

3. Enter a name for the cast member (**Figure 2.44**).

   or

   Type a name in the Name text box on the Cast or Member tab in the Property Inspector.

To rename a cast member:

1. In Thumbnail or List view, click the cast member that you want to rename.

2. Edit the name in the Name field at the top of the Cast window.

   or

   (In List view only) Click-pause-click (don't double-click) a cast member's name to activate editing.

To copy, move, or delete a cast member:

1. In either Thumbnail or List view, select one or more cast members that you want to copy, move to a different cast, or delete (**Figure 2.45**).

2. Duplicate the cast-member selection within a Cast window by holding down the Alt key (Windows) or Option key (Mac) while dragging and dropping the selection (**Figure 2.46**).

   or

   Delete the selection by pressing Delete.

   or

   Copy the cast-member selection to a *different* Cast window by dragging it there while holding down the Alt key (Windows) or Option key (Mac) (**Figure 2.47**).

   or

   Move the selection by dragging it to a different Cast window (**Figure 2.48**).

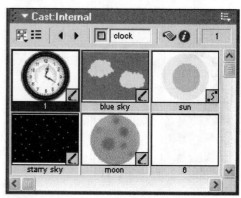

Figure 2.44 Type a name in the cast member Name field.

Figure 2.45 Make a cast-member selection.

Figure 2.46 Drag and drop the selection within the same Cast window while holding down the Alt key (Windows) or Option key (Mac) to duplicate the selection.

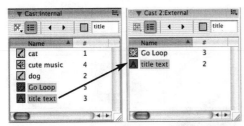

Figure 2.47 Drag the selection to a different cast while holding down the Alt key (Windows) or Option key (Mac) to copy it there.

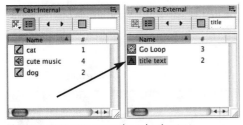

Figure 2.48 Drag to move the selection to a different cast.

✔ Tips

■ The last two options—copying and moving members to another cast—require that the second cast be in a completely separate window. You can't drag cast members between tabbed casts within a single Cast window. (For information on giving a tabbed panel its own window, see "To remove a panel from a panel group," in Chapter 1.)

■ You can't reorder cast members by dragging and dropping in list view, but you can do so in Thumbnail view.

■ You can also duplicate a cast-member selection in a Cast window by choosing Edit > Duplicate.

To reposition a cast member in a Cast window:

1. In Thumbnail view, select a cast member or members (**Figure 2.49**).

2. Drag the selected cast member (or cast members, in a multiple selection) to a new position in the Cast window (**Figure 2.50**).

   If you like, you can Alt+drag (Windows) or Option+drag (Mac) to copy the cast member instead of repositioning it.

   Multiple cast members are positioned sequentially from the point to which you drag them.

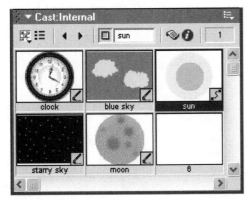

Figure 2.49 Make a cast-member selection. Here, the Sun cast member is selected.

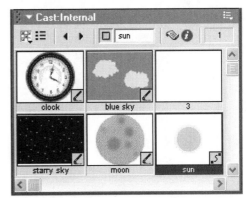

Figure 2.50 Reposition a cast member by dragging it to a new position in the cast. The Sun cast member is now in the lower-right corner of the Cast window.

The Place button

The Place button comes in handy when you want to move a cast member to a new position in a Cast window but it's not convenient to drag it—for example, when you can't see the place you're moving it to.

To move a cast member with the Place button:

1. In a Cast window, select the cast member you want to move (**Figure 2.51**).

2. Scroll through the Cast window to the position where you want to move the cast member.

3. Drag the Place button to the new position in the Cast window (**Figure 2.52**) or in a different Cast window.

   When you release the mouse button, the cast member moves to the destination.

✔ Tip

■ Hold down the Alt key (Windows) or Option key (Mac) while dragging the Place button to copy the selected cast member to its new position.

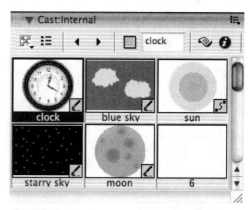

Figure 2.51 Select the cast member or cast members you want to move.

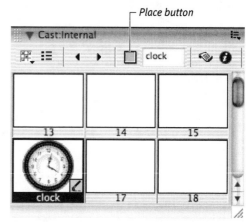

Figure 2.52 Drag the Place button to the new position in the Cast window or to a different Cast window.

Cast Member Properties button

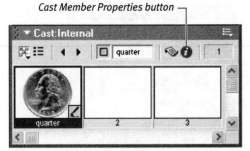

Figure 2.53 Click the Cast Member Properties button to open the Property Inspector.

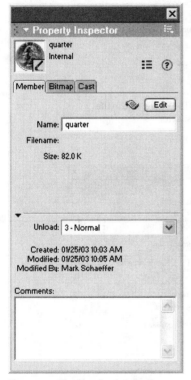

Figure 2.54 The Member tab for the Property Inspector.

Managing Cast and Cast Member Properties

You can use the Property Inspector to view and change the properties of individual cast members or entire casts.

To view or change cast and cast-member properties:

1. Select a cast member in the Cast window.

2. If the Property Inspector is not currently open, choose Modify > Cast Member > Properties or click the Cast Member Properties button in the Cast window (**Figure 2.53**).

   The Property Inspector appears, displaying three or four tabs at the top.

   The first tab is the Member tab, which contains the same set of generic properties for all cast members (**Figure 2.54**).

continues on next page

MANAGING CAST AND CAST MEMBER PROPERTIES

The second tab varies, depending on the type of cast member selected, and contains a specific set of properties for that type. If you select a bitmap cast member, for example, this tab contains properties such as palette and bit depth (**Figure 2.55**).

The last tab is the Cast tab, listing properties of the cast that contains the selected cast member (**Figure 2.56**).

If you've selected a text cast member, there will be an extra tab between the second and final tabs. This is the 3D Extruder, which displays the properties of 3D text. You'll find out more about this tab in Chapter 18, "Shockwave 3D."

3. Select the tab for which you want to set or view properties.

4. Click the List View Mode button to select either List or graphical view.

List view (**Figure 2.57**) generally shows a more complete set of properties than graphical view, which shows only the most commonly used properties.

5. Make any necessary changes in editable properties.

6. Close the Property Inspector.

The various cast-member–specific properties on the second tab are discussed throughout the book, in sections relating to the specific media type.

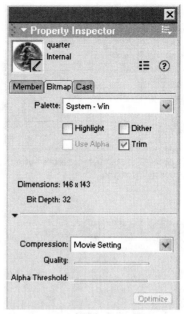

Figure 2.55 The Bitmap tab in the Property Inspector.

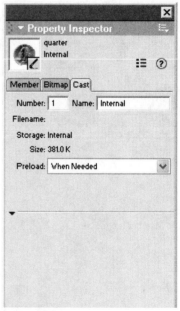

Figure 2.56 The Cast tab in the Property Inspector.

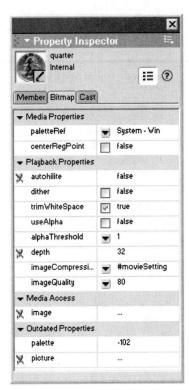

Figure 2.57 List view in the Property Inspector shows a more complete set of properties than graphical view.

✔ Tips

- When the Property Inspector is in List view, you can view a description of any property by holding the mouse pointer over the property name.

- When the Property Inspector is in List view, properties that can't be edited have a checkmark displayed next to their names.

Setting cast members and memory

When a user plays back your movie, Director sometimes must load and unload cast members from memory, juggling them to fit within the computer's memory constraints. You can control which cast members Director considers to be the most important to keep in memory—and which it considers to be the least important—by setting the cast members' Unload values in the Property Inspector (**Table 2.2**).

To set a cast member's priority in memory:

1. Select a cast member in a Cast window.

2. If the Property Inspector is not currently open, choose Modify > Cast Member > Properties to display it.

3. Select the Member tab.

4. Click the List View Mode button to select graphical view.

5. Choose a setting from the Unload pop-up menu (**Figure 2.58**).

   (Note that when the Property Inspector is in List view instead of graphical view, you set the Unload value by setting the purgePriority property). Unload settings range from 0 to 3. The 0 setting tells Director never to remove the cast member from memory; 3 means to unload this cast member from memory before anything with a 2 or 1 setting. Give the least important (or least frequently appearing) cast members a 2 or 3 setting. Give heavily used cast members a 0 setting.

Table 2.2

Cast-Member Memory Priority	
UNLOAD VALUE	PRIORITY IN MEMORY
0 (Never)	Cast member is never purged from memory
1 (Last)	Cast member is among the last group to be purged from memory
2 (Next)	Cast member is among the next group to be purged from memory
3 (Normal)	Cast member is purged from memory as necessary

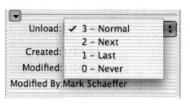

Figure 2.58 The Unload value determines the cast member's priority in memory.

Expander arrow

Figure 2.59 The asset-management fields are located in the lower pane of Member tab of the Property Inspector. If all you see is the upper pane (as shown here), click the expander arrow to reveal the lower pane.

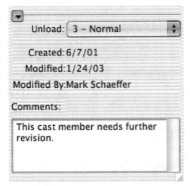

Figure 2.60 The asset-management fields.

Viewing cast member changes

The Property Inspector contains four asset-management fields that help you keep track of changes made in cast members. These fields are Created, Modified, Modified By, and Comments. They are particularly useful when a team of people is collaborating on a project.

To view and set asset-management fields for a cast member:

1. Select a cast member in a Cast window.

2. If the Property Inspector is not currently open, choose Modify > Cast Member > Properties to display it.

3. Select the Member tab (**Figure 2.59**).

4. Select graphical view (if necessary) by clicking the List View Mode button.

5. View the Created, Modified, and Modified By fields in the bottom pane of the Property Inspector (**Figure 2.60**). These fields cannot be edited.

6. *(optional)* Enter comments for the cast member by typing them in the Comments box.

Changing a cast member's thumbnail image

You can replace a cast member's thumbnail image to make it more meaningful to you and your project team. Replacing a thumbnail does not affect the actual cast member in any way. Creating custom thumbnails can be especially useful for cast members for which Director does not automatically create a thumbnail image, such as sounds and behaviors.

To set a cast-member thumbnail:

1. Copy a bit-mapped image that you want to use as the new thumbnail.

   You can copy this image from the Paint window or another source.

2. Select a cast member (**Figure 2.61**).

3. If the Property Inspector is not currently open, choose Modify > Cast Member > Properties to display it.

4. Right-click (Windows) or Ctrl+click (Mac) the thumbnail image in the top-left corner of the Property Inspector

   The Thumbnail pop-up menu appears (**Figure 2.62**).

5. Choose Paste Thumbnail.

   The Cast window shows the new thumbnail (**Figure 2.63**).

✔ Tips

- Choose Clear Thumbnail from the Thumbnail pop-up menu to return the cast member's original thumbnail image.

- You can copy and paste thumbnails by choosing the appropriate commands from the Thumbnail pop-up menu.

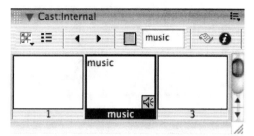

Figure 2.61 Select a cast member that needs a thumbnail.

Figure 2.62 Right-click (Windows) or Ctrl+click (Mac) the thumbnail image in the top-left corner of the Property Inspector to display a pop-up menu.

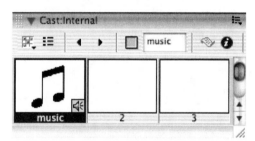

Figure 2.63 The new thumbnail is now in place.

BUILDING A SCORE

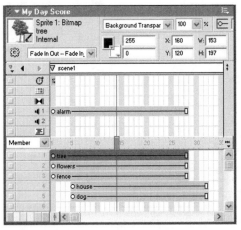

Figure 3.1 The Score provides a frame-by-frame record of all the components that form your Director movie.

Director's Score (**Figure 3.1**) works like the script of a Hollywood movie. It tells your cast members what they should do, and when and where they should do it.

You assemble a Director movie by placing cast members (such as graphics and sounds) and events (such as scene transitions and tempo changes) in the Score's frames, which represent brief segments of time in a movie.

Cast members placed in the Score or on the Stage are represented by images called *sprites*. In this chapter, you'll begin to work with sprites in the Score. You'll learn to arrange them in time and space, edit their properties, and use them to control activities on the Stage. You'll also learn how to view and customize the Score itself.

Using Frames and Channels

As you learned in Chapter 1, the Score shows how everything in your movie changes over time (**Figure 3.2**). The vertical columns, or *frames*, represent small slices of time, like the frames in a movie. The horizontal rows, called *channels*, represent places where you can put movie contents, such as graphics, animation scenes, text, buttons, sounds, and Lingo scripts.

The intersections of the frames and channels make a grid of little boxes called *cells*, like those in a spreadsheet. Each cell represents the smallest unit of a movie: one frame's worth of a sprite. The whole thing works together like a control panel for your movie, so that what you do in the Score actually manipulates what takes place on the movie Stage. When you start exploring the Score, you'll probably want the Stage to be open, too, so that you can see how the two work together.

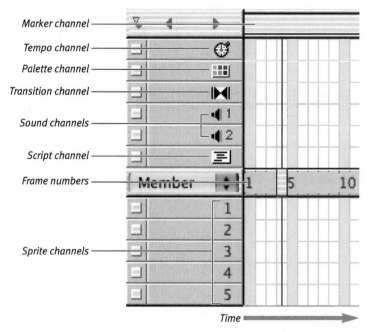

Marker channel

Tempo channel

Palette channel

Transition channel

Sound channels

Script channel

Frame numbers

Sprite channels

Time

Figure 3.2 The Score shows how all the elements of your movie appear—and how they change—over time.

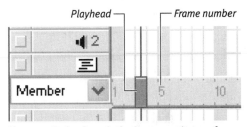

Figure 3.3 Each column in the Score constitutes a frame. Frames are numbered sequentially from left to right.

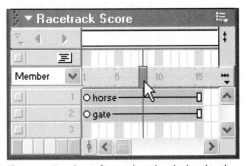

Figure 3.4 Even sprites that appear only briefly in a movie take up a series of frames in the Score.

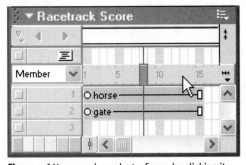

Figure 3.5 To select a frame, drag the playhead to the desired frame.

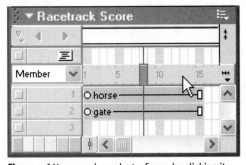

Figure 3.6 You can also select a frame by clicking it.

To open the Score:

◆ Choose Window > Score.

One frame in the Score, from top to bottom, is like a snapshot of the movie in time. The frames have numbers, visible between the effects and sprite channels, forming a horizontal band (**Figure 3.3**). The position of the *playhead* (the vertical line in the Score that advances as the movie plays) indicates which frame is currently displayed on the Stage.

There's no limit to the number of frames you can have in a movie, which means there's no technical limit to how long a Director movie can be (although there may be practical limits, such as how much room you have on a hard drive).

Because Director movies play at the speed of several (or many) frames per second, even sprites that appear only briefly in a movie take up a series of frames in the Score (**Figure 3.4**).

To select a frame:

◆ Drag the playhead left or right and release it in the desired frame (**Figure 3.5**).

  or

  Click the frame that you want to make active (**Figure 3.6**).

To open the Stage:

◆ Choose Window > Stage.

Score channels

You manage and direct your sprites and movie events by placing each of them in a channel of the Score (**Figure 3.7**). The first six channels at the top of the Score are reserved for specialized functions, as follows:

◆ **Tempo channel:** set the playback speed

◆ **Palette channel:** specify changes in color palettes

◆ **Transition channel:** set transition effects between scenes, such as dissolves and wipes

◆ **Sound channels (two):** add sound effects, music, and voice tracks

◆ **Script channel:** incorporate Lingo programming scripts

You'll find out more about these specialized channels later in this chapter and throughout the book.

The remaining channels—those below the frame-number bar—are called the *sprite channels*. For the most part, these channels are used for animating the visual elements of your movie.

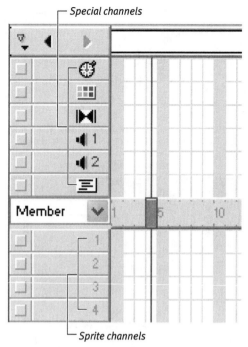

Special channels

Sprite channels

Figure 3.7 Each row of the Score constitutes a channel. Sprite channels are numbered from top to bottom along the left side of the Score.

Flash Talk: Channels vs. Layers

The channels in Director's Score work like the layers in Macromedia Flash's timeline, except that they're stacked in the opposite direction: Flash's layers are built upward from the bottom of the timeline, while Director's channels are built downward from the top of the Score. Unlike Flash's layers, Director's channels can't be named or grouped.

Director is more restrictive than Flash about the use of its channels. In Flash, you can place just about any sort of object (image, sound, script, or whatever) in any layer, and you can put multiple objects or symbols in a single layer. In Director, each object must be placed in its own layer, and specialized types of objects must be placed in specialized channels.

USING FRAMES AND CHANNELS

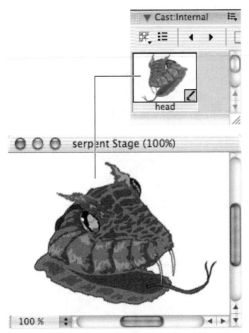

Figure 3.8 The sprite on the Stage has been flipped horizontally and rotated, but these changes in the sprite's properties do not affect the original cast member.

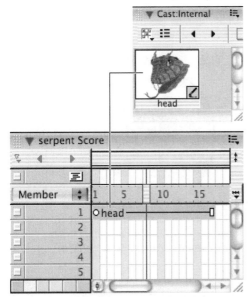

Figure 3.9 The same sprite is represented in the Score as a colored line spanning a range of frames.

Working with Sprites

You begin to construct a Director movie by dragging cast members from the Cast window. You can drop a cast member into a channel in the Score, or you can drop it on the Stage.

What you're actually dropping on the Stage or in the Score is not the cast member itself, but a *reference* to the cast member—a marker that points back to the original that's stored in the Cast window. This reference to the original cast member is known as a *sprite*.

You can create multiple sprites in your movie based on the same cast member. Every sprite has its own properties, which may be different from those of the original cast member. Except in the case of text, changing a sprite's properties does not alter the cast member (**Figure 3.8**).

Dragging a visual cast member to the Score or the Stage causes a sprite to appear both in the Score *and* on the Stage. On the Stage, the sprite looks like the original cast member. In the Score, the sprite takes the form of a colored line spanning a range of frames (**Figure 3.9**). But both are the same sprite. The Stage and the Score just provide two different ways of looking at the sprite.

To create a sprite in the Score:

1. Select one or more cast members (**Figure 3.10**).

2. Drag the cast-member selection to a cell in the Score.

   As you drag, Director outlines the range of cells where sprites will be created (**Figure 3.11**). Director outlines only cells that can accommodate your cast members (sounds can be dragged only to cells in the sound channels, for example) (**Figure 3.12**).

   When you release the mouse button, images of any visual cast members you dragged to the Score appear in the center of the Stage (**Figure 3.13**).

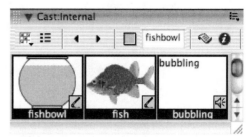

Figure 3.10 To create a sprite in the Score, you must first select one or more cast members.

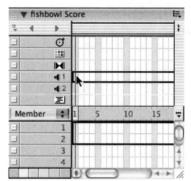

Figure 3.11 As you drag the cast-member selection into the Score, Director outlines the range of cells where sprites will be created.

Figure 3.12 The new sprites appear in the Score. Director is smart enough to drop sounds in the sound channel.

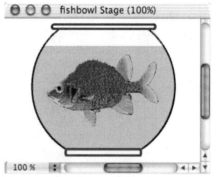

Figure 3.13 Visual cast members dragged into the Score appear at the center of the Stage.

WORKING WITH SPRITES

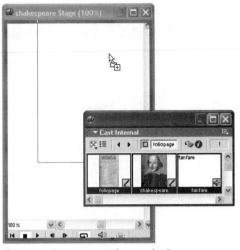

Figure 3.14 Drag cast members to the Stage.

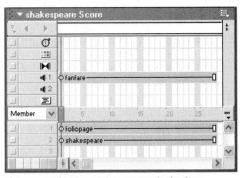

Figure 3.15 The new sprites appear in the Score.

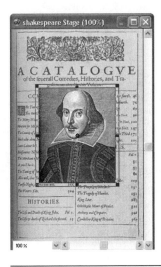

Figure 3.16 Visual cast members appear on the Stage at the location to which they were dragged.

To create a sprite by dragging cast members to the Stage:

1. Select one or more cast members.

2. In the Score, click the frame in which you want to place a sprite or group of sprites.

3. Drag the cast-member selection from the Cast window to the Stage (**Figure 3.14**).

   Your new sprites appear in the Score (**Figure 3.15**). Images of any visual cast members that were part of your selection appear stacked on the Stage in the location you dragged them to (**Figure 3.16**).

✔ Tip

■ Because a sprite is not a copy of a cast member, but simply a reference to it, sprites take up barely any disk space or memory. Adding cast members to a movie may greatly increase a movie's file size, but adding sprites will not.

WORKING WITH SPRITES

Adjusting sprite duration

Each new sprite you create has a default duration of 28 frames. You can change this default to any number of frames you like.

To change the default sprite duration:

1. Choose Edit > Preferences > Sprite (Windows), or Director > Preferences > Sprite (Mac).

   The Sprite Preferences dialog box opens (**Figure 3.17**).

2. Enter a value for the Span Duration option.

   or

   Choose Width of Score Window to have new sprites span the width of the Score.

3. Check the Terminate at Markers checkbox to have each new sprite end one frame before the next marker. (See "Setting Markers" later in this chapter for details on using markers.)

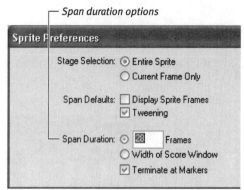

Span duration options

Figure 3.17 The Sprite Preferences dialog box.

Flash Talk: Sprite vs. Instance

A *sprite* in Director is roughly equivalent to an *instance of a symbol* in Flash. The main difference is that in Director, a sprite may refer to a representation either on the Stage or in the Score. In Flash, only the image on the Stage is called an instance; there's no equivalent term for the frames that the instance occupies in the timeline.

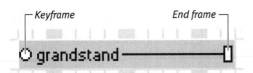

Figure 3.18 The first frame of a sprite is a keyframe, represented by a circle. The last frame of the sprite is represented by a rectangle. (The rectangle will change to a circle if the sprite is tweened. You'll find out about *tweening* in the next chapter.)

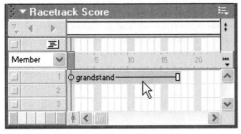

Figure 3.19 Click the horizontal line within a sprite to select the entire sprite.

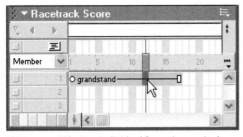

Figure 3.20 Select an individual frame in a sprite by Alt+clicking it (Windows) or Option+clicking it (Mac).

Selecting sprites

The first frame of a sprite is called a *keyframe*, represented in the Score by a small circle. (You'll learn about the significance of keyframes in the next chapter.) The last frame of a sprite is indicated by a rectangle (**Figure 3.18**). The first and last frames are connected by a solid line.

To select an entire sprite:

◆ Click the horizontal line (*not* the keyframe or end frame) within a sprite in the Score (**Figure 3.19**).

or

Click the sprite on the Stage.

✔ Tip

■ In the Score, the selected portions of a sprite appear in a darker color. If you intended to select the entire sprite, but most of the sprite still appears in a light color, chances are that you accidentally clicked the keyframe or end frame.

To select one frame in a sprite:

◆ Alt+click (Windows) or Option+click (Mac) the desired frame within the sprite in the Score (**Figure 3.20**).

or

Move the playhead in the Score to the desired frame, then Alt+click (Windows) or Option+click (Mac) the desired sprite on the Stage.

continues on next page

WORKING WITH SPRITES

✔ Tips

- If the single frame you want to select is a keyframe or end frame, simply click that frame in the Score. You don't need to hold down the Alt or Option key while you click.

- To select individual frames in a sprite without Alt+clicking or Option+clicking, see "To make sprite frames individually editable" later in this chapter.

To select multiple frames within a sprite in the Score:

- Ctrl+Alt+click (Windows) or Command+ Option+Click (Mac) to select multiple nonadjacent frames.

  or

  Shift+Alt+click (Windows) or Shift+Option+click (Mac) to select a continuous range of frames.

To select multiple sprites:

- Drag to select multiple sprites either in the Score (**Figure 3.21**) or on the Stage.

  You need not enclose a sprite completely within the selection rectangle to select all of it.

✔ Tip

- You can select a continuous range of sprites in the Score by clicking the first sprite and then Shift+clicking (Windows) or Command+clicking (Mac) the last sprite. Ctrl+click (Windows) or Command+click (Mac) to select multiple sprites that are not adjacent.

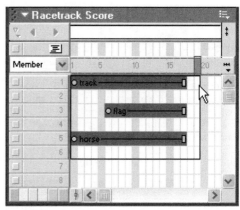

Figure 3.21 select multiple sprites in the Score. (You can do this on the Stage as well.)

Flash Talk: Spanning Frames

In Flash, if you want to place an instance of a symbol on the Stage for multiple frames, you must complete three steps: inserting a keyframe, dragging the symbol to the Stage, and inserting an end frame. In Director, the equivalent operation requires only *one* step: dragging a cast member to the Stage or to the Score. Director automatically inserts a keyframe, an end frame, and 26 intermediate frames.

WORKING WITH SPRITES

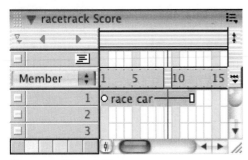

Figure 3.22 Click a sprite.

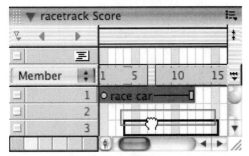

Figure 3.23 When you drag the sprite to a new frame and/or channel, you'll see an outline of the new range of frames.

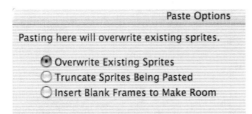

Figure 3.24 Specify in the Paste Options dialog box how sprites should be pasted.

Moving sprites within the Score

There are two main reasons why you might want to move a sprite within the Score. To make it appear earlier or later in the movie, you move it *horizontally* to a lower- or higher-numbered frame. To move the sprite farther from or closer to the foreground of the Stage, you move it *vertically* to a lower- or higher-numbered channel in the Score. (See "To change the order of overlapping sprites" later in this chapter).

To move a sprite to a new location in the Score:

1. In the Score, click a sprite (**Figure 3.22**).

2. Drag the sprite to a new frame and/or channel in the Score.

   Director outlines the new range of frames for the sprite (**Figure 3.23**).

3. Release the mouse button to place the sprite in the outlined frames.

You can also move sprites in the Score by cutting and pasting.

To cut and paste sprites in the Score:

1. In the Score, select the sprite or range of sprites.

2. Choose Edit > Cut Sprites, or Edit > Copy Sprites.

3. Click the cell in the Score where you want to paste the sprite selection.

4. Choose Edit > Paste Sprites.

   If the placement of the sprite selection threatens to overwrite any existing sprites, the Paste Options dialog box appears.

5. If the Paste Options dialog box appears, make one of the three choices and then click OK (**Figure 3.24**).

WORKING WITH SPRITES

✔ Tips

- The third option in the Paste Options is Insert Blank Frames to Make Room. If this is the option you want, you can accomplish the same thing (without seeing the dialog box) by choosing Edit > Paste Special > Insert.

- To delete a sprite selection instead of moving it, choose Edit > Clear Sprites in step 2, and ignore the remaining steps.

To reposition a sprite on the Stage:

1. Select an entire sprite in the Score.

   The sprite is highlighted in the Score and on the Stage (**Figure 3.25**).

2. Drag the sprite to its new position on the Stage (**Figure 3.26**).

   This step repositions the entire sprite (all of the frames in its span).

✔ Tip

- You can reposition selected frames of a sprite. First, select sprite frames (as described in "To select one frame in a sprite" earlier in this chapter); then reposition the sprite.

Figure 3.25 Selecting a sprite in the Score also highlights it on the Stage.

Figure 3.26 Drag the sprite to its new location on the Stage.

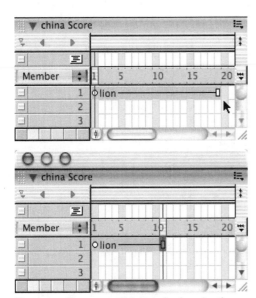

Figure 3.27 Change a sprite's span by dragging the frame at either end.

Figure 3.28 Change a sprite's span by entering new values in the Sprite toolbar or the Property Inspector.

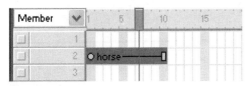

Figure 3.29 Select a sprite.

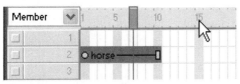

Figure 3.30 In the frame-number bar, click the frame in which you want the extended sprite to end.

Figure 3.31 After you choose Modify > Extend Sprite, the sprite extends to meet the playhead.

To change the length of a sprite's span:

◆ Drag the first or last frame of the sprite to a new frame (**Figure 3.27**).

✔ Tip

■ You can also change a sprite's span by entering new values in the Start or End fields in the Sprite toolbar, or in the Sprite tab of the Property Inspector (**Figure 3.28**). (See "To toggle the display of the Sprite toolbar" later in this chapter.)

To extend a sprite:

1. Select a sprite in the Score (**Figure 3.29**).

2. Click the number of the frame to which you want to extend the sprite (**Figure 3.30**).

   Director repositions the playhead in the selected frame.

3. Choose Modify > Extend Sprite.

   Director extends the sprite to meet the playhead (**Figure 3.31**).

✔ Tip

■ You can use the same process to shorten a sprite. Click a frame within the sprite to reposition the playhead where you want the sprite to end. When you choose Modify > Extend Sprite, the sprite shortens.

WORKING WITH SPRITES

Joining and dividing sprites

It's sometimes convenient to join several short sprites into one long sprite, or to divide one long sprite into several shorter sprites.

To join sprites:

1. Select two or more sprites in the Score.

   The sprites can have gaps between them, but they must all occupy the same channel (**Figure 3.32**).

2. Choose Modify > Join Sprites.

   The sprites merge into a single sprite (**Figure 3.33**).

To split a sprite:

1. In the Score, click a frame within a sprite (**Figure 3.34**).

   The playhead jumps to the frame that you clicked.

2. Choose Modify > Split Sprite.

   The sprite divides into two new sprites, dividing at the location of the playhead (**Figure 3.35**).

To make sprite frames individually editable:

1. In the Score, click a sprite.

2. Choose Edit > Edit Sprite Frames.

   The appearance of the sprite changes from a continuous span to a series of individual boxes. Now when you click a frame within the sprite, only that single frame is selected (**Figure 3.36**).

✔ Tip

- You can return the sprite to its normal state by selecting any frame in the sprite and then choosing Edit > Edit Entire Sprite.

Figure 3.32 In a single channel of the Score, select the sprites that you want to join.

Figure 3.33 The sprites merge into a single sprite.

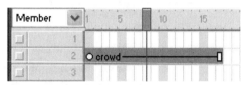

Figure 3.34 Click the frame in a sprite where you want the division to take place.

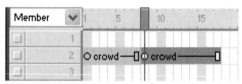

Figure 3.35 The sprite divides in two.

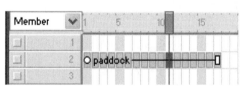

Figure 3.36 The boxy appearance of this sprite shows that its frames have been made individually editable by means of the Edit Sprite Frames command. A single frame of the sprite (frame 11) is selected; the rest remain unselected.

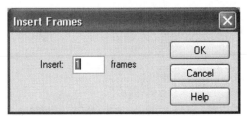

Figure 3.37 In the Insert Frames dialog box, type the number of frames you want to insert into the Score.

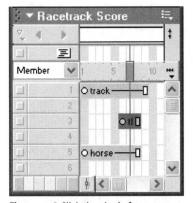

Figure 3.38 Click the single frame you want to remove.

Figure 3.39 The frame is deleted.

To insert frames into the Score:

1. Click the frame in the Score where you want to insert one or more frames.

2. Choose Insert > Frames.

   The Insert Frames dialog box opens (**Figure 3.37**).

3. Enter the number of frames to insert.

   If the frame you select contains sprites, Director inserts frames into each sprite, moving their end frames farther to the right. If the frame you select coincides with a keyframe in any sprite, new keyframes are inserted for those sprites.

To remove a frame from the Score:

1. Click the single frame that you want to remove (**Figure 3.38**).

   Note that the selected frame will be removed from sprites in *all* channels.

2. Choose Insert > Remove Frame.

   If any sprites span this frame, they are effectively shortened by one frame (**Figure 3.39**).

✔ Tip

- Keyframes are not removed by Insert > Remove Frame. If the keyframe of a sprite falls within the frame that's being removed, the first frame following the keyframe will be removed from that sprite.

WORKING WITH SPRITES

Reordering sprites

When sprites overlap on the Stage, the sprite in the higher-numbered channel appears in the foreground (**Figure 3.40**).

If you are animating a character walking down a street, for example, the character may appear to walk in front of buildings (**Figure 3.41**) but behind parked cars, street lamps, and signposts.

To change the order of overlapping sprites:

1. In the Score, select a sprite to be moved toward the foreground or the background of the Stage (**Figure 3.42**).

2. Choose Modify > Arrange, and select the appropriate command from the pop-up menu (**Figure 3.43**).

   Bring to Front places the selected sprite in front of all other sprites. Move Forward places the sprite one step closer to the foreground. The other two commands accomplish the opposite tasks.

✔ Tip

- Using Modify > Arrange sometimes leads to undesirable consequences when the sprites being rearranged are of different lengths. Longer sprites may be split into segments residing in different channels. To avoid these problems, it's often more convenient to move sprites to higher- or lower-numbered channels simply by dragging them.

Background ⌐ ⌐ Foreground

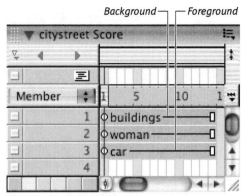

Figure 3.40 When sprites overlap on the Stage, the sprite in the highest-numbered channel appears in the foreground.

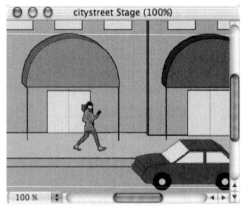

Figure 3.41 Here, the sprite of a car is in the foreground, the woman is in the middle ground, and the buildings are in the background.

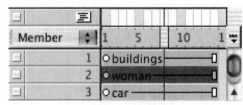

Figure 3.42 Select a sprite to move forward or backward.

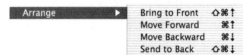

Figure 3.43 Use the Modify > Arrange menu to change the order of overlapping sprites.

WORKING WITH SPRITES

Changing Sprite Properties

Each sprite includes a set of properties that describes how the sprite looks in your Director movie. These properties include a sprite's Stage-location coordinates, size, blend percentage, ink effect, start frame and end frame, rotation, and skew angles, as well as animation options. You can vary these properties frame by frame as part of the animation process. (See Chapter 4, "Animating Sprites.")

You can change some sprite properties—such as size and Stage coordinates—by moving or resizing a sprite on the Stage. You can also change these properties, and others as well, by using the Property Inspector's Sprite tab or the Sprite toolbar in the Score. The Sprite toolbar contains the same set of properties as the Property Inspector; which one you use is a matter of preference.

While working on the Stage, you can view a set of commonly used sprite properties (coordinates, ink effect, and blend percentage) directly on the Stage in a small box called the *sprite overlay*. Using this overlay is often more convenient than having to go back and forth between the Stage and Property Inspector.

To open the Property Inspector for a sprite:

1. Select a sprite in the Score or on the Stage.

2. Choose Modify > Sprite > Properties. The Property Inspector opens, with the Sprite tab displayed (**Figure 3.44**).

To toggle the display of the Sprite toolbar:

1. Choose View > Sprite Toolbar (**Figure 3.45**).

2. Select a sprite to view its properties in the Sprite toolbar.

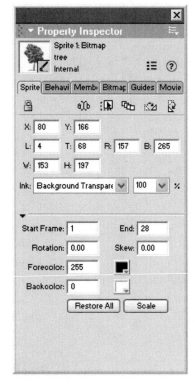

Figure 3.44 The Property Inspector's Sprite tab.

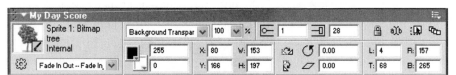

Figure 3.45 Set sprite properties in the Score's Sprite toolbar.

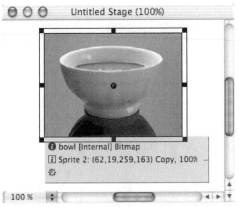

Figure 3.46 Turn on the Show Info option to view sprite details in a small rectangle below a sprite.

Figure 3.47 In the Overlay Settings dialog box, specify how Director displays the sprite information.

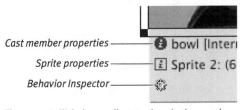

Cast member properties —— ❶ bowl [Inter

Sprite properties —— ⓘ Sprite 2: (6

Behavior Inspector —— ❀

Figure 3.48 Click the small center icon in the panel below the sprite to edit the sprite's properties.

To view sprite properties on the Stage:

1. Choose View > Sprite Overlay > Show Info.

   Sprite properties are displayed in a rectangle below each sprite (**Figure 3.46**).

2. Choose View > Sprite Overlay > Settings to open the Overlay Settings dialog box.

3. Choose an overlay setting to define how Director displays the sprite information (**Figure 3.47**):

   Click Roll Over if you want sprite properties to be displayed when you roll the mouse pointer over a sprite on the Stage.

   Click Selection if you want properties to be displayed only for selected sprites.

   Click All Sprites if you want properties to be displayed for all sprites on the Stage.

✔ Tip

■ Click the small center icon (**Figure 3.48**) on the left side of a Sprite Overlay panel to edit the sprite properties in the Property Inspector. Click the top icon to edit the cast member properties. Click the bottom icon to edit the behavior of the given sprite.

To resize a sprite:

1. In the Score or on the Stage, select a sprite.

   A rectangular outline with square resizing handles surrounds the sprite on the Stage (**Figure 3.49**).

2. On the Stage, drag one of the sprite's handles to stretch or squeeze the sprite (**Figure 3.50**).

   Hold the Shift key while dragging a corner handle of the sprite to resize it proportionately.

✔ Tips

■ Resizing a sprite affects only the selected sprite; the original cast member remains unchanged.

■ You can resize multiple sprites at the same time by selecting them together in the Score and then resizing one of the selected sprites on the Stage. All the selected sprites resize in the same way.

■ You can also resize a sprite by using the Scale Sprite dialog box (**Figure 3.51**). With a sprite selected, click the Scale button on the Sprite tab of the Property Inspector to open the dialog box. Enter an overall scale percentage or individual values for the width and height. You can check the Maintain Proportions option if you want to maintain the sprite's original width-to-height ratio.

Resize handle

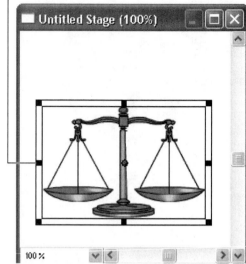

Figure 3.49 A selected sprite on the Stage has eight small resize handles.

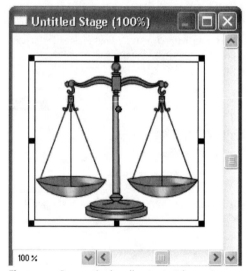

Figure 3.50 Drag resize handles to stretch or squeeze a sprite.

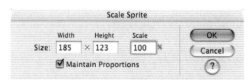

Figure 3.51 Resize a sprite by entering width and height dimensions in the Scale Sprite dialog box.

Figure 3.52 Select a sprite to rotate.

Figure 3.53 In the Property Inspector, type how many degrees to rotate the sprite.

Figure 3.54 The sprite, rotated 45 degrees clockwise.

Figure 3.55 You can also rotate sprites with the Rotation and Skew tool in the Tools palette.

To rotate a sprite:

1. Select a sprite in the Score or on the Stage. A rectangular outline surrounds the selected sprite on the Stage (**Figure 3.52**).

2. Choose Modify > Sprite > Properties to display the Property Inspector.

3. In the Property Inspector, type a number of degrees in the Rotation field and press Enter (**Figure 3.53**).

   A positive number rotates the sprite clockwise (**Figure 3.54**); a negative number rotates it counterclockwise.

✔ Tips

■ You can also rotate sprites with the Rotation and Skew tool in the Tool palette. First, choose Window > Tool Palette, and click the Rotation and Skew tool (**Figure 3.55**). Next, click a sprite to rotate on the Stage. Move the Rotation and Skew tool into the selected sprite to select the Rotation tool. Click and drag to rotate the sprite; release the mouse button when the result looks right to you.

■ To rotate a sprite in 90-degree increments, select a sprite and then choose Modify > Transform > Rotate Left, or Modify > Transform > Rotate Right.

CHANGING SPRITE PROPERTIES

To flip a sprite:

1. Select a sprite in the Score or on the Stage.

2. Choose Modify > Sprite > Properties.

3. Click Flip Horizontal or Flip Vertical (**Figure 3.56**) to flip the sprite either horizontally or vertically (**Figure 3.57**).

✔ Tip

- When you flip a sprite, you're creating a mirror image of that sprite.

Figure 3.56 The Flip Horizontal and Flip Vertical buttons of the Property Inspector's Sprite tab.

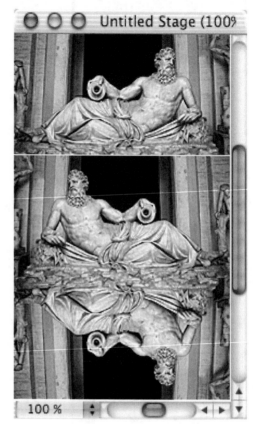

Figure 3.57 Sprites may be flipped horizontally or vertically.

Figure 3.58 Select a sprite to skew.

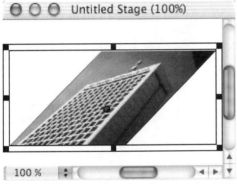

Figure 3.59 Type a value in the skew-angle field.

Figure 3.60 The sprite, skewed 45 degrees to the right.

Figure 3.61 The Rotation and Skew tool offers another way to skew sprites.

To skew a sprite:

1. Select a sprite in the Score or on the Stage (**Figure 3.58**).

2. Choose Modify > Sprite > Properties.

3. Type a value in the skew-angle box (**Figure 3.59**).

   A positive value skews the sprite to the right (**Figure 3.60**); a negative value skews it to the left. Entering 90 (degrees) flattens the sprite.

✔ Tips

- You can also skew sprites with the Rotation and Skew tool in the Tool palette. First, choose Window > Tool Palette, and click the Rotation and Skew tool (**Figure 3.61**). Next, click a sprite on the Stage. Move the Rotation and Skew tool to the border of the selected sprite to select the Skew tool. Click and drag to skew the sprite.

- After resizing, rotating, and skewing a sprite, you may want to restore its original shape and orientation. To do so, select the sprite and then choose Modify > Transform > Reset All.

To change a sprite's color:

1. Select a sprite in the Score or on the Stage.

2. Choose Modify > Sprite > Properties.

3. To change black portions of the sprite to a new color, open the foreground color menu (**Figure 3.62**).

   or

   To change white portions of the sprite to a new color, open the background color menu.

4. Choose a color from the available palette colors or from the color picker.

✔ Tips

■ You can change any sprite's color, but doing so is only recommended for sprites based on black-and-white cast members. Attempting to change the colors of sprites based on multicolored cast members will result in unpredictable and often undesirable color changes.

■ If you have a group of cast members that are identical except for their color, you can reduce the file size of your Director movie by deleting all but one of them. Change the remaining cast member to black and white by choosing Modify > Transform Sprite and selecting a color depth of 1 bit. You can then create multiple sprites of different colors from the single black-and-white cast member.

To change the transparency of a sprite:

1. Select a sprite in the Score or on the Stage.

2. Choose Modify > Sprite > Properties.

3. Type a new value in the Blend box, or select a value from the pop-up menu (**Figure 3.63**).

   A 100 percent blend makes a sprite completely opaque, while a 0 percent blend makes the sprite totally transparent.

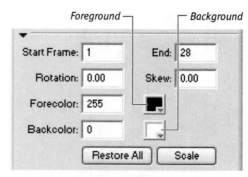

Figure 3.62 The foreground and background color menus in the Property Inspector can be used to change the colors of black-and-white sprites.

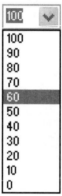

Figure 3.63 Set a new blend percentage by typing in a value or choosing one from the pop-up menu.

Trails

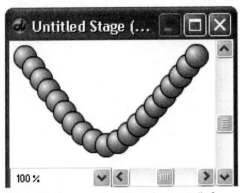

Figure 3.64 The Trails button in the Property Inspector.

Figure 3.65 You can set a sprite to leave a trail of images as it moves.

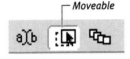

Moveable

Figure 3.66 The Moveable button in the Property Inspector.

To make a sprite leave a trail on the Stage:

1. Select a sprite in the Score or on the Stage.

2. Choose Modify > Sprite > Properties.

3. Click the Trails button in the Property Inspector (**Figure 3.64**).

    When you play the movie, the sprite will leave a trail of duplicates of itself (**Figure 3.65**).

✔ Tip

■ The Trails feature can be used to create an animated handwriting effect. See "Real-Time Recording" in Chapter 4, "Animating Sprites."

To set a sprite to be moveable during movie playback:

1. Select a sprite in the Score or on the Stage.

2. Choose Modify > Sprite > Properties.

3. Click the Moveable button in the Property Inspector (**Figure 3.66**).

    It now becomes possible for users to drag the sprite around the Stage while the movie is playing.

✔ Tip

■ This feature is useful in games or in educational applications in which you want to allow users to rearrange items on the screen.

CHANGING SPRITE PROPERTIES

Using Sprite Ink Effects

Director features a collection of ink effects that change the appearance of sprites on the Stage. Most of these effects are especially effective when sprites overlap. You can use ink effects to make sprites transparent, to darken or lighten them, or to apply a variety of color transformations. You can also use them to make the background of a sprite disappear (see Chapter 7, "Drawing Vector Shapes").

Note that sprite ink effects are different from those that you can apply to bitmaps in the Paint window. Ink effects in the Paint window (which you'll learn about in Chapter 6, "Using Paint Tools.") change the actual cast member. Sprite ink effects affect only sprites, not the cast members on which they are based. The names and functions of the ink effects in the two sets have differences as well.

To set an ink effect for a sprite:

1. Select a sprite in the Score or on the Stage.

2. Choose Modify > Sprite > Properties.

3. From the Ink pop-up menu, choose an ink effect (**Figure 3.67**).

   The "Score Ink Effects" sidebar describes the effects of the inks on sprites.

✔ Tip

■ Using ink effects other than the default Copy effect can slow your movie's animation. Try to use ink effects in strategic places, rather than across the board, if speedy animation is important in your project.

Figure 3.67 Use the Ink pop-up menu in the Property Inspector to choose an ink effect for a selected sprite.

Score Ink Effects

Although these explanations help you imagine the differences from one effect to another, the best way to understand them is to try them out.

Copy This is the default ink effect for all sprites. The sprite is displayed exactly like its corresponding cast member. If the cast member is not rectangular, the sprite is surrounded by a white rectangle (which is only evident if the sprite is placed against a nonwhite background).

Matte Sprites appear without the white rectangle associated with the Copy ink effect, but they use more memory and animate less quickly than those that use the Copy effect.

Background Transparent White pixels in the sprite are transparent. (If a background color other than white is selected, pixels of that color are transparent instead).

continues on next page

USING SPRITE INK EFFECTS

Score Ink Effects *continued*

Transparent White pixels are transparent, black pixels are opaque, and other colors have varying degrees of transparency depending on their lightness or darkness.

Reverse When a sprite with this ink effect overlaps another sprite, the overlapping areas change to the opposite of their normal color. White pixels become transparent.

Ghost This effect works like the Reverse ink effect, except that all non-overlapping areas of the sprite are transparent. (In other words, the sprite is invisible except where it overlaps another sprite.)

Not Copy, Not Transparent, Not Reverse, Not Ghost These ink effects act like the standard Copy, Matte, Transparent, and Ghost effects, except that they first reverse the foreground color of a sprite.

Mask This ink effect permits you to use another cast member (a mask) to specify which parts of a sprite are transparent. For more information, see "Using Ink Masks" in Chapter 7.

Blend White pixels in the sprite are transparent. All other colors take on the level of transparency specified in the Blend box on the Sprite tab of the Property Inspector.

Darkest When a sprite with this ink effect overlaps a sprite of a different color, the overlapping areas display the darker of the two colors.

Lightest This effect works like the Darkest ink effect, except the overlapping areas display the lighter of the two colors.

Add When a sprite with this ink effect overlaps another sprite, Director repaints the overlapping area with a new color that is created by adding the palette indexes of the overlapping pixels. If the new color has a palette index greater than 255 (the last color in the palette), Director subtracts 256 from the palette index and displays the resulting color.

Add Pin This effect works the same way as the Add ink effect, except that if the new color has a palette index greater than 255, Director changes it to the color whose index is 255 (which, in most palettes, is black).

Subtract When a sprite with this ink effect overlaps another sprite, Director repaints the overlapping area with a new color created by subtracting the palette index of the foreground color from that of the background color. If the new color has a palette index less than 0, Director adds 256 to the palette index and displays the resulting color.

Subtract Pin This effect works the same way as the Subtract ink effect, except that if the new color has a palette index less than 0, Director changes it to the color whose index is 0 (which, in most palettes, is white).

Darken The background color of the sprite is used to filter all areas of the sprite, and the foreground color of the sprite is added to all the filtered areas. The result looks similar to what print designers call a "duotone."

Lighten This effect works similarly to the Darken ink effect, except that the filtering action of the background color is used to lighten rather than darken the sprite.

Aligning Sprites on the Stage

To make your movie look neat and professional, you'll often want to align sprites cleanly—or distribute them evenly—across the Stage.

You can do either of these things by using the Align command. You can align sprites with respect to their centers, registration points (see "To view and set a cast member's registration point" later in this chapter), or any of the eight points around the bounding box that encompasses each sprite. Aligning sprites does not change their cast members' registration points.

You can use the Tweak command when you need to move sprites a precise number of pixels on the Stage.

When you construct an animation sequence from multiple cast members, the sprites may appear to jump or shift from one frame to the next. To eliminate this jerky motion, you can adjust the cast members' registration points. Every bitmapped cast member in your movie has a default registration point directly at its center (**Figure 3.68**).

If you are animating several frames of an athlete running, for example, you could reset the registration point for each cast member to the point where the character's feet touch the ground, to ensure that the runner's feet never hit above or below ground level.

To align sprites:

1. In the Score or on the Stage, select all the sprites that you want to align (**Figure 3.69**).

2. Choose Modify > Align to display the Align panel (**Figure 3.70**).

Figure 3.68 Cast members from an animation sequence of a flying bat. The registration point for each cast member is at its center (the default position). As a result, the bat's movements may not look smooth from frame to frame.

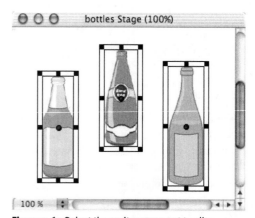

Figure 3.69 Select the sprites you want to align.

Figure 3.70 The Align Sprites panel.

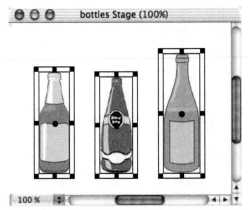

Figure 3.71 Sprites align with respect to the last sprite selected.

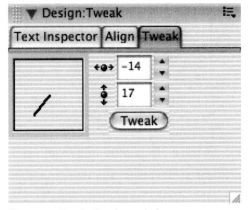

Figure 3.72 Use the Tweak panel when you want to move sprites a specific number of pixels.

3. In the Align panel, click one of the icons to specify how the sprites should aligned or distributed.

The sprites line up in relation to the last sprite you selected (**Figure 3.71**).

✔ Tip

- The last sprite you select is the sprite with which the others will be aligned. Therefore, you may want to select multiple sprites by Shift+clicking rather than by dragging.

To tweak a sprite:

1. Select a sprite in the Score or on the Stage.

2. Choose Modify > Tweak.

The Tweak panel opens (**Figure 3.72**).

3. Drag the image in the left side of the Tweak dialog box to specify visually how far to move the selected sprite.

or

Click the up and down arrows to specify how far (in pixels) to move the selected sprite in horizontal and vertical directions.

4. Click Tweak to move the sprite.

✔ Tip

- If you want to move a sprite by only a small number of pixels, it's usually faster to use the arrow keys on the keyboard than to use the Tweak command.

To view and set a cast member's registration point:

1. Double-click a visual cast member in the Cast window.

   If the cast member is a bitmap, it will open for editing in the Paint window; if it's a vector shape, it will open in the Vector Shape window.

2. Select the Registration Point tool (**Figure 3.73**).

   The current registration point appears at the intersection of the dotted lines.

3. Move the crosshair pointer where you want to place the new registration point, and click (**Figure 3.74**).

✔ Tip

■ To restore a registration point to its default position (the center of the cast member), open the cast member in the Paint or Vector Shape window; then double-click the Registration Point tool in the Paint Tool palette.

Figure 3.73 The Registration Point tool in the Paint window.

Figure 3.74 The same bat cast members, with the registration point moved to the center of each cast member's head. The bat's head will now remain steady while the wings flap.

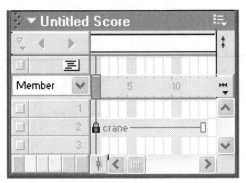

Figure 3.75 Locked sprites in the Score are dimmed and accompanied by a lock symbol.

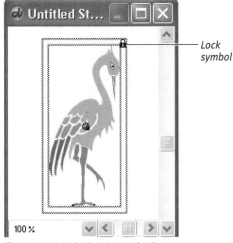

Lock symbol

Figure 3.76 A locked sprite on the Stage.

Figure 3.77 Click the Lock button to lock selected sprites.

Locking Sprites

Director allows you to lock a sprite, preventing any of its properties from being changed inadvertently. This feature can be particularly useful when you don't want to accidentally move or delete a carefully positioned sprite on the Stage. Locked sprites remain visible on the Stage but can't be selected from the Stage.

The locked sprites are displayed with a lock symbol in the Score (**Figure 3.75**). When selected in the Score, a locked sprite is surrounded by a red border on the Stage, which includes a lock symbol in the top-right corner (**Figure 3.76**). Property fields are dimmed for locked sprites in both the Property Inspector and the Sprite toolbar.

To lock a sprite or group of sprites:

1. In the Score or on the Stage, select a sprite or range of sprites that you want to lock.

   You can select multiple nonadjacent sprites. Note that you can't lock part of a sprite.

2. Choose Modify > Lock Sprite.

   or

   Click the Lock button in the Property Inspector (**Figure 3.77**) or Sprite toolbar.

To unlock a sprite or group of sprites:

1. In the Score, select a sprite or ranged of locked sprites that you want to unlock.

2. Choose Modify > Unlock Sprite.

✔ Tip

■ You can change a property (such as blend percentage) of a multiple-sprite selection consisting of both locked and unlocked sprites, but only the unlocked sprites change.

Changing the Score View

In addition to standard viewing controls, such as the scroll bars, you have several viewing options in the Score. You can hide the effects channels to use more of your screen for the sprite channels, zoom in or out, or open multiple Score windows so you can easily drag sprites between different parts of the Score without excess scrolling. If you find the circular keyframe indicators distracting, you can hide those from view as well.

To center the playhead in the window:

◆ Click the Center Current Frame button to reorient the Score so that the frame that contains the playhead is displayed at the center of the Score (**Figure 3.78**).

To hide or show the effects channels:

◆ Click the Hide/Show Effects Channels button to toggle the display of the effects channels (**Figure 3.79**).

To zoom in or out:

◆ Click the Zoom Menu button, and choose a magnification percentage from the pop-up menu (**Figure 3.80**).

Choose a percentage greater than 100 to zoom in and see more detail in each frame. Choose a percentage smaller than 100 to zoom out and see large portions of the Score.

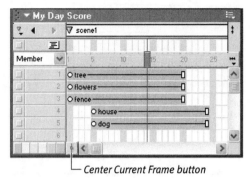

Center Current Frame button

Figure 3.78 Click the Center Current Frame button to center the frame that contains the playhead.

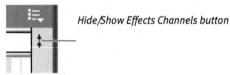

Hide/Show Effects Channels button

Figure 3.79 Toggle the Hide/Show Effects Channel button to hide or show the six effects channels.

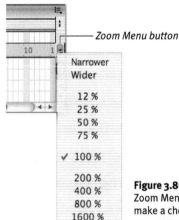

Zoom Menu button

Figure 3.80 Click the Zoom Menu button and make a choice from the pop-up menu.

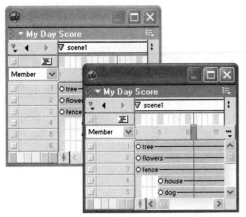

Figure 3.81 Open extra Score windows to view and edit different parts of the Score at the same time.

To view multiple Score windows:

1. Select the Score window. If it is docked to other panels, undock it.

2. Choose Window > New Window to display an additional Score window (**Figure 3.81**).

3. Use the scroll bars to navigate in the new window.

   You can open as many additional Score windows as you need.

To show or hide keyframe indicators in the Score:

1. Click on the Score to make it the active window.

2. Choose View > Keyframes to toggle the display of keyframe indicators in the Score.

Working with sprite labels

The text that identifies each sprite in the Score is called a *sprite label*. Sprite labels make it much easier to work with sprites and edit your movie by providing key information, such as the name or number of the cast member on which a sprite is based (**Figure 3.82**).

To view sprite labels in the Score:

1. Click on the Score to give it focus.

2. Choose View > Sprite Labels and then choose an option from the pop-up menu.

   The option determines where the sprite label appears (**Figure 3.83**). The actual information displayed by a sprite label is determined by the display option.

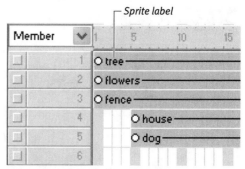

Figure 3.82 Sprite labels make it much easier to work with sprites in the Score.

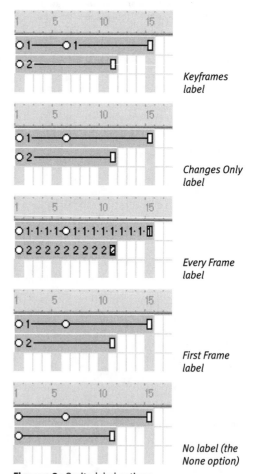

Keyframes label

Changes Only label

Every Frame label

First Frame label

No label (the None option)

Figure 3.83 Sprite-label options.

Score display options

Figure 3.84 Select sprite-label options in the Score.

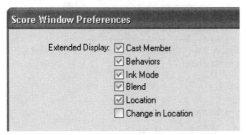

Figure 3.85 When you choose the Extended sprite-label option, you can specify which combination of display options appears by using the Score Window Preferences dialog box.

Channel On/Off button

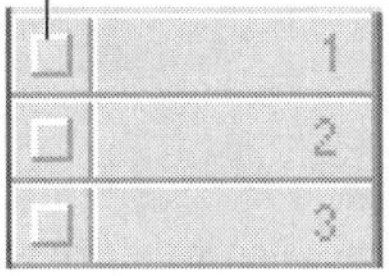

Figure 3.86 Turn a channel off or on to assist with testing.

To change the display option for sprite labels:

◆ Open the display options menu in the Score and make a choice (**Figure 3.84**).

or

Choose View > Display and then choose an option from the pop-up menu.

Following are the display options:

▲ *Member* displays each sprite's name and/or number (as they are displayed in the cast window).

▲ *Behavior* displays the behavior assigned to each sprite.

▲ *Location* displays the coordinates of each sprite's registration point, which Director uses to match up images in animation sequences.

▲ *Ink* displays the ink effect applied to sprites.

▲ *Blend* shows each sprite's blend percentage.

▲ *Extended* lets you view any combination of display options specified in the Score Window Preferences dialog box (**Figure 3.85**), which you open by choosing Edit > Preferences > Score (Windows) or Director > Preferences > Score (Mac).

To turn a channel on or off:

1. Click the button at the left side of a channel to turn the channel off during movie playback (**Figure 3.86**).

   Director ignores the contents of the disabled channel, allowing you to isolate other channels for testing.

2. To turn a channel back on, click the button again.

✔ Tip

■ By default, all channels in the Score are turned on, but you can turn a channel off to make it easier to test or work on a portion of the Score.

CHANGING THE SCORE VIEW

Setting Markers

One way to manage a movie composed of many frames is to use markers to label important sections of the Score (**Figure 3.87**).

To create a marker:

1. In the Score, click a frame in the marker channel where you want to insert a new marker (**Figure 3.88**).

2. Type a name for the marker.

3. Press Enter (Windows) or Return (Mac).

✔ Tip

■ Because marker names are often used by Lingo scripts to control the playback of a movie, it's a good idea to get into the habit of naming your markers in a Lingo-compatible style. Don't include spaces in your marker names, and don't begin them with uppercase letters. (For example, use "scene2" instead of "Scene 2.")

To reposition a marker:

◆ Drag the marker left or right to a new frame.

To delete a marker:

◆ Drag the marker out of the marker channel.

To navigate through a Score by markers:

1. Click the Previous Marker button to jump back to the marker before the current frame (**Figure 3.89**).

2. Click the Next Marker button to jump forward to the marker after the current frame.

3. Jump directly to a specific marker by opening the Markers pop-up menu and selecting the name of the marker.

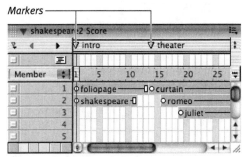

Markers

Figure 3.87 You can place markers in the Score to label sections of your movie.

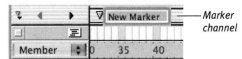

Marker channel

Figure 3.88 Click in the marker channel to insert a new marker.

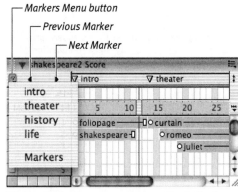

Markers Menu button
Previous Marker
Next Marker

Figure 3.89 To move to a marked position in the Score, use the Previous Marker or Next Marker buttons, or choose a marker name from the Markers pop-up menu.

SETTING MARKERS

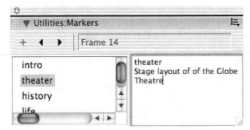

Figure 3.90 Select a marker in the left pane of the Markers window; then type an explanatory note in the right pane.

Director includes a Markers window that allows you to add descriptive comments to markers—scene descriptions or any other notes that might help someone understand the purpose of the marked frames.

To annotate markers in the Markers window:

1. With the Score open, choose Window > Markers to display the Markers window.

2. In the left pane of the window, click the name of the marker that you want to annotate.

   Director immediately moves the playhead to the frame that contains the selected marker; it also copies the name of the marker in the right pane of the window (**Figure 3.90**).

3. Click the right pane of the Markers window. You'll see a flashing cursor to the right of the repeated marker name.

4. Press Ctrl + Enter (Windows) or Return (Mac) to start the comments on a new line.

   Don't put your comments on the same line as the marker name. If you do, they'll become appended to the marker name and will be visible in the marker channel in the Score.

5. Type the comments.

6. To make your comments "stick," click another marker name in the left pane, or close the Markers window.

ANIMATING SPRITES

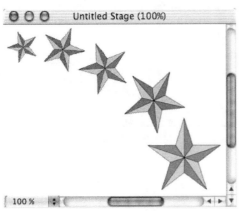

Figure 4.1 You can animate a sprite by changing its properties over a series of frames. This technique is called *tweening*.

Figure 4.2 You also can animate a sprite by having a series of slightly different cast members replace each other on the Stage. This technique is called *frame-by-frame animation*.

Traditionally, the word *sprite* means a lively supernatural being—an elf or a pixie. The sprites you put on the Stage and in the Score aren't very spritelike if they just sit there, are they? To give your sprites life, you need to animate them, which is one of the things Director does best.

You can animate sprites in two ways. The first way is to change a sprite's properties—for example, its size, rotation, color, or location on the Stage—over a series of frames to create the appearance of motion (**Figure 4.1**). The second way is to have the sprite represent a series of cast members in which each cast member is slightly different from the one before it (**Figure 4.2**).

The first of these methods is called *tweening*; the second is called *frame-by-frame animation*. Often, animators combine both methods in a single animated sequence, moving the image and changing it at the same time.

This chapter covers the basic techniques for accomplishing both types of animation. It also shows you how you can use animation to create film loops and custom cursors.

Setting Keyframes

When a sprite makes its first appearance in your movie, it has certain properties: It has a particular location on the Stage, and it has a particular size, degree of rotation, and so on. At some point, you may choose to change some of those properties; for example, you may move the sprite to a different location on the Stage, or you may enlarge or rotate it.

A *keyframe*—represented in the Score by a small circle—is a frame in which you specify or change the properties of a sprite (**Figure 4.3**). Since every sprite starts out with a certain set of properties, the first frame of every sprite is automatically a keyframe. If the sprite spans multiple frames in the Score, any of those additional frames can also be made into keyframes.

To create a keyframe:

1. Within a sprite in the Score, click the frame that you want to turn into a keyframe.

   The entire sprite will be selected, and the playhead will jump to your chosen frame (**Figure 4.4**).

2. Choose Insert > Keyframe.

   The frame becomes a keyframe (**Figure 4.5**).

✔ Tip

- Although the Keyframe command is on the Insert menu, you're not actually inserting anything—you're simply converting an existing "normal" frame to a keyframe. Therefore, the number of frames spanned by the sprite doesn't change.

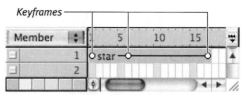

Figure 4.3 A keyframe is represented in the Score by a small circle within a sprite.

Figure 4.4 Click the frame that you want to turn into a keyframe.

Figure 4.5 The selected frame becomes a keyframe.

Where Did Those Words Come From?

The terms *keyframe* and *tweening* are not specific to Director; they're standard animation terms. In traditional animation, a lead animator draws the most important frames (the *key* frames) in a sequence, and an assistant animator draws the frames in between. The assistant animator's job became known as *in-betweening*, which eventually got shortened to *tweening*.

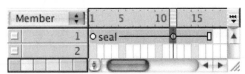

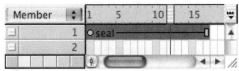

Figure 4.6 Click the keyframe that you want to remove.

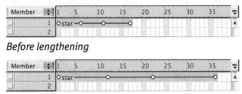

Figure 4.7 The keyframe turns back into a regular frame, and the entire sprite is selected.

Before lengthening

After lengthening

Figure 4.8 When you extend a sprite, its keyframes move proportionately farther apart.

To remove a keyframe:

1. Select a keyframe within a sprite in the Score (**Figure 4.6**).

2. Choose Insert > Remove Keyframe (**Figure 4.7**).

   The keyframe reverts to a regular frame.

✔ Tips

- Removing a keyframe doesn't shorten the sprite; it simply converts the keyframe to a "normal" frame.

- When you remove a keyframe, you remove any property settings that had been made in that keyframe. As a result, the sprite's appearance on the Stage is likely to change.

To reposition keyframes in the Score:

- ◆ Drag the keyframe left or right within the same channel.

✔ Tips

- When you drag the starting or ending keyframe to shorten or lengthen a sprite, all keyframes within the sprite move proportionately closer or farther apart (**Figure 4.8**). If you want to avoid this behavior—that is, if you want to drag only the selected keyframe while leaving the others alone—hold down the Ctrl key (Windows) or the Command key (Mac) as you drag.

- If you hold down the Alt key (Windows) or the Option key (Mac) while you drag a keyframe, you actually drag a *copy* of the keyframe, leaving the original where it was. This can be a handy way to add a keyframe to a sprite.

SETTING KEYFRAMES

Tweening

When a sprite contains two or more keyframes, Director automatically tweens them: That is, it compares the sprite's properties from one keyframe to the next, and it makes those changes happen incrementally over the intervening frames. For example, if a sprite is at the left side of the Stage in the first keyframe and is at the right side of the Stage in the next keyframe (**Figure 4.9**), Director changes the sprite's location gradually—moving it bit by bit with each frame. The result is a simple form of animation (**Figure 4.10**).

By default, Director will tween the following sprite properties:

◆ Location

◆ Size

◆ Rotation angle

◆ Skew angle

◆ Foreground and background colors

◆ Blend percentage

✔ Tip

■ If you want any of these properties *not* to be tweened, choose Modify > Sprite > Tweening and deselect the properties that you want Director to leave alone (**Figure 4.11**).

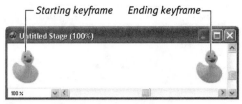

Starting keyframe   Ending keyframe

Figure 4.9 This sprite has two keyframes—one at the beginning, one at the end. The sprite's position on the Stage is different in the two keyframes.

Figure 4.10 Director tweens the sprite by changing its position incrementally between the two keyframes.

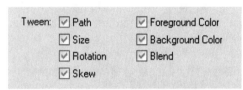

Figure 4.11 In the Sprite Tweening dialog box, you can select the properties that you want Director to tween. The settings may be different depending on which sprite is selected.

Flash Talk: Tweening

Director's tweening is virtually identical to *motion tweening* in Flash. (Director has no equivalent to Flash's *shape tweening*.) The main difference is that tweening in Director is automatic, while tweening in Flash must be set up manually.

Unlike Flash, in which only symbols can be motion-tweened, Director allows you to tween any visual cast member.

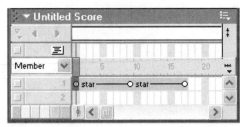

Figure 4.12 To tween a sprite, first select the initial keyframe.

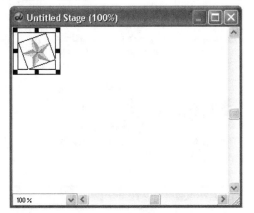

Figure 4.13 Set the sprite's properties (its location, rotation, size, and so on) the way you want them to look at the beginning of the tween.

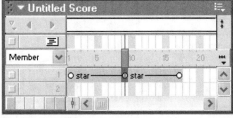

Figure 4.14 Select the next keyframe.

To tween a sprite:

1. Make sure that the sprite you want to tween has at least two keyframes.

2. In the Score, select the sprite's first keyframe (**Figure 4.12**).

3. Change any of the sprite's tweenable properties to the way you want them to be at the beginning of the tween (**Figure 4.13**).

   Some properties can be changed directly on the Stage. For example, you can drag the sprite to change its location, or you can rotate it, skew it, or resize it using the techniques described in Chapter 3, "Building a Score." In addition, all tweenable properties can be changed by using the Sprite toolbar in the Score or the Sprite tab in the Property Inspector.

4. Click to select the next keyframe within the sprite (**Figure 4.14**).

5. Change any of the sprite's tweenable properties to the way you want them to be at the end of the tween (**Figure 4.15**).

   Director automatically regenerates all frames between this keyframe and the preceding one.

6. Repeat steps 4 and 5 for each additional keyframe.

7. Rewind and play back the movie to see how the animation looks.

8. Refine the tweening, if necessary.

continues on next page

TWEENING

✔ Tips

■ Director tweens automatically. If you want to turn tweening off, choose Edit > Preferences > Sprite (Windows) or Director > Preferences > Sprite (Mac) and deselect the Tweening option.

■ To make a sprite appear to "fade in," tween its blend property from 0 (in the first keyframe) to 100 (in the next keyframe). To make it appear to fade out, do the opposite (**Figure 4.16**).

■ To make a sprite appear to rotate in three-dimensional space, tween its skew property from 0 (in the first keyframe) to 180 (in the next keyframe).

■ If you want to tween the size of a sprite, you'll be best off with sprites based on Flash or vector-shape cast members. Sprites based on bitmapped cast members may exhibit jaggedness or blockiness.

To create a keyframe and change a sprite property at the same time:

1. Select a single frame within a sprite by Alt+clicking (Windows) or Option-clicking (Mac) the frame (**Figure 4.17**).

   or

   Select a sprite, choose Edit > Edit Sprite Frames, and click one of the frames. (See "To make sprite frames individually editable" in Chapter 3.)

2. Change one or more of the sprite's tweenable properties.

   Director creates a keyframe in the selected frame (**Figure 4.18**) and then changes the sprite's properties in that keyframe.

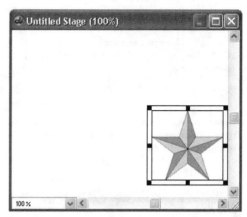

Figure 4.15 Set the sprite's properties the way you want them to look at the end of the tween.

Figure 4.16 This sprite's blend property has been tweened from 100 to 0.

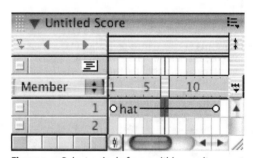

Figure 4.17 Select a single frame within a sprite.

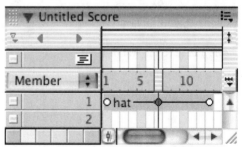

Figure 4.18 As soon as you change the properties of the sprite on the Stage, Director creates a keyframe in the Score.

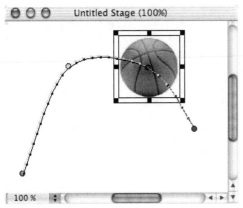

Figure 4.19 The motion path of a selected sprite is visible on the Stage.

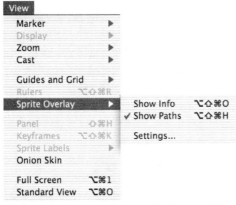

Figure 4.20 You can turn the path display on and off from the View menu.

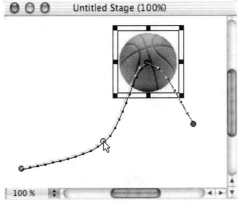

Figure 4.21 You can adjust the motion path by dragging any of the keyframe circles.

Adjusting Motion

When you tween a sprite's location so that it moves around the Stage, the path that the sprite follows is known as a *motion path*. If the Show Paths feature is turned on (which it is by default), you can see a selected sprite's complete motion path in the form of a dotted line on the Stage (**Figure 4.19**). Keyframes within the path are represented by colored circles; regular frames are represented by black dots.

Using that dotted line as a visual reference, you can make adjustments to the shape, curvature, and acceleration of the sprite's motion path.

To change the shape of a sprite's motion path:

1. In the Score, select the sprite whose path you want to view or adjust.

2. If the sprite's motion path isn't visible on the Stage, choose View > Sprite Overlay > Show Paths to turn it on (**Figure 4.20**).

3. Drag any of the keyframe circles to a new position (**Figure 4.21**).

   The sprite's path adjusts immediately.

✔ Tip

- If you select an entire sprite in the Score (rather than just a single keyframe), you can then drag the sprite *and its entire motion path* to a different location on the Stage.

To smooth a sprite's movement:

◆ Drag the sprite's last keyframe to the right. Doing so causes all the keyframes to move apart from each other.

When you drag keyframes farther apart, you increase the number of frames between the keyframes. This makes the movement less jerky, but it also slows down the animation; so you may want to increase the frame rate to compensate. (See "Setting a Movie's Tempo" in Chapter 5.)

✔ Tip

■ If some keyframes are close together and others are far apart, the sprite may abruptly speed up and slow down as the movie is played. To minimize the abruptness of these speed changes, choose Modify > Sprite > Tweening and select Smooth Changes (**Figure 4.22**).

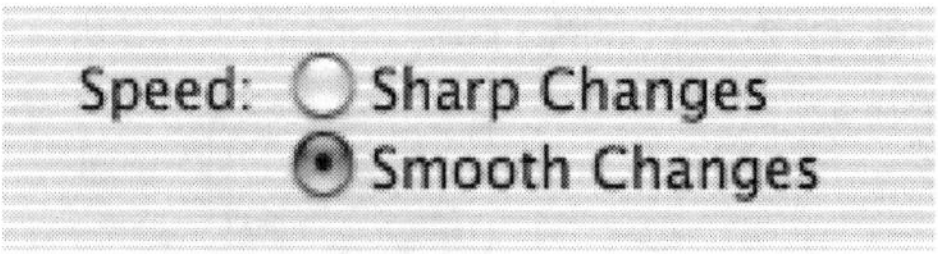

Figure 4.22 Click Smooth Changes in the Sprite Tweening dialog box to make the sprite's speed changes more gradual.

Keyframe Color Coding

The circles that represent keyframes on the Stage are color-coded to help you determine the direction of the sprite's motion path. A sprite's first keyframe is green, and its last keyframe is red. All other keyframes are yellow (if the entire sprite is selected) or white (if the sprite is unselected).

If a particular keyframe—rather than the entire sprite—is selected in the Score, the circle representing that keyframe on the Stage turns blue.

Preview pane   *Curvature slider*

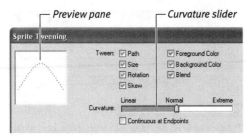

Figure 4.23 Preview the sprite's motion path in the preview pane of the Sprite Tweening dialog box.

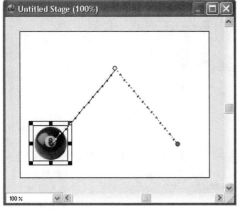

Figure 4.24 Linear settings produce straight-line motion.

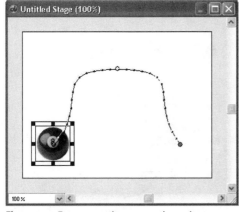

Figure 4.25 Extreme settings cause the sprite to curve outside of the positions set by its keyframes.

To adjust the curvature of a sprite's motion path:

1. In the Score, select a sprite whose motion path you wish to adjust.

2. Choose Modify > Sprite > Tweening.

   The Sprite Tweening dialog box opens.

3. In the Sprite Tweening dialog box, drag the Curvature slider to adjust how much curvature is in the sprite's path.

   You can preview the adjusted path on the left side of the Sprite Tweening dialog box (**Figure 4.23**).

   Drag the slider to the Linear end to move the sprite in straight lines between keyframes (**Figure 4.24**).

   Drag the slider to Normal to give the sprite's path moderate curvature.

   Drag to the Extreme end for maximum curvature in the path between keyframes (**Figure 4.25**).

✔ Tips

- The curvature settings affect only sprites that have three or more keyframes and whose motion path isn't a straight line.

- If you want greater control over the shape or curvature of a sprite's motion path, create additional keyframes within the sprite and make the adjustments by hand.

ADJUSTING MOTION

103

To create a circular path for a sprite:

1. Create a new sprite by dragging a cast member to the Stage or Score.

2. Insert three keyframes in the sprite (**Figure 4.26**). (Including the default first keyframe, this makes a total of four keyframes.)

   Leave the end frame alone—don't turn it into a keyframe.

3. If the sprite's motion path isn't visible on the Stage, choose View > Sprite Overlay > Show Paths to turn it on.

4. On the Stage, position the sprite's keyframes as corners of a diamond (**Figure 4.27**).

5. Select the sprite in the Score and choose Modify > Sprite > Tweening.

   The Sprite Tweening dialog box opens.

6. Select the Continuous at Endpoints checkbox (**Figure 4.28**).

   That option closes the path.

7. Drag the Curvature slider to the right to make the sprite's path resemble a circle.

   Use the path preview on the left side of the Sprite Tweening box as a guide.

8. Click OK.

9. Fine-tune the circular path, if necessary, by dragging the keyframes (represented by circles) to new locations on the Stage (**Figure 4.29**).

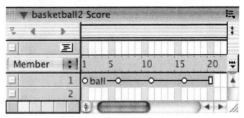

Figure 4.26 Create a sprite with exactly four keyframes.

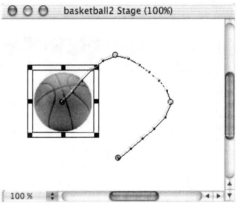

Figure 4.27 Position the sprite's keyframes in a diamond pattern.

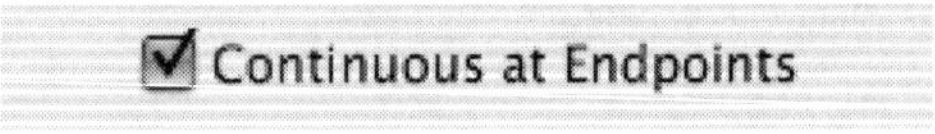

☑ Continuous at Endpoints

Figure 4.28 Selecting Continuous at Endpoints closes the path.

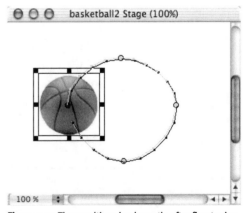

Figure 4.29 The resulting circular path, after fine-tuning.

ADJUSTING MOTION

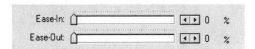

Figure 4.30 Drag the Ease-In and Ease-Out slider bars in the Sprite Tweening dialog box to control a sprite's acceleration and deceleration.

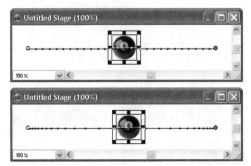

Figure 4.31 A sprite's motion path with default settings (above), and with Ease-In and Ease-Out settings of about 40 percent (below).

To accelerate or decelerate a sprite along its path:

1. In the Score, select a tweened sprite whose movement you want to adjust.

2. Choose Modify > Sprite > Tweening.
   The Sprite Tweening dialog box opens.

3. Drag the Ease-In and Ease-Out slider bars to control the sprite's acceleration along its path (**Figure 4.30**).

   The Ease-In slider controls the beginning of the sprite's motion: High settings make the sprite take a longer time to reach "cruising speed." The Ease-Out slider controls the end of the sprite's motion: High settings make the sprite take a longer time to slow down (**Figure 4.31**).

To reverse the direction of a sprite:

1. In the Score, select a tweened sprite whose direction you want to reverse.

2. Choose Modify > Reverse Sequence.
   The order of the keyframes within the sprite is reversed, causing the animation to run backward.

ADJUSTING MOTION

Step Recording

If you've seen old monster movies, you're probably familiar with a technique called stop-motion animation. The animator places a miniature model in front of the camera, poses it, shoots a frame of film, alters the model's pose slightly, shoots another frame of film...and so on, until the sequence is finished.

Step recording is Director's version of stop-motion animation. Instead of manipulating a physical model, you change a sprite's properties slightly, one frame at a time, and Director saves those changes in a series of keyframes. Step recording gives you much more precise control over a sprite's movement than Director's automatic tweening does.

To perform step recording:

1. Within a sprite in the Score, click the frame in which you want step recording to begin.

   The entire sprite will be selected, and the playhead will jump to your chosen frame.

2. Choose Control > Step Recording.

   An indicator appears to the left of the sprite in the Score (**Figure 4.32**).

3. Arrange the sprite on the Stage the way you want it to appear in the first frame (**Figure 4.33**).

4. Click the Step Forward button in the Control Panel (**Figure 4.34**) or in the secondary control panel attached to the bottom of the Stage.

   Director creates a keyframe in the Score and advances to the next frame.

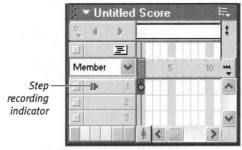

Step recording indicator

Figure 4.32 Select a sprite for step recording, and click the frame where you want to start. An indicator appears to the left of the sprite.

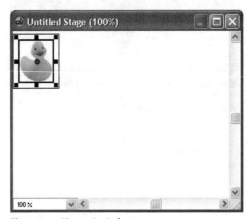

Figure 4.33 The sprite in frame 1.

Step Forward button

Figure 4.34 Click the Step Forward button to record a frame.

STEP RECORDING

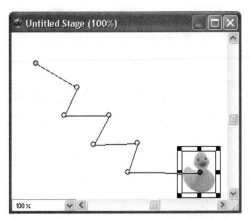

Figure 4.35 The motion path of a step-recorded sprite consists entirely of keyframes. (Each keyframe is represented by a small circle on the Stage.) The rubber ducky's zig-zag path was created by repositioning the sprite manually, keyframe by keyframe, during the step-recording process.

5. Arrange the selected sprite the way you want it to appear in the current frame.

6. Repeat steps 4 and 5 to step-record as many frames as you need (**Figure 4.35**).

7. When you're finished, choose Control > Step Recording.

8. Rewind and play the movie to see the animation.

✔ Tips

■ If you step past a sprite's last frame, Director automatically extends the sprite.

■ Step recording can be done with several sprites at once—just select them all before you start recording. At any time, you can cancel step recording for one of the sprites (while continuing it for the others) by selecting the sprite and deselecting Step Recording in the Control menu.

Real-Time Recording

The real-time recording feature is like a video camcorder—it allows you to drag a sprite around the Stage while Director records the sprite's movements to the Score. Real-time recording is most appropriate for sprites that need to be animated along a natural, free-flowing path with many changes in direction.

To perform real-time recording:

1. Make sure the sprite whose movements you want to record is in a channel by itself. (Director will record indefinitely in a clear channel but will cut recording short if the playhead encounters another sprite.)

2. Within the sprite, click the frame in which you want real-time recording to begin.

   The entire sprite will be selected, and the playhead will jump to your chosen frame.

3. Arrange the sprite on the Stage the way you want it to appear in the first frame of the recording.

4. Choose Control > Real-Time Recording. An indicator appears to the left of the sprite in the Score (**Figure 4.36**), and a red-and-white striped frame surrounds the sprite on the Stage (**Figure 4.37**).

5. Whenever you're ready, start dragging the sprite around the Stage.

   Director begins recording at the moment you first move the sprite.

6. When you're finished, release the mouse button.

   Director stops recording (**Figure 4.38**).

7. Rewind and play the movie to see the animation.

8. Adjust individual frames, if necessary, to refine the sprite's motion path.

Real-time recording indicator

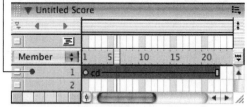

Figure 4.36 Select a sprite for real-time recording, and click the frame where you want to start. When you choose Control > Real-Time Recording, an indicator appears to the left of the sprite.

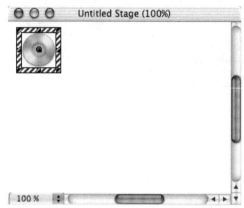

Figure 4.37 The attention-getting frame around the sprite on the Stage means that Director is standing by to begin real-time recording.

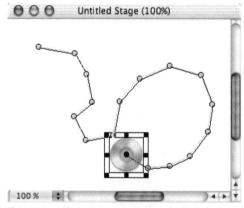

Figure 4.38 When Director stops recording, the sprite's motion path becomes visible on the Stage. It's a record of the movements you made to the sprite while recording.

REAL-TIME RECORDING

Tempo box

Figure 4.39 Slow the recording tempo in the Control Panel for more control.

Figure 4.40 Select the Trails option in the Sprite toolbar for a real-time recorded sprite to create a handwriting effect.

✔ Tips

- The drawback of real-time recording is that the resulting animation never looks as smooth as you might like. You can always go back and refine individual frames, but if you're going to fix numerous frames manually, it probably makes sense to use step recording instead.

- Unless you have lightning-fast reflexes, it's a good idea to record real-time animation at a very slow frame rate—perhaps two or three frames per second. To change the frame rate, open the Control Panel by choosing Window > Control Panel; then enter a value (in frames per second) in the Tempo box (**Figure 4.39**). You can reset the tempo to a higher rate to play back the animation.

- You can create a handwriting effect by selecting a real-time recorded sprite and clicking the Trails box in the Sprite toolbar or the Property Inspector. As the sprite moves across the Stage, it leaves a trail (**Figure 4.40**).

- Like step recording, real-time recording can be done with several sprites at once.

Animating Frame by Frame

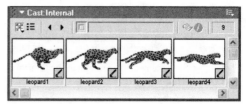

Figure 4.41 A series of cast members designed for frame-by-frame animation.

Dragging sprites around the Stage, or changing their properties, produces only the most basic kind of animation. Doing *real* animation—the traditional kind, in which characters move in lifelike ways—still requires the labor-intensive task of making a series of drawings, each of which differs slightly from the one before, and playing them in sequence to create the illusion of motion (**Figure 4.41**).

Teaching the artistic skills needed to create a series of animation drawings is beyond the scope of this book. So let's assume that you already have the set of images, which you've either created within Director or (more likely) imported into Director, and that you've arranged them in order in the Cast window. Now what?

Each image needs to be on the Stage for a short amount of time—one frame or perhaps several frames—and then replaced by the next image in the series. You could do this by having a separate sprite for each image, but it's more efficient to create a *multiple-member sprite*—a sprite that contains references to two or more cast members. Doing so allows the entire animated sequence to be contained within a single sprite, which can then be edited or tweened like any other sprite.

There are several ways to create a multiple-member sprite: You can exchange cast members within a sprite, or you can use specialized Director commands called Cast to Time and Space to Time. The Cast to Time command is generally appropriate for animation that's fixed in one place, while the Space to Time command lends itself more to animation that moves around the Stage.

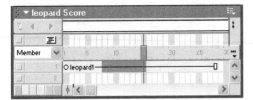

Figure 4.42 Select the frames in which you want to substitute a different cast member.

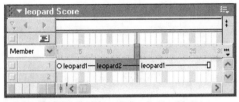

Figure 4.43 As you can see from the sprite label, the selected frames in the sprite now refer to a different cast member (leopard2).

To exchange cast members within a sprite:

1. Within a sprite in the Score, select the range of frames whose cast-member reference you want to change (**Figure 4.42**).

2. In the Cast window, select the cast member that you want to substitute for the existing cast member.

3. Choose Edit > Exchange Cast Members. The cast member is exchanged, and sprite labels in the Score are updated (**Figure 4.43**).

4. Repeat steps 1 through 3 as many times as necessary until the full animated sequence has been added to the sprite.

✔ Tip

- You can also use the Exchange Cast Members command to change the cast member for a standard, single-member sprite. Just select the entire sprite rather than a range of frames within the sprite.

ANIMATING FRAME BY FRAME

111

To create a multiple-member sprite using Cast to Time:

1. In the Score, click the cell in which you want the first frame of the sprite to fall (**Figure 4.44**).

2. In the Cast window, select the sequence of cast members that you want to combine into a sprite (**Figure 4.45**).

   You can choose adjacent cast members or make noncontiguous selections; however, the cast members must be in the proper order within the Cast window.

3. With the Cast window still active, choose Modify > Cast to Time.

   Director creates a sprite that consists of as many frames as there are cast members in your selection, with a new cast member in each frame (**Figure 4.46**).

✔ Tips

- If you want each cast member within the sprite to occupy more than one frame, drag the sprite's last keyframe to the right. Doing so will cause all the keyframes to move apart from each other, allowing each one to remain in effect for several frames (**Figure 4.47**).

- As a shortcut for the Modify > Cast to Time command, you can hold down the Alt key (Windows) or Option key (Mac) while dragging the selected cast members into the Score.

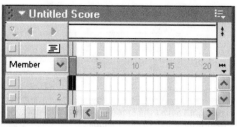

Figure 4.44 Select the cell in which you want the first frame of the multiple-member sprite to fall.

Figure 4.45 Select a series of cast members.

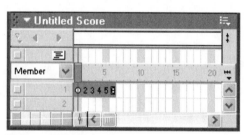

Figure 4.46 Director creates one sprite from the series of cast members.

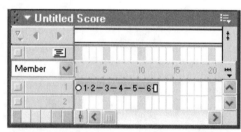

Figure 4.47 The sprite has been doubled in length by dragging the last keyframe. As a result, each cast member referenced by the sprite will be on the Stage for two frames rather than one.

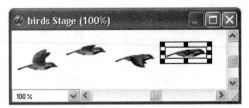

Figure 4.48 Drag cast members for the sequence to the Stage—in order.

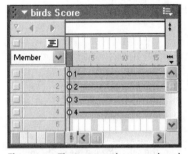

Figure 4.49 The cast members are placed in sequential channels in the Score.

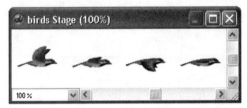

Figure 4.50 Position the sprites on the Stage as they should appear in the animated sequence.

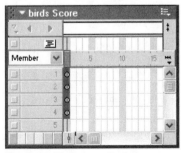

Figure 4.51 Limit the sprites' span duration to one frame.

To create a multiple-member sprite using Space to Time:

1. In the Score, click the cell in which you want the first frame of the sprite to fall.

2. One by one, drag the cast members for the animated sequence from the Cast window to the Stage (**Figure 4.48**).

   Be sure to drag the cast members to the Stage in the correct order. Director automatically places the cast members in sequential channels in the Score, creating separate sprites (**Figure 4.49**).

3. Arrange the sprites on the Stage as they should appear in the animated sequence (**Figure 4.50**).

4. Select all the sprites that you just created in the Score.

5. Limit the selected sprites' span duration to one frame (**Figure 4.51**) by entering the same frame number for the start frame and end frame in the Property Inspector or the Score's Sprite toolbar.

6. Choose Modify > Space to Time.

continues on next page

7. In the Space to Time dialog box, enter a Separation value to indicate how many frames should separate the sprites within the new combined sprite.

8. Click OK.

All the selected sprites combine into a multiple-member sprite in a single channel (**Figure 4.52**).

✔ Tips

■ Space to Time can also be used to animate a single cast member. Simply drag multiple copies of the cast member onto the Stage and arrange them as desired.

■ If you use Space to Time to create an animated sequence that moves in a single direction across the Stage, you can extend that sequence by using the Paste Relative command (see the following).

To extend an animated sequence using Paste Relative:

1. In the Score, select a sprite that contains an animated sequence, preferably one with linear movement.

2. Choose Edit > Copy Sprites.

3. In the Score, choose the cell immediately after the last cell of the selected sprite (**Figure 4.53**).

4. Choose Edit > Paste Special > Relative (**Figure 4.54**).

Your animated sequence repeats on the Stage, beginning exactly where the previous sequence ends (**Figure 4.55**).

✔ Tip

■ The Paste Relative command is appropriate only for animated sequences that contain linear movement. Another (and much more versatile) way to extend an animated sequence is to use Film Loop, described in the next section.

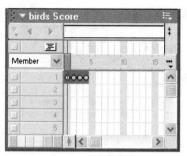

Figure 4.52 The multiple sprites are converted to a single sprite.

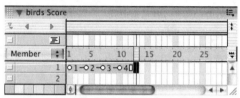

Figure 4.53 Select the cell following the sprite you copied.

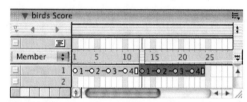

Figure 4.54 Using Paste Relative, copy the sprite into place.

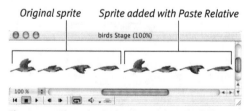

Original sprite   Sprite added with Paste Relative

Figure 4.55 The animated sequence is extended.

Figure 4.56 These six cast members, showing a running figure...

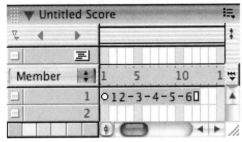

Figure 4.57 ...are combined into a multiple-member sprite.

Figure 4.58 The multiple-member sprite is made into a film loop.

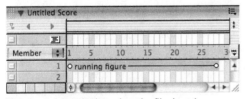

Figure 4.59 A sprite based on the film loop is tweened in the Score.

Figure 4.60 In the final result, the figure appears to run across the Stage.

Making Film Loops

Director allows you to turn any animated scene—no matter how many frames or channels it occupies in the Score—into a single cast member called a *film loop*. Film loops work best with repetitive movements, such as walking (**Figures 4.56** and **4.57**). If you create a film loop (**Figure 4.58**) of a man taking two strides (one with the left foot and one with the right), the film loop will repeat those strides endlessly, causing the man to run in place.

Like any other cast member, a film loop can be dragged to the Stage or Score and tweened (**Figure 4.59**). If the film loop of the walking man is tweened from one side of the Stage to the other, the man will appear to be walking across the Stage (**Figure 4.60**).

A film loop can contain other film loops. Suppose you have two film loops in the Score: one of the walking man and the other of his running dog. You can create a single film loop to include both loops. In this way, film loops make it easy to assemble complex movies.

To create a film loop:

1. In the Score, select all the sprites for the film loop.

   You can include effects sprites from the effects channels.

2. Choose Insert > Film Loop.

   The Create Film Loop dialog box opens (**Figure 4.61**).

3. Type a name for the film loop.

4. Click OK.

   Director puts the film loop in the next available position in the Cast window.

✔ Tips

- A shortcut for creating a film loop is to drag the selected sprites directly from the Score to the Cast window.

- After creating a film loop, you can, if you wish, delete the original sprites from which the film loop was made.

- Do *not* delete the cast members that are used in the film loop. If you delete them from the Cast window, they will vanish from the film loop as well.

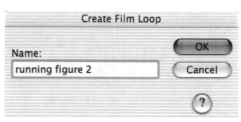

Figure 4.61 Choose a name for the film loop.

Flash Talk: Film Loops vs. Movie Clips

A film loop is the closest equivalent Director has to a Flash movie clip. Both allow a complex sequence to be reduced to a single, tweenable object that repeats the same series of frames indefinitely. However, since a film loop stops playing when the movie ends, it's closer to an animated graphic symbol than to a movie clip.

In Flash, one of the significant features of movie clips is that they are scriptable. In Director, *everything* is scriptable, including film loops.

Unlike Flash symbols, a film loop doesn't have its own timeline, so the only way to edit a film loop is to paste it into the Score, make your changes, and then convert it back to a film loop. This is one area in which Director is noticeably more primitive than Flash.

To use a film loop in a movie:

1. Create a sprite by dragging the film loop from the Cast window to the Score or the Stage.

2. If necessary, extend the sprite by dragging its end frame to the right.

   The sprite should be at least long as the original sprite (or sprites) from which the film loop was made, so the action of the film loop will be able to play at least once. The longer you extend the sprite, the more times the action of the film loop will repeat. (**Figure 4.62**).

3. *(optional)* Tween the film loop as you would any other sprite.

✔ Tips

- Film loops animate only when you play your movie; you won't see the animation if you step through the frames or drag the playhead across the frames.

- You can't apply ink effects to film loops. You must apply ink effects to the individual sprites before you include them in a film loop.

Figure 4.62 If the action in the film loop is 12 frames long, this 36-frame sprite will repeat the action two more times.

To edit a film loop:

1. Select the film loop in the Cast window (**Figure 4.63**).

2. Choose Edit > Copy Cast Members.

3. Click a cell in a clear part of the Score.

4. Choose Edit > Paste Sprites.

   The sprites that make up the film loop will be pasted into the Score (**Figure 4.64**).

5. Edit or adjust the sprites as necessary (**Figure 4.65**).

6. Select the sprites.

7. Choose Insert > Film Loop.

   The Create Film Loop dialog box opens.

8. Type a name for the revised film loop. You may, if you wish, give it the same name that you gave the original film loop.

9. Click OK.

   Director puts the revised film loop in the next available position in the Cast window (**Figure 4.66**).

10. Select the new film loop in the Cast window.

11. Choose Edit > Cut Cast Members.

12. Select the old film loop in the Cast window.

13. Choose Edit > Paste.

    The new (edited) film loop replaces the old one.

✔ Tips

- If you haven't deleted the original sprites from which the film loop was made, you can skip steps 1 through 4.

- If you want to keep both the old and new versions of the film loop, you can skip steps 10 through 13.

Figure 4.63 Select the film loop whose contents you want to edit.

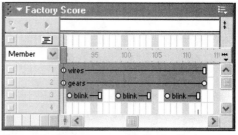

Figure 4.64 The sprites contained in the film loop are pasted into the Score.

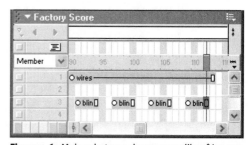

Figure 4.65 Make whatever changes you like. (You can even add or delete sprites.)

Figure 4.66 The revised film loop doesn't overwrite the original; it simply gets added as a new cast member.

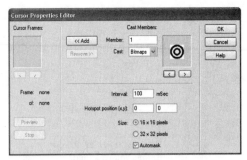

Figure 4.67 Use the Cursor Properties Editor to create an animated cursor.

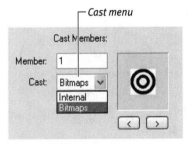

Figure 4.68 Choose a cast.

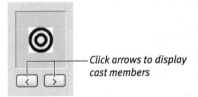

Figure 4.69 Find the cast member that you want to use for the first frame of the cursor.

Figure 4.70 Click Add to add the selected cast member to the series of frames in the cursor. Click Remove to delete a frame from the cursor.

Animating Cursors

Director allows you to create animated color cursors that can replace the standard black-and-white mouse pointer. You might activate an animated cursor during a rollover, for example, as a way to communicate to your users that some action is possible when the mouse pointer is over a certain icon. An animated cursor consists of a frame-by-frame animated sequence in which each frame is a separate bitmapped cast member.

Once you've created an animated cursor, you need to activate it by writing a Lingo script. (See "Lingo for Animated Cursors" in Chapter 15.)

To create an animated cursor:

1. Create or import the series of cast members that will make up the animated sequence.

   The cast members must be 8-bit bitmapped images with dimensions of 16 x 16 pixels (Windows or Mac) or 32 x 32 pixels (Windows only). (For an explanation of "8-bit," see the "What Is Color Depth?" sidebar in Chapter 2.)

2. Choose Insert > Media Element > Cursor.

   The Cursor Properties Editor dialog box opens (**Figure 4.67**).

3. From the Cast pop-up menu, choose the cast that contains the cast members for the animated cursor (**Figure 4.68**).

   You can use members from more than one cast.

4. Click the arrows below the Cast Members section (on the right side of the dialog box) to browse choices and select a cast member (**Figure 4.69**).

   Only suitable cast members (8-bit color bitmapped images) show up as choices.

5. Click Add (**Figure 4.70**).

   The selected cast member is added to the series of frames in the cursor.

continues on next page

ANIMATING CURSORS

6. Repeat steps 4 and 5 to add all the cast members you need.

7. Use the arrows in the Cursor Frames section of the dialog box to review the frames you've added (**Figure 4.71**).

8. Click Remove to delete a previewed frame if necessary.

9. Enter a value (in milliseconds) in the Interval field to set the time delay between frames of the cursor (**Figure 4.72**).

This interval applies only to the cursor and is independent of the movie's play-back tempo.

10. Enter *x* and *y* values in the Hotspot Position field to define your cursor's hot spot—the place that activates whatever you click.

(0,0) marks the top-left corner.

11. Click a size option to select the maximum size of your cursor.

Depending on your system, only one option may be available.

12. Check Automask to make white pixels in the cursor transparent.

13. Click Preview to see the cursor animation.

14. When you're satisfied with the cursor animation, click OK.

The cursor goes into the internal cast (**Figure 4.73**).

✔ Tips

■ You can create an animated cursor that appears to have a variable frame rate by creating identical consecutive cursor frames. For example, if your Interval is 100 milliseconds, you can create a cursor frame that appears to last 500 milliseconds (half a second) by using five identical cursor frames in a row.

Figure 4.71 Review the cursor frames you've added.

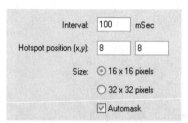

Figure 4.72 Specify values for the interval between cursor frames, the position of the cursor's hot spot, and the size of the cursor.

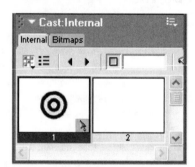

Figure 4.73 Your newly created custom cursor appears in the Cast window.

■ If you select Automask to make white pixels transparent, you still can have opaque "white" pixels in your cursor by selecting the lightest shade of gray from the color palette for those pixels. They will appear white on the screen.

ANIMATING CURSORS

Playing & Refining Movies

5

While authoring a Director movie, you repeatedly play back the movie to check results and make improvements. This chapter will show you how to use the Control Panel to play back your movie in different ways.

This chapter also covers *tempo*—how fast the movie plays back. You'll learn how to set tempos in the tempo channel, and how to test playback to compare actual performance with the assigned tempo.

When you play a movie, you'll sometimes notice places where one scene jumps abruptly to another. That's a good place to choose a transition effect—also explained in this chapter. Transitions range from simple *wipes* (in which a new frame slides in from one side to replace the original frame) and *dissolves* (one frame melts into another) to more elaborate effects.

Using the Control Panel

Director's Control Panel resembles the controls for a videotape or CD player (**Figure 5.1**). It allows you to play, rewind, step forward, and step backward through the frames of your movie. It also allows you to adjust volume and set loop playback.

A new feature of Director MX is an additional, abbreviated control panel attached to the bottom of the Stage. Except where noted, all of the tasks in this section can be accomplished from either the "real" Control Panel or the secondary control panel (**Figure 5.2**).

Though the instructions in this book usually don't include keyboard shortcuts, this section will be an exception. Since playing a movie is the most common task you'll be doing in Director, you'll want to be able to do it quickly and effortlessly from the keyboard.

To open the Control Panel:

◆ Choose Window > Control Panel.

   or

   Press Ctrl+2 (Windows) or Command+2 (Mac).

To rewind the movie to frame 1:

◆ In the Control Panel, click the Rewind button (**Figure 5.3**).

   or

   Press Ctrl+Alt+R (Windows) or Command+Option+R (Mac).

✔ Tip

■ If you rewind the movie while it's playing, it will stop and rewind.

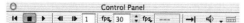

Figure 5.1 You can play back movies, set tempo and volume, and specify looping with the Control Panel.

Figure 5.2 In Director MX, an additional control panel is located at the bottom of the Stage.

Figure 5.3 Click the Rewind button to return to the start of a movie.

Figure 5.4 Click the Play button to start playback.

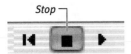

Stop

Figure 5.5 The Stop button halts the playback of a movie.

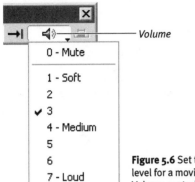

Volume

0 - Mute

1 - Soft

2

✔ 3

4 - Medium

5

6

7 - Loud

Figure 5.6 Set the sound level for a movie with the Volume control.

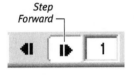

Step Forward

1

Figure 5.7 Click to move ahead one frame at a time, or hold down the button to step forward continuously.

To start playback:

◆ Click the Play button (**Figure 5.4**).

or

Press Ctrl+Alt+P (Windows) or Command+Option+P (Mac).

To stop playback:

◆ Click the Stop button (**Figure 5.5**).

or

Press Ctrl+period (Windows) or Command+period (Mac).

To set the volume of your movie:

1. Click the Volume button (**Figure 5.6**).

2. Select a volume level from the pop-up menu.

✔ Tip

■ The volume setting in the Control Panel applies only at the time the movie is being played. It is not saved as part of the movie file.

To step through a movie, one frame at a time:

◆ Click the Step Forward button (**Figure 5.7**).

or

Press Ctrl+Alt+right arrow (Windows) or Command+Option+right arrow (Mac).

✔ Tips

■ Holding down the Step Forward button (or the corresponding keyboard shortcut) causes the movie to step forward continuously.

■ When a Score channel is in step-recording mode, clicking the Step Forward button copies the contents of the current frame to the next frame.

USING THE CONTROL PANEL

To step backward through a movie:

- Click the Step Backward button (**Figure 5.8**).

  or

  Press Ctrl+Alt+left arrow (Windows) or Command+Option+left arrow (Mac).

✔ Tip

- Holding down the Step Backward button (or the corresponding keyboard shortcut) causes the movie to step backward continuously.

To make the movie loop (or stop looping):

- Click the Loop Playback button (**Figure 5.9**).

  or

  Press Ctrl+Alt+L (Windows) or Command+Option+L (Mac).

  If looping is turned on, the movie will start again from frame 1 when the playhead reaches the last frame. If looping is turned off, the movie will stop when the playhead reaches the last frame.

✔ Tip

- To find out whether looping is turned on or off, look at the symbol on the Loop Playback button (**Figure 5.10**).

Step Backward

Figure 5.8 Click to move back one frame at a time, or hold down the button to step back continuously.

Loop Playback

Figure 5.9 Click to toggle looping on or off.

Looping disabled   Looping enabled

Figure 5.10 The Loop Playback button changes to show whether looping is turned on or off.

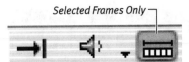

Figure 5.11 The Selected Frames Only button tells Director to play back only part of the movie.

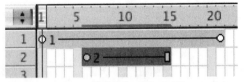

Figure 5.12 When you click the Selected Frames Only button, a green bar appears in the Score.

Figure 5.13 The Frame box shows the current frame number, which you can replace with your desired frame number.

To play only part of a movie:

1. In the Score, select the frames you want to play.

   It doesn't matter which channel (or channels) you make the selection in; Director will play all channels for the selected frames.

2. In the Control Panel, click the Selected Frames Only button (**Figure 5.11**).

   A green bar appears in the Score above the selected frames (**Figure 5.12**).

3. Click the Play button.

   Only the selected frames play.

4. When you finish viewing the movie segment, click the Selected Frames Only button again to remove the green bar and turn off the selection.

To jump to a specific frame:

1. Open the Control Panel. (You can't accomplish this task from the secondary control panel.)

2. Double-click the number displayed in the Frame box (**Figure 5.13**).

   By default, this box displays the number of the frame where the playhead currently resides.

3. Type the number for the frame you want to view.

4. Press Enter (Windows) or Return (Mac).

   The playhead will jump to the desired frame.

   or

   Click the Play button (or use the keyboard shortcut).

   The movie will begin playing from the desired frame.

USING THE CONTROL PANEL

Setting a Movie's Tempo

Director plays your movie at a particular tempo, or speed, which is displayed in the Control Panel. The movie's tempo is usually measured in *frames per second* (fps). The fastest tempo Director supports is 999 fps, though it's unlikely any movie could actually play at this rate. Most movies have tempos in the range of 10 to 30 fps.

The tempo you set affects the speed at which visual sprites are animated on the Stage. It does not affect the playback rate of audio or video cast members. (For more information, see Chapter 10, "Adding Digital Video.")

You can apply one tempo to an entire movie via the Control Panel, or you can vary the tempo within the movie by using the tempo channel in the Score.

To set the units in which tempo is displayed:

1. Open the Control Panel. (You can't accomplish this task in the secondary control panel.)

2. Use the Tempo Mode pop-up menu (**Figure 5.14**) and choose either Frames Per Second or Seconds Per Frame.

   Changing this setting has no effect on the movie's tempo, only on how it's displayed.

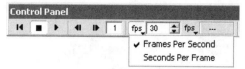

Figure 5.14 Use the pop-up menu to set the units for the tempo display.

Flash Talk: Tempo vs. Frame Rate

Tempo is one area in which Director has a huge advantage over Macromedia Flash. When you set a frame rate in Flash, it applies to the entire movie—there's no way to alter it if you want a particular sequence to move more quickly or slowly. In Director, you can use the tempo channel to change the tempo at any point during the movie.

Figure 5.15 To set a tempo in the Control Panel, click the arrows or enter a new number in the Tempo box.

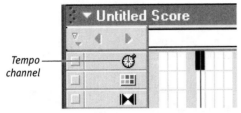

Figure 5.16 In the tempo channel (identified by a stopwatch icon), select a cell for the new tempo.

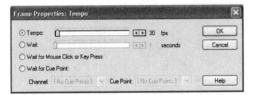

Figure 5.17 The Frame Properties: Tempo dialog box.

Figure 5.18 Drag the slider or click the arrows to set a new tempo.

To set one tempo for an entire movie:

1. Open the Control Panel. (You cannot accomplish this task in the secondary control panel.)

2. Click the up or down arrows to the right of the Tempo box to select a new tempo for the movie (**Figure 5.15**).

   or

   Enter a new number in the Tempo box.

✔ Tips

■ The tempo setting in the Control Panel is saved with your movie file.

■ You can also set a tempo for an entire movie by placing a tempo setting in frame 1 of the tempo channel (see the next task "To set the tempo for any part of a movie.") below).

To set the tempo for any part of a movie:

1. In the tempo channel of the Score, select the frame in which you want the new tempo to begin (**Figure 5.16**).

2. Choose Modify > Frame > Tempo.

   The Frame Properties: Tempo dialog box opens (**Figure 5.17**).

3. In the dialog box, click the Tempo button if it's not already selected.

4. Drag the slider or click the arrows to set the movie's tempo in frames per second (**Figure 5.18**).

5. Click OK.

   The tempo setting appears in the Score.

6. Play the movie.

   The specified tempo takes effect in the frame you selected. The movie will continue to play at that tempo until the playhead encounters another setting in the tempo channel.

continues on next page

SETTING A MOVIE'S TEMPO

✔ Tips

- You can select a frame and open the Tempo dialog box in one move by double-clicking the desired cell in the tempo channel.

- If no tempo is set in frame 1 of the tempo channel, Director will use the tempo from the Control Panel. If the playhead encounters a tempo setting in a later frame, that new tempo will override the tempo setting in the Control Panel.

To insert a pause in a movie:

1. In the tempo channel, select the frame in which you want the pause to take place.

2. Choose Modify > Frame > Tempo.

    The Frame Properties: Tempo dialog box appears.

3. In the dialog box, select a wait option (**Figure 5.19**):

    ▲ Select the first wait option if you're creating a timed pause. You can use the adjacent slider or arrows to specify the duration in seconds (**Figure 5.20**).

    ▲ Select the Wait for Mouse Click or Key Press option if you want the movie to remain paused until the user clicks the mouse or presses a key (**Figure 5.21**).

    ▲ Select the Wait for Cue Point option if you want the movie to pause until a specific cue point is reached in an audio or video cast member (**Figure 5.22**). (See the "Using Cue Points" sidebar for more information.)

4. If you selected the Wait for Cue Point option, choose a cast member and a cue point from the Channel and Cue Point pop-up menus.

5. Click OK.

    The pause setting appears in the Score.

Figure 5.19 Three options are available for setting pauses in a movie.

Figure 5.20 Set the length for the pause by dragging the slider or clicking the arrows.

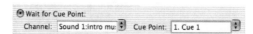

Figure 5.21 Select this option to pause until the user either clicks the mouse or presses a key.

Figure 5.22 The Wait for Cue Point option pauses your movie until a specified cue point is reached.

SETTING A MOVIE'S TEMPO

Using Cue Points

It's possible to insert specialized markers called *cue points* in certain types of audio or video files. These cue points are invisible and inaudible, but Director can detect them and use them with the Wait for Cue Point option. This feature is useful for synchronizing events in a Director movie with specific cues in a music or dialog track.

When Director's playhead reaches a frame that includes a Wait for Cue Point setting, the movie pauses. All action comes to a halt, except for any audio or video cast members that are already playing. (For information on using audio and video cast members in movies, see Chapter 10, "Adding Digital Video," and Chapter 13, "Adding Sound.") When the specified audio or video cast member reaches the specified cue point, Director's playhead starts moving again and the action of the movie resumes.

Director can't insert cue points in audio or video files—to do that, you have to use third-party software. In Windows, you can use Sound Forge 4.0 or later, or Cool Edit 96 or later, to insert cue points in audio files. On the Macintosh, you can use SoundEdit 16 2.07 or later, or Peak LE 2 or later, to insert cue points in audio or QuickTime video files.

If you don't have access to these third-party programs, you can still use the Wait for Cue Point feature, because every audio and video cast member already contains one cue point: the end of the file. In the Frame Properties: Tempo dialog box, if you select an audio or video cast member from the Channel pop-up menu and choose {End} from the Cue Point pop-up menu, the Director movie will pause until the specified audio or video cast member plays through to the end of the file.

SETTING A MOVIE'S TEMPO

Comparing Target Tempo with Actual Tempo

If you set a fast tempo for a movie—say, anything over 30 fps—keep in mind that not every computer that plays back your movie will be able to play it at that speed. The tempo you set in the Control Panel or the tempo channel is considered the *target tempo*. Director will try to achieve the target tempo, but the actual playback speed may fall short when the movie includes elements that place a heavy load on the processor. (See the sidebar "Reducing Processor Load.") Because some computers are more powerful than others, the playback speed of your movie often will vary from computer to computer.

Director's Control Panel allows you to compare the movie's target tempo with the actual playback tempo. Using this information, you can make whatever changes are necessary (either slowing the target tempo or simplifying the movie) to make the two numbers match. But even if the movie can achieve its target tempo on *your* computer, this doesn't mean it will be able to achieve it on other computers. If you know that some of your users will be using older or slower computers, test the movie on computers similar to those as well.

In many cases, when you're testing a movie, the actual tempo won't match the target tempo but you'll decide the movie looks fine anyway. In that case, you can lock the frame durations so that the movie will play back on other computers the same way it played on yours.

Reducing Processor Load

If the playback speed of your movie—or a particular part of your movie—is unacceptably slow, try doing one or more of the following things to reduce the load on the computer's processor:

◆ Reduce the number of sprites in motion at the same time.

◆ Replace high-color-depth cast members with lower-color-depth ones.

◆ Reduce the use of blends in the Score.

◆ Reduce the use of ink effects other than the default Copy.

◆ Reduce the use of sprites that are resized on the Stage.

◆ Use the Direct-to-Stage option for Flash and digital-video sprites. (For more information, see Chapter 11, "Using Flash Movies in Director.")

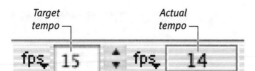

Target tempo   *Actual tempo*

Figure 5.23 The Control Panel shows both the target tempo and the actual tempo.

To compare the target tempo with the actual tempo:

1. Open the Control Panel.

2. If Looping is turned on, turn it off by clicking the Loop Playback button.

3. Click the Rewind button to rewind the movie to the first frame.

4. Play the movie once through to the end.

   Behind the scenes, Director records the actual playback speed for each frame in the movie.

5. Rewind the movie to the first frame.

6. Click the Step Forward button.

7. Compare the target-tempo and actual-tempo displays (**Figure 5.23**).

   The Tempo box displays the target tempo for the frame you just played. This may be the tempo from the most recent setting in the tempo channel, or—if no tempo has been set in the tempo channel—the tempo that was set in the Control Panel.

   The Actual Tempo box displays the speed at which Director was able to play the frame when you played the movie in step 4.

8. Repeat steps 6 and 7 for each frame of the movie.

✔ Tips

- Director is sometimes unable to record the actual tempo for a particular frame. In those cases, the Actual Tempo box displays three dashes (---). If you play the movie again, Director may be able to get a reading the second time.

- If you don't want to compare the tempos for each individual frame, you can make the comparisons "on the fly" by keeping an eye on the actual-tempo display as you play all or part of the movie.

COMPARING TARGET TEMPO WITH ACTUAL TEMPO

To change how the actual tempo is displayed:

1. Open the Control Panel.

2. Choose an option from the Actual Tempo Mode pop-up menu (**Figure 5.24**):

   ▲ Frames Per Second and Seconds Per Frame are self-explanatory.

   ▲ Running Total indicates the total elapsed time, in seconds, from the start of your movie to the current frame.

   ▲ Estimated Total is similar to Running Total, but it's theoretically more accurate in tracking time variations caused by pauses and transitions.

✔ Tip

■ Because Estimated Total mode requires Director to do complex calculations while the movie plays, this mode can actually slow down your movie.

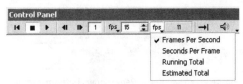

Figure 5.24 Use this pop-up menu to set the mode for the actual-tempo display.

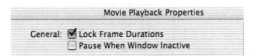

Figure 5.25 To lock the playback speed of a movie, select the Lock Frame Durations checkbox in the Movie Playback Properties dialog box.

To lock playback speed:

1. In the Control Panel, rewind the movie to the first frame.

2. If Looping is on, turn it off.

3. Play the movie all the way through.

   If the movie branches off into multiple segments (in an interactive presentation, for example), make sure you play through all those segments. Behind the scenes, Director records the actual playback speed for each frame in the movie.

4. Choose Modify > Movie > Playback.

   The Movie Playback Properties dialog box appears (**Figure 5.25**).

5. Select the Lock Frame Durations option.

6. Click OK.

   Each frame is now locked to play at the actual speed recorded when the movie was played back.

✔ Tips

- To unlock the movie's playback speed, reopen the Movie Playback Properties dialog box, deselect the Lock Frames Duration checkbox, and click OK.

- Locking the playback speed can't turn a slow computer into a fast one. If parts of your movie are too processor-intensive for a user's computer, they may play more slowly than the speed you locked in.

COMPARING TARGET TEMPO WITH ACTUAL TEMPO

Using Scene Transitions

Director offers more than 50 different transitions—such as dissolves, wipes, and motion effects—that you can use to move smoothly from one frame to the next. Use them whenever you have an abrupt change in subject matter that might otherwise create a jarring effect for the viewer.

Attempting to describe all the transition styles individually would require more space than is available here. The best way to find out what each transition looks like is to try them out. Experiment with a number of different transition types before selecting one for your scene change.

If you can't find a transition you like among those that come with Director, a variety of other transitions are available as Xtras from third-party developers on Macromedia's Web site.

To set a transition:

1. In the transition channel of the Score, select the frame in which you want to place the transition (**Figure 5.26**).

   Important: The transition occurs between the frame that you select and the frame that precedes it. In other words, to transition between two scenes, you place the transition at the first frame of the second scene, not the last frame of the first scene.

2. Choose Modify > Frame > Transition.

   The Frame Properties: Transition dialog box opens (**Figure 5.27**).

3. In the left pane of the dialog box, choose the category from which you'd like to select a transition. (If you don't want to limit your selection to a specific category, choose All.)

   The transitions from the category you've selected appear in the right pane of the dialog box. Each has a descriptive name—and, on the Macintosh, an illustrative icon as well (**Figure 5.28**).

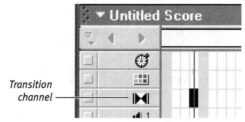

Transition channel

Figure 5.26 In the transition channel (identified by a bow-tie icon), select a frame for the transition.

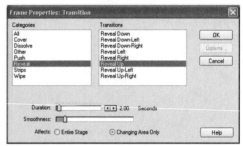

Figure 5.27 The Frame Properties: Transition dialog box lists categories of transitions on the left. When you select a category, the transitions in the category appear in the list on the right.

Figure 5.28 On the Macintosh, transition names are accompanied by icons.

USING SCENE TRANSITIONS

Figure 5.29 These controls allow you to specify the duration and smoothness of the transition, as well as which part of the Stage the transition affects.

Transition icon

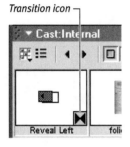

Figure 5.30 When a transition is used in the Score, it is automatically added to the movie's Cast.

4. Choose a transition from the right pane.

5. Use the Duration slider or the adjacent arrows to specify how long, in seconds, the transition should last (**Figure 5.29**).

The duration of a transition is completely independent of the movie's tempo.

6. Use the Smoothness slider to set the "chunkiness" of the transition.

The Smoothness control has different effects on different transitions, but higher levels of smoothness are always more processor-intensive and thus may cause the transition to take longer than the duration you specified in step 5.

7. Specify where on the Stage to apply the transition.

Choose the Entire Stage option to apply the transition to the entire Stage.

Choose the Changing Area Only option to apply the transition only to the area of the Stage that changes from one frame to the next.

8. Click OK.

The transition appears in the Score and also becomes a member of the current Cast (**Figure 5.30**).

✔ Tips

■ Once a transition has been added to the Cast, you no longer have to choose it from the Frame Properties: Transition dialog box. The next time you want to use that transition in your movie, simply drag it from the Cast window to the desired frame in the transition channel.

■ You can select a frame and open the Transition dialog box in one move by double-clicking the desired cell in the transition channel.

USING SCENE TRANSITIONS

To use Xtra transitions:

1. If Director is running, choose File > Exit (Windows) or Director > Quit Director (Mac) to close it.

2. Install the transitions by copying them to the Xtras folder inside the Director MX program folder. (For more information on finding and importing Xtras, see Chapter 19, "Using Xtras.")

3. Restart Director.

   From now on, whenever you open the Transition dialog box, the Xtra transitions will be available in a custom category (**Figure 5.31**).

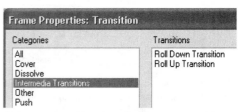

Figure 5.31 Transitions installed as Xtras are made available in the Transition dialog box.

What About the Palette Channel?

Since the tempo channel and the transition channel have both been covered in this chapter, you'd expect the third special-effects channel—the palette channel (**Figure 5.32**)—to be covered as well. It won't be, however, for the simple reason that it really isn't used anymore.

Years ago, when many computers could display only 256 colors at a time, it was common to create Director movies that had an 8-bit color depth. In those movies, the palette channel was used to specify which set of colors would be available for display in each frame of the movie.

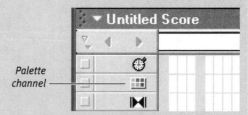

Figure 5.32 The palette channel is now obsolete.

Because computers with 8-bit displays have virtually disappeared, there's no need to make 8-bit Director movies anymore, and Director MX no longer supports them. The palette channel is included primarily to maintain backward compatibility with older movie files.

Note that it's still possible—and often desirable—to use 8-bit *cast members* in Director movies. When you use an 8-bit cast member, its associated palette will sometimes show up in the palette channel; but the palette's presence or absence there has no effect on the movie.

Using Paint Tools

Director's Paint window is a museum piece—a perfectly preserved bit of 1988 technology in a 21st-century program. Except for a slight cosmetic brush-up to give it the MX "look," the Paint window literally has not been changed since Director's earliest days. Looking for layers? Forget about it. Antialiasing? Never heard of it.

With much more sophisticated paint tools—such as Adobe Photoshop or even Macromedia Fireworks—so widely available, why would anyone use Director's primitive Paint window to create cast members?

Well, for the most part, they don't. Most Director users import their bitmapped cast members from other programs. And yet, the Paint window remains an integral part of Director, chiefly because of the convenience factor: Anything created in the Paint window automatically becomes a cast member, with no importing or cutting and pasting necessary. And if you need to make changes in a cast member, you can do it in the Paint window with a simple double-click.

continues on next page

Beyond convenience, the Paint window has features that you won't find in Photoshop. There are unusual ink effects, such as Switch and Cycle, that let you use color in creative ways. There's an Auto Distort feature that creates tweened versions of cast members. Perhaps most useful of all is the Onion Skinning feature, which makes frame-by-frame animation easier by letting you use existing cast members as a guide for painting new ones.

If you know you'll be importing cast members from other programs, you can ignore Director's paint tools—and this chapter—altogether. But if the convenience of creating your cast members within Director appeals to you, this chapter will show you how to use Director's built-in paint tools to create, edit, and apply effects to your images.

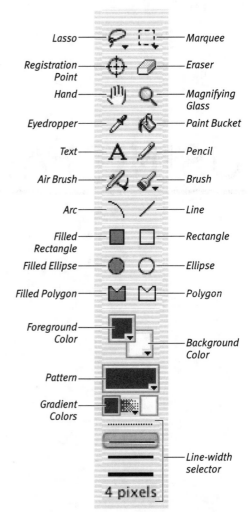

Figure 6.1 The Paint Tool palette should look familiar to you if you've used any other paint or image-editing programs.

USING PAINT TOOLS

Paint Window Basics

This chapter assumes that you already have some experience using paint programs. (Even if you haven't used Photoshop, you've probably at least used Microsoft Paint, included with every version of Windows.) Based on that experience, you'll probably find most of the items on the Paint window's tool palette comfortably familiar (**Figure 6.1**).

Just about all of the paint tools—the Pencil, Paint Bucket, Rectangle, and so on—work the same in Director's Paint window as they do in other paint programs, and therefore

won't be covered in this chapter. The Brush and the Air Brush, which do have some unique features in Director, *will* be covered.

Nearly all of the tasks in this chapter take place in the Paint window (**Figure 6.2**). Therefore, most of the directions for each task will assume you're already in the Paint window.

Before you start using individual tools, you should become familiar with the general way the Paint window operates.

Effects toolbar

Paint Tool palette

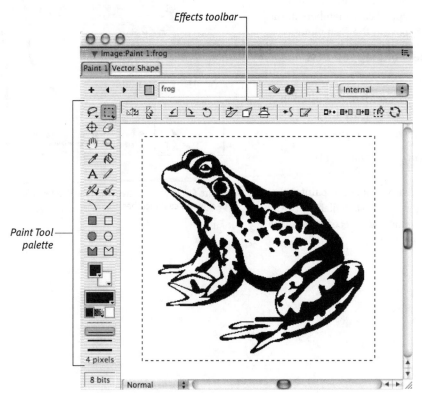

Figure 6.2 If you've used previous versions of Director, you'll find the Paint window largely unchanged, save for the new MX interface.

To open the Paint window:

◆ Choose Window > Paint.

To view or edit an existing bitmapped cast member:

◆ Double-click the cast member in the Cast window.

The Paint window opens (if it's not open already) and displays the selected cast member.

or

If the Paint window is already open and displaying a different cast member, click the Next Cast Member or Previous Cast Member button (**Figure 6.3**) to step through bitmapped cast members in the order they appear in the Cast window.

To create a new bitmapped cast member:

1. Click the New Cast Member button in the Paint window (**Figure 6.4**).

   A new, blank work area appears.

2. Create an image, using any of the paint tools.

   At the moment you begin to paint, your image occupies the first available position in the Cast window and becomes available for use in your movie.

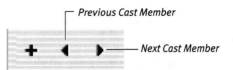

Previous Cast Member

Next Cast Member

Figure 6.3 Use these buttons to cycle through existing bitmapped cast members in the order they appear in the Cast window.

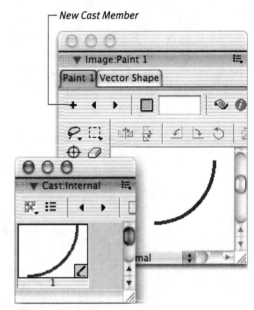

New Cast Member

Figure 6.4 Any image created in the Paint window becomes a cast member.

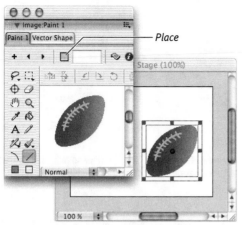

Figure 6.5 Drag the Place button from the Paint window to the Stage to place the current image there.

Figure 6.6 You can display horizontal and vertical rulers to help you align and measure your artwork.

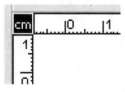

Figure 6.7 Click the upper-left-hand box where the rulers intersect to change the unit of measurement.

To turn an image in the Paint window into a sprite on the Stage:

1. Create or open an image in the Paint window.

2. Drag the Place button (**Figure 6.5**) onto the Stage.

   Director places the image from the Paint window on the Stage and in the Score.

To show or hide the Paint Tools palette:

◆ Choose View > Paint Tools.

To show or hide rulers:

◆ Choose View > Rulers (**Figure 6.6**).

✔ Tips

■ You can set a ruler's zero point by dragging anywhere within the ruler and releasing the mouse button where you want the new zero point to be.

■ To cycle the rulers' unit of measurement from inches to centimeters to pixels, click in the box where the two rulers meet (**Figure 6.7**).

To zoom in or out:

◆ Choose View > Zoom (**Figure 6.8**).

or

1. Select the Magnifying Glass in the tool palette (**Figure 6.9**).

   The mouse pointer becomes a magnifying glass.

2. Click within the work area to zoom in, or Shift+click to zoom out.

   When you're zoomed in at any level greater than 100 percent, a navigation rectangle appears in the upper-right corner of the Paint window, showing the artwork at its actual size (**Figure 6.10**). Clicking within this rectangle returns the zoom level to 100 percent.

✔ Tips

■ If the navigation rectangle blocks part of your artwork, use the Hand tool to move the artwork around within the work area.

■ To zoom in on an image at the maximum zoom level, double-click the Pencil tool in the Paint Tool palette.

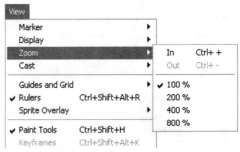

Figure 6.8 The View > Zoom command lets you choose a specific zoom level, or simply zoom in or out.

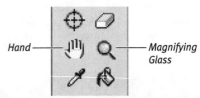

Figure 6.9 Use the Magnifying Glass tool to zoom in and out, and the Hand tool to move your artwork around within the visible portion of the work area.

Figure 6.10 When you zoom into an image, the navigation rectangle at the upper right shows the same image at its actual size, to help you recognize the area you're editing.

Figure 6.11 The Marquee tool.

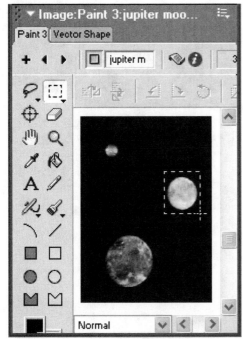

Figure 6.12 Drag diagonally to make a rectangular selection.

Selecting and Moving Images

When you edit an image, selection is almost always the first step of the operation: First you select the area you want to operate on, and then you do something to it (for example, move it to another region of the Paint window, cut or copy it, or change its dimensions).

The Paint window offers two selection tools: the Marquee tool, which selects a rectangular area, and the Lasso, which allows you to make a selection of any shape. Each has a number of options that can significantly change the tool's behavior.

To select with the Marquee tool:

1. In the Paint Tool palette, select the Marquee tool (**Figure 6.11**).

   The pointer becomes a crosshair pointer.

2. In the Paint window, position the crosshairs pointer at one corner of your selection.

3. Hold down the mouse button and drag the pointer diagonally to the opposite corner to create a selection box around the artwork (**Figure 6.12**).

   A dotted rectangle called a *marquee* appears as you drag.

4. Release the mouse button when the marquee encloses what you want to select.

✔ Tip

■ Double-click the Marquee tool to select everything in the Paint window.

To choose Marquee tool options:

1. Select the Marquee tool and hold down the mouse button until the Options pop-up menu appears (**Figure 6.13**).

Figure 6.13 Open the Marquee tool's Options pop-up menu.

2. Select one of the four options (**Figure 6.14**).

   ▲ **Shrink** makes the rectangular selection marquee tighten around whatever object you've selected.

   ▲ **No Shrink** leaves the selection exactly as you draw it.

   ▲ **Lasso** creates a form-fitting selection around whatever object you've selected, as though you had used the Lasso tool.

   ▲ **See Thru Lasso** is similar to the Lasso option, but it makes all white pixels in the selection transparent. This is useful if you want to copy and paste the selected area on top of another image, and you want portions of the background to show through.

Shrink *No Shrink* *Lasso*

Figure 6.14 The first three Marquee tool options.

✔ Tip

■ Though it seems odd for the Marquee tool to behave like a lasso, the Lasso and See Thru Lasso options have the advantage of combining the versatility of lasso-style selection with the simplicity of marquee-style selection.

Lasso

Figure 6.15 The Lasso tool gives you greater freedom, letting you select any shape, no matter how irregular.

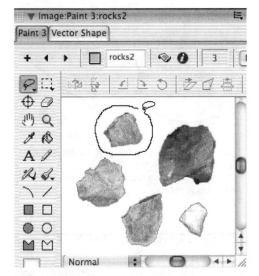

Figure 6.16 To select an irregularly shaped item, drag the Lasso tool around it.

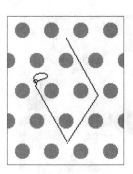

Figure 6.17 To select a polygonal shape, hold down the Alt or Option key while dragging, adding line segments as you go along.

To select with the Lasso tool:

1. In the Paint Tool palette, click the Lasso tool (**Figure 6.15**).

2. In the Paint window, position the Lasso wherever you want to begin your selection.

3. Hold down the mouse button and drag the Lasso around the area you want to select (**Figure 6.16**).

4. Release the mouse button.

   Director highlights the selected area.

   If you did not entirely enclose your selection, Director automatically connects its starting and ending points.

✔ Tip

■ You can use the Lasso tool to select a polygon. Hold down the Alt key (Windows) or Option key (Mac) while dragging the Lasso to create an anchor point and draw a straight selection line. Add line segments to enclose the artwork. Double-click to end your selection (**Figure 6.17**).

To choose Lasso options:

1. Select the Lasso tool and hold down the mouse button until the Options pop-up menu appears (**Figure 6.18**).

2. Select an option (**Figure 6.19**):

   ▲ **No Shrink** selects the entire area that you enclose with the Lasso.

   ▲ **Lasso** makes the selection marquee tighten around whatever object you've selected. Director tries to identify an object's border by looking for color differences among pixels.

   ▲ **See Thru Lasso** makes all the white pixels in your selection transparent.

To reposition a selected area:

1. In the Paint window, make a selection with the Marquee or Lasso tool.

2. Drag the selection to a new location (**Figure 6.20**).

To copy a selected area:

1. Make a selection with the Marquee or Lasso tool.

2. Hold down the Alt key (Windows) or Option key (Mac), and drag the selection to a new place.

   The original image is left in place.

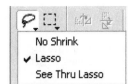

Figure 6.18 To further fine-tune your Lasso selections, use the Options pop-up menu.

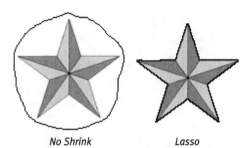

No Shrink   Lasso

Figure 6.19 Use the Lasso Tool's No Shrink option when you want to select the entire area that you enclose with the Lasso tool. For a tighter selection, use the Lasso option.

Figure 6.20 To reposition a selected item, simply drag it.

SELECTING AND MOVING IMAGES

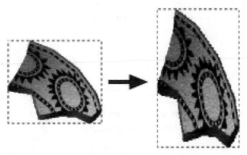

Figure 6.21 Drag while holding down the Ctrl or Command key to stretch a selection.

To stretch or compress a selected area:

1. Make a selection with the Marquee tool (you can't use the Lasso for this task).

2. Hold down the Ctrl key (Windows) or Command key (Mac), click anywhere in the selection, and drag (**Figure 6.21**). Drag away from the center to stretch the image; drag toward the center to compress.

✔ Tip

■ To maintain the selection's original proportions when you stretch or compress, press Ctrl+Shift (Windows) or Command+ Shift (Mac) while dragging.

To erase a selected area:

1. Make a selection with the Marquee or Lasso tool.

2. Press the Backspace or Delete key. The selected area is erased.

✔ Tip

■ To erase the entire contents of the Paint window, double-click the Eraser tool in the Paint Tool palette.

Setting Line Widths

The line-width selector (**Figure 6.22**) allows you to specify the width of lines painted by the Line tool, the Arc tool, and the various shape tools (**Figure 6.23**).

To choose a line width:

◆ In the Paint Tool palette, click one of the options in the line-width selector. (The dotted line represents a zero line width—that is, no line.)

The next time you use the Line, Rectangle, Arc, Ellipse, or Polygon tools, they will paint with the specified line width.

To create a custom line width:

1. Choose Edit > Preferences > Paint (Windows) or Director > Preferences > Paint (Mac).

   or

   Double-click the Other Line Width button in the Paint Tool palette. (It's the only option in the line-width selector that's displayed as text.)

   The Paint window Preferences dialog box opens.

2. Use the "Other" Line Width slider or the adjacent arrows to set the line width (**Figure 6.24**).

3. Click OK.

   The Other Line Width button on the Paint Tool palette displays the line width you selected.

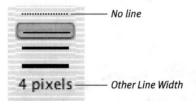
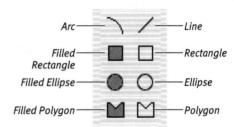

Figure 6.22 Use the line-width selector to set the thickness of lines, arcs, and borders.

Figure 6.23 These tools make use of the current line-width selection.

Figure 6.24 Create a custom line thickness by dragging the slider or clicking the arrows in the Paint Preferences dialog box.

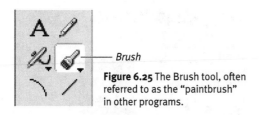

Brush

Figure 6.25 The Brush tool, often referred to as the "paintbrush" in other programs.

Figure 6.26 Select the Brush tool and hold down the mouse button to open a pop-up menu of shape selections.

Customizing the Brush Tool

The tool known as a "paintbrush" in most paint programs is simply called the Brush in Director (**Figure 6.25**). It's the most versatile of the paint tools.

By default, Director offers five different shapes for the Brush. You can replace any or all of these with shapes chosen from the Brush Shapes dialog box, or you can create custom brush shapes.

You can set the Brush to "remember" the last color it used, in which case it will paint with that color regardless of the current foreground color setting.

To choose a brush shape:

1. Select the Brush tool in the Paint Tool palette and hold down the mouse button.

   A pop-up menu appears, listing (but not describing) the brush shapes that you can choose (**Figure 6.26**).

2. Select a brush shape.

✔ Tip

■ The mouse pointer instantly takes on the brush shape you've chosen. So, if you want to know what Brush 3 looks like, select it; then move the mouse pointer into the work area and look at its shape.

To change the set of available brush shapes:

1. Select the Brush tool in the Paint Tool palette and hold down the mouse button.
   The Brush pop-up menu appears.

2. Select the brush shape that you want to replace.
   Because the menu is limited to five choices at any one time, your new shape must replace one of the currently listed shapes.

3. Open the Brush pop-up menu again and choose Settings.
   or
   Double-click the Brush tool in the Paint Tool palette.
   The Brush Settings dialog box opens (**Figure 6.27**).

4. Select a brush shape to add to the menu.

5. Click OK.
   The new brush shape takes its place in the pop-up menu.

To create a custom brush shape:

1. Double-click the Brush tool to open the Brush Settings dialog box.
   You'll create a new brush shape by editing an existing brush shape.

2. If it's not already selected, choose Custom from the pop-up menu (**Figure 6.28**).
   The set of custom shapes is initially identical to the set of standard shapes, except that the Custom set is editable and the Standard set is not.

3. Select a custom brush shape to edit.
   An enlarged version of the selected brush appears in the Brush Shape edit box (**Figure 6.29**).

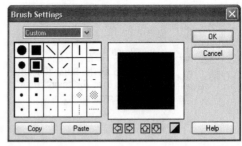

Figure 6.27 Select a new brush shape in the Brush Settings dialog box.

Brush Shape edit box —

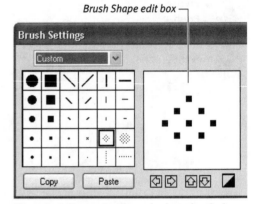

Figure 6.28 Choose Custom and select a brush shape to edit.

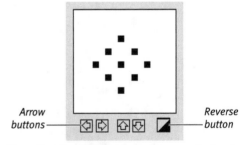

Arrow buttons — — *Reverse button*

Figure 6.29 Use the arrow buttons to move the brush around within the edit box, or the Reverse button to create a negative image.

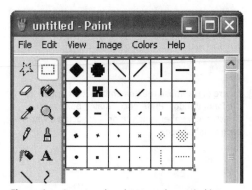

Figure 6.30 A custom brush set can be copied into a third-party paint program (such as Microsoft Paint, shown here) and saved as a single image file.

4. In the Brush Shape edit box, click empty spaces to add pixels to the brush or click existing pixels to erase them.

You can click the arrow buttons to move the brush within the space, or the Reverse button to change all black pixels to white (and vice versa).

5. When you're happy with your new brush design, click OK.

6. Add your custom brush shape to the Brush pop-up menu by following the steps in the previous task, "To change the set of available brush shapes."

To store a set of custom brush shapes:

1. Double-click the Paint Brush tool to open the Brush Settings dialog box.

2. In the Brush Settings dialog box, click Copy.

3. Open a new, blank document iany third-party image-editing or paint program.

4. Still in the image-editing or paint program, Choose Edit > Paste.

The entire custom brush set is pasted as a single image (**Figure 6.30**).

5. Save the image as a file, with whatever name you like.

✔ Tip

■ If you're using a PC that has the Windows Clipboard Viewer installed, you can skip steps 3 and 4. Just open the Clipboard Viewer and save the file from there.

CUSTOMIZING THE BRUSH TOOL

To retrieve a stored set of custom brush shapes:

1. Open the stored custom brush file in an image-editing or paint program.

   or

   Import the file into Director and open it in the Paint window.

2. In the Paint window, select the entire custom brush set, using the Marquee tool or its equivalent.

3. Choose Edit > Copy.

4. In Director's Paint window, double-click the Brush tool to open the Brush Settings dialog box.

5. Click Paste to install the stored brush set.

To assign a color to a brush shape:

1. Open the Paint Window Preferences dialog box by choosing Edit > Preferences > Paint (Windows) or Director > Preferences > Paint (Mac).

2. Select the Remember Color checkbox (**Figure 6.31**).

   From now on, when you choose one of the five brush shapes from the Brush pop-up menu, it will paint with whatever color was last used with that brush shape. (To change the color associated with a brush shape, choose a new foreground color from the color menu *after* selecting the brush shape. See "Using Colors and Patterns" later in this chapter.)

✔ Tip

- If Remember Color is selected in Paint window Preferences, it will apply to the Air Brush tool as well as the Brush tool.

Figure 6.31 Choose the Remember Color option in the Paint Window Preferences dialog box to make Director remember which color is associated with each brush shape.

Air Brush

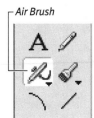

Figure 6.32 The Air Brush tool.

Spray-area preview

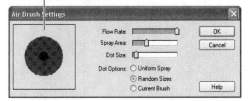

Figure 6.33 Use the Air Brush Settings dialog box to adjust and preview the Air Brush tool's spray pattern.

Current Brush   Random Sizes   Uniform Spray

Figure 6.34 The Air Brush can spray three different types of dots.

Customizing the Air Brush Tool

The Air Brush (**Figure 6.32**) paints with a "spatter" pattern. You can adjust the size of the Air Brush's spray area, the size of the dots it sprays, and the speed at which it sprays them. Five Air Brush settings are available as presets. You can choose from the default presets, or replace any or all of them with custom presets.

To adjust the Air Brush spray pattern:

1. In the Paint Tool palette, select the Air Brush tool while holding down the mouse button, and choose Settings from the pop-up menu that appears.

   or

   Double-click the Air Brush tool.

   The Air Brush Settings dialog box opens (**Figure 6.33**).

2. Drag the Flow Rate slider to adjust the speed at which the Air Brush sprays.

3. Drag the Spray Area slider to change the diameter of the Air Brush spray (represented by a gray circle in the preview area).

4. Drag the Dot Size slider to adjust the size of the dots sprayed by the Air Brush (represented by a black circle in the preview area).

5. Choose a dot option (**Figure 6.34**):

   ▲ **Uniform Spray** makes dots of identical size.

   ▲ **Random Sizes** randomly varies the size of dots sprayed.

   ▲ **Current Brush** causes the Air Brush to spray in the shape that's currently selected for the Brush tool. (Yes, the *Brush* tool—not the Air Brush tool, which has no brush shapes.)

6. Click OK.

   The new Air Brush settings take effect.

153

To choose an Air Brush preset:

1. In the Paint Tool palette, select the Air Brush tool and hold down the mouse button.

   A pop-up menu appears (**Figure 6.35**), listing the five presets.

2. Choose a preset.

✔ Tip

■ Since the presets are listed only as Air Brush 1, Air Brush 2, and so on, there's no way to know what each one looks like. The only way to find out is to choose one, then open the Air Brush Settings dialog box and look at the preview. If you don't want to make any changes in the settings, you can click Cancel to exit the dialog box.

To create a custom preset:

1. In the Paint Tool palette, select the Air Brush tool and hold down the mouse button.

2. Select the preset that you want to replace.

3. Open the Air Brush pop-up menu again and choose Settings.

   or

   Double-click the Air Brush tool.

   The Air Brush Settings dialog box opens.

4. Change the Air Brush's Flow Rate, Spray Area, Dot Size, and Dot Options settings as desired.

5. Click OK.

   Your new settings are stored as a preset.

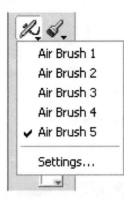

Figure 6.35 Click the Air Brush tool and hold down the mouse button to display the presets.

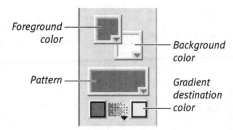

Figure 6.36 Color and pattern settings in the Paint Tool palette.

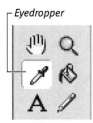

Figure 6.37 Click the Eyedropper tool to sample the color you want to replace.

Paint Window Color Settings

Foreground Color: This is the Paint window's most important color. Nearly all of the paint tools (with the exception of the Text tool) paint with the foreground color exclusively. The foreground color also is the fill color for solid patterns, and it serves as the primary color in multicolor patterns.

Background Color: The only paint tool that makes use of the background color is the Text tool, which uses it as a backdrop for foreground-colored text. (See "Adding Text," later in this chapter.) Otherwise, the background color serves mainly as the secondary color in multicolor patterns.

Gradient Destination Color: This color serves as the ending color for gradients (whose beginning color is always the same as the foreground color). It also plays a role in several specialized ink effects, which you'll read about later in this chapter.

Using Colors and Patterns

Every paint tool is capable of painting solid colors, and some—the Paint Bucket, Brush, and Air Brush—are able to paint with patterns as well. You select colors and patterns using the pop-up menus in the Paint Tool palette (**Figure 6.36**).

When you use a paint tool, the color of the pixels you paint depends on the choice you've made most recently from the Foreground Color menu. Depending on the tool you're using, you may also have to make choices from the Background Color and Gradient Destination Color menus. (For information on the roles of these colors, see the "Paint Window Color Settings" sidebar.)

If you want to paint with a pattern, you can select one from any of three default pattern sets. You can also create your own custom patterns, or use a piece of a cast member as a building block for a pattern (called a *tile*).

To choose a paint color:

◆ In the Paint Tool palette, select the desired color from the Foreground Color, Background Color, or Gradient Destination Color menus. (For more information on using color menus, see "Selecting Colors" in Chapter 1.)

The color you select will remain in effect for all tools in the Paint window until you choose another color.

To switch colors in a cast member:

1. Make sure that your cast member is displayed in the Paint window.

2. In the Paint Tool palette, select the Eyedropper tool (**Figure 6.37**).

The mouse pointer takes the form of an eyedropper.

continues on next page

USING COLORS AND PATTERNS

3. Click on the color in your cast member that you want to replace (**Figure 6.38**).

The color you selected becomes the new foreground color.

4. In the Paint Tool palette, select a new color from the Gradient Destination Color menu.

This will become the replacement color in your cast member.

5. Use the Marquee or Lasso tool to select the portion of the image in which the color switch should take place.

6. Click the Switch Colors button in the Effects toolbar, which is located at the top of the Paint window (**Figure 6.39**).

The original color is replaced by the new color.

To choose a pattern:

1. In the Paint Tool palette, click to open the Pattern menu (**Figure 6.40**).

2. Choose a pattern.

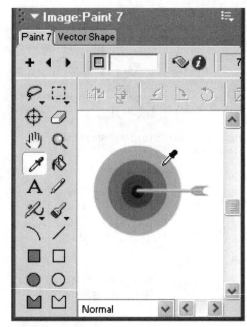

Figure 6.38 Sample a color by clicking on it.

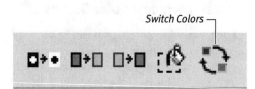

Figure 6.39 Click the Switch Colors button in the Effects toolbar.

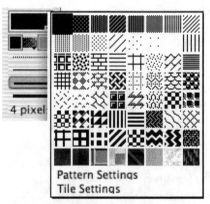

Figure 6.40 Click on the Pattern pop-up menu (it looks like a black rectangle).

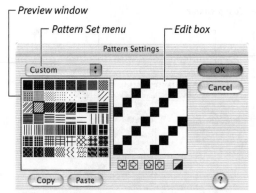

Preview window

Pattern Set menu

Edit box

Figure 6.41 If you can't find a pattern you want, open the Pattern Settings dialog box to choose a different pattern set.

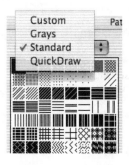

Figure 6.42 Choose from one of the four pattern sets that appear in the Pattern pop-up menu.

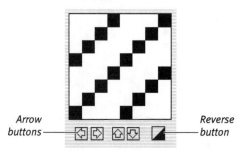

Arrow buttons

Reverse button

Figure 6.43 The Pattern editor works exactly like the Brush Shape editor.

To make a different pattern set available:

1. In the Paint Tool palette, click to open the Pattern menu.

2. Choose Pattern Settings from the bottom of the menu.

   The Pattern Settings dialog box opens (**Figure 6.41**).

3. Choose a pattern set from the pop-up menu. (**Figure 6.42**)

   The patterns in each set display in the window underneath the menu.

4. Click OK.

   The pattern set you selected becomes available on the Pattern pop-up menu.

To create a new pattern:

1. In the Paint Tool palette, click to open the Pattern menu.

2. Choose Pattern Settings from the bottom of the menu.

   The Pattern Settings dialog box opens.

3. Choose Custom from the pop-up menu.

   The Custom set of patterns is initially identical to the Standard set.

4. Select a pattern to edit.

   An enlarged version of the selected pattern appears in the edit box (**Figure 6.43**).

5. In the Pattern edit box, click empty spaces to add pixels to the pattern or click existing pixels to erase them.

   You can click the arrow buttons to move the brush within the space, or the Reverse button to change all black pixels to white (and vice versa).

continues on next page

6. When you're happy with the new pattern, click OK.

The Custom pattern set, including the pattern you just created, becomes available on the Pattern pop-up menu.

✔ Tips

■ If you want to edit a pattern from one of the noncustom pattern sets, open the desired set in the Pattern Settings dialog box, copy and paste your selected pattern into the Custom set, and edit it there.

■ Custom pattern sets can be saved and retrieved just like custom Brush Shape sets. Follow the steps in "To store a set of custom brush shapes" and "To retrieve a stored set of custom brush shapes," substituting the Pattern Settings dialog box for the Brush Settings dialog box.

To create a tile from a cast member:

1. Find a color cast member on which you want to base your tile, and open it in the Paint window.

Creating a tile has no effect on the cast member.

2. In the Paint Tool palette, click to open the Pattern menu.

3. Choose Tile Settings from the bottom of the menu.

The Tile Settings dialog box opens (**Figure 6.44**).

4. Select the Cast Member option (**Figure 6.45**).

(The other option, Built-in, allows you to preview—but not edit—the default tiles built in to Director.)

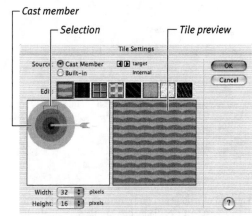

Figure 6.44 The Tile Settings dialog box.

Figure 6.45 Select the Cast Member option to create a tile from a cast member.

Sidebar: USING COLORS AND PATTERNS

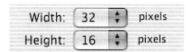

Figure 6.46 Set the dimensions of your tile.

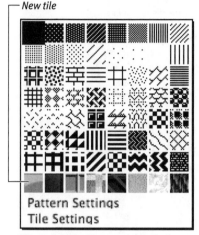

Figure 6.47 The Pattern menu displays the new tile.

Figure 6.48 Here, the Brush tool is painting with the new tile.

5. Use the Width and Height menus to set the dimensions (in pixels) of the tile you want to create (**Figure 6.46**).

Your choices for each dimension are 16, 32, 64, or 128 pixels. It's not necessary for the two dimensions to be the same.

6. In the left pane of the dialog box, drag the selection marquee to the part of the cast member you want to use as a tile.

You can preview the pattern built from the tile in the right pane of the dialog box.

7. When you're satisfied with the tile, click OK.

Your new tile appears in the bottom row of the Pattern menu (**Figure 6.47**), where it can be selected and used like any other pattern (**Figure 6.48**).

✔ Tip

■ While you're in the Tile Settings dialog box, if you want to use a different cast member as the basis for your tile, click the left and right arrows to step through available cast members in the order they appear in the Cast window.

Using Ink Effects

Ink effects are special color effects that can be applied by paint tools when you create or edit an image. Each paint tool offers a different set of ink effects. (The only tool that offers *every* ink effect is the Brush, and the only ink effect offered by *every* paint tool is Normal.)

Ink effects in the Paint window should not be confused with ink effects in the Score. (See Chapter 3, "Building a Score," for information on the latter.) Ink effects applied to sprites in the Score can be changed at any time. By contrast, ink affects applied in the Paint window affect the actual pixels that make up a cast member, and therefore are permanent.

Even though ink effects in the Paint window are different from those used in the Score, some of them may have names in common. See the sidebar "Paint window Ink Effects" for a description of what each ink effect does.

To use an ink effect:

1. Select a tool in the Paint Tool palette.

2. Click the Ink menu at the bottom of the Paint window (**Figure 6.49**).

   The Ink pop-up menu appears (**Figure 6.50**).

3. Choose an ink effect.

   Depending on the tool you've chosen, some of the ink effects may be unavailable.

✔ Tip

■ When you choose an ink effect for a tool, that ink effect "sticks" to the tool—that is, it will remain in effect whenever you use that tool unless you explicitly choose a different ink effect. To turn off this behavior, open the Paint Preferences dialog box and deselect Remember Ink.

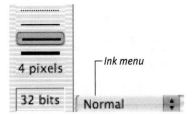

Figure 6.49 The Ink menu is located at the bottom of the Paint window. Here's how it looks when it's closed...

Figure 6.50 ...and here's how the Ink menu looks when it's open.

USING INK EFFECTS

Paint Window Ink Effects

Normal This is the default setting, which is no ink effect at all. Paint tools use the currently selected foreground color and pattern.

Transparent The background color used in patterns becomes transparent, allowing you to see artwork behind the pattern.

Reverse Any color that you paint over changes to its opposite color. Reverse ink is not affected by the currently selected foreground and background colors.

Ghost Instead of the foreground color, tools paint with the currently selected background color.

Gradient Tools paint with two or more smoothly blended colors, specified by the current gradient settings.

Reveal Reveal ink makes use of the previous cast member. As you paint with Reveal ink, you "uncover" the bitmapped cast member that precedes this one in the Cast window.

Cycle As you paint with Cycle ink, the color constantly changes, cycling through all the colors in the color palette between the current foreground color and the current gradient destination color.

Switch If you paint over any pixels of the current foreground color, they are changed to the gradient destination color. Pixels of other colors are unaffected.

Blend All pixels that you paint over (including white background pixels) are mixed with the current foreground color. You can set the degree of blending in the Paint window Preferences dialog box.

Darkest When you paint over pixels of a different color, the overlapping areas display the darker of the two colors.

Lightest This effect works like the Darkest ink effect, except the overlapping areas display the lighter of the two colors.

Darken Darken ink reduces the brightness of artwork as you paint over it. You can set the rate of darkening in the Paint window Preferences dialog box.

Lighten Lighten ink increases the brightness of artwork as you paint over it. You can set the rate of lightening in the Paint window Preferences dialog box.

Smooth Smooth ink blurs artwork as you paint over it. It's useful for smoothing out jagged edges.

Smear Smear ink works only with the Brush tool. It causes existing artwork to spread or smear as you drag the Brush across it. The smear occurs in the direction you drag the Brush.

Smudge Smudge ink is similar to smear ink, but spreads colors in a manner resembling charcoal or pastels.

Spread Spread ink works only with the Brush tool. It paints with whatever color or pattern is beneath the Brush when you start to drag it.

Clipboard This ink uses the contents of the Clipboard as a substitute for the current brush shape and color.

Painting with Gradient Ink

Gradients are probably the most frequently used ink effect in the Paint window. A *gradient* is a gradual transition from one color to another. Gradients may be linear (traveling in a straight line) or radial (radiating inward toward a central point) (**Figure 6.51**), and are extremely useful for creating artistic or perspective effects.

In Director, the starting color of a gradient is always the current foreground color. The ending color can be any color you select from the Gradient destination color menu. Other aspects of the gradient (for example, its direction and blending method) are set in the Gradient Settings dialog box.

Gradient ink is available for use with the Paint Bucket, Text, and Brush tools, and the three filled-shape tools (Filled Rectangle, Filled Ellipse, and Filled Polygon).

To paint with gradient ink:

1. In the Paint Tool palette, select a tool that works with gradients.

    Select one of the following tools: Paint Bucket, Text, Air Brush, Brush, Filled Rectangle, Filled Ellipse, or Filled Polygon.

2. Choose Gradient from the Ink pop-up menu (**Figure 6.52**).

3. In the Paint window, paint with the selected tool.

    The tool will paint with a gradient defined by the current gradient settings.

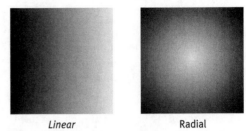

| Linear | Radial |

Figure 6.51 The two basic kinds of gradients.

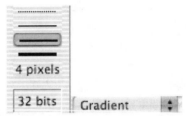

Figure 6.52 Choose Gradient from the Ink pop-up menu.

Clash of the Metaphors

When you think about it, the idea of using ink effects in the Paint window is rather incongruous. So which is it, *ink* or *paint?*

What we have here is an unfortunate collision between two of Director's guiding metaphors. In the world of theater and film, stage sets are painted, but in the world of traditional animation, characters are inked onto transparent cels. Director's original developers drew from both traditions, and Director users have been painting with ink ever since.

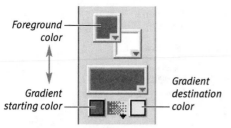

Figure 6.53 The foreground color and the starting gradient color are always the same.

Figure 6.54 Click between the gradient color menus to open the Gradient pop-up menu.

Figure 6.55 Use the Gradient Settings dialog box to set specific characteristics of a gradient.

To create a gradient:

1. Choose the first color for the gradient from either the Foreground Color menu or the Gradient starting color menu (**Figure 6.53**).

   Making a choice from either menu will set the same color for both.

2. Choose the ending color for the gradient from the Gradient destination color menu.

3. Click between the gradient color menus to open the Gradient pop-up menu (**Figure 6.54**).

4. Choose Gradient Settings from the bottom of the menu.

   The Gradient Settings dialog box opens (**Figure 6.55**).

5. Make any desired changes to the settings.

   As you change the gradient's settings, you can preview the results on the left side of the dialog box. For information on each of the settings, see the tasks that follow.

6. Click OK.

7. To use your new gradient, follow the steps for the previous task, "To paint with gradient ink."

✔ Tip

■ Gradient settings can't be saved. If you want to use the same gradient settings later, make a note of them so you can recreate them in the Gradient Settings dialog box.

To set the gradient direction:

1. Open the Gradient Settings dialog box.

2. Make a choice from the Direction pop-up menu (**Figure 6.56**):

   ▲ **Top to Bottom**, **Bottom to Top**, **Left to Right**, and **Right to Left** result in linear gradients that travel vertically or horizontally in the specified direction.

   ▲ The **Directional** option allows you to create a linear gradient that isn't necessarily horizontal or vertical. See the sidebar "Using a Directional Gradient."

   ▲ **Sun Burst** results in a radial gradient that's always circular, regardless of the shape of the area it's filling (**Figure 6.57**).

   ▲ **Shape Burst** (Mac only) results in a radial gradient that follows the contours of the area it's filling.

3. Click OK.

✔ Tip

■ If you don't plan to change any other settings, you can choose a gradient's direction directly from the Gradient pop-up menu, without having to open the Gradient Settings dialog box.

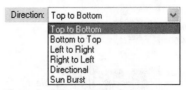

Figure 6.56 The Direction pop-up menu.

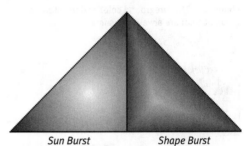

Sun Burst   Shape Burst

Figure 6.57 A triangle filled with a Sun Burst gradient (left) and a Shape Burst gradient (right).

PAINTING WITH GRADIENT INK

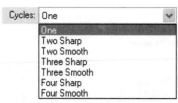

Figure 6.58 The Cycles pop-up menu controls how the gradient repeats within an area.

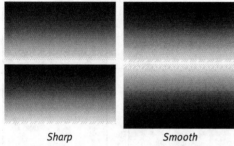

Sharp   *Smooth*

Figure 6.59 Sharp gradient repeat cycles display hard-edged transitions, while smooth gradient repeat cycles provide a softer, more gradual blend of repeats.

To set the gradient repeat settings:

1. Open the Gradient Settings dialog box.

2. Make a choice from the Cycles pop-up menu to determine how frequently, and in what manner, the gradient repeats (**Figure 6.58**).

   You can set the gradient to repeat up to four times in a given area. **Sharp** cycles repeat from start to finish with a crisp edge between repeats. **Smooth** cycles repeat with the colors reversed, giving a gradual transition between repeats (**Figure 6.59**).

3. Click OK.

Using a Directional Gradient

When you use a paint tool with Gradient ink, and the current gradient settings specify a directional gradient, the tool will operate somewhat differently than you're used to.

Paint with the tool as usual. When you release the mouse button, the mouse pointer will turn into crosshairs. A solid line will connect the center of the crosshairs to the center of the shape you're painting (**Figure 6.60**).

Move the crosshairs to the point where you want the gradient to end. (The solid line will indicate the direction of the linear gradient.) When you press and release the mouse button, the gradient will appear (**Figure 6.61**).

Figure 6.60 When you paint with a directional gradient, these crosshairs appear when you release the mouse button.

Figure 6.61 The final directional gradient.

PAINTING WITH GRADIENT INK

To set the gradient type and method:

1. Open the Gradient Settings dialog box.

2. Click either the Dither or Pattern radio button in Type settings (**Figure 6.62**).

   Dither, the default choice, creates the smoothest possible gradient through the use of intermingled pixels of different colors.

   Choose **Pattern** if you want to base the gradient on the currently selected pattern (**Figure 6.63**).

3. Still in the Gradient Settings dialog box, use the Method pop-up menu to determine which colors will be included in the gradient:

   ▲ **Best Colors** uses colors that, by Director's calculations, will create the smoothest possible transition between your foreground and destination colors.

   ▲ **Best Colors Transparent** (available for pattern gradients only) is similar to Best Colors, but any white pixels in the gradient are made transparent.

   ▲ **Adjacent Colors** uses all the colors that happen to lie between the foreground and destination colors in the current palette, even if those colors don't contribute to a smooth transition.

   ▲ **Adjacent Colors Transparent** (available for pattern gradients only) is similar to Adjacent Colors, but any white pixels in the gradient are made transparent.

   ▲ **Two Colors** includes only the foreground and destination colors in the gradient. (All the intermediate steps are achieved by dithering the two colors.)

Figure 6.62 Use the Type and Method settings to specify how the gradient will be constructed and which colors will be included.

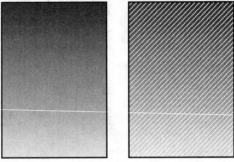

Figure 6.63 These are examples of dithered (left) and patterned (right) gradients.

Figure 6.64 The Spread pop-up menu provides options for spacing the colors of a gradient within a region.

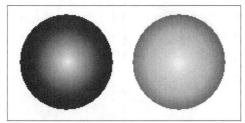

Figure 6.65 These are examples of two kinds of gradient spreads: More Foreground (left) and More Destination (right) increase the amount of foreground and background color, respectively, used in the gradient.

▲ **One Color** uses only the foreground color (ignoring the selected destination color), and fades that color to white by dithering.

▲ **Standard Colors** and **Multi Colors** are holdovers from the days when Director movies often had an 8-bit color depth. In today's 24- or 32-bit movies, these methods are indistinguishable from Best Colors.

4. Click OK.

To set the gradient spread:

1. Open the Gradient Settings dialog box.

2. Make a choice from the Spread pop-up menu to control how Director distributes the colors of the gradient (**Figure 6.64**):

▲ The **Equal** option spaces the gradient's colors evenly throughout an area.

▲ **More Foreground** and **More Destination** (**Figure 6.65**) increase the amount of foreground or destination color in a gradient.

▲ **More Middle** devotes more space to the gradient's middle colors, which are determined by the gradient's Method setting.

3. Click OK.

PAINTING WITH GRADIENT INK

To set the gradient range:

1. Open the Gradient Settings dialog box.

2. Make a choice from the Range pop-up menu to determine whether all or only part of the gradient will be visible in your artwork (**Figure 6.66**).

   If you choose **Paint Object,** the entire gradient will appear within the boundaries of the area you're painting (**Figure 6.67**).

   If you choose **Cast Member** or **Window,** only a portion of the gradient will be visible in the area you're painting (**Figure 6.68**). (Which portion will depend on the size and location of the area you're painting in relation to the full cast member or Paint window.)

3. Click OK.

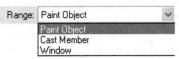

Figure 6.66 The Range pop-up menu.

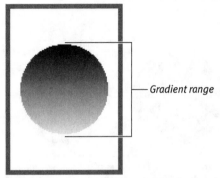

Figure 6.67 A circle within a rectangle. The circle has been painted with a gradient with a range setting of Paint Object—meaning the entire gradient appears within the confines of the circle.

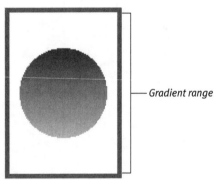

Figure 6.68 The same circle and rectangle. This time the circle has been painted with a gradient whose range setting is Cast Member—meaning the circle contains only a portion of the gradient.

Text

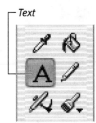

Figure 6.69 Use the Text tool to create bitmapped text within the Paint window.

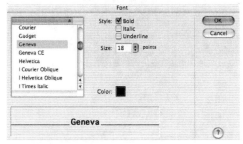

Figure 6.70 Set the typeface, size, and style of text in the Font dialog box.

Creating Bitmapped Text

The Text tool (**Figure 6.69**) allows you to create bitmapped text within the Paint window. Unlike regular text (which you'll learn about in Chapter 12, "Adding Text"), bitmapped text isn't editable. If you want to correct a misspelling, use a different font, or make any other changes, your only option is to erase what's there and start over. (That's why it's often a good idea to choose the size, style, and typeface of your text before you start typing.) Also, most text created in the Paint window also has a bad case of the "jaggies."

On the positive side, text created in the Paint window is extremely versatile. You can transform and manipulate it—by rotating, distorting, or flipping, for example—just as you would any other bitmapped image. You can create bitmapped text with gradients or other ink effects. Best of all, since bitmapped text is just a bunch of pixels, it will look exactly the same on every computer, regardless of what fonts are installed.

To set the typeface, size, and style of text before you create it:

1. Choose Modify > Font.

   or

   Double-click the Text tool in the Paint Tool palette.

   The Font dialog box opens (**Figure 6.70**).

2. Select the desired typeface, style, and size of your text.

3. Click OK to close the dialog box.

To create bitmapped text:

1. In the Paint Tool palette, click the Text tool.

2. In the Paint window, click where you want the text to appear.

   A text box appears, with a blinking insertion point.

3. If you wish to set the typeface, size, or style of the text, choose Modify > Font.

   The Font dialog box opens.

4. Make whatever choices you like, and click OK to close the dialog box.

5. Type the text (**Figure 6.71**).

   If you want multiple lines of text, press Return to start each new line.

   If you need to make changes as you type, use the Backspace key. Don't try to use the left or right arrows or the mouse to move the insertion point within the text box—you'll just "freeze" the text prematurely.

6. If you wish, move the text to another location by dragging the border of the text box (**Figure 6.72**).

7. Proofread the text carefully.

   This is the last point at which your text will be editable.

8. Click anywhere outside the text box.

   The text becomes a bitmap.

✔ Tip

- The Text tool uses the current foreground color as the text color and the current background color as a background. If you want your text to be against a white background, be sure to set the background color to white.

Figure 6.71 Type directly in the text box.

Figure 6.72 You can reposition a text box by dragging it by its border.

Applying Effects

Director's Effects toolbar (**Figure 6.73**) offers a variety of effects and transformations that you can apply to existing artwork. They include flips, rotations, edge traces, image distortions, and other modifications. You may want to make a copy of your cast member before applying any of these effects, in case you're not satisfied with the results.

You can increase the usefulness of your effects by using the Auto Distort command, which applies an effect in gradual steps and creates a new cast member for each step. The result is a series of tweens that can be used to create a sequence of frame-by-frame animation.

You must select an area before you can apply any effects to it. And for most effects, you must use the Marquee tool, not the Lasso, to make the selection.

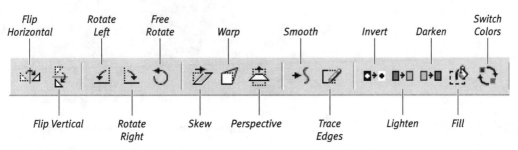

Figure 6.73 The Effects toolbar lets you flip, warp, rotate, and skew, to name a few features.

To rotate artwork 90 degrees:

1. In the Paint window, make a selection with the Marquee tool (**Figure 6.74**).

2. Click Rotate Right or Rotate Left in the Effects toolbar (**Figure 6.75**).

   The selected image rotates 90 degrees (**Figure 6.76**).

3. Click anywhere outside the marquee to lock in the transformation.

To freely rotate artwork in 1-degree increments:

1. Make a selection with the Marquee tool.

2. Click Free Rotate in the Effects toolbar. Director places handles at each corner of your selection.

3. Drag one of the handles to rotate your art selection in 1-degree increments (**Figure 6.77**).

4. Click anywhere outside the marquee to lock in the transformation.

Figure 6.74 Select the artwork (here, a fine-looking eagle) to rotate.

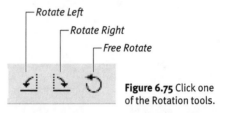

Figure 6.75 Click one of the Rotation tools.

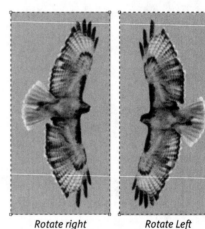

Rotate right   Rotate Left

Figure 6.76 The image rotates to the left or right.

Figure 6.77 Drag a handle to rotate a selection in 1-degree increments with the Free Rotate tool.

APPLYING EFFECTS

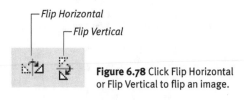

Figure 6.78 Click Flip Horizontal or Flip Vertical to flip an image.

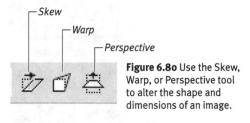

Original

Flip Horizontal   *Flip Vertical*

Figure 6.79 Here, you can see the results of flipping a tour bus.

Figure 6.80 Use the Skew, Warp, or Perspective tool to alter the shape and dimensions of an image.

To flip artwork:

1. Make a selection with the Marquee tool.

2. Click the Flip Horizontal or Flip Vertical tool in the Effects toolbar (**Figure 6.78**). The selected image flips horizontally or vertically (**Figure 6.79**).

To distort artwork:

1. Make a selection with the Marquee tool.

2. Click the Skew, Warp, or Perspective tool in the Effects toolbar (**Figure 6.80**):

   ▲ The **Skew** tool slants the selected area into a parallelogram shape (**Figure 6.81**).

   ▲ The **Warp** tool allows the selected area to be stretched in any number of directions.

   ▲ The **Perspective** tool bends the selected area into a trapezoidal shape, which can be used to make parts of an image seem to recede into the distance.

   When you click a tool, Director places handles at each corner of the selected area.

3. Drag any of the handles to apply the desired effect to the selection.

4. Click anywhere outside the marquee to lock in the transformation.

APPLYING EFFECTS

Original   *Skew*   *Warp*   *Perspective*

Figure 6.81 This bottle of poison gets a fierce workout with Director's four distortion tools.

To apply other toolbar special effects:

1. Use the Marquee or Lasso tool to make a selection.

   The Lasso tool works for all of the following effects except Trace Edges.

2. Choose the Smooth, Trace Edges, Invert Colors, Lighten, Darken, Fill, or Switch Colors tool in the Effects toolbar (**Figure 6.82**):

   ▲ **Smooth** softens the edges of your artwork by adding pixels that blend the colors at the edges (**Figure 6.83**).

   ▲ **Trace Edges** creates an outline around the edges of the artwork you've selected. Select Trace Edges repeatedly to increase the number of outlines in the trace.

   ▲ **Invert Color** replaces each color with its opposite.

   ▲ **Lighten** and **Darken** change the brightness of the artwork.

   ▲ **Fill** fills the selected area with the current foreground color and pattern.

   ▲ **Switch Colors** lets you swap out an unwanted color for a new one. (See "To switch colors in an existing cast member" earlier in this chapter.)

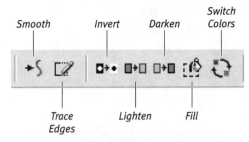

Figure 6.82 More effects tools in the Effects toolbar.

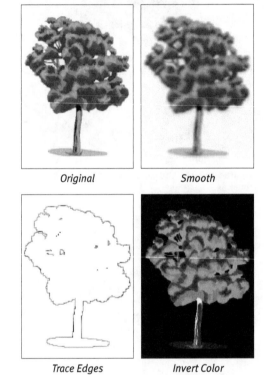

Figure 6.83 Here, a tree sports three different paint effects.

APPLYING EFFECTS

Figure 6.84 In the Auto Distort dialog box, enter the number of in-between cast members you want to create.

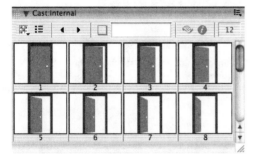

Figure 6.85 The results of using Auto Distort with the Warp tool to create a series of in-between images.

To create a sequence of tweens:

1. Make a selection with the Marquee tool.

2. Click the Skew, Warp, Perspective, or Rotate tool in the Effects toolbar.

   Director places handles at each corner of the selection.

3. Drag any of the handles to rotate or distort the selected art.

   Do not click outside the marquee; the selection handles must remain active.

4. Choose Xtras > Auto Distort.

   The Auto Distort dialog box opens.

5. Type the number of in-between cast members that you want to create (**Figure 6.84**).

6. Click Begin.

   Director applies the effect in the number of steps you specified. For each step, Director creates a new cast member and places it in the next available position in the Cast window (**Figure 6.85**).

✔ Tip

■ There's usually no reason to use Auto Distort with the Skew or Rotate effects, since sprites can be skewed or rotated easily on the Stage. Auto Distort is better used with the Warp and Perspective effects, which can't be duplicated on the Stage.

APPLYING EFFECTS

Onion Skinning

The Onion Skinning feature allows you to create a new cast member in the Paint window while using one or more existing cast members as a reference. The reference images appear dimmed in the background, as though you had tracing paper over them. (In fact, the name of this feature comes from the onion-skin tracing paper that animators traditionally used when drawing animation sequences.) Onion skinning comes in handy when you need to create a sequence of frame-by-frame animation in which each new cast member varies only slightly from the one before.

To use onion skinning:

1. In the Paint window, create the first cast member in the sequence.

   This cast member will be used as your first reference image (**Figure 6.86**).

2. Choose View > Onion Skin.

   The Onion Skin toolbar appears (**Figure 6.87**).

3. Turn on the Onion Skinning feature by clicking the Toggle Onion Skinning button in the Onion Skin toolbar.

   Nothing will look any different, since you still have only one cast member in the sequence.

4. Click the New Cast Member button in the Paint window (**Figure 6.88**).

   The preceding cast member now appears dimmed in the background.

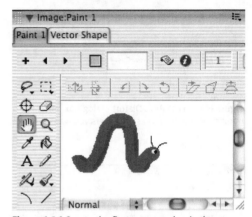

Figure 6.86 Create the first cast member in the sequence.

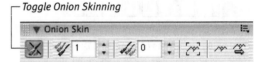

Figure 6.87 The Onion Skin toolbar.

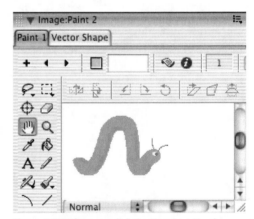

Figure 6.88 When you click the New Cast Member button, an empty cast member opens with a dimmed reference image in the background.

ONION SKINNING

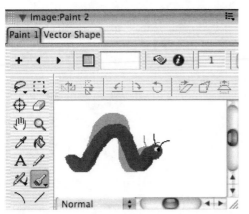

Figure 6.89 Paint a new cast member on top of the reference image.

Preceding Cast Members

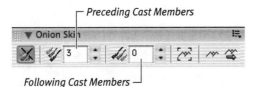

Following Cast Members

Figure 6.90 Display multiple reference images by entering a number in the Preceding Cast Members or Following Cast Members box.

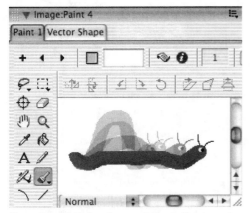

Figure 6.91 Multiple reference cast members appear on top of each other, with earlier ones dimmer than later ones.

5. Draw the new cast member on top of the dimmed image (**Figure 6.89**).

The cast member being used as the reference image won't be affected.

6. Repeat steps 4 and 5 as many times as necessary to create your series of cast members.

To view more than one reference image at a time:

◆ Enter a number in the Preceding Cast Members box (or click the arrows) to specify how many of the preceding cast members you want to see at one time. (**Figure 6.90**).

The specified number of cast members appears in the background, one on top of the other. Earlier cast members are dimmer than later ones (**Figure 6.91**).

✔ Tip

■ If you wish to use cast members as reference images *following* the current cast member (for example, if you've gone back to edit an earlier cast member), enter a number in the Following Cast Members box.

DRAWING VECTOR SHAPES

For many years, vector graphics—which are made up of mathematically defined lines and fills—were considered a "poor cousin" to bitmapped graphics. (For more on the difference between vectors and bitmaps, see the "Vectors Compared with Bitmaps" sidebar later in this chapter.) Because they lack the subtlety and texture of bitmapped images, vector images were used primarily for technical illustration, where aesthetic considerations were less important.

Director had no vector drawing capability at all until the Vector Shape window was added in version 7. This late addition was most likely a response to the boost in popularity that vector graphics received from the success of Macromedia Flash.

Flash—whose developers had realized that vector graphics, with their minimal data requirements, were ideal for use on the Web—was designed from the beginning with vectors in mind. It included a set of high-powered drawing tools that made vector artwork, which had previously been somewhat tricky to create, as easy to draw as bitmapped artwork.

continues on next page

Director's Vector Shape window gives
Director users, like Flash users, the ability
to use vector images in their movies. Other
than that, however, Director's implementation
of vector graphics is rudimentary. Director's
vector drawing tools, in strong contrast to
Flash's, are cumbersome to use and extremely
limited in what they can do. In addition,
Director offers virtually no support for importing vector images. (With the exception of
vector PICT files, a rare and outdated format
limited to the Mac, Director can import
vector images only if they're included in
Flash SWF files.)

If you want to do any sort of serious vector
animation, use Flash. Flash movies can be
imported into Director in their entirety,
allowing them to be integrated fully with
your Director movies. (See Chapter 11, "Using
Flash Movies in Director.") Use Director's
Vector Shape window only when you need
simple, no-frills vector shapes that can be
edited within Director.

Vectors Compared with Bitmaps

A *bitmapped graphic*—the kind of image you've worked with so far in this book—is a rectangular array of pixels (**Figure 7.1**). The visual content of a bitmapped graphic is created by changing the colors of individual pixels in the rectangle. Bitmapped graphics are created in image-editing programs such as Photoshop and Fireworks, or in Director's Paint window.

Bitmapped circle (enlarged)   *Vector circle*

Figure 7.1 A bitmapped circle is made from a rectangular array of square pixels, colored to approximate a circle. A vector circle is an actual, mathematically defined circle.

A *vector graphic* is a set of mathematical instructions for drawing and filling geometric shapes. The software that displays vector graphics must do the "work" of converting those instructions into a visual image. Hence, vector graphics put more of a load on the processor than bitmapped graphics do. Vector graphics are created in illustration programs such as Illustrator or Freehand, in Flash, or in Director's Vector Shape Window.

Functionally, bitmapped and vector graphics differ in two major ways:

◆ **File size:** A bitmapped graphic file has to store information about each individual pixel in the image. As the dimensions of a bitmapped graphic increase, the file size increases balloons even more rapidly. (For example, a 10-by-10-pixel image contains 100 pixels, but a 20-by-20-pixel image contains 400 pixels.) A vector graphic file, by contrast, contains only mathematical formulas, which don't take up much space to begin with and which remain the same size regardless of the size of the image.

◆ **Scalability:** When you enlarge a bitmapped image, the image-editing software has to make educated guesses about where and how to insert pixels. The result of this guesswork is usually roughness and jagged edges—called *jaggies*. When a vector graphic is enlarged, there is no guesswork: New values are inserted in the formulas, but the formulas remain the same, so the vector image retains its quality at any size.

Vector Shape Window Basics

The Vector Shape window (**Figure 7.2**) works much like the Paint window, though it has a much simpler tool palette (**Figure 7.3**).

There are several things you can do in the Paint window that you *can't* do in the Vector Shape window: You can't hide the tool palette, you can't use rulers, and you can't drag a cast member directly to the Stage. Otherwise, if you're comfortable with the basic operations of the Paint window, you'll be at home in the Vector Shape window as well.

To open the Vector Shape window:

◆ Choose Window > Vector Shape.

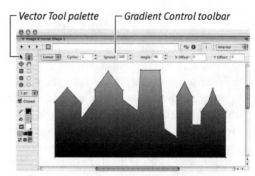

Vector Tool palette   Gradient Control toolbar

Figure 7.2 The Vector Shape window contains a tool palette and workspace for creating vector shapes.

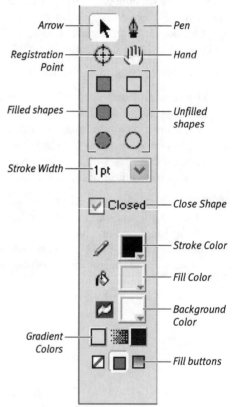

Arrow — Pen
Registration Point — Hand
Filled shapes — Unfilled shapes
Stroke Width — 1 pt
Closed — Close Shape
Stroke Color
Fill Color
Background Color
Gradient Colors
Fill buttons

Figure 7.3 Here's a closer look at the Vector Shape window's tool palette.

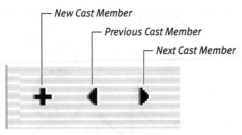

New Cast Member

Previous Cast Member

Next Cast Member

Figure 7.4 Use these buttons to step through existing vector-shape cast members in the order they appear in the Cast window.

Figure 7.5 The View > Zoom command lets you choose a specific zoom level, or simply zoom in or out.

To view or edit an existing vector-shape cast member:

◆ Double-click the cast member in the Cast window.

The Vector Shape window opens (if it's not open already) and displays the selected cast member.

or

If the Vector Shape window is already open and displaying a different cast member, click the Next Cast Member or Previous Cast Member button (**Figure 7.4**) to step through vector-shape cast members in the order they appear in the Cast window.

To create a new vector-shape cast member:

1. In the Vector Shape window, click the New Cast Member button.

A new, blank work area appears.

2. Use one of the shape tools, either filled or unfilled, or the Pen tool to draw a shape. (See "Creating Vector Shapes" on the next page.)

Your newly created vector shape automatically occupies the first available position in the Cast window and becomes available for use in your movie.

To zoom in or out:

◆ Choose View > Zoom, and select a zoom value from the submenu (**Figure 7.5**).

VECTOR SHAPE WINDOW BASICS

Creating Vector Shapes

The Vector Shape window offers two basic ways to create a shape: You can use one of the shape tools (the Rectangle, Rounded Rectangle, or Polygon, either filled or unfilled) to draw a simple geometric shape, or you can use the Pen tool to draw a custom shape. The Pen tool, modeled after similar pen tools in Illustrator, Photoshop, and Flash, requires some practice to use: You click to plot points along a path, and you drag to control the curvature of the line that connects those points.

Other tools allow you to specify a shape's line width; line color, fill color, and background color; and whether the shape is open or closed. You can choose what kind of fill a shape will have (none, solid, or gradient), and you can specify the colors for a gradient fill. You can draw multiple shapes within a single cast member, but all of them must share the same line and fill settings (**Figure 7.6**).

To create a simple vector shape:

1. Select one of the shape tools, either filled or unfilled (**Figure 7.7**).

2. Drag diagonally in the Vector Shape window to draw the shape.

✔ Tips

- Hold down the Shift key while dragging to constrain the shape. A constrained rectangle makes a square; a constrained ellipse makes a circle.

- It doesn't really matter whether you choose a filled or unfilled shape tool; you can always fill or unfill a shape later by selecting one of the Fill buttons at the bottom of the palette.

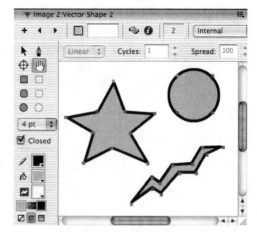

Figure 7.6 You can draw multiple shapes within a single cast member, but all of them must share the same line and fill settings.

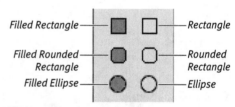

Figure 7.7 The shape tools.

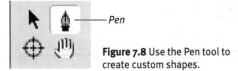

Figure 7.8 Use the Pen tool to create custom shapes.

Figure 7.9 An open path. Each click of the Pen tool creates a new corner point, connected to the previous point by a straight line.

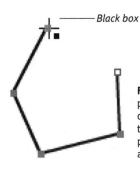

Black box

Figure 7.10 To close a path, position the crosshairs directly over the first point in the path so that a black box appears, and click.

Figure 7.11 The same path, closed.

Figure 7.12 When this check box is selected, the first and last points in a path are automatically connected.

To draw a custom shape composed of straight lines:

1. Select the Pen tool in the Vector Shape window (**Figure 7.8**).

   The mouse pointer turns into a crosshairs.

2. Click in the work area to begin the first line segment.

   A small square appears, indicating a corner point. (See the following sidebar, "Types of Points.")

3. Position the mouse pointer where you want the line segment to end, and click.

   Another corner point appears, connected to the first point by a straight line.

4. Repeat step 3, as many times as desired, until you have the path you want (**Figure 7.9**).

5. If you want to leave the path open, double-click the last point you added.

   or

   If you want to close the path, position the mouse pointer directly over the first point in the path—a black box (**Figure 7.10**) appears next to the crosshairs when you're in the right position—and single-click (**Figure 7.11**).

✔ Tips

- It doesn't really matter whether you initially decide to close a path or leave it open. You can always toggle a shape between its open and closed states by selecting or deselecting the Close Shape check box on the palette (**Figure 7.12**).

- If you include multiple shapes in a single cast member, all must be open or all must be closed.

CREATING VECTOR SHAPES

Types of Points

A vector shape consists of a series of points connected by straight or curved lines. A shape you draw with the Pen tool may contain various kinds of points, indicated by different shapes and colors (**Figure 7.13**).

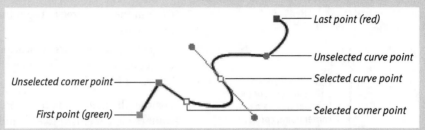

Figure 7.13 Different types of points are indicated by different shapes and colors.

A *corner point* is the endpoint of a straight line segment. It's represented by a small square.

A *curve point* is the endpoint of a curved line segment. It's represented by a small circle.

If a point is selected, the circle or square is hollow; if a point is unselected, the circle or square is solid. (In most cases, a selected curve point also has two control handles attached to it.)

Points are color-coded as follows:

◆ The first point in a path is green.

◆ The last point in a path—or the point you've added most recently—is red.

◆ All other points are blue.

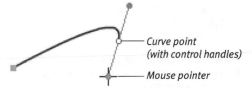

Figure 7.14 When you drag the mouse outward, a curve point with two control handles appears.

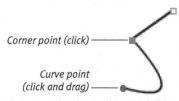

Figure 7.15 You can combine straight and curved segments in a single path.

To draw a custom shape composed of curved lines:

1. In the Vector Shape window, select the Pen tool.

2. Click in the work area to begin the first curved line segment.

   A corner point appears.

3. Position the mouse pointer where you want the segment to end, depress the mouse button, and drag outward.

   A curve point with two control handles appears (**Figure 7.14**), with your mouse pointer "gripping" one of them.

4. Keeping the mouse button depressed, drag the control handle until the curved line looks the way you want it to; then release the mouse button.

5. Repeat steps 3 and 4 as many times as desired until you have the path you want.

6. If you want to leave the path open, double-click the last point you added.

   or

   If you want to close the path, single-click the first point in the path. (See step 5 in the preceding task for more details.)

✔ Tip

- You can combine straight and curved segments in a single path. Just click if you want the preceding line segment to be straight, or click and drag if you want the preceding segment to be curved (**Figure 7.15**).

To set the line width for a vector-shape cast member:

◆ Choose a value from the Stroke Width menu (**Figure 7.16**).

✔ Tip

■ If you want your shapes to have no outline, select 0 from the Stroke Width menu.

To set the line color for a vector-shape cast member:

◆ Choose a color from the Stroke Color menu (**Figure 7.17**).

To set the background color for a vector-shape cast member:

◆ Choose a color from the Background Color menu.

✔ Tip

■ When you put a vector-shape cast member on the Stage with the default Copy ink effect, the background color fills the rectangular bounding box surrounding the sprite (**Figure 7.18**).

Figure 7.16 In the Vector Shape window, select a value from the Stroke Width menu. Choosing a larger value results in a wider stroke width.

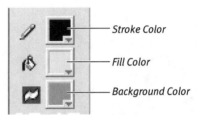

Figure 7.17 Use these menus to select line, fill, and background colors.

Figure 7.18 When you use the Copy ink effect, the background color fills the rectangular bounding box that surrounds a sprite on the Stage.

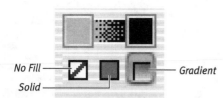

No Fill — Solid — Gradient

Figure 7.19 Use these buttons to choose the type of fill for your vector shape.

Gradient starting color — Gradient destination color

Figure 7.20 The gradient starting color is always the same as the fill color.

To set the fill type for a vector-shape cast member:

1. Click the No Fill, Solid, or Gradient button in the Vector Shape window (**Figure 7.19**).

2. If you clicked Solid, choose a fill color from the Fill Color menu.

   or

   If you clicked Gradient, follow the steps for "To set the characteristics of a gradient fill," below.

✔ Tip

■ If the shapes in a cast member are open, the fill buttons are dimmed.

To set the characteristics of a gradient fill:

1. In the Vector Shape window, choose the first color for the gradient from either the Fill Color menu or the Gradient starting color menu (**Figure 7.20**).

   Making a choice from either menu will set the same color for both.

2. Choose the ending color for the gradient from the Gradient destination color menu.

3. Choose Linear or Radial from the Gradient Type menu.

   This and other gradient controls are on a toolbar across the top of the Vector Shape window (**Figure 7.21**).

   continues on next page

Gradient Type — Gradient Cycles — Gradient Spread — Gradient Angle — Gradient X Offset — Gradient Y Offset

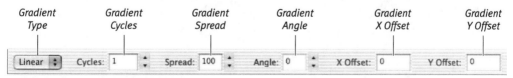

Linear ⬍ Cycles: 1 ⬍ Spread: 100 ⬍ Angle: 0 ⬍ X Offset: 0 Y Offset: 0

Figure 7.21 Choose settings for your gradient on the Gradient toolbar.

4. Enter a value for Cycles.

The Cycles setting specifies how many times the gradient repeats within the cast member (**Figure 7.22**).

5. Enter a Spread value.

The Spread value controls whether the gradient is weighted more toward the starting color or the destination color. Values of less than 100 weight the gradient toward the destination color; values of greater than 100 weight it toward the starting color. A value of 100 distributes the gradient evenly (**Figure 7.23**).

6. If you've chosen a linear gradient, determine its direction by entering a value in the Angle field.

An angle of 0 specifies a gradient that goes horizontally from left to right.

7. To offset a gradient within a vector shape, enter values in the X Offset and Y Offset fields (**Figure 7.24**).

The starting point of the gradient moves horizontally or vertically by the number of pixels you specify.

✔ Tips

- Radial gradients in the Vector Shape window travel in the opposite direction from those in the Paint window: In the former, the destination color is at the outer edge, while in the latter, the destination color is in the center.

- You can have only one gradient per vector-shape cast member. If you have multiple shapes in a cast member, the gradient is stretched across all the shapes.

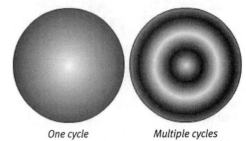

One cycle | Multiple cycles

Figure 7.22 Gradient cycles control how many times the gradient repeats in a shape.

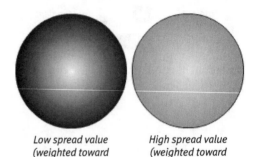

Low spread value (weighted toward destination color) | High spread value (weighted toward starting color)

Figure 7.23 The Spread value controls whether a gradient is weighted more toward the starting color or the destination color.

X and Y offsets set to 0 | Positive X and Y offsets

Figure 7.24 You can create gradients with different offsets.

CREATING VECTOR SHAPES

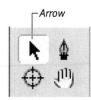

—Arrow

Figure 7.25 The Arrow tool is used for selecting and moving points.

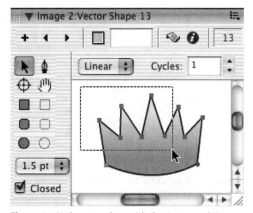

Figure 7.26 When you drag with the Arrow tool, it creates a rectangular marquee that you can use to select multiple points.

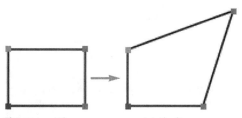

Figure 7.27 When you move a point, the lines connecting to the point adjust dynamically.

Figure 7.28 Deleting a point can drastically change a shape.

Editing Vector Shapes

After you create a vector-shape cast member, you can modify it by moving, adding, and deleting points; changing corner points to curve points (or vice versa); or resizing the entire cast member. You can also split a vector shape in two, or join two shapes into one.

To select one or more points:

1. With a vector shape open in the Vector Shape window, click the Arrow tool (**Figure 7.25**).

2. Click on a single point to select it.

   or

   Drag across multiple points to select them (**Figure 7.26**).

✔ Tip

■ You can add to a selection by Shift+clicking additional points.

To move points:

1. Select one or more points of a vector shape.

2. Drag the point or points to a new location (**Figure 7.27**).

   The lines connecting to the point or points adjust dynamically.

✔ Tip

■ You can nudge selected points one pixel at a time by using the arrow keys.

To delete points:

1. Select one or more points of a vector shape.

2. Press Delete.

   The lines connecting to the point or points you delete are also removed (**Figure 7.28**).

✔ Tip

■ If you select all the points in a shape and press Delete, the entire shape is deleted.

191

To adjust a curve:

1. Select a curve point attached to the curve you want to adjust.

   Two control handles appear (**Figure 7.29**).

Figure 7.29 When you select a curve point, its handles appear.

2. Shorten or lengthen the curve on either side of the point by dragging the corresponding handle inward or outward (**Figure 7.30**).

3. Rotate the curve around the point by dragging either control handle along a circular path (**Figure 7.31**).

✔ Tips

- To rotate only one side of a curve while leaving the other side unaffected, hold down the Ctrl key (Windows) or Command key (Mac) while you drag the control handle (**Figure 7.32**).

- Hold down the Shift key while dragging a control handle to constrain it to 45-degree increments.

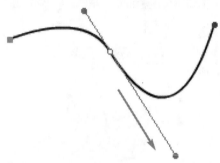

Figure 7.30 Drag a handle to shorten or lengthen the adjacent curve.

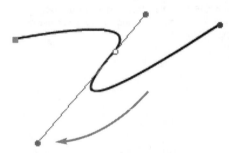

Figure 7.31 Rotate the curve around a corner point by dragging a control handle along a circular path.

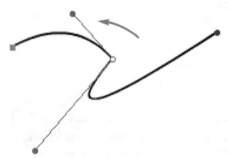

Figure 7.32 You can independently rotate either control handle by holding down the Ctrl key (Windows) or Command key (Mac) as you drag the handle.

Figure 7.33 Select a corner point.

Figure 7.34 Convert a selected corner point to a curve point by Alt+dragging (Windows) or Option+dragging (Mac) outward from the point.

Figure 7.35 Select a curve point.

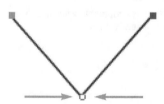

Figure 7.36 Convert the curve point to a functional corner point by dragging the handles into the point.

To convert a corner point to a curve point:

1. Select a corner point of a vector shape (**Figure 7.33**).

2. Alt+drag (Windows) or Option+drag (Mac) outward from the selected corner point.

   The corner point converts to a curve point, a control handle extends in the direction that you're dragging, and the adjacent straight line becomes a curve (**Figure 7.34**).

3. *(optional)* Alt+drag (Windows) or Option+drag (Mac) in the other direction from the curve point to extend the second control handle.

To convert a curve point to a corner point:

1. Select a curve point of a vector shape (**Figure 7.35**).

2. Drag one control handle into the point to make it disappear.

3. Drag the second control handle into the point.

   The point technically remains a curve point (still represented by a circle), but with its handles collapsed it functions as if it were a corner point (**Figure 7.36**).

To resize a vector-shape cast member:

1. In the Vector Shape window, click the arrow tool.

2. Ctrl+Alt+drag (Windows) or Command+Option+drag (Mac) anywhere within the cast member to scale it proportionally (**Figure 7.37**).

   Dragging outward enlarges the cast member; dragging inward reduces it.

✔ Tip

- If your cast member includes multiple shapes, you must resize all of them at once.

To add a point to a closed vector shape:

1. Click the Pen tool in the Vector Shape window.

2. Click anywhere on the outline of the shape to create a new corner point (**Figure 7.38**).

   or

   Click and drag anywhere on the outline of the shape to create a new curve point.

To add a new endpoint to an open vector shape:

1. Select either endpoint (**Figure 7.39**).

2. Click the Pen tool.

3. Click anywhere to create a new corner endpoint (**Figure 7.40**).

   or

   Drag anywhere to create a new curve endpoint.

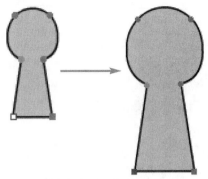

Figure 7.37 Ctrl+Alt+drag (Windows) or Command+Option+drag (Mac) to rescale a vector-shape cast member.

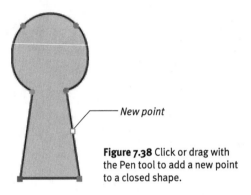

New point

Figure 7.38 Click or drag with the Pen tool to add a new point to a closed shape.

Selected endpoint

Figure 7.39 To add a new endpoint to a vector shape, you must first select an endpoint.

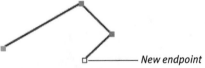

New endpoint

Figure 7.40 With the Pen tool, click to create a new corner endpoint or drag to create a new curve endpoint.

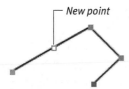

New point

Figure 7.41 Alt+click (Windows) or Option+ click (Mac) anywhere on an open path to add a new corner point.

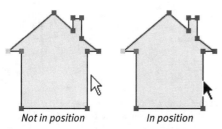

Not in position   In position

Figure 7.42 When the "hot spot" of the mouse pointer is over the edge of a shape, the color of the pointer inverts. The shape can now be dragged to a new location.

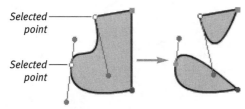

Selected point

Selected point

Figure 7.43 You can split a vector shape to create two new shapes. The first selected point becomes the start and endpoint of one new shape; the second selected point becomes the start and endpoint of another new shape.

To add a new intermediate point to an open vector shape:

1. Click the Pen tool.

2. Alt+click (Windows) or Option+click (Mac) anywhere on the path to add a new corner point (**Figure 7.41**).

   or

   Alt+drag or Option+drag anywhere on the path to add a new curve point.

To move a single shape within a multi-shape cast member:

1. In the Vector Shape window, click the Arrow tool.

2. Position the mouse pointer over the edge of a shape that you want to move.

   The color of the pointer inverts when it's in the right position (**Figure 7.42**).

3. Drag the shape to its new location.

✔ Tips

■ If the shape that you want to move is filled, you can move it simply by dragging its interior.

■ You can move multiple shapes at the same time by first selecting all their points with the Selection tool and then dragging a selected point to a new location.

To split a vector shape into two separate shapes:

1. Select any two adjacent points in a vector shape.

2. Choose Modify > Split Curve.

   The selected points become new start and endpoints. If the shape you split is closed, the new start and endpoints connect to the previous start and endpoints to form two closed shapes (**Figure 7.43**).

To join two vector shapes or curves:

1. Select one point in each of the vector shapes or curves that you want to join.

2. Choose Modify > Join Curves.

   If the points you selected were start or endpoints, those points become joined (**Figure 7.44**).

   If the points you selected were intermediate points, the start point of the second shape (the one most recently drawn) becomes joined to the endpoint of the first shape (**Figure 7.45**).

   If the shapes you joined were open, you get a new open shape. If the shapes were closed, you get a new closed shape (**Figure 7.46**).

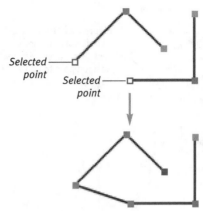

Figure 7.44 If start or endpoints were selected, they become joined to each other.

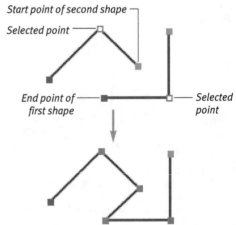

Figure 7.45 If intermediate points were selected, the start point of the second shape is joined to the endpoint of the first shape.

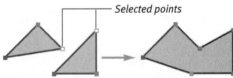

Figure 7.46 Joining two closed shapes results in a new closed shape.

COMPOSITING IMAGES

Figure 8.1 This gigantic pumpkin, superimposed against a field, is an example of compositing.

The Stage in **Figure 8.1** shows a gigantic pumpkin sitting in a field. Needless to say, there are no pumpkins quite that large—the image was faked by taking a photo of a pumpkin, removing its background, and placing it in front of a photo of a field to give the appearance of a unified whole. The technique of combining one or more foreground images with one or more background images in this way is called *compositing*.

In the days before computers, compositing was a difficult, expensive operation involving duplicate negatives, high-contrast photographic masks, and expensive photographic printing equipment. Even when computers changed the way compositing was done, it remained a time-consuming and processor-intensive task. One of the amazing things about Director is that it handles compositing on the fly—with multiple layers of moving sprites—tens or hundreds of times per second.

continues on next page

Any time you have sprites in more than one channel—which is to say, in just about every Director movie—the way the foreground sprites appear against the background sprites is important. If you have a car driving across the screen, and it's surrounded by a white rectangle, or its windows are opaque, your movie won't have a convincing, professional appearance.

Though compositing is relatively simple when done with vector images, compositing bitmaps is a trickier business, and this is one area where Director really shines. There are several ways to handle compositing in Director, each with its advantages and drawbacks. This chapter will take you through them.

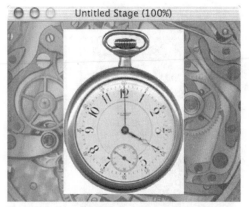

Figure 8.2 Most sprites are surrounded by a white rectangle when they first appear on the Stage.

Figure 8.3 If the sprite itself is perfectly rectangular, then the white rectangle isn't visible.

Figure 8.4 This sprite looks fine against a white background (left), but the white rectangle becomes visible when the background is changed (right).

Using Ink Effects for Transparency

When you place a visual cast member on the Stage, it's automatically surrounded by a rectangular bounding box. This bounding box usually appears as a white rectangle behind the sprite (**Figure 8.2**). (If the sprite is based on a vector-shape cast member, the rectangle is filled with the cast member's background color, which is usually—but not necessarily—white.)

If the sprite itself is perfectly rectangular, the rectangle is completely hidden behind the sprite (**Figure 8.3**). But with most sprites, at least part of the rectangle remains visible, resulting in unsatisfactory compositing against anything other than a pure white background (**Figure 8.4**).

continues on next page

You can easily solve this problem by changing the ink effect applied to the sprite. (For more information on ink effects, see "Sprite Ink Effects" in Chapter 3.) The default ink effect applied to every new sprite is Copy. If you change the ink effect to Background Transparent, the white rectangle disappears (**Figure 8.5**). This is because the Background Transparent ink effect makes all white pixels in a sprite (or all pixels of the background color you specify) invisible, allowing whatever is behind those pixels to show through.

The Background Transparent ink effect is a quick, simple way to composite a sprite against a background. However, it only works for sprites based on a specific kind of cast member:

◆ The cast member must have a pure, flat-white or solid-color background. (Note that many backgrounds that *seem* to be solid actually have slight color variations. Uneven color backgrounds are especially common in cast members imported from JPEG files. **Figure 8.6** shows what happens to background color variations when you use Background Transparent ink.)

◆ If the cast member is a bitmap, it must have sharp boundaries, with no anti-aliasing, blurring, or smoothing. If the edges of the cast member are blended into the background in any way, there will be a "halo" around the sprite when Background Transparent ink is applied. (See "Eliminating Halos in Imported Images," later in this chapter.)

Figure 8.5 Changing the sprite's ink effect from Copy to Background Transparent makes the rectangle disappear.

Figure 8.6 Because the background in this JPEG file isn't consistently white, parts of it remain visible when Background Transparent ink is applied.

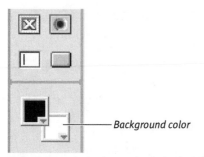

Background color

Figure 8.7 Set the background color in the Tool palette to match the background color of the cast member.

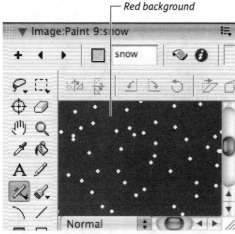

Red background

Figure 8.8 This falling snow was made with the Air Brush tool. Because the snow is white, it was sprayed onto a red background instead of the usual white background.

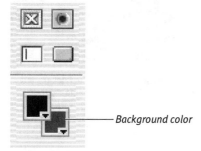

Background color

Figure 8.9 The background color in the Tool palette is set to match the red used for the background of the snow.

To make a sprite's background transparent:

1. Select the sprite on the Stage or in the Score.

2. Set the background color in the Tool palette to match the background color of the sprite's cast member (**Figure 8.7**).

   If the cast member's background is white, make sure the background color in the Tool palette is set to white.

   If the cast member's background is a color other than white (**Figure 8.8**), set the background color in the Tool palette to match that color (**Figure 8.9**). (Use the color picker if necessary.)

3. In the Property Inspector, select the Sprite tab.

   continues on next page

4. In the Sprite tab's Ink menu, choose Background Transparent (**Figure 8.10**).

The sprite's background becomes invisible on the Stage (**Figure 8.11**).

If there are pixels in the sprite that are the same color as the background, they become invisible as well (**Figure 8.12**).

✔ Tip

■ In order for the Background Transparent ink effect to work, the background color set in the Tool palette must match the cast member's background color exactly. If necessary, sample the sprite's background color in the Paint window or in an external image-editing program to get the color's exact RGB values. Then match those RGB values in the Tool palette, using the color picker if necessary.

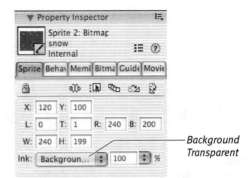

Background Transparent

Figure 8.10 Select Background Transparent ink in the Property Inspector.

Figure 8.11 The snow's red background becomes invisible, allowing the falling snow to be composited into the scene.

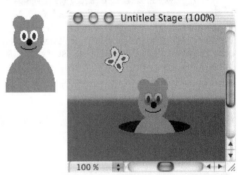

Figure 8.12 Left: a cast member whose background and eyes are both white. Right: the same cast member as a sprite on the Stage, with Background Transparent ink applied. The background and eyes both become transparent.

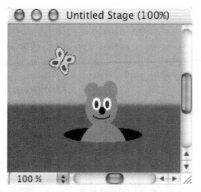

Figure 8.13 The same sprite using Matte ink instead of Background Transparent. The Matte ink makes the background transparent but leaves untouched the pixels that were the same color as the background—such as the eyes, in this case.

Figure 8.14 Repainting the eyes with a slightly off-white color allows them to stay visible when Background Transparent ink is used.

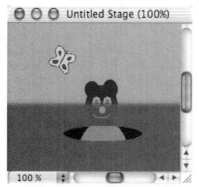

Figure 8.15 Other ink effects (such as Reverse, shown here) also make a sprite's background disappear, but they affect the foreground as well.

To make a sprite's background transparent without affecting pixels that are the same color as the background:

◆ Follow the steps in the previous task, "To make a sprite's background transparent," but use the Matte ink effect instead of Background Transparent (**Figure 8.13**).
or
Change the pixels (either foreground or background) to a different color (**Figure 8.14**); then follow the steps in the previous task.

✔ Tips

■ The Matte ink effect takes more processing power than Background Transparent and can slow down your movie, so avoid it if you can.

■ There are other ink effects that will make background pixels transparent, such as Transparent, Reverse, and Ghost. (See the "Score Ink Effects" sidebar in Chapter 3 for descriptions of all the ink effects.) However, unlike Background Transparent and Matte, these other effects may change the appearance of foreground pixels as well (**Figure 8.15**).

■ The Background Transparent and Matte ink effects work for both vector and bitmapped cast members. The remaining compositing techniques in this chapter are for bitmapped cast members only.

Using Ink Masks

Another ink effect, called Mask ink, can also be used to composite a sprite. Mask ink is unusual in that it requires a second cast member—an *ink mask*—as a reference. An ink mask is essentially a map that shows Director which parts of a sprite to make transparent and which to leave opaque. Director always looks for the ink mask in the same place: in the Cast window, directly following the cast member that the sprite refers to (**Figure 8.16**).

You can create an ink mask in Director's Paint window, or you can import it from an external paint program. If you create your cast members in Photoshop or another image-editing program that supports masks, you can create the ink mask at the same time you create the original cast member. (For one way to do this, see the sidebar, "A Quick Detour into Photoshop," later in this chapter.)

Using the Mask ink effect has a couple of advantages over using the Background Transparent or Matte ink effects. First, through the use of an ink mask, *any* part of a sprite can be made transparent, regardless of the color of its pixels. And second, the Mask ink effect allows for levels of semi-transparency, which the Background Transparent and Matte ink effects do not.

The main drawback of using the Mask ink effect is that creating an ink mask requires some time and effort. Also, each ink mask you use increases the number of cast members and therefore adds to the size of your movie file.

Cast member to be masked
Ink mask

Figure 8.16 An ink mask must always be placed in the Cast window immediately following the cast member it's associated with.

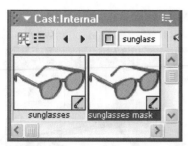

Figure 8.17 Create a duplicate cast member that will become an ink mask.

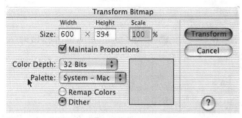

Figure 8.18 The Transform Bitmap dialog box, showing appropriate settings for an 8-bit ink mask.

Figure 8.19 Open the cast member in the Paint window.

To create and use an ink mask:

1. In the Cast window, select the cast member for which you want to create an ink mask.

2. Choose Edit > Duplicate.

   Director creates a duplicate cast member and selects it in the Cast window.

   This cast member will be the ink mask, so you may want to give it a name that identifies it as a mask (**Figure 8.17**).

3. With the duplicate cast member still selected, choose Modify > Transform Bitmap.

   The Transform Bitmap dialog box opens (**Figure 8.18**).

4. Make a selection from the Color Depth pop-up menu:

   Choose 8 bits if you want to create a mask that has varying levels of transparency.

   or

   Choose 1 bit if you want to create a mask with only fully opaque and fully transparent areas. (A 1-bit mask adds barely anything to the movie's file size.)

5. If you selected 8 bits as your color depth, choose Grayscale from the Palette pop-up menu.

6. Click the Remap Colors radio button.

7. Click Transform.

   A dialog box asks you to confirm that you want to transform the cast member.

8. Click OK.

9. Double-click the transformed cast member to open it in the Paint window (**Figure 8.19**).

continues on next page

USING INK MASKS

205

10. In the Paint Tool palette, click the Paint Bucket, Paint Brush, or any other paint tool.

11. "Color in" the cast member as follows:

Use white to indicate areas where you want the sprite to be fully transparent.

Use black to indicate areas where you want the sprite to be fully opaque.

Use varying levels of gray to indicate semi-transparent areas, with lighter grays indicating greater transparency and darker grays indicating greater opacity (**Figure 8.20**).

12. In the Cast window, make sure that the duplicate cast member immediately follows the original version of the cast member.

13. If you haven't done so already, drag the original cast member to the Stage or Score to create a sprite. (The ink mask does *not* get placed on the Stage or in the Score.)

14. Select the sprite.

15. In the Property Inspector, select the Sprite tab.

16. From the Ink menu, choose Mask (**Figure 8.21**).

Portions of the sprite become transparent or semi-transparent as specified in the ink mask (**Figure 8.22**).

Semi-transparent

Transparent — — Opaque

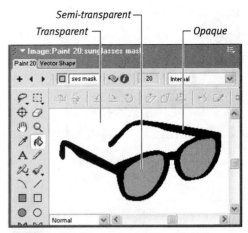

Figure 8.20 The same cast member, repainted to serve as an ink mask.

Figure 8.21 Choose Mask from the Ink menu.

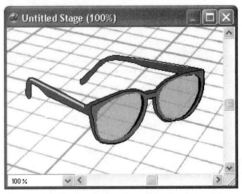

Figure 8.22 The masked sprite on the Stage contains both opaque and transparent areas, resulting in a more realistic image.

Figure 8.23
This mask, imported from Photoshop, has values opposite from those that Director expects. This glass full of beer, for example, has transparent areas appear as black.

Invert Colors tool

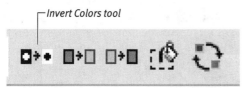

Figure 8.24 Click to invert the colors in the mask.

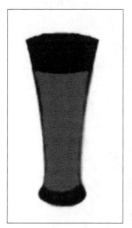

Figure 8.25 The revised mask, suitable for use as a Director ink mask.

To use an imported ink mask:

1. Create an image in an external program, such as Photoshop.

   At the same time you create the image, follow the instructions in your image-editing program to create a mask for the image. (For one way to do this, see the "Quick Detour into Photoshop" sidebar later in this chapter.)

2. In your image-editing program, save the image and the mask as separate files.

   The mask should be saved as a 1-bit file (if it contains no gray areas) or an 8-bit grayscale file.

   To save on file size, you may also want to save the image as an 8-bit file rather than a 32-bit file.

3. Import the image and the mask into Director.

4. Double-click the mask in the Cast window to open it in the Paint window.

5. Look at the mask to make sure the colors are displayed correctly for Director.

   Depending on how the mask was made and where it was imported from, it may show opaque areas in white and transparent areas in black (**Figure 8.23**). This is the reverse of the way ink masks work in Director.

   If the colors in the mask are indeed reversed, do the following:

   ▲ Double-click the Marquee tool in the Paint Tool palette to select the entire mask.

   ▲ Click the Invert Colors tool on the Effects toolbar (**Figure 8.24**).

   Each color in the mask changes to its opposite (**Figure 8.25**).

6. Follow steps 10 through 13 of the previous task, "To create and use an ink mask."

USING INK MASKS

Eliminating Halos in Imported Images

If you compare an image created in Director's Paint window with a similar image created in Photoshop, you'll see a striking difference. In the image created in Director, the diagonal and curved lines display a stair-step effect referred to as *jaggies*. In the image created in Photoshop, the same diagonal and curved lines appear smooth (**Figure 8.26**).

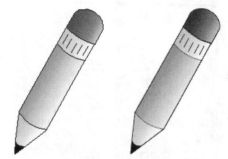

Figure 8.26 This image of a pencil created in Director's Paint window (left) looks a little jagged, while the Photoshop version (right) appears much smoother.

The superior quality of the Photoshop image results from a visual trick called anti-aliasing. *Anti-aliasing* is a careful blending of the foreground and background colors with intermediate colors in a way that fools the eye into seeing smooth lines and curves (**Figure 8.27**). Photoshop does an excellent job of anti-aliasing, while Director's Paint window doesn't do it at all.

Anti-aliasing is handled differently with vector images than with bitmapped images. When Director displays a vector image, it performs anti-aliasing in real time while the image is on the screen. With a bitmapped image, however, the anti-aliasing is done at the time the image is created, and the color-blended pixels are stored as part of the image file.

Figure 8.27 A closer inspection of the Photoshop version of the pencil reveals the use of anti-aliasing to create the appearance of smooth edges.

Although anti-aliasing greatly improves the appearance of bitmapped images, it can make compositing difficult in Director. If you create an image on a white background in Photoshop, import it into Director, and apply the Background Transparent or Matte ink effect, you may see a white halo around the sprite (**Figure 8.28**). This occurs because when the ink effect turns the pixels of the white background transparent, it ignores the blended-color pixels around the edges.

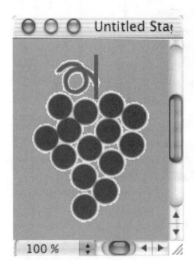

Figure 8.28 These grapes, created in Photoshop on a white background, display unwanted "halos" when the Background Transparent ink effect is applied.

Figure 8.29 To eliminate the dreaded halo effect, create an ink mask for the grapes, leaving the anti-aliased edges as shades of gray.

Figure 8.30 The grapes lose their halos when the Mask ink effect is applied.

There are two basic ways to eliminate the halo. One is to create and use an ink mask; the other is to edit or re-create the anti-aliased cast member. Each of these solutions has several variations. All require time and effort, but—unless you choose to eliminate anti-aliasing entirely—all yield good-looking results. Choose the method that best fits your particular situation and your preferred way of working.

To eliminate a halo by using an ink mask:

1. Create an 8-bit ink mask for the haloed cast member according to the steps in "To create and use an ink mask," earlier in this chapter.

   In the mask, make the background solid white and the interior of the cast member solid black, but leave the anti-aliased edges as shades of gray (**Figure 8.29**).

2. If you haven't done so already, create a sprite from the cast member.

3. Apply the Mask ink effect to the sprite.

   The blended gray edges in the ink mask will largely cancel out the blended colors in the halo (**Figure 8.30**).

To eliminate a halo by altering the cast member:

1. Re-create the cast member from scratch, without anti-aliasing.

   You can do this in Director's Paint window (which has no anti-aliasing capability), or you can do it in an external program such as Photoshop by turning off anti-aliasing for each of the tools you use.

   or

   Re-create the cast member in an external program, anti-aliased against a colored background. The color of the background should be similar to the color or colors that the sprite will be composited with in Director (**Figure 8.31**).

   or

   Re-create the cast member in an external program, anti-aliased against a transparent background, and save it as a 32-bit image with an alpha channel. (For more on alpha channels, see the following section, "Working with Alpha Channels.")

2. Reimport the cast member into Director.

3. Create a sprite from the cast member.

4. Apply the Background Transparent or Matte ink effect to the sprite (**Figure 8.32**).

✔ Tips

■ The three options in step 1 are included for the sake of completeness, but you probably won't want to use the first one. There's no good reason to eliminate anti-aliasing entirely, unless you happen to like jaggies.

■ The second option—anti-aliasing against a colored background—does not yield results as good as the third. However, it does add less data to your Director movie. That's because the second option allows you to save the cast member as an 8-bit file, while the third option requires a 32-bit file. (All other things being equal, an 8-bit file is only one-quarter the size of a 32-bit file.)

Figure 8.31 Because this bird is intended to be composited into a background of green leaves, it was created against a green background in Photoshop.

Figure 8.32 The bird has a slight green halo when Background Transparent ink is applied, but the halo isn't noticeable because it's so similar to the color of the leaves.

Working with Alpha Channels

Figure 8.33 Here, this image of a smokestack appears on what *looks* like a transparent background in Photoshop.

Figure 8.34 But behind this smokestack, a hidden Photoshop mask helps create the illusion of transparency.

Image-editing programs such as Photoshop and Fireworks allow you to create an image against a "transparent" background (**Figure 8.33**). In reality, there's no such thing as a transparent background—the pixels in a bitmapped image are always opaque. What these programs really do is create a mask at the same time you create your image, and then use this mask to give the illusion of transparency when the image is displayed on your screen (**Figure 8.34**).

When you save the file in the program's native file format (for example, a PSD file in Photoshop or a PNG file in Fireworks), the mask is saved with the file in the form of an alpha channel. In essence, an *alpha channel* functions much like an ink mask in Director, except that its contents are stored as part of the image file.

You can import images with alpha channels into Director. When you do so, Director automatically recognizes the alpha channel and uses it to provide transparency.

Cast members with alpha channels are extremely well suited for compositing in Director. Because the mask in the alpha channel was created at the same time as the image, it's flawless and seamless. It allows anti-aliased edges to blend perfectly into any background.

The drawback of images with alpha channels is that they use a lot of disk space and require extra processing power. To store an alpha channel with an image, you must save the image as a 32-bit file, which means that 32 bits of information are used to describe each pixel in the image. When Director animates the image, it must process all 32 bits of information for each pixel over and over again, frame by frame. This can put a heavy load on the computer's processor and slow down the movie.

If the file size or processor load of a 32-bit file is a problem for your movie, you can open the image in an external image-editing program and save it as two separate files: one 8-bit file for the image and another for the mask (See the sidebar, "A Quick Detour into Photoshop," later in this chapter) You can then import both files into Director and use them as described in "To use an imported ink mask," earlier in this chapter.

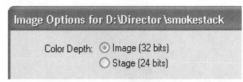

Figure 8.35 When you import a file that has an alpha channel, be sure to import it as a 32-bit image.

To use an image that has an alpha channel:

1. Import the image file into Director.

   When the Image Options dialog box appears, be sure to set the color depth to 32 bits. If you specify a lower color depth, you'll lose the alpha channel (**Figure 8.35**).

2. Drag the image from the Cast window to the Stage or Score.

   Director automatically recognizes the alpha channel and uses it to provide transparency (**Figure 8.36**).

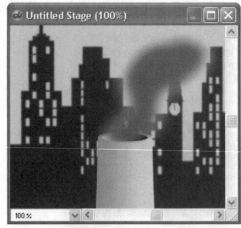

Figure 8.36 Director uses the alpha channel to composite the image.

✔ Tips

- A sprite with an alpha channel will look exactly the same on the Stage regardless of whether its ink effect is set to Copy, Background Transparent, or Matte.

- Occasionally, Director will have trouble importing a native Photoshop (PSD) file. If this happens, go back into Photoshop and save the image as a PICT or TIFF file, following the directions in the sidebar "A Quick Detour into Photoshop."

- If you want Director to disregard a cast member's alpha channel, go to the Property Inspector's Bitmap tab and deselect Use Alpha (**Figure 8.37**).

Figure 8.37 The Use Alpha option is selected by default, but you can deselect it if you want Director to ignore a cast member's alpha channel.

Figure 8.38 When you edit a cast member in the Paint window, its alpha channel is unaffected. As a result, even if you edit it sloppily (left), the out-of-bounds brushstrokes are masked out by the alpha channel on the Stage (right).

Figure 8.39 Choose Launch External Editor from a cast member's contextual menu to launch Fireworks (the default) or whatever image-editing program you prefer.

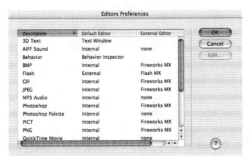

Figure 8.40 In the Editors Preferences dialog box, you can specify which program will be launched by the Launch External Editor command when you edit a particular cast member.

To edit a cast member that has an alpha channel:

◆ Edit the image in Director's Paint window.

The Paint window doesn't recognize or let you edit alpha channels, so it will leave existing alpha channels intact (**Figure 8.38**).

or

Edit the image in an external program such as Photoshop or Fireworks if you *do* want to modify the alpha channel along with the image.

✔ Tips

■ If you want to edit a cast member in Fireworks, right-click (Windows) or Control+click (Mac) the cast member in the Cast window and choose Launch External Editor from the contextual menu (**Figure 8.39**). If Fireworks is installed on your computer, Director will automatically launch it and open the selected cast member for editing.

■ If you want to edit a cast member in Photoshop—or in any image-editing program other than the default Fireworks—choose Edit > Preferences > Editors (Windows) or Director > Preferences > Editors (Mac) and specify the program you want to use to edit each file type (**Figure 8.40**). Thereafter, when you choose Launch External Editor from a cast member's contextual menu, the specified program will be launched.

WORKING WITH ALPHA CHANNELS

A Quick Detour into Photoshop

OK, we know this is a Director book, not a Photoshop book. But since most Director users do their image editing in Photoshop, you'll probably find this information useful.

When you create an image, Photoshop stores the transparency information for each layer in a hidden channel called the *transparency channel*. If you want to save this transparency information in a file format other than Photoshop's native PSD, or if you want to export a separate mask file, you have to convert the various layers' transparency channels into one standard alpha channel. Here's an easy way to do it:

1. If your image has any alpha channels—that is, if there's anything on the Channels palette other than RGB, Red, Green, and Blue—select those extra channels on the Channels palette and delete them.

2. If your image has a Background layer, double-click it in the Layers palette.
   The New Layer dialog box appears, with Layer 0 displayed as the layer name.

3. Click OK.
   The Background layer is converted to a normal layer.

4. If your image has more than one layer, choose Layer > Merge Visible to merge them into a single layer with a single transparency channel.

5. Choose Select > Load Selection.
   The Load Selection dialog box appears (**Figure 8.41**). Make sure Layer *X* Transparency (where *X* represents the name of your layer) is displayed on the Channel pop-up menu, and the New Selection radio button is selected under Operation.

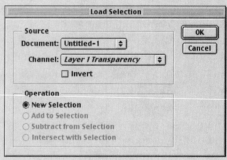

Figure 8.41 The Load Selection dialog box in Photoshop.

6. Click OK.
   The transparent and semi-transparent areas of your image are selected on the screen.

7. Choose Select > Save Selection.
   The Save Selection dialog box appears (**Figure 8.42**). Make sure New is displayed on the Channel pop-up menu, and New Channel is selected under Operation.

8. Click OK.
   The transparency information is converted to an alpha channel called Alpha1.

continues on next page

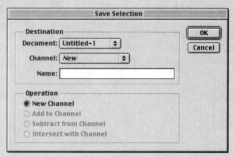

Figure 8.42 Click Save in the Save Selection dialog box.

A Quick Detour into Photoshop *continued*

Now, if you save the image as a PICT (Macintosh only) or TIFF file, the alpha channel will be saved with the image.

If you want to save the transparency information as a separate mask file rather than as an alpha channel, you can choose Split Channels from the Options menu on the Channel palette. (Make sure you've saved your image before you do this, because the Split Channels command is not reversible.) You can then select the image window containing the alpha channel and save it separately.

WORKING ON THE STAGE

Figure 9.1 The Stage's default appearance.

The Stage is by far the simplest part of Director's interface: It's just a plain white rectangle in a frame (**Figure 9.1**). But there's more to the Stage than meets the eye. By means of a number of controls scattered throughout Director—in menus, in the Property Inspector, and on the Tool palette—the Stage can be resized, repositioned, zoomed, scrolled, and gridded. Not only is the Stage the place where your movie plays; it's also a place where you can create cast members such as buttons, text fields, and shapes.

This chapter will show you how to customize the Stage and use its hidden features to show off your movie to its best advantage.

Setting Stage Properties

One of the most important decisions you make in Director is determining the size of the Stage for a movie. For example, if the movie is going to be incorporated into a Web page, you may want to make the Stage relatively small to leave room for other elements in the browser window (**Figure 9.2**). If the movie is going to be used for a kiosk, you'll want the Stage to be the same size as the screen it will be viewed on. Make your size decision carefully: Even though you can easily change the Stage size at any time, reworking the rest of your movie to fit the new size is not nearly as easy.

You can also decide where you want the Stage to be on the screen when your movie is played back. (The two most common choices are the center of the screen, or the upper left corner.) Note, however, that the Stage Location setting applies only to movies that will be played from a projector file (which means, for the most part, movies that are distributed on CD- or DVD-ROM). When you're making a Shockwave movie, you need to determine the location of the movie in the browser window, which you set as part of the publishing process. (See Chapter 17, "Making Movies for the Web.")

You can set the background color for the Stage, but you're limited to one background color for the entire movie. If you want the background color to change during the movie, you can create a colored rectangle as a cast member and place it in channel 1 of the Score at the point where you want the new color to begin (**Figure 9.3**).

Embedded movie

Figure 9.2 A Shockwave movie incorporated into a Web page. The Stage size here is 300 by 240 pixels.

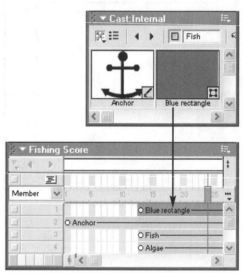

Figure 9.3 You can change the Stage color in the middle of a movie by using a colored rectangular cast member as a backdrop.

Figure 9.4 Set the Stage size, location, and color on the Movie tab of the Property Inspector.

To change the size, location, and background color of the Stage:

1. Select the Movie tab in the Property Inspector.

   If the Movie tab isn't available, click anywhere on the Stage or in the Score, and it will appear.

2. Click the List View Mode button, if necessary, to place the Property Inspector in Graphical mode.

3. Choose a size from the Stage Size pop-up menu, or type in your own values for the width and height (**Figure 9.4**).

   The Stage takes on the new size immediately.

4. Choose a Stage location from the Location pop-up menu.

   Your choices are Centered, Upper Left, and Other. If you choose Other, specify coordinates by entering them in the adjoining boxes.

   The Stage jumps to the new location.

5. Choose a background color from the Color menu (or type in your own color in hexadecimal format).

   The Stage immediately takes on the new color. The "offstage area" (the gray rectangle surrounding the Stage) is not affected.

   continues on next page

SETTING STAGE PROPERTIES

✔ Tips

■ The Stage size, location, and color settings are saved with each movie. Therefore, don't be surprised if your Stage changes size or jumps to another part of the screen when you open a previously saved movie.

■ If you move the Stage manually by dragging it with the mouse, its new position is *not* saved with the movie. In order for a Stage location to take effect on playback, it must be explicitly entered in the Property Inspector.

■ If you begin a new movie (by choosing File > New Movie, or by starting Director without double-clicking an existing movie file), the Stage will retain whatever characteristics it had in the last movie you were working on.

To view the Stage in Full Screen mode:

◆ Choose View > Full Screen.

The Stage jumps to the location specified in the Property Inspector. Everything else on the screen is masked out by the current background color (**Figure 9.5**).

✔ Tips

■ Despite its name, Full Screen mode doesn't change the size of the Stage to match the dimensions of your screen; it merely makes the Stage the only thing on the screen.

■ The menu bar disappears in Full Screen mode, so how do you turn Full Screen mode *off*? Easy—click at the top of the screen where the menu bar should be, and it reappears. Choose View > Full Screen again to toggle your screen back to its normal state.

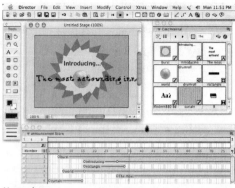

Normal

Full Screen

Figure 9.5 The Stage in normal mode and in Full Screen mode.

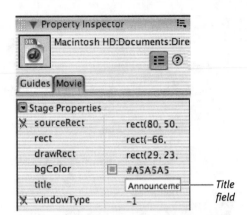

Figure 9.6 The Title field appears only when the Property Inspector is in List view.

To show or hide the control panel at the bottom of the Stage:

◆ Choose View > Control Toolbar.

To set the title of the Stage:

1. Select the Movie tab in the Property Inspector.

2. Click the List View Mode button, if necessary, to place the Property Inspector in List view.

3. In the Title field, type a name to appear in the title bar above the Stage (**Figure 9.6**).

✔ Tip

■ If you don't enter a title, Director uses the name of the current movie file (or *Untitled,* if the movie hasn't yet been given a filename), followed by the word *Stage.*

Zooming and Scrolling the Stage

While working on your movie, you may find it helpful to zoom your view of the Stage in and out (**Figure 9.7**). The zoom level of the Stage is not saved with your movie file and does not affect the way the movie looks when it's distributed.

When you zoom in the Stage, you can scroll to unseen parts of the Stage by using the Hand tool or the scroll bars. (If you've placed any sprites in the gray offstage area, for example, you may need to scroll the Stage even when it's at its normal zoom level.) If you find the scroll bars distracting, you can hide them.

To zoom in or out:

◆ Choose View > Zoom, and select a magnification level.

or

1. Select the Magnifying Glass tool in the Tool palette (**Figure 9.8**).

2. Click anywhere on the Stage to zoom in, or Alt+click (Windows) or Option+click (Mac) to zoom out.

✔ Tips

■ If you zoom with the View menu, Director zooms in on the center of the Stage. If you zoom with the Magnifying Glass, Director zooms in on the area you click.

■ To restore the Stage to normal zoom level, choose View > Standard View, or double-click the Magnifying Glass tool in the Tool palette. (Doing so not only restores the zoom level to 100 percent; but it also moves the Stage to the location specified in the Property Inspector, regardless of where you might have moved it manually.)

Figure 9.7 You can zoom in and out when working on the Stage. Here is the same scene at 50 percent, 100 percent, and 200 percent.

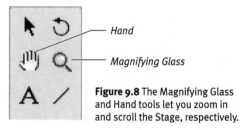

Hand

Magnifying Glass

Figure 9.8 The Magnifying Glass and Hand tools let you zoom in and scroll the Stage, respectively.

Scroll bars visible   *Scroll bars hidden*

Figure 9.9 The Stage, with and without scroll bars.

To scroll the Stage:

◆ Use the horizontal and vertical scroll bars to scroll left, right, up, or down on the Stage.

or

1. Select the Hand tool in the Tool palette.

2. Drag the Stage to scroll it in any direction.

✔ Tip

■ To re-center the Stage after it's been scrolled, double-click the Hand tool.

To hide or show the Stage's scroll bars:

1. Choose Edit > Preferences > General (Windows) or Director > Preferences > General (Mac).

2. Select or deselect Show Stage Scrollbars (**Figure 9.9**).

✔ Tips

■ If you hide the scroll bars, the gray off-stage area becomes hidden as well.

■ Even when the scroll bars are hidden, you can still scroll the Stage with the Hand tool.

Using Grids and Guides

Director allows you to place a grid on the Stage for help in aligning sprites (**Figure 9.10**). You can use the grid as a visual reference, or you can use the Snap To setting to make sprites snap to the grid.

Sometimes you need to align sprites to a specific position on the Stage that doesn't coincide with a grid line. In this case, you can add custom guide lines, much like those in a page-layout program, and align sprites to them (**Figure 9.11**).

All of the controls for the grid and guides are on the Guides tab in the Property Inspector. (If the Guides tab isn't available, click anywhere on the Stage or in the Score, and it will appear.) The grid controls are in the lower half of the window, so you may have to click the expander arrow to make them visible (**Figure 9.12**).

The grid and guides are visible only in the Director application; they don't show up in distributed versions of your movie.

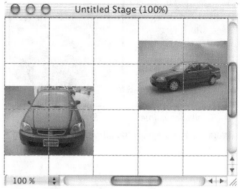

Figure 9.10 Placing a grid on the Stage can help you align sprites.

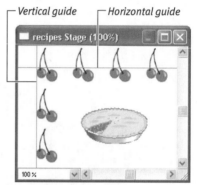

Figure 9.11 You can place guides wherever you need them on the Stage.

Figure 9.12 Use the Guides tab in the Property Inspector to adjust settings for both guides and grids.

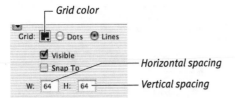

Grid color

Horizontal spacing

Vertical spacing

Figure 9.13 Specify grid settings in the Grid section of the Guides tab.

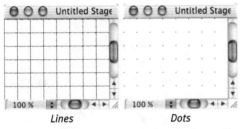

Lines　　　*Dots*

Figure 9.14 Director offers two ways to display a grid.

To show or hide the grid:

◆ Choose View > Guides and Grid > Show Grid.

or

Select or deselect the Visible check box in the Grid section of the Guides tab in the Property Inspector (**Figure 9.13**).

To configure the grid:

(All of these settings are done in the Grid section of the Guides tab in the Property Inspector.)

1. In the Grid section of the Property Inspector's Guides tab, select either Dots or Lines.

The Lines option shows a normal grid. The Dots option shows only the points where the lines in the grid intersect (**Figure 9.14**).

2. Specify the spacing of the grid lines, in pixels.

For horizontal spacing, enter a value in the W (for Width) box. For vertical spacing, enter a value in the H (for Height) box.

USING GRIDS AND GUIDES

To add a guide to the Stage:

1. On the Guides tab of the Property Inspector, position your mouse pointer over the horizontal or vertical guide symbol (**Figure 9.15**).

   The mouse pointer becomes a hand.

2. Depress the mouse button and drag the mouse to the Stage (**Figure 9.16**).

   The mouse pointer is now dragging a guide.

3. Release the mouse button when the guide is in the desired position.

✔ Tips

- Guides are automatically made visible when you drag a new guide to the Stage. If you want to toggle the guides' visibility, choose View > Guides and Grid > Show Guides, or use the Visible check box on the Guides tab of the Property Inspector.

- The visibility settings of guides and the grid are not saved with the movie file. However, the positions of any guides that you place on the Stage *are* saved with the movie file.

To reposition a guide on the Stage:

1. Select the Arrow tool on the Tool palette.

2. On the Stage, position the mouse pointer over the guide you want to move.

   The mouse pointer becomes a double-headed arrow (**Figure 9.17**).

3. Drag the guide to its new location.

✔ Tips

- To remove a guide, drag it off the Stage.

- To remove all guides, click the Remove All button on the Guides tab of the Property Inspector.

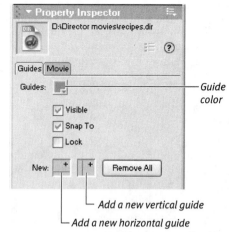

Guide color

Add a new vertical guide

Add a new horizontal guide

Figure 9.15 The Guides tab lets you choose a vertical or horizontal guide for the Stage.

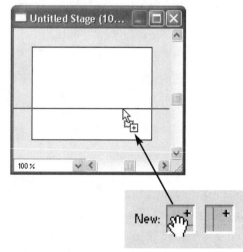

Figure 9.16 Place a horizontal or vertical guide on the stage by dragging it from the Guides tab in the Property Inspector.

Figure 9.17 When you reposition a guide, the mouse pointer becomes a double-headed arrow.

To lock or unlock guides:

◆ Choose View > Guides and Grid > Lock Guides.

or

Select or deselect the Lock check box on the Guides tab of the Property Inspector.

✔ Tips

■ Locking the guides prevents you from accidentally repositioning or removing them.

■ The locked setting applies to all guides on the Stage. You can't lock or unlock individual guides.

To toggle snapping to the grid or guides:

◆ Choose View > Guides and Grid > Snap to Grid (or Snap to Guides).

or

Select or deselect the Snap To check box in the appropriate section of the Guides tab in the Property Inspector.

To change the color of the grid or guides:

◆ Choose a color from the appropriate color menu on the Guides tab in the Property Inspector.

USING GRIDS AND GUIDES

Creating Shapes on the Stage

Although you normally create sprites by dragging a cast member from the Cast window to the Stage, it's possible to draw very simple sprites directly on the Stage. You do this by using the Line and shape tools in the Tool palette (**Figure 9.18**). When you draw a shape on the Stage, it appears automatically in the Cast window.

Shapes drawn on the Stage are essentially vector graphics, but they use a different (and older) technology than what's used in the Vector Shape window. They lack anti-aliasing, and they animate a bit more slowly than standard vector or bitmapped sprites. On the positive side, they consume virtually no memory and add practically nothing to a movie's file size. They're also quick and easy to create.

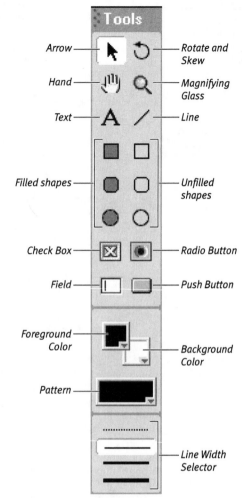

Figure 9.18 The full Tool palette.

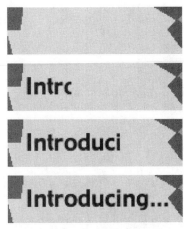

Figure 9.19 The word *Introducing...* is covered by a rectangular shape the same color as the Stage background, then gradually revealed through tweening.

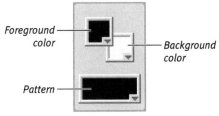

Figure 9.20 Click a line to choose a line width.

Foreground color

Background color

Pattern

Figure 9.21 Select a foreground color, background color, and pattern.

These simple shapes come in handy for a variety of tasks—for example, creating colored backdrops for a movie (see **Figure 9.3**) or temporarily hiding other sprites (**Figure 9.19**).

To choose a line width:

◆ Click a line in the line-width selector in the Tool palette (**Figure 9.20**). (The dotted line represents no line.)

The next time you use the Line tool or any of the shape tools, the tool will draw with the specified line width.

To choose a color and pattern:

1. Select the desired colors from the Foreground and Background Color menus (**Figure 9.21**) in the Tool palette.

The selected foreground color applies to all lines, to the fill color of filled shapes, and to the foreground color of patterns.

The background color applies only to the background of patterns.

2. Select the desired pattern from the Pattern menu.

The selected pattern appears only in filled shapes. The default setting is a solid pattern (which is to say no pattern at all).

✔ Tip

■ The color and pattern you select will remain in effect for all tools until you choose another color or pattern.

To draw a line:

1. In the Tool palette, click the Line tool (**Figure 9.22**).

2. Drag on the Stage to draw a line.

3. Release the mouse button when the line has the desired length and direction.

✔ Tip

■ Hold down the Shift key while dragging to constrain the Line tool to horizontal, vertical, and 45-degree lines.

To draw a shape:

1. Click one of the shape tools in the Tool palette (**Figure 9.23**).

2. On the Stage, drag diagonally to make a shape.

3. Release the mouse button when the shape has the desired height and width.

✔ Tip

■ Hold down the Shift key to constrain a rectangle to a square, or an ellipse to a circle.

To edit the characteristics of a line or shape:

1. Click the Arrow tool in the Tool palette.

2. On the Stage, select the line, shape, or group of lines and shapes that you want to adjust.

3. Choose a new color, pattern, or line width from the Tool palette.

   The selected sprites change to reflect the new setting.

✔ Tip

■ Sprites drawn on the Stage can be resized, rotated, skewed, and so forth like any other sprite. See "Changing Sprite Properties" in Chapter 3.

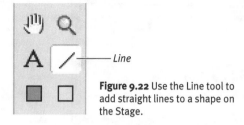

Figure 9.22 Use the Line tool to add straight lines to a shape on the Stage.

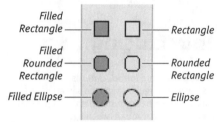

Figure 9.23 The shape tools.

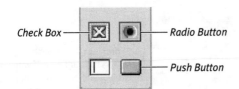

Check Box ———— Radio Button

Push Button

Figure 9.24 Use these tools to create push buttons, check boxes, and radio buttons for your movie.

Creating Buttons on the Stage

With the tools in the Tool palette, you can create working push buttons, check boxes, and radio buttons, along with the text that accompanies them (**Figure 9.24**). For a description of each of these kinds of buttons, see the sidebar, "Button Types."

When you play back your movie, you can click the buttons and they'll respond to your clicks (for example, an *X* will appear in a check box), but they won't actually do anything. In order for a button to accomplish a task, you have to assign a behavior to it (see Chapter 14, "Adding Behaviors") or attach a script to it (see Chapter 15, "Scripting Lingo").

Note that these buttons are fairly primitive graphically. They're based on the buttons used in early versions of the Mac operating system—pure black and white, with none of the shading or 3D effects that are typical of present-day buttons. The push button, in particular, is probably too old-fashioned-looking to be useful. Instead, you'll probably want to create or import your own push-button cast members and attach a button behavior to them. (See Chapter 14, "Adding Behaviors.")

CREATING BUTTONS ON THE STAGE

Button Types

A *push button* is what most of us have in mind when we simply refer to "a button" (**Figure 9.25**). It's an object that may or may not look like a physical button, but it performs a specific action when clicked.

Clicking a *check box* causes an *X* to appear in the center of the box. It's possible to select more than one check box in a group, so that any number (including all or none) of the boxes may end up with *X*'s in them (**Figure 9.26**). Check boxes usually appear in groups, allowing a user to select any number of options, though a single check box may be used in a yes-or-no situation.

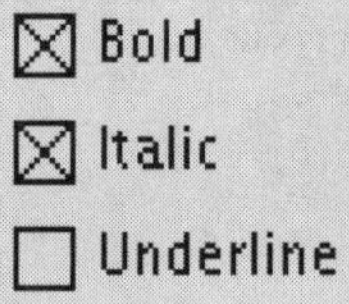

Figure 9.25 Add a push button to your movie if you want an action performed when a button is clicked.

Figure 9.26 Add check boxes to your movie when you want users to select any number of options.

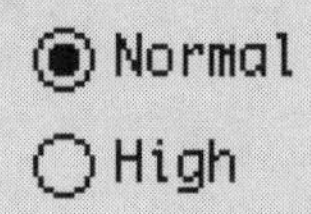

Figure 9.27 Add radio buttons to your movie when you want your users to choose only one option.

Radio buttons always occur in groups. Clicking a radio button causes a dot to appear in its center and causes the dot to disappear in any other buttons in the group. Thus, only one radio button can be chosen at a time (**Figure 9.27**). Radio buttons require a user to make a single choice from among several options.

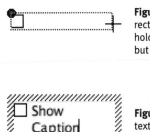

Figure 9.28 Drag a rectangle big enough to hold not just the button but a text label as well.

Figure 9.29 Type the text that goes with the button.

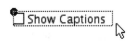

Figure 9.30 Resize the rectangle if necessary to accommodate the text.

To create a button or check box:

1. Depending on your preference, click the radio button, push button, or check box tool in the Tool palette.

2. On the Stage, drag horizontally to create the button. Drag a rectangle big enough to contain not just the button but the text label that accompanies it (**Figure 9.28**).

   Check boxes and radio buttons are always the same size no matter how far you drag. You can change the width of push buttons by dragging farther, but the height remains the same.

3. Release the mouse button.

   A blinking insertion point appears at the place where the text label will go. If you're creating a push button, the insertion point is inside the button; if you're creating a check box or radio button, the insertion point is to the right.

4. If you wish, select the font, size, and style for the text label: Choose Modify > Font and use the Font dialog box; alternatively, you can specify these text settings in the Text Inspector.

   For more information about each of these options, see Chapter 12, "Adding Text."

5. Type the text (**Figure 9.29**).

6. If you need more room for the text, expand the rectangle by dragging the gray striped border that surrounds it.

   The text inside will automatically rewrap (**Figure 9.30**).

7. Click outside the rectangle.

   The button and text become a sprite on the Stage and are added to the Cast window.

✔ Tip

- To edit the text in a button, double-click it. The insertion point and gray border will reappear.

Creating Text on the Stage

You can use the Text and Field tools (**Figure 9.31**) to create text or text fields on the Stage. The text you create in this way is indistinguishable from text created in the Text and Field windows.

See Chapter 12, "Adding Text," for a complete discussion of using text in Director, including the use of these tools.

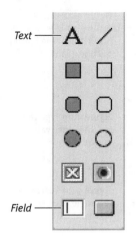

Text

Field

Figure 9.31 Use the Text and Field tools to add text to your movie.

ADDING

DIGITAL VIDEO

Figure 10.1 You can import many kinds of digital video files into Director such as the QuickTime VR movie at the center of the Stage.

To say that Director can import digital video files doesn't seem like that big a deal. After all, we're accustomed to seeing digital video on our computers. But when you discover that you can import a wide variety of video files—including streaming video, QuickTime VR panoramas, DVD-quality MPEG-4 video—into Director, place them on the Stage, and animate them just like any other sprite, you may find your imagination flooding with new ideas about what you can accomplish with Director (**Figure 10.1**).

Director imports video in QuickTime, RealMedia, and AVI formats. (For a summary of the advantages and disadvantages of using each format in Director, see the following "Video File Formats" sidebar.) Keep in mind that digital video is extremely processor-intensive, so keep your use of video to a minimum unless you know that everyone who's going to view your movie has a fast, up-to-date computer.

Director gives you precise control over how your digital video files appear and behave on the Stage. This chapter will look at the ways you can control video cast members in the Score and in the Property Inspector. You can exert even more power over video cast members by using specialized Lingo commands—although that's beyond the scope of this book.

continues on next page

Director provides very basic video-editing tools in its QuickTime window, where you can rearrange frames by cutting, copying, and pasting. (AVI and RealMedia files can't be edited in Director.) Keep in mind, however, that Director is not intended to be a video-editing program. Most people do all their video editing in Final Cut Pro, Premiere, or a similar program before importing video files into Director.

Video File Formats

QuickTime

QuickTime, which works both on the Mac and in Windows, is more than just a digital video format. It supports a variety of media, including MIDI (Musical Instrument Digital Interface) audio, virtual-reality scenes, and even Director-style sprites—as well as high-quality video and audio. Because QuickTime is so flexible and robust, it's the format of choice for most Director developers.

If you want to include QuickTime files in a Director movie, you must have the QuickTime Player installed on your computer, and so must anyone who wants to view your movie. Director MX supports QuickTime 2 and later, but QuickTime 6 is recommended. (QuickTime 4 or later is required if you want to use streaming video.) You can download the latest version of the QuickTime Player free from Apple's Web site, www.apple.com.

RealMedia

The RealMedia format is especially well suited for streaming video and audio over low-bandwidth connections. If you want to include RealMedia files in a Director movie, you must have version 8 or higher of RealMedia's player (formerly called RealPlayer, now called RealOne Player) installed on your computer, and so must anyone who wants to view your movie. The latest version of the player can be downloaded free from www.real.com.

Director won't recognize RealMedia files unless the RealMedia Xtras are installed in the Xtras folder. This installation is done automatically in Windows. But on the Mac, you must do it manually: On the Mac Director installation CD, look inside the Goodies folder for a folder called RealXtra and follow the directions in the read-me file inside. (See Chapter 19, "Using Xtras.")

If you distribute your Director movie over the Web via Shockwave, users who want to view the movie must download the RealMedia Asset Xtra. In most cases, the Shockwave player handles this download automatically.

AVI

AVI is a no-frills, Windows-only format. (The Mac version of Director can import AVI files, but it immediately converts them to QuickTime format.) Unlike QuickTime and RealMedia files, AVI files require no third-party software in order to be playable in Director. Use AVI files in your Director movie only if your movie's intended audience includes no Mac users.

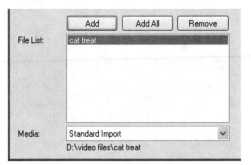

Figure 10.2 Even though the Media menu says "Standard Import," this video file will be imported as a linked external file.

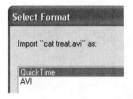

Figure 10.3 You can choose to import an AVI file in AVI or QuickTime format.

Importing and Previewing Digital Video Files

So far as Director is concerned, a digital video file is just another cast member—it doesn't require any special handling. Once a video file has been imported, it occupies a slot in the Cast window along with all the other cast members.

Just as you can double-click a bitmapped cast member to open it in the Paint window, or a vector cast member to open it in the Vector Shape window, you can double-click a video cast member to open it in a video preview window. (There are actually three different video preview windows, one for each of the video file formats that Director imports.)

To import a digital video file:

◆ Follow the same procedure that you use to import other kinds of cast members. (See "Importing Cast Members" in Chapter 2)

   However, there are two things to keep in mind when you import digital video files:

   ▲ Video files are always imported as linked external files, regardless of what the Media pop-up menu says (**Figure 10.2**). If you import a video file from your hard drive, the file must always be in the same place relative to your Director movie file; otherwise, Director won't be able to find it. If you import a video file from the Web, it must always be available at the same URL.

   ▲ When you import an AVI file in the Windows version of Director, a dialog box asks whether you want the file to be in AVI or QuickTime format (**Figure 10.3**). If you choose AVI, your movie will be playable only on Windows computers; if you choose QuickTime, your movie will be playable on any computer that has the QuickTime Player installed. (When you import on the Mac, there's no choice: AVI files are always converted to QuickTime format.)

To preview a QuickTime video file:

1. In the Cast window, double-click a QuickTime cast member (**Figure 10.4**).

   The video file opens in the QuickTime preview window (**Figure 10.5**).

2. Click the Play button to play the video.

   While the video is playing, the Play button becomes a Stop button (**Figure 10.6**).

3. Click the Stop button to stop the movie.

   The button returns to being a Play button.

4. If you wish, use the slider to move forward or back to any point in the video file.

5. If you want to preview the movie frame by frame, use the Step Forward and Step Backward buttons.

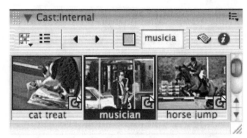

Figure 10.4 To preview a QuickTime video file, you must first double-click a QuickTime cast member.

Play   Slider   Step Backward

Step Forward

Figure 10.5 The video file opens in the QuickTime preview window.

Play   Stop

Figure 10.6 A single button changes appearance to serve as a Play button (when the video isn't playing) and a Stop button (when it is).

Play
Stop
Slider — *Rewind*

Figure 10.7 The RealMedia preview window looks a little different from the QuickTime preview window. You won't find a "Step Forward" button here, for example.

Figure 10.8 Unlike the RealMedia and QuickTime preview windows, the AVI preview window has no playback controls.

To preview a RealMedia file:

1. In the Cast window, double-click a RealMedia cast member.

   The video file opens in the RealMedia preview window (**Figure 10.7**).

2. Click the Play button to play the video.

3. Click the Stop button to stop the video.

4. Use the slider to move forward or back to any point in the video file, or use the Rewind button to rewind it to the beginning.

To preview an AVI file (Windows only):

1. Double-click an AVI cast member in the Cast window.

   The video file opens in the AVI preview window (**Figure 10.8**). Unlike the QuickTime and RealMedia windows, the AVI window has no playback controls.

2. Double-click the video image in the AVI window to play the video.

3. Single-click the image to stop the video.

Working with Video Sprites

You place a video cast member in your movie by dragging it to the Stage or Score, just as you would any cast member. Thereafter, you can treat it as you would any other sprite. Though you can't rotate or skew a digital video sprite, you can move it, resize it, or tween it (**Figure 10.9**). You can also apply ink effects to it or change its blend percentage, unless the Direct to Stage option is selected (see "Setting Digital Video Properties," later in this chapter). Be aware that doing any of these things may take a toll on playback performance. (See the sidebar "Reducing Processor Load with Video Sprites" later in this chapter.)

To understand the behavior of a video sprite in a Director movie, it's useful to think of the sprite as a little TV set. When you tween the sprite or change its properties, you're affecting only the TV set—you're not changing what's playing on the TV screen. If what's playing on the TV is a 60-minute videotape, the running time of the tape will *always* be 60 minutes, regardless of whether the TV gets moved around, gets bigger or smaller, or is taken out of the room.

The same is true of the video content of your sprite. Every video cast member that you import has a specific duration. When you drag the cast member to the Stage, you create a sprite. You can keep the sprite on the Stage for as many or as few frames as you want, and do whatever you want with it during that time, but the duration of the sprite's video content will always be the same.

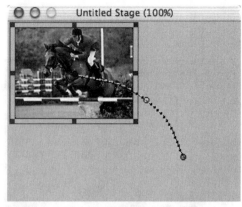

Figure 10.9 As you can see by its motion path, this video sprite has been tweened across the Stage.

When you play a tape in a VCR, you can continue to watch the tape until the TV is turned off or the tape runs out, whichever comes first. The same is true in Director. When the playhead enters a video sprite in the Score, the sprite's video content begins to play. It continues to play until either the playhead leaves the sprite or the duration of the video file is reached, whichever comes first.

The relationship between the time-based content of a video sprite and the frame-based Score can sometimes be complex. The following are examples of the more common tasks that you might want to accomplish with video sprites. In some cases, the behavior of the video sprite may not be what you expect, but it will begin to make more sense after some experimentation.

To display a video sprite for a fixed amount of time (regardless of the length of its content):

1. Decide how long you want the sprite to remain on the Stage.

   For this example, let's assume you want the sprite to be visible for 3 seconds.

2. Multiply the number of seconds from step 1 by the current tempo of the movie. (See "Setting a Movie's Tempo" in Chapter 5)

   Let's assume the current tempo is 10 frames per second (fps). In that case, 3 times 10 equals 30.

continues on next page

3. Extend the video sprite in the Score to span the number of frames you arrived at in step 2.

In this case, you'd make the video sprite 30 frames long.

4. Play the movie.

When the playhead enters the video sprite, the sprite appears on the Stage, shows 3 seconds of video content, then disappears.

If the sprite's video file has a duration of more than 3 seconds, only the first 3 seconds of the content is seen (**Figure 10.10**).

If the sprite's video file has a duration of less than 3 seconds, the content of the video file is seen in its entirety. For the remainder of the time, the last frame of the video file is displayed in the sprite (**Figure 10.11**).

To loop a sprite's video content (QuickTime and AVI only):

1. In the Score, extend the sprite so that its duration is longer than that of the sprite's video content.

The longer the sprite, the more times the video content will repeat.

2. In the Cast window, select the cast member represented by the video sprite.

3. In the Property Inspector, click the QuickTime tab (for a QuickTime cast member) or the AVI tab (for an AVI cast member).

4. Select the Loop option in the Property Inspector (**Figure 10.12**).

5. Play the movie.

The sprite's video content loops repeatedly for as long as the sprite is on the Stage (**Figure 10.13**).

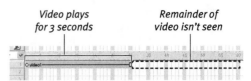

Figure 10.10 A 3-second sprite in a movie whose tempo is 10 fps. If the sprite's video file is 6 seconds long, only half of the video content will be seen.

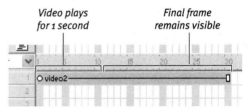

Figure 10.11 A 3-second sprite in a movie whose tempo is 10 fps. If the sprite's video file is 1 second long, the video content will be seen in its entirety, followed by 2 seconds in which the video file's last frame is displayed in the sprite.

Figure 10.12 The Loop option on the QuickTime tab in the Property Inspector. (This option is also available on the AVI tab).

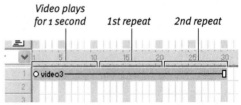

Figure 10.13 A 3-second sprite in a movie whose tempo is 10 fps. If the sprite's video file is 1 second long, and the Loop option is selected, the video content will play 3 times.

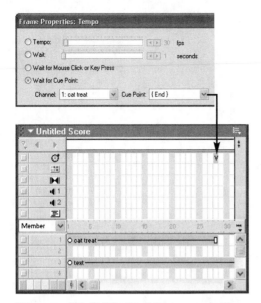

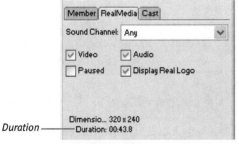

Figure 10.14 This Wait for Cue Point command will cause the Director movie to pause until the video sprite has played in its entirety.

Duration ——

Figure 10.15 The duration of the selected cast member can be found on the RealMedia tab of the Property Inspector.

To make a sprite's video content play through just once:

◆ **For a QuickTime or AVI sprite:**
In the Score, place a Wait for Cue Point command in the tempo channel in the video sprite's last frame (**Figure 10.14**). (See the "Using Cue Points" sidebar in Chapter 5.)

or

◆ **For any type of video sprite:**

1. Find out the duration of the video cast member in either of the following ways.

   ▲ Open the cast member's linked external file in an external player (such as the QuickTime Player, the RealOne Player, or the Windows Media Player) and read the duration from the player's display.

   ▲ If the cast member is a RealMedia cast member, select it in the Cast window and read the duration from the RealMedia tab in the Property Inspector (**Figure 10.15**).

2. Multiply the duration of the video file (in seconds) by the tempo of the Director movie (in frames per second) to get the number of frames the video sprite needs to span in the Score.

continues on next page

WORKING WITH VIDEO SPRITES

3. Extend the sprite in the Score to span the number of frames you arrived at in step 2.

✔ Tip

■ Remember that Director movies often play at less than the intended tempo. Therefore, don't design your movie with the expectation that the length of a sprite will correspond exactly with the duration of a video file. If you do need the sprite to disappear precisely when the video content ends, use a cue point.

Reducing Processor Load with Video Sprites

If the mere presence of a video sprite on the Stage puts a heavy load on the computer's processor, changing any of the sprite's properties—particularly its dimensions—increases those processing demands significantly. If your movie is played on an insufficiently powerful computer, its playback tempo may slow drastically, and the video itself may hesitate and sputter.

You can reduce the processor load in the following ways:

◆ Eliminate unnecessary property changes. (For example, keep the video sprite at its actual size instead of resizing it on the Stage.)

◆ Eliminate unnecessary tweening.

◆ Use video files with smaller dimensions (for example, 240 by 180 pixels instead of 320 by 240).

◆ Have only one video sprite on the Stage at a time.

◆ Use the Direct to Stage option (see "Setting Digital Video Properties" on the following page).

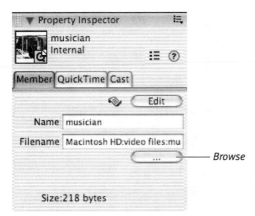

Figure 10.16 In the Property Inspector's Member tab, click the Browse button.

— *Browse*

Figure 10.17 Use the "Locate replacement..." dialog box to select a file that you want to link to a cast member. In the Mac version, shown here, select the file and click Choose.

Setting Digital Video Properties

Digital video cast members have a wide range of properties that affect their playback performance and appearance. You can set the most commonly used properties in the Property Inspector. (You must set others through Lingo, which won't be covered in this chapter.)

The Property Inspector also allows you to change the external file that a video cast member is linked to.

To change a video cast member's linked external file:

1. Select a digital video cast member in the Cast window.

2. Select the Member tab in the Property Inspector.

3. Click the Browse button (labeled with three dots, as shown in **Figure 10.16**). A "Locate replacement..." dialog box appears (**Figure 10.17**).

4. In the dialog box, navigate to and select the file that you want to link to the cast member.

5. Click "Open" (Windows) or "Choose" (Mac). The new path and filename appear in the Filename field.

✔ Tips

■ If you know the complete path and filename for the file you want to link to, you can skip steps 3 through 5 and enter the information directly into the Filename field in the Property Inspector.

■ If you've moved or renamed the file that's linked to a movie's cast member, Director will automatically offer you the "Locate replacement..." dialog box the next time you open the movie.

To set a video cast member's properties:

1. Select a digital video cast member in the Cast window.

2. Select the appropriate tab in the Property Inspector: QuickTime for a QuickTime cast member (**Figure 10.18**), RealMedia for a RealMedia cast member (**Figure 10.19**), or AVI for an AVI cast member (**Figure 10.20**).

3. Change properties as desired.

Here are the properties you can set:

◆ **Video:** This option is selected by default. It allows the video content of the cast member to be seen and played on the Stage. If you're using a "digital video" file that contains only audio, deselect this option to improve playback performance.

◆ **Audio:** This option is selected by default. It allows the audio track (or tracks) of the cast member to be heard. If your digital video file contains no sound, deselect this option.

◆ **Paused:** If this option is selected, the video will be paused when it first appears on the Stage. In that case, the only way to start playing the video is through a command in a Lingo script.

◆ **DTS** (QuickTime and AVI only): DTS stands for Direct to Stage and is selected by default. It significantly reduces the load on the computer's processor by handing control of video playback to the QuickTime Player or to Windows, rather than to Director. In essence, when DTS is selected, the video content is superimposed in front of the Stage rather than appearing *on* the Stage. As a result, the video sprite always appears in the foreground regardless of which channel it's in in the Score, and ink effects don't affect it. The DTS

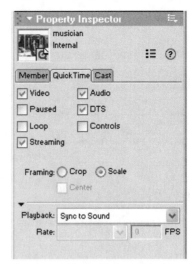

Figure 10.18 The QuickTime tab in the Property Inspector.

Figure 10.19 The RealMedia tab in the Property Inspector.

Figure 10.20 The AVI tab in the Property Inspector.

Figure 10.21 When the Controls property is selected, this controller bar appears at the bottom of a QuickTime video sprite.

option may cause problems with tweened video sprites, so if playback is unsatisfactory, try turning it off.

◆ **Loop** (QuickTime and AVI only): This option causes the video content to loop (repeat from the beginning) when the sprite has a longer duration than the video file. See "To loop a sprite's video content," earlier in this chapter.

◆ **Controls** (QuickTime only): When this option is selected, a controller bar is displayed at the bottom the sprite, giving users control of video playback (**Figure 10.21**). This option is available only if the DTS option is selected. (Note: It's possible to add controls to RealMedia sprites as well, using behaviors from the Library palette. See Chapter 14, "Adding Behaviors.")

◆ **Streaming** (QuickTime only): This option, which is selected by default, allows QuickTime movies to be streamed. *Streaming* means that when a user views your Director movie from the Web, the video content of a sprite can start playing as soon as the sprite appears on the Stage, while the rest of the video file loads in the background. The following things must be true in order for this option to have any effect: The Director movie must be distributed over the Web via Shockwave and must be configured as a streaming movie (see Chapter 17, "Making Movies for the Web"); the DTS option must be selected; and QuickTime 4 or later must be installed on the user's computer. (Note: Although there's no Streaming option on the RealMedia tab, RealMedia video files stream automatically—their streaming property can't be turned off.)

continues on next page

◆ **Display Real Logo** (RealMedia only): This option is selected by default. It causes the RealMedia logo to be displayed briefly before a sprite's video content begins to play. If you don't want to see the logo (and why would you?), deselect it.

◆ **Preload** (AVI only): When this option is selected, Director loads as much of the video file as possible into RAM before playing. Preload improves playback performance but causes a delay while the video loads.

◆ **Playback** (QuickTime and AVI only): There are two options on this pop-up menu, stemming from the fact that audio places much less of a load on the processor than video does. **Sync to Sound**, the default, causes Director to give priority to the audio tracks of the video file, skipping video frames if necessary to keep the video in sync with the audio. The other option, **Play Every Frame (No Sound)**, causes Director to turn off the audio tracks and to play every frame of the video, even if doing so causes the video content to exceed its intended duration.

◆ **Rate** (QuickTime and AVI only): This pop-up menu becomes available only when Play Every Frame is selected in the Playback menu (**Figure 10.22**). **Normal**, the default option, plays the video content at its normal rate, slowing down only when necessary to avoid skipping frames. **Maximum** plays the video content as quickly as possible without skipping frames. **Fixed** plays the video content at whatever rate you specify in the FPS (frames per second) box to the right of the menu.

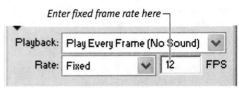

Enter fixed frame rate here

Figure 10.22 The Rate pop-up menu becomes available if Play Every Frame is selected in the Playback menu. If you choose Fixed, enter your desired frame rate in the FPS box.

Scale

Crop

Crop + Center

Figure 10.23 Here, this video sprite has been resized with the Scale, Crop, and Crop + Center options.

◆ **Framing** (QuickTime and AVI only): These options determine what happens when you resize a video sprite on the Stage (**Figure 10.23**). If **Scale** (the default) is selected, the sprite behaves as most visual sprites do: The entire image expands or shrinks to match the new dimensions of the sprite. If **Crop** is selected, the image remains the same size, and portions of it are cropped (cut away) when the sprite is resized. (The Crop option places less of a demand on the computer's processor.) By default, the sprite is cropped from the right side and the bottom, but if **Center** is selected, it's cropped from all four sides.

Editing QuickTime Files

Director allows you to perform simple video editing operations in the QuickTime preview window. Editing a QuickTime cast member makes permanent changes to the linked external file, so be sure to make a backup copy of the file before you begin. (Important: The Undo command doesn't work for QuickTime editing.)

Editing in the QuickTime window is essentially a two-stage process: First, you select one or more frames and cut or copy them to your computer's clipboard; then you paste those frames into a new location. That new location may be within the same QuickTime cast member, in a different QuickTime cast member, or in a brand-new cast member (in which case you're actually creating a new, external QuickTime file).

To edit a QuickTime cast member:

1. Double-click a QuickTime cast member in the Cast window.

   The cast member opens in the QuickTime preview window.

2. Drag the slider at the bottom of the window to the frame preceding the first frame that you want to cut or copy.

3. While holding down the Shift key, drag the slider to the last frame in the range that you want to cut or copy. (If you wish, the range may consist of a single frame.)

   The range of frames is selected, as indicated by a gray bar in the controller (**Figure 10.24**).

4. Choose Edit > Copy or Edit > Cut.

   If you choose Cut, an alert box warns you that this operation will change the linked file (**Figure 10.25**).

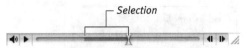

Figure 10.24 The frames you've selected in the QuickTime cast member are indicated by a gray bar.

Figure 10.25 This alert box appears when you cut frames from, or paste frames into, a QuickTime cast member.

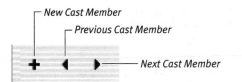

Figure 10.26 Use these buttons (located in the upper-left corner of the QuickTime preview window) to select a cast member that you want to paste frames into.

Figure 10.27 This dialog box allows you to name a new QuickTime file.

5. If necessary, click OK to close the dialog box.

6. If you intend to paste the frames into a different cast member, use the Previous Cast Member or Next Cast Member buttons to step through QuickTime cast members until you reach the one you want (**Figure 10.26**).

   or

   If you want to paste the selected frames into a new, empty cast member, click the New Cast Member button and skip step 7.

7. Drag the slider to the frame preceding the spot where you want to paste the range of frames.

8. Choose Edit > Paste.

   If you're pasting into an existing cast member, an alert box warns you that this operation will change the linked file.

   If you are pasting into a new cast member, a dialog box allows you to name the new linked file (**Figure 10.27**).

9. Click OK to close the warning dialog box.

   or

   Name the new QuickTime file and click Save.

Importing Animated GIFs

An animated GIF file is a type of image file that contains multiple frames. It's often used to display simple animations on Web sites.

You can import animated GIF files into Director and use them in a movie, just as you'd use digital video files. No third-party software is required.

To import an animated GIF file:

1. Choose File > Import, and follow the same steps you'd follow to import any other file. (See "Importing Cast Members" in Chapter 2 for more information.)

   Instead of the normal Image Options dialog box, Director presents you with a Select Format dialog box, asking whether you want to import the file as an animated GIF or as a bitmapped image (**Figure 10.28**).

   The Animated GIF option is selected by default.

2. Click OK.

   The animated GIF file appears in the Cast window.

✔ Tip

■ If you select Bitmap Image instead of Animated GIF, Director imports the first frame of the animated GIF file as a standard bitmapped cast member.

Figure 10.28 This dialog box appears whenever you import a GIF file (animated or otherwise).

Figure 10.29 The Animated GIF tab in the Property Inspector lets you adjust the frame rate and other properties for an animated GIF.

Figure 10.30 The Animated GIF Asset Properties window.

To set an animated GIF file's properties:

1. Select an animated GIF cast member in the Cast window.

2. Select the Animated GIF tab in the Property Inspector (**Figure 10.29**).

3. Choose an option from the Rate pop-up menu.

   Normal, the default, plays the GIF animation at its original frame rate.

   The Lock-Step option plays the animation at the same rate as your Director movie.

   If you want to specify a different frame rate, choose Fixed, and enter the desired frame rate in the FPS box below the menu.

4. If you want the animated GIF file to be played Direct to Stage, select the DTS option.

   Playing the animation Direct to Stage reduces the load on the computer's processor, but it has significant drawbacks. (See "To set a video cast member's properties" earlier in this chapter for more information.) Animated GIF files are typically small and not especially processor-intensive, so selecting DTS usually isn't necessary.

5. If you want to preview the GIF animation, click the More button.

   The Animated GIF Asset Properties window opens, displaying the same properties that were displayed on the Animated GIF tab in the Property Inspector (**Figure 10.30**).

6. Click the Play button at the bottom left of the window to preview the animation.

7. Click OK to close the window.

USING FLASH MOVIES IN DIRECTOR

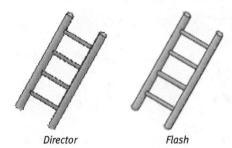

Director   *Flash*

Figure 11.1 A bitmapped image rotated in Director and in Flash. As you can see, Flash rotates bitmaps more smoothly.

If you have experience using both Director and Macromedia Flash, you're no doubt aware that Flash simply does certain things better. Flash's drawing tools make Director's look like a stone-age hammer and chisel. Motion tweening is often smoother in Flash. Resizing, rotation, and skewing of bitmaps are smoother as well (**Figure 11.1**). Text in Flash can be stretched, squeezed, and rotated. Making rollover buttons is a piece of cake. And the list goes on.

Of course, there are also lots of things that Director does better than Flash. (See "Who uses Director?" in the introduction to this book.) Fortunately, you don't have to choose between the two: If you have both products, you can use them together to create a movie that has the best features of each.

Use Flash to create the elements that look better in Flash—anything from a single vector image to a complex, animated, interactive movie. You can publish the Flash movie as an SWF file, then import the SWF file into Director. All of the SWF file's features—including any ActionScript it may contain—function in Director just as they do in Flash. It's not necessary for Flash to be installed on your computer (or on the computers of those to whom you distribute your movies) for Flash sprites to function in Director.

Tips on Exporting from Flash

Director users tend to use Flash in two different ways. Sometimes, they create a full-fledged movie in Flash—including animation and possibly interactivity—with the intention of playing it on the Director Stage. In this case, Flash plays a role similar to that of video-editing programs such as Adobe Premiere or Apple's Final Cut Pro—as a tool for producing self-contained cast members with time-based content.

At other times, Flash is used to create high-quality vector cast members that you can then animate in Director. In this case, you can use Flash as a substitute for an image-creation program such as Adobe's Photoshop or Illustrator.

If you're planning on creating a Flash movie and exporting it to Director, there are several things you can do in Flash MX to make your movie work better in Director:

- If the movie includes digital video files, delete them. (You'll get better performance by importing them separately as Director cast members).

- Edit the movie's scripts to remove any use of the `loadMovieNum` command to load movies into levels above Level 0. (The movies won't load in Director.)

- Set the frame rate of the Flash movie to be no faster than the frame rate of the Director movie you'll be importing it into.

- Choose File > Publish Settings, and deselect the Compress Movie option (to avoid memory problems in Director).

You can then export an SWF file from Flash in any of the usual ways: by choosing Control > Test Movie, File > Publish, or File > Export Movie.

In the second case—in which you want to export only a vector image, with no animation or interactivity—the best way to do it is to follow these steps:

1. Make the Stage as small as possible, following the steps in the "Optimizing the Flash Stage" sidebar, later in this chapter.

2. If any of the objects you want to export are symbols with scripts attached to them, delete the attached scripts.

3. In the Timeline, select the frame that you want to export. (If your movie has only one frame, this obviously isn't necessary.)

4. If there are any frame scripts attached to the selected frame, delete them.

continues on next page

Tips on Exporting from Flash *continued*

5. Choose File > Export Image. (The advantage of Export Image over Export Movie is that it exports only the frame you've selected.)

The Export Image dialog box opens (**Figure 11.2**).

6. Select Flash Movie from the Format pop-up menu. (Even though you're only exporting a single frame, the SWF file is still considered a "movie.")

From this point on, you can continue the export process as you would with any other Flash movie. The result will be a single-frame SWF file.

When you import the resulting file into Director, be sure to select the Static option on the Property Inspector's Flash tab. (See "To set a Flash cast member's properties," later in this chapter.)

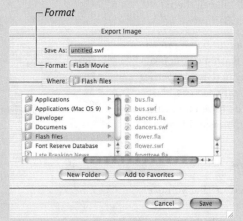

Figure 11.2 In Flash MX's Export Image dialog box, select the Flash files you want to import into Director.

Importing and Configuring Flash Movies

Though we often talk informally about importing "Flash movies" into Director, it should be stressed that Director imports only SWF files, not FLA files. (SWF is the file format in which Flash movies are distributed via the Web; FLA files are used for authoring and editing Flash movies. To use FLA files in Director, see "Editing Flash Cast Members," later in this chapter.) SWF files from applications other than Flash (such as Adobe's Freehand or Illustrator) can be imported as well, though Director will still call them "Flash movies" (**Figure 11.3**).

Flash cast members have a number of properties that affect the way the Flash movie appears and plays in Director. Many of these properties can be set on the Property Inspector's Flash tab. Others (which won't be covered in this book) can be set only by means of Lingo commands.

To import a Flash movie:

◆ Follow the same procedure that you use to import other kinds of cast members. (See "Importing Cast Members" in Chapter 2.)

Unlike digital video files, Flash movies may be imported with either the Standard Import option (in which the cast member becomes part of the Director movie file) or the Link to External File option.

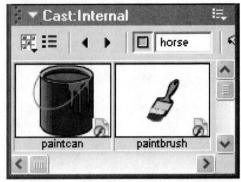

Figure 11.3 SWF files exported from Flash (left) and Freehand (right), together in the Cast window. Both have Flash movie icons in their lower-right corners.

Figure 11.4 Use the Flash tab in the Property Inspector to adjust properties for your Flash cast member.

To set a Flash cast member's properties:

1. Select a Flash cast member in the Cast window.

2. Select the Flash tab in the Property Inspector (**Figure 11.4**).

3. Change properties as desired.

   The last two properties on the tab, Normal FPS and Frames, can't be changed. They tell you the frame rate of, and the number of frames in, the imported Flash movie.

You *can* set the following properties in the Flash tab:

◆ **Image:** This option is selected by default. It allows the visual content of the Flash movie to be seen on the Stage.

◆ **Loop:** This option is selected by default. It causes the Flash movie to loop (repeat from the beginning) if it's on the Stage for a period of time that exceeds the duration of the Flash movie.

◆ **Paused:** If this option is selected, the Flash movie will be paused at its first frame when it first appears on the Stage. Thereafter, the only way to start playing the movie is by means of a command in a Lingo script.

◆ **Audio:** This option is selected by default. It allows the audio content of the Flash movie to be heard.

continues on next page

IMPORTING AND CONFIGURING FLASH MOVIES

◆ **DTS:** *DTS* stands for Direct to Stage. When this option is selected, the Flash movie is placed in front of the Stage instead of interacting with other sprites on the Stage. Ink effects and the Blend property don't work when DTS is turned on, and motion tweening may not work properly. However, by reducing the load on the computer's processor, this option may improve the playback performance of your Director movie.

◆ **Preload:** This option affects only Flash cast members that are linked to external files. If selected, it causes the entire Flash movie to be loaded into memory before the first frame of your Director movie is played. The Preload option improves playback performance but causes a delay while the Flash movie loads.

◆ **Static:** This option allows Director to display only the first frame of the Flash movie. If you've imported a single-frame Flash movie, selecting this option tells Director not to bother updating the movie in every frame, and thus improves playback performance.

◆ **Rate:** Choose an option from the pop-up menu (**Figure 11.5**). **Normal,** the default, plays the Flash movie at its original frame rate (shown at the bottom of the Property Inspector). The **Lock-Step** option plays the Flash movie at the same frame rate as your Director movie. If you want to specify a different frame rate, choose **Fixed** and enter the desired frame rate in the FPS box to the right of the menu. (Director will not play the Flash movie at a frame rate faster than that of the Director movie, even if you enter a higher number here.)

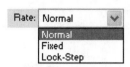

Figure 11.5 In the Rate pop-up menu, choose the frame rate of your Flash movie.

IMPORTING AND CONFIGURING FLASH MOVIES

Show All   No Border

Figure 11.6 A Flash sprite resized disproportionately with the Show All and No Border options.

Exact Fit   No Scale

Figure 11.7 A Flash sprite resized disproportionately with the Exact Fit and No Scale options.

Exact Fit   Auto Size

Figure 11.8 A Flash sprite resized and rotated with the Exact Fit and Auto Size options.

◆ **Scale:** This pop-up menu determines what happens when you resize a Flash sprite on the Stage. (Note that the dimensions of a Flash cast member are those of the Flash Stage at the time the SWF file was exported. To eliminate unnecessary space within the cast member, see the sidebar "Optimizing the Flash Stage.") Here are the menu options you can choose from:

▲ The **Show All** and **No Border** options both allow the Flash movie to keep its original proportions if the sprite is resized disproportionately. The former does it by "letterboxing" the Flash movie, using the background color of the Flash Stage; the latter does it by cropping out parts of the movie that don't fit within the sprite (**Figure 11.6**).

▲ The **Exact Fit** option resizes the Flash movie to match the sprite exactly, regardless of its original proportions. The **No Scale** option does the opposite: It always keeps the Flash movie at its original size, regardless of the size of the sprite (**Figure 11.7**).

▲ **Auto Size**, the default option, acts like Exact Fit, but it makes the Flash movie fit entirely within the sprite's bounding rectangle if the movie is rotated or skewed (**Figure 11.8**).

continues on next page

◆ **Quality**—This pop-up menu determines how Director applies anti-aliasing to the Flash movie. (Anti-aliasing greatly improves the appearance of the movie but puts a greater load on the computer's processor.) The **High** and **Low** settings turn anti-aliasing on and off, respectively (**Figure 11.9**). The **Auto-High** setting turns anti-aliasing on to begin with, but turns it off if Director is unable to play the movie at the tempo specified by the Rate setting. The **Auto-Low** setting turns anti-aliasing off to begin with, but turns it on later if Director is able to achieve the tempo specified by the Rate setting.

✔ Tip

■ If you want to set the properties for a Flash movie *before* you import it, use Insert > Media > Flash Movie to import the file (instead of the usual File > Import). The Flash Asset Properties window opens (**Figure 11.10**), allowing you to set the same properties that can be set on the Flash tab of the Property Inspector. You can then select a file to import by using the Browse button.

Anti-aliasing on

Anti-aliasing off

Figure 11.9 A Flash sprite with and without anti-aliasing. While anti-aliasing presents a smoother appearance, it places greater demands on the computer's processor.

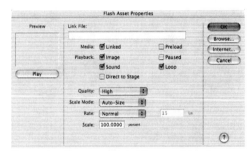

Figure 11.10 If you want to set the properties for a movie before importing it into Director, choose Insert > Media > Flash Movie to open the Flash Asset Properties window, shown here.

Optimizing the Flash Stage

When you import a Flash movie into Director, the cast member has the same dimensions that the Flash Stage had at the time the movie was exported (**Figure 11.11**). To avoid inconvenience and wasted space, follow these steps to make the Flash Stage as small as possible before exporting your movie from Flash MX:

1. Move the objects in your Flash movie as close as possible to the upper-left corner of the Stage.

2. Choose Modify > Document.

   The Document Properties dialog box opens (**Figure 11.12**).

3. In the row of buttons headed by the word *Match,* click the Contents button.

   The Stage dimensions shrink to the minimum necessary to accommodate the objects on the Stage.

4. Click OK to close the dialog box.

| Before | After |

Figure 11.11 A Flash cast member with a Stage size of 320 by 240 pixels, and the same cast member reexported from Flash with a smaller Stage size. The smaller version is easier to work with when you place it on the Stage in Director.

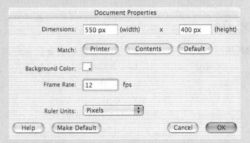

Figure 11.12 The Document Properties dialog box in Flash MX.

To change the dimensions of a Flash cast member:

1. Select a Flash cast member in the Cast window.

2. Select the Flash tab in the Property Inspector.

3. Type a new value into the Scale box (**Figure 11.13**).

   The default value is 100 percent. Enter a lower percentage to shrink the cast member or a higher percentage to enlarge it.

4. Press Enter.

   The cast member is scaled to the percentage you specified, keeping its original proportions.

✔ Tip

■ Although the Scale box is next to the Scale pop-up menu, the two have nothing to do with each other. By entering a number in the Scale box, you resize the *cast member*. The selection you make from the Scale pop-up menu (see "To set a Flash cast member's properties," earlier in this chapter) governs the resizing of individual *sprites*.

To preview a Flash movie:

1. Select a Flash cast member in the Cast window.

2. Select the Flash tab in the Property Inspector.

3. Click the Options button.

   The Flash Asset Properties window opens.

4. Click the Play button at the left side of the window to preview the Flash movie (**Figure 11.14**).

   The movie plays, and the Play button becomes a Stop button.

5. Click the Stop button to end the preview.

6. Click OK to close the window.

Figure 11.13 The Scale box on the Property Inspector's Flash tab.

Figure 11.14 The preview area of the Flash Asset Properties window.

Figure 11.15 A Flash sprite (left), and the same sprite rotated and skewed (right).

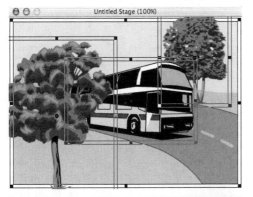

Figure 11.16 Multiple Flash sprites selected on the Director Stage (top), and the same images combined into a single sprite (bottom).

Working with Flash Sprites

As with digital video sprites, you can resize and tween Flash sprites without interfering with their content. Unlike video sprites, Flash sprites can also be rotated and skewed (**Figure 11.15**).

If a Flash cast member includes time-based content (that is, animation with a frame rate and duration independent of the Director movie, as described in the sidebar "Tips on Exporting from Flash"), you may have to make special calculations when deciding how many frames a Flash sprite should span. For more information on this subject, see "Working with Video Sprites" in Chapter 10.

Because of the way Director handles memory for Flash movies, having too many Flash sprites on the Stage at the same time can slow your Director movie's performance. If you find that you have more than a few Flash sprites on the Stage at once, go back into Flash and combine them into a single movie whenever possible (**Figure 11.16**).

To turn a Flash cast member into a sprite:

◆ Drag it to the Stage or Score. (See "Working with Sprites" in Chapter 3, "Building a Score.")

To make the background of a Flash sprite invisible:

1. Select a Flash sprite on the Stage or in the Score.

2. Select the Sprite tab in the Property Inspector.

3. Open the Ink menu and choose Background Transparent, Transparent, or Blend.

   The background of the Flash sprite—which is, in fact, the Flash Stage itself—disappears (**Figure 11.17**). It doesn't matter what color the Flash Stage is, and it doesn't matter what the background color is set to in Director's Tool palette.

✔ Tip

■ The Background Transparent, Transparent, and Blend ink effects are the only ones that work with a Flash sprite. Their only effect is to make the Flash Stage disappear; they don't change the appearance of the Flash movie in any other way.

To make the content of a Flash sprite play through just once:

1. Select a Flash sprite in the Score.

2. Select the Flash tab in the Property Inspector.

   Look at the values for Normal FPS and Frames, at the bottom of the Property Inspector.

3. If the frame rate (Normal FPS) of the Flash movie is the same as the current tempo of your Director movie, do the following:

   1. Select Lock-Step from the Rate pop-up menu (**Figure 11.18**).

   2. Extend the Flash sprite in the Score to span the number of frames indicated by the Frames value.

   or

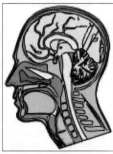
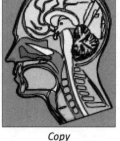

Copy   Background Transparent

Figure 11.17 A Flash sprite with the default Copy ink effect and with the Background Transparent ink effect.

Figure 11.18 Selecting Lock-Step from the Rate pop-up menu locks the frame rate of the Flash sprite to the actual tempo of the Director movie.

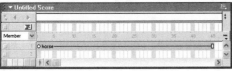

Figure 11.19 Divide the Frames value by the Normal FPS value to get the duration of the Flash movie—in this case, 3 seconds.

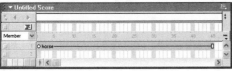

Figure 11.20 If the tempo of the Director movie is 15 fps, the optimal sprite length for a 3-second Flash movie would be 3 times 15, or 45 frames.

If the frame rate (Normal FPS) of the Flash movie is *different than* the current tempo of your Director movie, do the following:

1. Divide the Frames value by the Normal FPS value to get the duration of the Flash movie, in seconds (**Figure 11.19**).

2. Multiply the number of seconds you arrived at in step 1 by the current tempo (in frames per second) of your Director movie.

   This gives you the optimal number of frames for the Flash sprite.

3. Extend the Flash sprite in the Score to span the number of frames you arrived at in step 2 (**Figure 11.20**).

4. Play the movie.

The Flash sprite plays once, then disappears.

✔ Tips

- Because of variations in the playback speed of the Flash sprite and your Director movie, they're unlikely to synchronize exactly if their frame rates are different. Therefore, it's much preferable to give the Flash movie the same frame rate as the Director movie, and to use the Lock-Step method.

- The Wait for Cue Point command, which you might use in this situation with a digital video sprite, doesn't work with Flash sprites.

WORKING WITH FLASH SPRITES

To loop the content of a Flash sprite:

1. Follow the steps for the previous task, "To make the content of a Flash sprite play through just once," to arrive at the minimum number of frames for the Flash sprite.

2. In the Score, extend the sprite so that it spans *more* frames than the number you arrived at in step 1.

   The longer the sprite, the more times the Flash movie will repeat.

3. With the sprite still selected, click the Property Inspector's Flash tab.

4. Select the Loop option, if it's not selected already (**Figure 11.21**). (It's selected by default when you import a Flash movie.)

5. Play the movie.

   The sprite's content loops repeatedly for as long as the sprite is on the Stage.

Figure 11.21 The Loop option on the Flash tab of the Property Inspector is selected by default.

Figure 11.22 The Editors Preferences dialog box lets you specify an external editor.

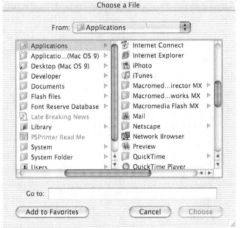

Figure 11.23 The Choose a File dialog box appears.

Editing Flash Cast Members

Wouldn't it be convenient to be able to double-click on a Flash movie in the Cast window and have it open for editing, just as you can with bitmapped cast members? Well, you can—sort of. There's just a slight obstacle: SWF files, the only kind of Flash files Director imports, aren't editable. FLA files, however—the Flash authoring files from which SWF files are exported—*are* editable. So if Director knows the location of the FLA file to which a particular SWF file belongs, it can do the file-swapping behind the scenes, and make the SWF file act as if it's editable.

In order for this juggling act to work, Flash MX must be installed on your computer. When Director is installed, it automatically checks for the presence of Flash on your computer; if it finds it, it adds Flash to its list of available editing programs. If you install Flash *after* you install Director, you must inform Director manually that Flash is now available.

To add Flash to the list of external editors:

1. Choose Edit > Preferences > Editors (Windows) or Director > Preferences > Editors (Mac).
   The Editors Preferences dialog box opens (**Figure 11.22**).

2. In the first column, select Flash.

3. Click the Edit button.
   The Select Editor for Flash dialog box appears.

4. Click the Use External Editor radio button.

5. Click the Browse button.
   The Choose a File dialog box opens (**Figure 11.23**).

continues on next page

EDITING FLASH CAST MEMBERS

6. Navigate to the Flash MX application and click Open (Windows) or Choose (Mac).

Flash now is listed as the external editor for Flash files (**Figure 11.24**).

7. Click OK to close the dialog box.

To associate an FLA file with an SWF file:

1. Select a Flash cast member in the Cast window.

2. Select the Flash tab in the Property Inspector.

3. In the lower pane of the Property Inspector, click the Browse button (labeled with three dots, as in **Figure 11.25**).

A "Locate Flash source file for member" dialog box appears (**Figure 11.26**).

4. Navigate to the FLA file that you want to link to the cast member.

5. Click Open (Windows) or Choose (Mac).

The new path and filename appear in the Filename field on the Property Inspector's Flash tab.

✔ Tip

■ If you know the complete path and filename for the file that you want to link to, you can skip steps 3 through 5 and enter the information directly into the Filename field on the Property Inspector's Flash tab.

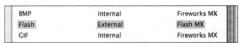

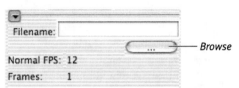

Figure 11.24 After you select the Flash MX application icon, Flash MX is listed as the external editor for Flash files in the Editors Preferences dialog box.

Figure 11.25 Click the Browse button, located in the lower pane of the Flash tab in the Property Inspector.

Figure 11.26 The "Locate Flash source file for member" dialog box.

EDITING FLASH CAST MEMBERS

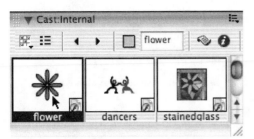

Figure 11.27 Double-click a Flash cast member that you want to edit.

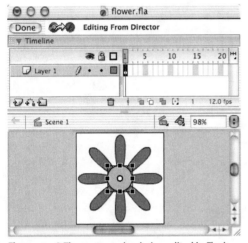

Figure 11.28 The cast member being edited in Flash.

Figure 11.29 This button and header appear above the timeline in Flash.

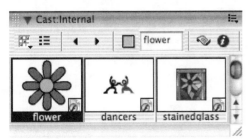

Figure 11.30 The revised cast member in Director's Cast window.

To edit a Flash cast member:

1. In the Cast window, double-click the Flash cast member that you want to edit (**Figure 11.27**).

   The FLA file associated with the cast member opens in Flash (**Figure 11.28**). Above the Flash timeline, there is a header bar that says "Editing from Director," accompanied by a Done button (**Figure 11.29**).

2. Edit the Flash movie.

3. Click the Done button.

   Flash automatically exports a new SWF file.

   Director becomes the active application and automatically imports the new SWF file. The edited cast member appears in the Cast window (**Figure 11.30**).

continues on next page

EDITING FLASH CAST MEMBERS

271

✔ Tips

- When you double-click a Flash cast member, if you haven't previously associated an FLA file with that cast member, Director will bring up the "Locate Flash source file for member" dialog box so you can choose one.

- If you switch back to Director while the Flash editing session is still in progress, you'll see the alert box shown in **Figure 11.31**. Don't click the Done button here—doing so will cancel the editing operation. Instead, switch back to Flash, finish editing, and then click the Done button above the Flash timeline.

Figure 11.31 This alert box appears if you switch to Director while in the process of editing a Flash cast member.

ADDING TEXT

Director MX
Regular text

Director MX
Field text

Figure 12.1 Regular text can be anti-aliased for a smoother appearance; field text can't.

A picture may be worth a thousand words, but sometimes you really *need* those thousand words. Fortunately, Director makes it easy to add words to your movies, either by importing text from other programs or by creating text within Director.

You can use three kinds of text in Director:

- **Regular text** (sometimes called *vector text*, or just plain *text*) is exactly like the text you use in word-processing programs. You can edit and format it easily, and anti-alias it for a smoother appearance (**Figure 12.1**). You can create regular text in Director or import it from ASCII, RTF, or HTML files.

- **Field text** requires less memory and downloads more quickly than regular text, but it offers few formatting options, can't be anti-aliased, and can't be imported.

continues on next page

◆ **Bitmapped text** is technically not text at all, but rather a bitmapped image that *looks* like text. It can be warped, distorted, filled with a gradient, and enhanced in numerous other ways (**Figure 12.2**). Bitmapped text created within Director can't be anti-aliased and is generally less readable than other kinds of text, but bitmapped text imported from programs such as Photoshop is often quite present-able. (The process of creating bitmapped text in Director's Paint window is explained in Chapter 6, "Using Paint Tools," and won't be covered in this chapter.)

Figure 12.2 You can create bitmapped text directly in Director's Paint window. And you can treat bitmapped text just like any other bitmapped image, rotating it or adding effects.

To decide which kind of text to use for a particular purpose, see the sidebar "Choosing the Right Text for the Job," or look at the feature-by-feature comparison in **Table 12.1**.

Table 12.1

Comparing Director's varieties of text			
	REGULAR TEXT	FIELD TEXT	BITMAPPED TEXT
Cast member size	Large	Small	Medium
Animation speed	Medium	Fast	Fastest
Word processing tools	Yes	—	—
Author can revise easily	Yes	Yes	—
Can set for users to edit during playback	Yes	Yes	—
Where it's created	Text window, Stage	Field window, Stage	Paint window
May need embedded fonts	Yes	Yes	—
Supports hyperlinks	Yes	—	—
Can be anti-aliased	Yes	—	—
Movie viewers see the same font as author, even without embedding fonts	—	—	Yes
Modifiable with paint tools/effects	—	—	Yes

Choosing the Right Text for the Job

To decide which kind of text to use in a particular situation, ask yourself these questions:

Will the text need to be formatted?

Regular text is the only kind of text that gives you control over tabs, indents, kerning, and line spacing.

Will I need to edit the text later?

Regular text and field text are editable; bitmapped text isn't.

Will I be using large-sized characters?

Text at large point sizes needs anti-aliasing to look presentable, and only regular text can be anti-aliased in Director. (However, you can create anti-aliased bitmapped text in an image-editing program such as Photoshop and then import it as an image file.)

How much text will there be?

Bitmapped text is practical for only small amounts of text. Field text and regular text work well at any length.

Will my movie be played on older, slower computers?

Field text requires the least amount of disk space, memory, and processing power.

Does the text require special effects?

Field text can be given a rudimentary drop shadow. Other than that, if you need to color text with a gradient or pattern, rotate or skew the text, or do anything else out of the ordinary, bitmapped text is your only option.

Do I plan to use the text as a hyperlink?

Only regular text can be used as a link to a Web page.

The Fourth Way: Flash

As an alternative to the three types of text Director handles, consider creating your text in Macromedia Flash and importing it as a Flash cast member. (See Chapter 11, "Using Flash Movies in Director.") Like regular text, Flash text is anti-aliased and perpetually editable. And like bitmapped text, Flash text can be rotated, skewed, stretched, and squeezed with no loss in quality (**Figure 12.3**).

Figure 12.3 As an alternative, you can create text in Flash and import it into Director. Here, this Flash text has been rotated, skewed, and stretched.

Creating and Importing Text

In Director, text (whether regular or field) can be created in either of two ways:

◆ You can type the text directly on the Stage.

◆ You can create a cast member by typing text in the Text or Field window. (Afterward, you can create a sprite by dragging the cast member from the Cast window to the Stage.)

If you want to format your text with custom tab settings or hanging indents, you'll need to use the Text window. Otherwise, typing directly on the Stage is usually more convenient.

With either method, you can type text just as you would in a word processor. You can use the Tab key to create an indent and the Return key to start a new paragraph (**Figure 12.4**).

You can also create text outside Director and then import it. Imported text automatically becomes a regular text cast member; field text can't be imported.

To create text directly on the Stage:

1. Choose Window > Text Inspector.

   The Text Inspector opens (**Figure 12.5**). (You'll use this later for setting the font, size, and other text attributes, but right now its controls are dimmed until you select the Text tool.)

2. In the Score, select the cell where you want the text sprite to begin (**Figure 12.6**).

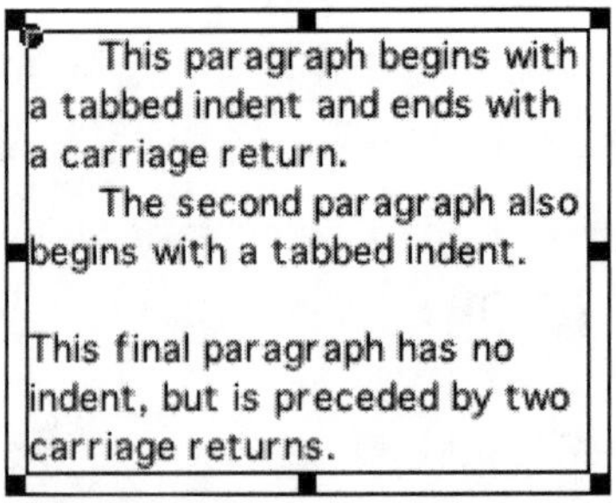

This paragraph begins with a tabbed indent and ends with a carriage return.

The second paragraph also begins with a tabbed indent.

This final paragraph has no indent, but is preceded by two carriage returns.

Figure 12.4 A text cast member may include tabbed indents and multiple paragraphs.

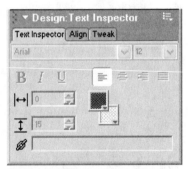

Figure 12.5 The controls in the Text Inspector remain dimmed until you start using the Text tool.

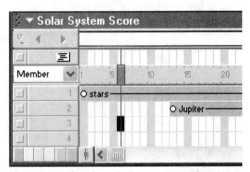

Figure 12.6 Select the cell where you want the text sprite to begin.

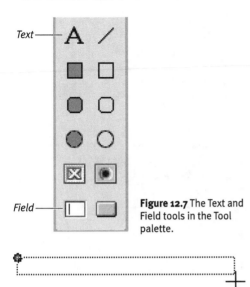

Text —

Field —

Figure 12.7 The Text and Field tools in the Tool palette.

Figure 12.8 A rectangle appears as you drag the mouse across the Stage.

3. Click the Text tool (for regular text) or the Field tool (for field text) in the Tool palette (**Figure 12.7**).

4. On the Stage, position the mouse pointer at the place where you want the text to begin.

5. Press the mouse button and drag horizontally to set the desired line length for the text.

   A rectangle appears on the Stage, serving as a bounding box for the text (**Figure 12.8**).

6. Release the mouse button.

   The border of the rectangle widens, and a flashing insertion point appears inside. At the same time, a new, empty text cast member appears in the Cast window, and the controls in the Text Inspector become active.

7. Set the font, size, style, and other attributes, using the controls in the Text Inspector (**Figure 12.9**). (See "Setting Text Attributes," later in this chapter.)

   If you wish, you can skip this step and Director will use whatever text attributes are currently set. You can change them at any time.

   continues on next page

CREATING AND IMPORTING TEXT

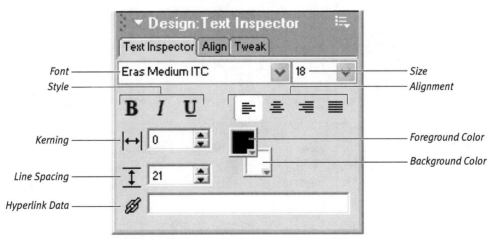

Font ——
Style ——
Kerning ——
Line Spacing ——
Hyperlink Data ——

—— Size
—— Alignment
—— Foreground Color
—— Background Color

Figure 12.9 Set attributes for the text in the Text Inspector.

8. Type the text.

If the text you type exceeds the width of the rectangle, Director automatically wraps it to a new line (**Figure 12.10**).

9. When you're finished, click anywhere on the Stage outside the rectangle.

The rectangle disappears. The text remains on the Stage, just as you typed it. The text also appears as a cast member in the Cast window (**Figure 12.11**).

To create text in the Text or Field window:

1. Choose Window > Text (for the Text window) or Window > Field (for the Field window).

The window opens (**Figures 12.12 and 12.13**).

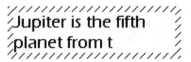

Figure 12.10 Type text inside the rectangle. Director wraps text to a new line as necessary.

Regular text cast member

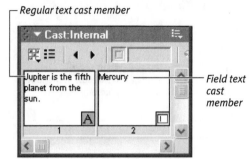

Field text cast member

Figure 12.11 When you create text on the Stage, it also appears in the Cast window.

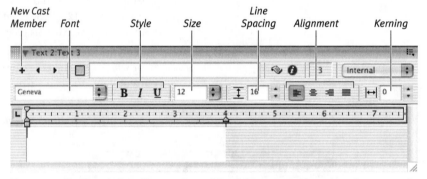

Figure 12.12 The Text window offers an alternative way to create and format text for your movie.

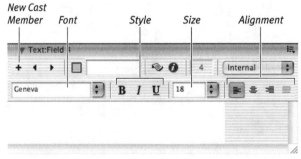

Figure 12.13 The Field window.

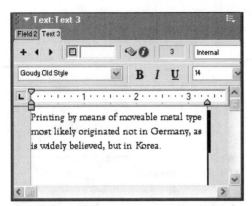

Figure 12.14 The Text and Field windows work like a word processor. Lines wrap automatically as you type.

If a text cast member is currently selected in the Cast window, that text appears in the Text or Field window when it opens.

If no text cast member is selected in the Cast window, the Text or Field window opens empty and a blank text cast member appears in the Cast window. In this case, you can skip step 2.

2. If necessary, click the New Cast Member button to empty the Text or Field window.

Doing so creates a new cast member in the Cast window.

3. Set the font, size, style, and other attributes for the text you're about to type, using the controls on the toolbar at the top of the Text or Field window. (See "Setting Text Attributes," later in this chapter.)

If you wish, you can skip this step and Director will use whatever text attributes are currently set. You can change them at any time.

4. Type the text (**Figure 12.14**).

As you type, the text appears simultaneously in the current cast member in the Cast window.

The text cast member is available for use at any time. You don't have to save the text, close the Text or Field window, or do anything else.

✔ Tip

■ To show or hide the Text or Field window's toolbar, choose View > Text Toolbar while the window is active.

CREATING AND IMPORTING TEXT

To import text:

◆ Follow the same procedure that you use to import other kinds of cast members. (See "Importing Cast Members" in Chapter 2)

You can import text from plain ASCII text files, Rich Text Format (RTF) files, and HTML files. Director preserves the formatting as much as possible.

✔ Tip

■ Tables imported from RTF and HTML documents will be preserved in Director, even though tables can't be created in Director (**Figure 12.15**).

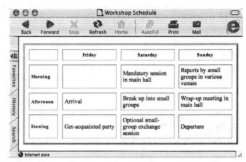

HTML file in a browser

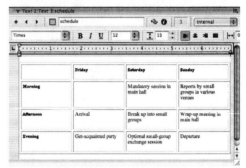

Same file imported into Director

Figure 12.15 Director does its best to preserve the formatting of imported text files, even if they include tables.

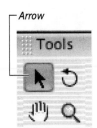

Arrow

Figure 12.16 Use the Arrow tool to select text for editing.

Editing Text

You can edit regular text either on the Stage or in the Text window, regardless of where it was created. Similarly, you can edit field text either on the Stage or in the Field window, regardless of where it was created.

You can convert either type of text to bitmapped text if you decide belatedly that you'd like to rotate it or add effects.

To edit text on the Stage:

1. Click the Arrow tool in the Tool palette (**Figure 12.16**).

2. On the Stage, double-click the text sprite that you want to edit.

   A rectangle appears around the text, and a flashing insertion point appears inside.

3. Edit the text.

4. When you're finished, click anywhere on the Stage outside the rectangle.

✔ Tips

- Any changes you make to a text sprite affect the original text cast member and all other sprites based on the same text cast member.

- If you double-click bitmapped text on the Stage, Director will open it in the Paint window, just as it would any bitmapped image.

EDITING TEXT

To edit in the Text or Field window:

1. In the Cast window, double-click a text cast member.

   Depending on which kind of cast member it is, the Text or Field window opens, displaying the text.

2. Edit the text.

   The changes you make take effect immediately; you don't have to do anything special to make them "stick."

To convert regular text or field text to bitmapped text:

1. Select a text cast member in the Cast window.

2. Choose Modify > Convert to Bitmap.

   The text becomes a bitmapped image (**Figure 12.17**).

Before

After

Figure 12.17 A line of text in the Field window (top); the same line of text converted to a bitmap and distorted in the Paint window (bottom).

EDITING TEXT

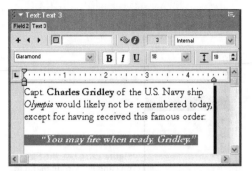

Figure 12.18 You can change the formatting of selected text within a cast member.

Formatting Text

When text is displayed in the Text or Field window, or is in editing mode on the Stage, you can make selections within the text just as you would in a word processor. Once you've selected some text, you can change its font, size, style, alignment, and color, and (for regular text only) its kerning and line spacing (**Figure 12.18**). If you want to change these attributes for an entire cast member, select all the text.

If you're editing text in the Text window, you can also change the text's tab and indent settings. These settings can't be changed on the Stage.

A number of other properties, including scrolling and anti-aliasing, can be set in the Property Inspector. These settings apply to the cast member as a whole and not to selected text within the cast member.

To format selected text:

1. Double-click a text sprite on the Stage or a text cast member in the Cast window.

   If the text cast member is on the Stage, it enters editing mode; if it's in the Cast window, it opens for editing in the Text or Field window. (See "To edit text on the Stage" or "To edit in the Text or Field window," earlier in this chapter.)

continues on next page

FORMATTING TEXT

2. Using the controls in the Text Inspector (if you're editing the text on the Stage) or on the Text toolbar (if you're editing the text in the Text or Field window), set any of the following attributes:

▲ **Font:** You can choose from any of the fonts that are installed on your computer or from any fonts that are embedded in the Director file. (See "Embedding Fonts," later in this chapter.)

▲ **Size:** Choose a point size from the pop-up menu, or type a size directly in the Size box (**Figure 12.19**).

▲ **Style:** Click the buttons to select Bold, Italic, Underlined, or any combination (**Figure 12.20**).

▲ **Alignment:** Click a button to left-align, center-align, right-align, or fully justify the text. Your choice will affect the entire paragraph in which the selected text appears (**Figure 12.21**).

▲ **Kerning** (regular text only): Use this setting to change the horizontal spacing between characters. You can click the up or down arrows to increment or decrement the value by 1, or you can just enter a number in the Kerning box. Positive values move characters farther apart; negative values move them closer together. To change the spacing between a pair of characters, select the first character only (**Figure 12.22**).

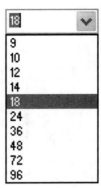

Figure 12.19 Use the Size box and its pop-up menu to adjust the size of your text.

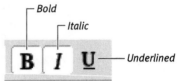

Figure 12.20 You can select any combination of style buttons (in this case, bold and italic).

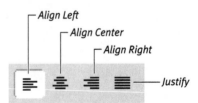

Figure 12.21 Select a button to align the selected text. Your choice will affect the entire paragraph.

Value

Before

Value

After

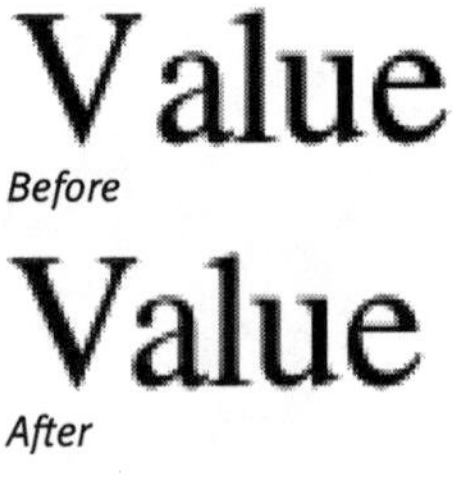

Figure 12.22 The *V* and the *a* were moved closer together by selecting the *V* and giving it a kerning value of -4.

Tours of the Paramount Theatre take place on the first and third Saturday of every month.

Default value

Tours of the Paramount Theatre take place on the first and third Saturday of every month.

Less than default

Tours of the Paramount Theatre take place on the first and third Saturday of every month.

Greater than default

Figure 12.23 Changing the Line Spacing value moves lines of text closer together or farther apart.

▲ **Line Spacing** (regular text only): Use this setting to change the vertical spacing between lines (traditionally called *leading*). You can click the up or down arrows to increment or decrement the value by 1, or enter a number in the Line Spacing box. Values higher than the default move the lines farther apart; values lower than the default move them closer together (**Figure 12.23**). If you choose a value of 0, Director will automatically restore the default value.

▲ **Color:** Text color can be changed only in the Text Inspector. However, you can use the Text Inspector to change the color of *any* text, whether it's selected on the Stage or in the Text or Field window. Select a foreground color from the Foreground Color menu and a background color from the Background Color menu. The foreground color will affect only the selected text, but the background color will affect the entire cast member (**Figure 12.24**).

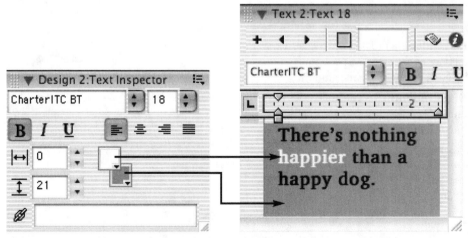

Figure 12.24 You can change the foreground color of selected text within a cast member, but your choice of background color affects the entire cast member.

To change the indent and tab settings for selected paragraphs (regular text only):

1. In the Cast window, double-click a text cast member.

   The Text window opens, displaying the text.

2. If the ruler isn't visible beneath the Text toolbar, display it by choosing View > Ruler (**Figure 12.25**).

3. Select the paragraphs whose indent or tab settings you want to change.

   Selecting any text within a paragraph will cause the indents and tabs to be changed for the entire paragraph. If you want to change the indents or tabs for only a single paragraph, you don't have to select anything; just click within the paragraph.

4. Change the indents by dragging the appropriate controls (**Figure 12.26**):

   ▲ **Left Indent** (first line only): This control causes the first line of each of the selected paragraphs to be indented by the amount you specify.

   ▲ **Left Indent** (all but first line): This control causes all lines *except* the first line of the selected paragraphs to be indented by the amount you specify.

   ▲ **Left Indent** (all): This control causes all lines of the selected paragraph to be indented by the same amount.

   ▲ **Right Indent:** This control causes all lines of the selected paragraph to be indented from the right.

   Note: The second and third controls—Left Indent (all but first line) and Left Indent (all)—move as a unit, but their effect depends on which one you drag.

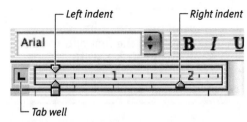

Figure 12.25 The ruler in the Text window contains controls for margin and tabs.

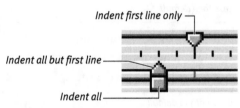

Figure 12.26 The left-indent controls.

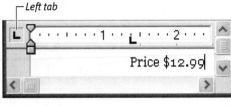

—Left tab

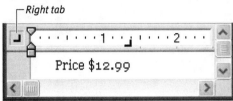

—Right tab

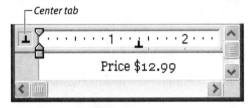

—Center tab

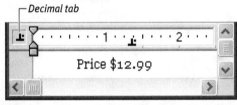

—Decimal tab

Figure 12.27 Click in the tab well until you see the icon for the type of tab you want to set.

5. To select the type of tab you want to set, click the tab well.

Click as many times as necessary. Each time you click, the icon in the tab well changes. It cycles, in order, through the Left tab, the Right tab, the Center tab, and the Decimal tab (**Figure 12.27**).

6. Click the ruler at the place where you want to set a tab.

A new tab, of the type displayed in the tab well, appears at the spot you clicked.

7. If necessary, change the tab's location by dragging it along the ruler.

✔ Tip

■ You can remove a tab by dragging it off the ruler.

To change the properties of a regular text cast member:

1. Select a text cast member in the Cast window.

2. Click the Text tab in the Property Inspector (**Figure 12.28**).

3. Change properties as desired.

You can change the following properties:

- **Display:** There are only two options on this pop-up menu: Normal, the default, displays text normally. The 3D Mode option gives the text the illusion of depth. (For information on 3D text, see Chapter 18, "Shockwave 3D.")

- **Framing:** The options on this menu determine how text is displayed in relation to its bounding box. (See the task that follows, "To adjust the dimensions of a text cast member.") The default setting, **Adjust to Fit**, causes the bounding box to expand vertically as far as necessary to display all the text (thus giving you control over the width of the bounding box, but not its height). **Fixed** allows you to adjust the bounding box to any dimensions you like, even if some of the text gets hidden as a result. **Scrolling** does the same but provides a vertical scroll bar to make the hidden text accessible (**Figure 12.29**).

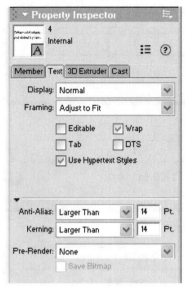

Figure 12.28 The Text tab in the Property Inspector.

```
Active Ingredient:
Ibuprofen
Inactive Ingredients:
Colloidal Silicon Dioxide,
Croscarmellose Sodium,
Hydroxpropyl
Methyl-cellulose,
Microcrystalline
Cellulose, Iron Oxides,
Corn Starch, Stearic Acid,
Titanium Dioxide.
```
Adjust to Fit

```
Active Ingredient:
Ibuprofen
Inactive Ingredients:
Colloidal Silicon Dioxide,
Croscarmellose Sodium,
Hydroxpropyl Methyl-
```
Fixed

```
Active Ingredient:
Ibuprofen
Inactive Ingredients:
Colloidal Silicon Dioxide,
Croscarmellose Sodium,
Hydroxpropyl Methyl-
```
Scrolling

Figure 12.29 A text cast member with the Adjust to Fit, Fixed, and Scrolling properties.

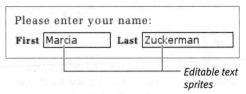

Editable text
sprites

Figure 12.30 Editable text is normally used in conjunction with Lingo scripts that allow Director to process a user's input.

◆ **Editable:** This option allows people who view your movie to enter or edit text while the movie plays. It's generally used in conjunction with a Lingo script that can process the user's input. Unless you have such a script, it's best to leave this option unselected (**Figure 12.30**).

◆ **Tab:** If the Editable option (above) is selected, the Tab option causes Director to move the insertion point to the next editable cast member when the user presses the Tab key.

◆ **Wrap:** This option, selected by default, causes text to wrap automatically when it's typed into a cast member. Unless you're using editable text in conjunction with a Lingo script (in which case Lingo can "see" the text even if it runs past the edge of the bounding box), you should always leave this option selected.

◆ **DTS:** DTS stands for Direct to Stage. When this option is selected, the text cast member is placed in front of the Stage instead of interacting with other sprites on the Stage. Ink effects and the Blend property don't work when DTS is turned on, and motion tweening may not work properly. However, by reducing the load on the computer's processor, this option may improve the playback performance of your movie.

◆ **Use Hypertext Styles:** This option is selected by default. If the cast member contains hyperlinked text, this option causes the links to change color when they're clicked, as the links in a Web browser do. (See "Creating Hyperlinked Text," later in this chapter.)

continues on next page

- **Anti-Alias:** This pop-up menu tells Director which text to anti-alias. The default is **Larger Than**, which tells Director to anti-alias text only if it's larger than a specified point size. (The default is 14 points, as shown in **Figure 12.31**, but you can enter a different value in the Points box). The **All Text** option anti-aliases all text in a cast member regardless of its point size, but this is generally a bad idea, because anti-aliasing can make small-sized text difficult to read (**Figure 12.32**). The **None** option turns off anti-aliasing for the cast member. (Note to Mac users: Even when anti-aliasing is turned off in Director, the Mac operating system may apply its own anti-aliasing.)

- **Kerning:** This pop-up menu tells Director when to apply kerning rules that adjust the spacing between certain combinations of characters. The option you choose here affects the entire cast member, unlike the kerning settings you may apply to selected text. (See "To change the attributes of selected text," earlier in this chapter.) The Kerning pop-up menu is identical to that for the Anti-Alias property (**Figure 12.33**). As with anti-aliasing, kerning small-sized text often reduces readability.

- **Pre-Render:** Applying anti-aliasing to text requires a good deal of processing power. When a large amount of anti-aliased text appears on the Stage, playback of the movie may slow down. By selecting a pre-render option, you can tell Director to prepare the text for display *before* it appears on the Stage, thus improving play-back speed. Select the **Copy Ink** option to pre-render a cast member whose sprite will have the default Copy ink effect applied. Select the **Other Ink** option to pre-render a cast member whose sprite will have any other ink effect applied. Select **None** to turn off pre-rendering.

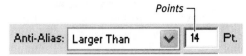

Points

Figure 12.31 The default setting for the Anti-Alias property tells Director to anti-alias text within a cast member only if it's larger than 14 points.

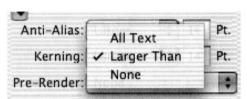

With anti-aliasing

Without anti-aliasing

Figure 12.32 A sample of 10-point text, with and without anti-aliasing. The anti-aliased text is more difficult to read.

Figure 12.33 The Kerning pop-up menu is identical to the Anti-Alias pop-up menu.

FORMATTING TEXT

Figure 12.34 The Field tab in the Property Inspector.

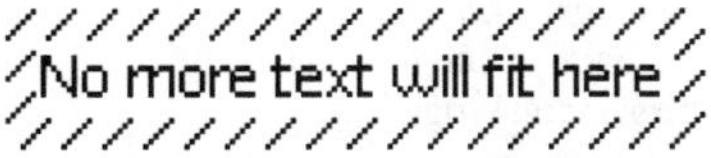

Figure 12.35 The Limit to Field Size property limits the amount of text that can be typed into a field text cast member.

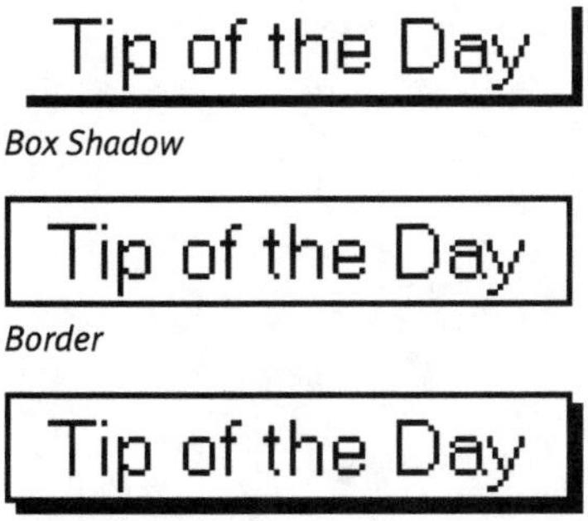

Tip of the Day

Box Shadow

Tip of the Day

Border

Tip of the Day

Box Shadow and Border

Figure 12.36 Field text with a box shadow, a border, and both.

To change the properties of a field text cast member:

1. Select a field text cast member in the Cast window.

2. Click the Field tab in the Property Inspector (**Figure 12.34**).

3. Change the following properties as desired:

   ▲ **Framing:** The first three options on this pop-up menu—**Adjust to Fit**, **Scrolling**, and **Fixed**—are identical to those on the Text tab of the Property Inspector. (See "To change the properties of a regular text cast member," above.) The last option, **Limit to Field Size**, allows only as much text to be entered as can fit in the cast member's bounding box (**Figure 12.35**).

   ▲ **Editable, Wrap, and Tab:** These options are identical to those on the Text tab of the Property Inspector. (See "To change the properties of a regular text cast member," above.)

   ▲ **Box Shadow:** This option allows you to add a simple drop shadow—in the form of black lines to the right and underneath—to a field text cast member's bounding box. It looks best if the Border option (see below) is also selected (**Figure 12.36**). The pop-up menu gives you a range of 1 to 5 pixels for the width of the shadow, or **None** for no shadow.

   continues on next page

FORMATTING TEXT

▲ **Border:** This option places a border around the cast member's bounding box. The pop-up menu, offering a width selection of 1 to 5 pixels (or **None** for no border), is identical to that for the Box Shadow property (above) and the Drop Shadow and Margin properties (below) (**Figure 12.37**).

▲ **Drop Shadow:** This option allows you to add a simple drop shadow to the text within a field text cast member. It looks better with larger-sized text. The drop shadow consists of a copy of the text, in black, offset by 1 to 5 pixels (**Figure 12.38**). Choose **None** if you don't want a drop shadow.

▲ **Margin:** This option sets the distance between the text and the edges of the bounding box from 0 pixels (**None**) to 5 pixels (**Figure 12.39**).

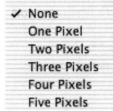

Figure 12.37 The Box Shadow, Border, Drop Shadow, and Margin properties all have identical pop-up menus.

Figure 12.38 Field text with a 2-pixel drop shadow.

No margin   5-pixel margin

Figure 12.39 Field text with the Border option selected, with no margin (left) and with a 5-pixel margin (right).

FORMATTING TEXT

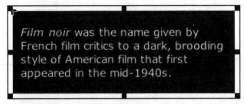

Before

After

Figure 12.40 As you change the size of the bounding box, Director automatically rewraps the text.

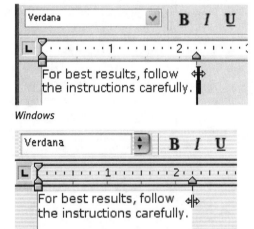

Windows

Mac

Figure 12.41 Drag the right side of the white rectangle to change the width of the cast member. In Windows, the boundary is marked by a heavy black bar (top); on the Mac (bottom), it's not.

To adjust the dimensions of a text cast member:

1. Select a text sprite (either regular or field text) on the Stage.

2. Drag any of its resize handles to change the dimensions of the sprite's bounding box.

   If the Adjust to Fit option is selected for this cast member (see the description of the Framing property in "To change the properties of a regular text cast member" or "To change the properties of a field text cast member," above), you'll only be able to resize the box horizontally, not vertically.

   The text will automatically rewrap as you change the size of the box (**Figure 12.40**). Any changes you make to the dimensions of the text sprite will be applied to the original cast member.

   or

1. Double-click a text cast member in the Cast window.

   The Text or Field window opens, displaying the text.

2. Position the mouse pointer over the right edge of the white rectangle that encloses the text.

   The mouse pointer becomes a double-headed arrow (**Figure 12.41**).

3. Drag left or right to change the width of the cast member.

   You can't change the height of the cast member in the Text window; that can only be done on the Stage.

Embedding Fonts

When you add a regular text or field text cast member to a movie, Director uses the fonts installed on your computer. When you distribute your movie, Director will look for those same fonts on the computer it's being played on. If those fonts aren't available, Director will substitute a different font—generally Arial (on a PC) or Geneva (on a Mac)—greatly diminishing the artistic quality of your movie (**Figure 12.42**).

One way to prevent such substitutions is to use only common fonts in your movie (such as Times, Arial, and Courier) that are likely to be found on every computer. However, that may cramp your style. A more palatable solution is to *embed* fonts in the movie. When you embed a font, Director compresses the font outline that's used to display characters in the font and stores it as a cast member. Thereafter, Director can always use it to display text in the movie, even if the font isn't installed on the user's computer. Embedded fonts work equally well on Macs and PCs, regardless of which platform the fonts originated on.

The drawback to embedding fonts is that each font you embed adds significantly to your movie's file size, often adding as much as 25K. Therefore, when possible, it's a good idea to embed only a part of a font. (For example, if you don't use any numbers, don't embed the font's numerals.) If you want to be really parsimonious, you can embed only the characters that are used in your movie.

THE REAL DEAL

Your computer

The Real Deal

Someone else's computer

Figure 12.42 A text sprite using an exotic font (above), and the same sprite—displayed with a substitute font—on a computer that doesn't have the specified font installed (below).

Flash Talk: Font Embedding

When you publish a movie in Flash, Flash automatically embeds all the fonts used in the movie in the SWF file—and does so in a "smart" way, embedding only the characters that are used in the movie. By contrast, Director requires that you embed fonts manually and that you manually specify which characters to embed.

Though Director's way is obviously less convenient than Flash's, it has a significant advantage. Flash allows fonts to be embedded only in the SWF file, not in the authoring (FLA) file. If you pass your FLA file to someone else, you have to supply the fonts as well. Director allows fonts to be embedded in the authoring (DIR) file, so they so they're always available when you're working on a movie, even if the file is passed from one computer to another. When you create a Shockwave or projector file to distribute your movie, any fonts embedded in the DIR file are automatically passed on to the distribution files.

EMBEDDING FONTS

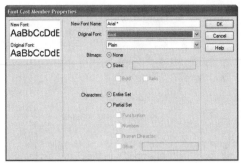

Figure 12.43 The Font Cast Member Properties dialog box is used to embed fonts.

Figure 12.44 Choose the font you want to embed from the Original Font pop-up menu, which lists all the fonts on your computer.

Figure 12.45 Choose the specific style of the font you want to embed.

Figure 12.46 The font and style that you've chosen to embed are displayed in the New Font Name field, followed by an asterisk.

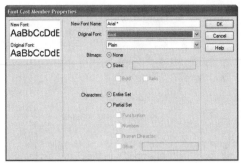

Figure 12.47 If you want Director to embed bitmaps, type the desired point sizes, separated by commas.

To embed a font:

1. Choose Insert > Media Element > Font. The Font Cast Member Properties dialog box opens (**Figure 12.43**).

2. From the Original Font pop-up menu— which lists all the fonts available on your computer—choose the font you want to embed (**Figure 12.44**).

   The font you select appears in the New Font Name field at the top of the dialog box, followed by an asterisk. (The asterisk after the font name is Director's standard way to indicate an embedded font.)

3. If the selected font has custom styles, such as Bold, Italic, or Bold Italic, choose the specific style you want to embed from the pop-up menu below the Original Font menu (**Figure 12.45**). (The regular, roman version of a font is listed as Plain.)

   If you choose a style other than Plain, it appears after the font name in the New Font Name field (**Figure 12.46**).

4. If you want to give the embedded font a new name, edit the name in the New Font Name field. (Unless you have a good reason to rename the font, it's a good idea to leave the name as is, to help you identify the embedded font in the future.)

5. If you want to embed bitmapped versions of the font (in addition to the normal font outline), select the Sizes option under Bitmaps and list the sizes for which you want to embed bitmaps (**Figure 12.47**).

   Embedding bitmaps sometimes improves the readability of a font at small sizes, but it adds significantly to the file size. In most cases, you'll want to choose None.

6. Indicate whether you want to embed the entire font or only part of the font by clicking either Entire Set or Partial Set.

continues on next page

EMBEDDING FONTS

7. If you chose Partial Set in step 6, indicate which parts of the font you want to embed by selecting Punctuation, Numbers, Roman Characters, or Other. (You can select any number of these options.)

If you select Other, list the specific characters you want to embed (**Figure 12.48**). List each character only once, no matter how many times it appears on your movie. If your text cast members include spaces, be sure to include a space here (unless you've also selected Punctuation).

8. Click OK to close the dialog box.

The embedded font appears in the Cast window (**Figure 12.49**).

✔ Tip

■ Once you've embedded a font, be sure to choose the embedded font from the Font menu when you create text cast members (**Figure 12.50**). If you created text cast members before you embedded the font, go back and change them to use the embedded font.

To edit the properties of an embedded font:

1. Double-click the embedded font in the Cast window.

The Font Cast Member Properties dialog box opens.

2. Change any of the settings you made when you embedded the font.

3. Click OK to close the dialog box.

✔ Tip

■ It's usually a good idea to embed an entire font while you're working on a movie, so you'll have all the characters at your disposal. Then, when the movie is finished, edit the embedded font, choose the Other option, and list only the characters you ended up using in your movie.

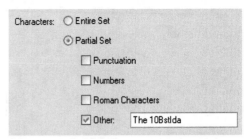

Figure 12.48 Selecting the Other option gives you the opportunity to embed only the characters that are used in the movie.

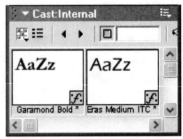

Figure 12.49 Embedded fonts in the Cast window.

Figure 12.50 Once you've embedded a font, make sure your text cast members *use* the font by selecting it from the Font menu.

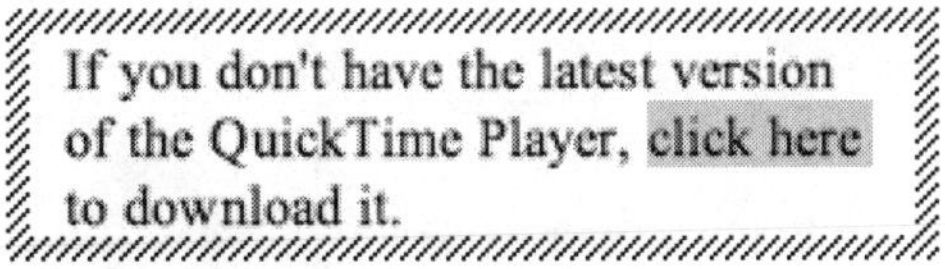

If you don't have the latest version
of the QuickTime Player, click here
to download it.

Figure 12.51 Select the portion of text that you want to turn into a hyperlink.

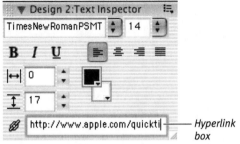

Design 2:Text Inspector
TimesNewRomanPSMT
14
B I U
0
17
http://www.apple.com/quickti
Hyperlink box

Figure 12.52 Type the URL or other message in the hyperlink box at the bottom of the Text Inspector.

If you don't have the latest version
of the QuickTime Player, click here
to download it.

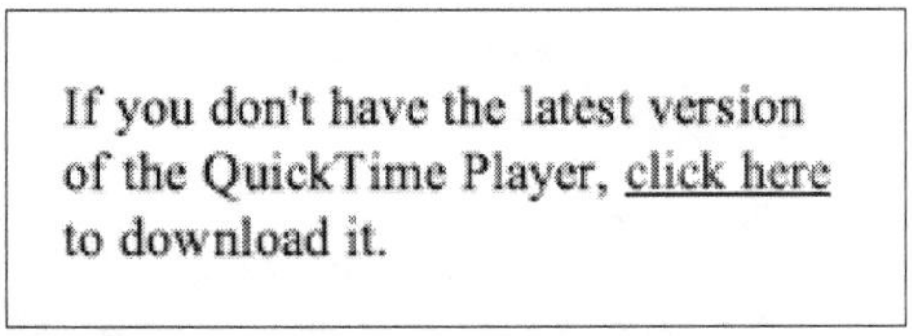

Figure 12.53 Text formatted as a hyperlink is blue and underlined.

Creating Hyperlinked Text

Any text within a regular text cast member can be made into a *hyperlink*, similar to the text links on a Web page. Assuming that the Use Hypertext Styles property is selected for the cast member (as it is by default), Director applies the Web's standard link formatting to the text: The link appears underlined, with a blue color before it's been clicked and a purple color after.

For anything to happen when the user clicks the link, you must assign the Text > Hypertext - General behavior to the cast member, or write an equivalent Lingo script. (See Chapter 14, "Adding Behaviors.") The behavior will cause the link to go to a Web URL or perform some other action.

To format text as a hyperlink:

1. Double-click a regular text sprite on the Stage or a regular text cast member in the Cast window.

   If the text cast member is on the Stage, it enters editing mode; if it's in the Cast window, it opens for editing in the Text window. (See "To edit text on the Stage" or "To edit in the Text or Field window," earlier in this chapter.)

2. Select the portion of text that you want to make into a hyperlink (**Figure 12.51**).

3. If the Text Inspector isn't currently open, Choose Window > Text Inspector to display it.

4. In the hyperlink box at the bottom of the Text Inspector, type the URL that you want to send to the Lingo script (**Figure 12.52**).

5. Press Enter.

   The selected text is formatted as a hyperlink (**Figure 12.53**).

13

ADDING SOUND

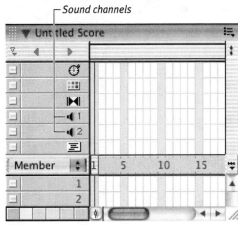

Sound channels

Figure 13.1 The Score has two channels intended only for sound sprites.

Sounds—including music, narration, and sound effects—can bring your Director movie to life. Adding sounds to Director movies is easy: You simply import a sound file and place it in one of the two sound channels in the Score (**Figure 13.1**).

Director offers very limited sound-recording capability (on the Mac only) and no sound-editing capability. In most cases, you'll want to use a third-party sound-editing program to record and edit the sound before you bring it into Director. If you're serious about sound, you'll probably want professional-level recording and editing software such as Digidesign's Pro Tools. In the middle range, there are capable sound-editing programs such as Sonic Foundry's Sound Forge, Bias's Peak LE, and SoundEdit 16 (a Macromedia product that's no longer being developed but is still on the market). In a pinch, you can use the Sound Recorder application that comes with Windows for rudimentary sound editing. You can also find a variety of inexpensive or free sound-editing programs on the Web.

Once you've prepared your sound files, this chapter will show you how to import them, synchronize them to animation in the Score, and compress them for faster download. You'll also learn how certain sound files can be streamed over the Web.

Importing and Previewing Sound Files

You can import most commonly used sound file formats into Director, including AIFF, WAV, AU, Shockwave Audio, and MP3 (**Figure 13.2**). Macromedia recommends using sounds with an 8- or 16-bit depth and with a sampling rate of 11.025 kHz, 22.050 kHz, or 44.1 kHz.

To import a sound file:

◆ Follow the same procedure that you use to import other kinds of cast members. (See "Importing Cast Members" in Chapter 2.)

Director handles internal and external sounds differently when a movie is played, so keep the following guidelines in mind when deciding whether to choose Standard Import or Link to External File:

▲ Standard Import embeds the sound file in your Director movie. When you play a movie that contains an embedded sound file, Director must load the entire sound into memory before playing it. If the sound file is large, the loading time may produce a pause in the playback of your movie. Therefore, it's best to use Standard Import only for small sound files.

▲ Link to External File allows a sound file to be *streamed*—that is, the beginning of the sound file starts to play even while the rest of the sound is loading. Streaming allows a sound to play without delay and is therefore appropriate for larger files. However, the playback of linked external sounds may not be as smooth as that of embedded sounds.

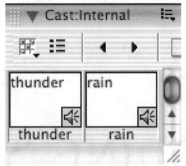

Figure 13.2 No matter what their original file format, sound cast members all look the same in the Cast window. (The cast member on the left is an AIFF file; the one on the right is an MP3 file.)

Figure 13.3 When importing a sound as a linked external file, don't use the Internet button.

✔ **Tip**

■ When you're importing a sound as a linked external file, don't use the Internet button in the Import Files dialog box (**Figure 13.3**). If you do, Director will import the file but will lose the link when the movie is closed. Instead, to use an external sound file located at a URL, follow the instructions in "Using Streaming Sounds" later in this chapter.

Inserted and Streaming Sounds

Before we go any further, it's important to sort out some confusing terminology—specifically, Director's use of *inserted* and *streaming* in regard to its handling of sounds.

An *inserted sound* is any sound file imported by means of the standard import procedure noted on the previous page and described thoroughly in Chapter 2. An inserted sound may be either embedded in the Director movie file or linked to an external file. If it's linked to an external file, the file must be local—that is, directly accessible via a relative path (in practice, this usually means that it's somewhere on the same computer).

A *streaming sound* is a Shockwave Audio or MP3 file that Director accesses from a URL or via an absolute path. That means the file may be anywhere—on the same computer or halfway around the world. The file is imported by a special procedure described in "Using Streaming Sound," later in this chapter.

Despite the difference in their names, both kinds of sound files may, in fact, stream. If an inserted sound is linked to an external file on a local disk, it will stream from the disk. If it's part of a streaming Shockwave movie (see Chapter 17, "Making Movies for the Web"), it will stream along with the rest of the movie.

What's different about the type of sound that Director refers to as a *streaming sound* is that it streams directly from the specified URL, independent of the streaming of the rest of the Director movie.

In general, when we talk about sound in this book, we're talking about inserted sound files. *Streaming sound*, in Director's use of the term, is a special case that will be discussed in "Using Streaming Sound," later in this chapter.

To preview a sound:

1. In the Cast window, select a sound cast member.

2. Click the Sound tab in the Property Inspector (**Figure 13.4**).

3. Click the Play button in the Property Inspector.

4. To stop the preview, click the Stop button in the Property Inspector.

✔ Tip

- In addition to letting you preview the sound, the Property Inspector gives you information about its duration, sampling rate, and bit depth, and whether it's a stereo or mono sound.

To set the playback volume of a sound:

1. On the Control Panel (or on the secondary control panel attached to the bottom of the Stage), click the Volume button (**Figure 13.5**).

2. Select a volume level from the pop-up menu.

✔ Tip

- The volume setting in the Control Panel applies to the entire movie, including sounds played on the Stage and previewed in the Property Inspector. It applies only at the time the movie is being played. If you want to apply volume settings that "stick" when the movie is saved, you must use Lingo.

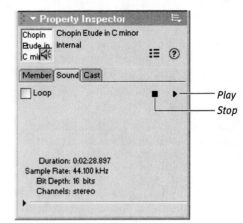

Figure 13.4 The Sound tab in the Property Inspector.

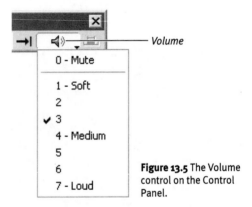

Figure 13.5 The Volume control on the Control Panel.

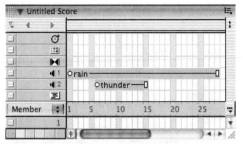

Figure 13.6 By placing sound sprites in both sound channels, you can have two sounds play at the same time—like rain and thunder, for example.

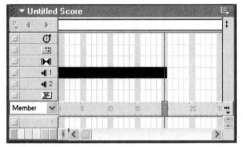

Figure 13.7 Select the frames in the Score where you want the sound sprite to go.

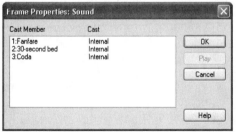

Figure 13.8 The Frame Properties: Sound dialog box.

Working with Sound Sprites

The Score contains two sound channels in which sprites can be placed. It doesn't matter which channel you use for a particular sound sprite; the sound will play the same way in either channel. If you place sprites in both channels, you can have two sounds play at the same time (**Figure 13.6**). (Director actually allows eight sounds to play at the same time, but the additional six sound channels can be accessed only via Lingo.)

Sound sprites, like digital video sprites, have time-based content, and therefore the same ground rules apply:

◆ Every sound file has a fixed duration that's independent of the tempo of the Director movie.

◆ When the playhead enters a sound sprite in the Score, the content of the sound begins to play. It continues to play until either the playhead leaves the sprite or the duration of the sound file is reached, whichever comes first.

◆ If the duration of the sprite is less than the duration of the sound file, you'll hear only part of the sound.

For a more thorough discussion of these issues, see "Working with Video Sprites" in Chapter 10.

To turn a sound cast member into a sprite:

1. In the Score, select the frames in a sound channel where you want to place the sound (**Figure 13.7**).

2. Choose Modify > Frame > Sound.

   The Frame Properties: Sound dialog box opens, displaying all the sound cast members in the movie (**Figure 13.8**).

continues on next page

WORKING WITH SOUND SPRITES

3. From the list in the dialog box, select the sound you want to place in the Score.

   If you don't remember what a particular sound sounds like, you can click Play to preview it.

4. Click OK to place the selected sound in the Score.

   The sprite occupies the frames you selected in step 1 (**Figure 13.9**).

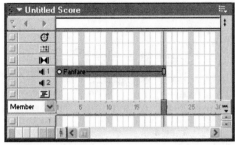

Figure 13.9 The sound sprite occupies the frames you selected in the Score.

✔ Tip

- You can drag a sound directly into one of the Score's sound channels from a Cast window, just as you would with other types of cast members. When you do so, you get a sound sprite that's 28 frames long (or whatever duration you're previously chosen—see "To change the default sprite duration" in Chapter 3).

To play a sound for a fixed amount of time (regardless of the duration of the sound file):

1. For a particular sound sprite in the Score, decide how long you want the sound to play.

   For this example, let's assume you want to hear the sound for 2 seconds.

2. Multiply the number of seconds from step 1 by the current tempo of the movie. (See "Setting a Movie's Tempo" in Chapter 5.)

   Let's assume the current tempo is 15 frames per second (fps). In that case, 2 times 15 equals 30.

3. Extend the sound sprite in the Score to span the number of frames you arrived at in step 2.

   In this case, you'd make the sprite 30 frames long.

Figure 13.10 A 2-second sprite in a movie whose tempo is 15 fps. If the sprite's audio file is 4 seconds long, only half of the audio content will be heard.

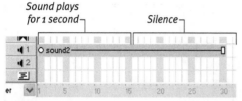

Figure 13.11 A 2-second sprite in a movie whose tempo is 15 fps. If the sprite's audio file is 1 second long, the sound will be heard in its entirety, followed by 1 second of silence.

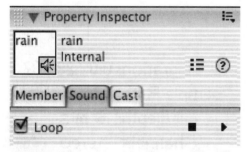

Figure 13.12 The Loop option on the Sound tab in the Property Inspector.

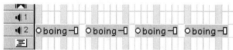

Figure 13.13 You can repeat a sound by placing it in the Score multiple times. Make sure to separate the sprites by at least one frame.

4. Play the movie.

When the playhead enters the sound sprite, the sound begins to play. If the sprite's sound file has a duration of more than 2 seconds, only the first 2 seconds of the content is heard (**Figure 13.10**).

If the sprite's sound file has a duration of less than 2 seconds, the audio content of the video file is heard in its entirety, followed by silence (**Figure 13.11**).

To loop a sprite's audio content:

1. In the Score, extend the sprite so that its duration is longer than that of the sprite's audio content.

The longer the sprite, the more times the video content will repeat.

2. Click the Sound tab in the Property Inspector.

If there is no Sound tab, select the sound sprite in the Score (or its corresponding cast member in the Cast window) to make the tab available.

3. Select the Loop option in the Property Inspector (**Figure 13.12**).

4. Play the movie.

The sound begins to play when the playhead enters the sprite and repeats until the playhead leaves the sprite.

✔ Tip

■ You can also repeat a sound by placing multiple copies of a sound sprite next to one another in the Score (**Figure 13.13**). For this technique to work, you must separate the sprites by at least one frame. Separating the sprites tells Director to start playing the sound again at the start of each sprite.

To make a sound sprite play its full audio content just once:

♦ In the Score, place a Wait for Cue Point command in the tempo channel in the sound sprite's last frame, using {End} as the cue point (**Figure 13.14**). (For details, see the "Using Cue Points" sidebar in Chapter 5; see also the "Synchronizing Sound to Actions" section later in this chapter.)

  or

1. Select the sound sprite in the Score.

2. In the Property Inspector, click the Sound tab.

3. If the Loop option is selected in the Property Inspector, deselect it.

   While you're in the Property Inspector, look at the value for Duration (**Figure 13.15**). It's displayed to the thousandth of a second, but you'll probably want to round it to the nearest second, since sprite durations are not an exact science.

4. Multiply the sound file's duration (in seconds) by the current tempo of your Director movie (in frames per second).

5. Extend the sound sprite in the Score to span *more than* the number of frames you arrived at in step 4.

   Since the Loop option is turned off, adding more frames to the sprite does no harm, and it adds an extra cushion in case the actual tempo of your movie is less than the target tempo.

✔ Tip

■ If you're using music as a background, instead of playing one long sound file all the way through, it's usually a better idea to take a smaller chunk of music and loop it. (See "To loop a sprite's audio content" on the previous page.) Doing so keeps your file size down, reduces download time, and improves playback performance.

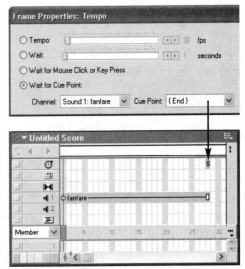

Figure 13.14 This Wait for Cue Point command will cause the Director movie to pause until the sound sprite has played in its entirety.

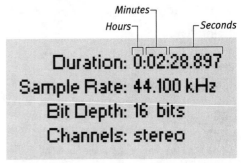

Figure 13.15 The duration of a sound cast member, as displayed on the Sound tab in the Property Inspector.

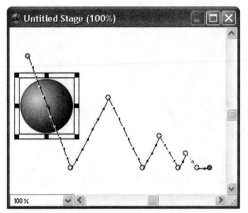

Figure 13.16 An animated ball bounces on the Stage. To synchronize the sound of the bouncing ball with the animation, you must first make note of each frame in the Score in which the ball hits the floor.

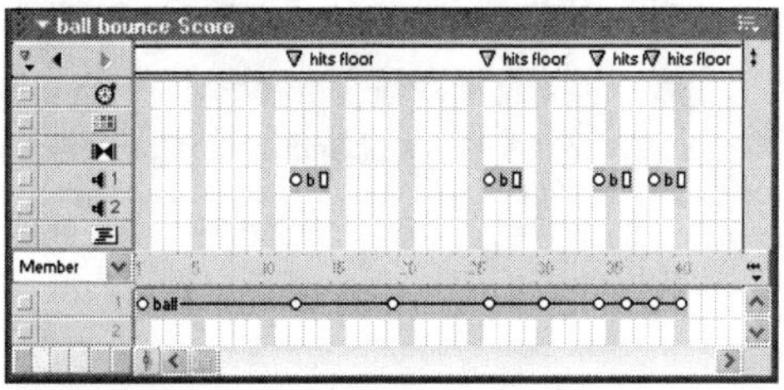

Figure 13.17 Sprites representing the ball-bounce sound effect have been placed in a sound channel. Each sprite begins in a frame in which the ball hits the floor.

Synchronizing Sound to Actions

Most sounds in Director movies don't need to be precisely synchronized. If you have background music playing while action is happening on the Stage, it usually doesn't matter whether particular points in the music coincide with particular points in the action.

Occasionally, however, you *do* want sounds to be synchronized with events on the Stage. For example, you may have an animation of a ball bouncing, and you want an impact sound to be heard each time the ball hits the floor (**Figure 13.16**). In this case, you can note the frames in which the ball hits the floor, and place a sound sprite in each of those frames (**Figure 13.17**). Though this technique works well with brief sounds, it doesn't work nearly as well with longer sounds, which often take an unpredictable amount of time to load into memory or to begin streaming.

Because of the ways tempo and loading times vary from computer to computer, it's a good idea to avoid situations where you need to synchronize longer sound files to action on the Stage. If you do need to synchronize sound precisely to animation, you might consider exporting your movie as a QuickTime file. (See the sidebar "Exporting an Animation Sequence as a QuickTime File" later in this chapter.)

You'll find it much easier to do the opposite—synchronize action on the Stage to a sound track. Through the use of cue points, you can make the playhead pause and wait for a particular point in a sound file, then resume playing when that point is reached. (See the sidebar "Using Cue Points" in Chapter 5.)

If you don't have access to one of the third-party programs that allow you to insert cue points in a sound file, you can achieve a similar result by using any sound-editing program to divide the sound file into smaller segments. Then, in Director, you can synchronize your action to the {End} cue point for each segment.

To synch animation to sound by using cue points:

1. Using a third-party program, create cue points in your sound file at the points where visual elements of your movie need to be synchronized to the sound (**Figure 13.18**).

   The Windows programs that allow you to insert cue points are Sound Forge 4.0 or later, or Cool Edit 96 or later. On the Mac you can use SoundEdit 16 version 2.07 or later, or Peak LE 2 or later. (In some of these programs, cue points are called Markers.)

2. Save the sound file in WAV format (Windows) or AIFF or Shockwave Audio format (Mac).

3. Import the sound file into Director. (See "Importing and Previewing Sound Files" at the beginning of this chapter.)

   The sound file appears in the Cast window.

4. If you haven't done so already, create the animation that will be synchronized to the cue points in the sound file.

   Include natural places for the animation to pause while Director waits for a cue point (**Figure 13.19**). Be sure that each portion of the animation is shorter than the corresponding portion of the sound file, so there's time to include a pause.

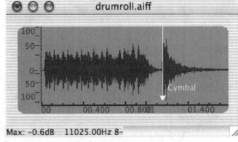

Figure 13.18 This is a window in Peak LE, displaying a sound file containing a drum roll followed by a cymbal crash. A cue point has been placed at the beginning of the cymbal crash.

Figure 13.19 In this animation sequence of a rabbit being pulled out of a hat, you can see that once the hand is fully in the hat, the animation will pause until the end of the drum roll.

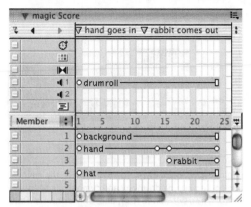

Figure 13.20 The drum-roll sound sprite containing the cymbal cue point is placed in the Score, with its first and last frames corresponding with the first and last frames of the animation.

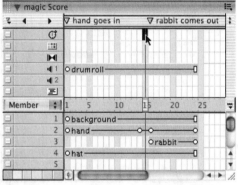

Figure 13.21 In the tempo channel, double-click the frame in which you want the animation to pause.

Figure 13.22 The cue point settings for the cymbal crash in the Frame Properties: Tempo dialog box.

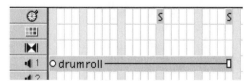

Figure 13.23 There are now two Wait for Cue Point commands in the Tempo channel: one to pause the animation before the cymbal crash, the other to pause it at the end so that the sound file can play to completion.

5. Drag the sound cast member to either of the two sound channels in the Score, placing its first frame wherever you want the sound to start in the movie.

6. Drag the last frame of the sound sprite to line up with the last frame of the corresponding animation (**Figure 13.20**).

7. In the tempo channel of the Score, double-click the frame where you want the playhead to pause and wait for a cue point (**Figure 13.21**).

   The Frame Properties: Tempo dialog box opens.

8. Choose the Wait for Cue Point option (**Figure 13.22**).

9. From the Channel pop-up menu, choose the sound channel that contains the sound sprite.

10. From the Cue Point pop-up menu, choose the cue point to wait for.

11. Click OK to close the dialog box.

12. Repeat steps 7 through 11 for each additional cue point to which you want to synchronize an action.

    If nothing else, you'll probably want to place a Wait for Cue Point command in the last frame of the sound sprite, using {End} as the cue point, so that the sound file can play to completion (**Figure 13.23**).

13. Rewind and play the movie.

    The playhead pauses at each frame where you inserted a Wait for Cue Point command, and resumes playing when the specified cue point is reached in the sound file.

SYNCHRONIZING SOUND TO ACTIONS

To synch animation to sound without using cue points:

1. Using any third-party sound-editing program, divide your sound file into individual segments. Make the divisions at the points where visual elements of your movie need to be synchronized to the sound (**Figure 13.24**).

2. Save the segments as individual sound files in any format that Director can import.

3. Import the sound files into Director. The sound files appear in the Cast window.

4. If you haven't done so already, create the animation that will be synchronized to the segmented sound file.

   Be sure that each portion of the animation is shorter than the corresponding segment of the sound file, so there's time to include a pause.

5. Drag the sound cast members, in sequence, to either of the two sound channels in the Score.

6. Drag the last frame of each sound sprite to line up with the last frame of the corresponding animation (**Figure 13.25**).

Figure 13.24 In Windows Sound Recorder, the sound file containing the drum roll and cymbal has been divided into two sound files, one for the drum roll and one for the cymbal.

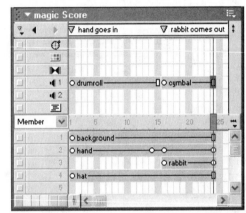

Figure 13.25 The drum roll and cymbal sound sprites together in the Score. The last frame of the drum roll sprite is dragged to the frame where the animation is intended to pause. The last frame of the cymbal sprite is dragged to the last frame of the animation.

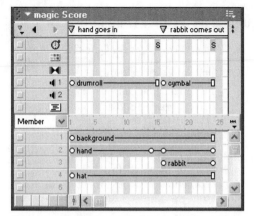

Figure 13.26 A Wait for Cue Point command corresponds with the end of each sound sprite.

7. In the tempo channel of the Score, double-click the frame in which the first sound sprite ends.

   The Frame Properties: Tempo dialog box opens.

8. Choose the Wait for Cue Point option.

9. From the Channel pop-up menu, choose the sound channel that contains the sound sprite.

10. From the Cue Point pop-up menu, choose {End}.

11. Click OK to close the dialog box.

12. Repeat steps 7 through 11 for each additional sound sprite (**Figure 13.26**).

13. Rewind and play the movie.

    The playhead pauses at each frame where you inserted the Wait for Cue Point command, and resumes playing when the corresponding sound file comes to an end.

Exporting an Animation Sequence as a QuickTime File

If you have a movie that relies on precise correspondence between animation and sound, you may be unpleasantly surprised when you test the movie on other hardware. Because the tempo of a Director movie varies from computer to computer (see "Comparing Target Tempo with Actual Tempo" in Chapter 5), the synchronization that seemed perfect on your computer may be a mess on someone else's.

It this situation, one option you might consider is exporting your animation sequence as a QuickTime file. By doing so, you capture the movie exactly as it plays on your computer and "freeze" it in QuickTime format—which, unlike Director, is designed to keep the video and audio tracks in perfect sync at all times.

To export a QuickTime file, do the following:

1. In the Score, select the frames that you want to export.

   (If you want to export the entire movie, you can skip this step.)

2. Choose File > Export. The Export dialog box opens (**Figure 13.27**).

3. Under Export, choose Selected Frames (if you selected frames in step 1) or All Frames (if you didn't).

4. Under Format, choose QuickTime movie.

5. Click the Options button.
   The QuickTime Options dialog box opens (**Figure 13.28**).

6. Under Frame Rate, choose Real Time.

7. *(optional)* Set the other QuickTime export options as desired. (See the Director documentation or Help menu for details.)

8. Click OK.
   The QuickTime Options dialog box closes.

9. In the Export dialog box, click Export.
   A Save As dialog box appears.

10. Choose a name and location for the QuickTime file and click Save.
    An alert box appears, warning you to disable any screensavers.

11. Click OK to close the alert box.
    Director switches to full-screen mode, plays the animation, and captures it to QuickTime. The new QuickTime file appears in the location you specified in step 10.

You can now import the QuickTime file into your Director movie and use it to replace the animated scene. (Be sure to save the original first!)

Figure 13.27 The Export dialog box.

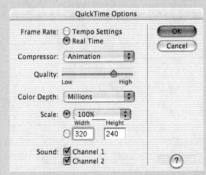

Figure 13.28 The QuickTime Options dialog box appears.

music.wav
1,286 KB

music.swa
177 KB
Macromedia Director Shockwave

Figure 13.29 Two music files displayed in Windows: a standard WAV file (above), and the same piece of music compressed in Shockwave Audio format (below). Note the significant difference in file sizes.

Compressing Sounds

The Shockwave Audio (SWA) format was originally developed as a way to compress sound cast members in Director movies. It reduces sound cast members to as little as one-twelfth of their original size, with minimal loss in sound quality (**Figure 13.29**).

Sound cast members embedded in a Director movie file are automatically compressed in SWA format when you publish your Director movie as a Shockwave movie. (See Chapter 17, "Making Movies for the Web.") The same is true when you create a projector file, but only if the Compress (Shockwave format) option is selected in the Projector Options dialog box. (See Chapter 16, "Creating a Projector.") The only exceptions in both cases are sound cast members that are already compressed, such as MP3 files.

SWA compression of embedded cast members is one-size-fits-all. You can't choose different settings for different cast members, or choose to compress some sound files and not others.

External sound files may also be converted to SWA format, but the conversion must be done manually. In Windows, WAV files may be converted to SWA within Director. On the Mac, a variety of file formats can be converted, but only in a third-party program, Peak LE.

These days, there's very little reason to use SWA. SWA format is very similar to MP3 format, which was based on SWA and has since become the most popular format for music files on the Internet. If you want to compress sound files, you'll get better quality by using one of many third-party programs (such as Apple's free iTunes) to convert them to MP3 format. You can then import them normally into Director (using either the Standard Import or Link to External File option), or use them as streaming audio files (see "Using Streaming Sounds," later in this chapter).

Keep in mind that using either SWA or MP3 compression may cause a slight delay at the beginning of your Director movie while the files are decompressed.

To convert external sound files to SWA format (Windows):

1. In Director, choose Xtras > Convert WAV to SWA.

   The "Convert .WAV files..." dialog box opens (**Figure 13.30**).

2. Click Add Files.

   The "Select .WAV Files..." dialog box opens (**Figure 13.31**).

3. Select one or more WAV files to convert.

   To select multiple files, hold down the Control key as you click each additional file.

4. Click Open.

   The selected files appear in the Files to Convert window in the "Convert .WAV files..." dialog box (**Figure 13.32**).

5. Choose compression settings (**Figure 13.33**).

   The settings you specify apply to all the selected files.

   The **Bit Rate** may be set to any value from 8 to 160. Lower values mean more compression but lower sound quality.

   Accuracy may be set to Normal or High. High accuracy improves sound quality but increases conversion time significantly.

   If the bit rate is set to 48 or higher, you have the option to select **Convert Stereo to Mono**. (Below 48, stereo files are automatically converted to mono.) Choosing this option halves the amount of data in a stereo sound file.

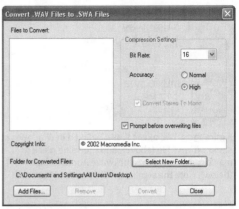

Figure 13.30 The "Convert .WAV files..." dialog box opens.

Figure 13.31 The "Select .WAV files..." dialog box, with multiple files selected.

Figure 13.32 The selected files appear in the Files to Convert window of the "Convert .WAV files..." dialog box.

Figure 13.33 Choose settings for the bit rate and accuracy, and decide whether you want stereo files to be converted to mono.

Figure 13.34 In the "Select an Output Folder..." dialog box, select the folder in which you want the converted files to be saved.

6. Click the Select New Folder button.

A "Select an Output Folder..." dialog box opens (**Figure 13.34**).

7. Select a folder to which you want the converted sound files to be saved, and click Select Folder.

The "Select an Output Folder..." dialog box closes.

8. In the "Convert .WAV files..." dialog box, click Convert.

A progress bar tracks the conversion process.

9. Click Close to close the dialog box.

The converted files are in the folder you specified in step 7.

To convert an external sound file to SWA format (Mac):

1. Open the file in Peak LE (version 2 or later).

2. In Peak LE, choose File > Save As.

A Save Audio Document dialog box opens.

3. Choose Shockwave from the File Type pop-up menu.

4. Choose compression settings as desired.

5. Click Save to save the file.

Using Streaming Sounds

As explained in the "Inserted and Streaming Sounds" sidebar at the beginning of this chapter, any externally linked sound file can be streamed. However, only *some* sounds can be streamed over the Web, directly from their source files, independent of the streaming of the rest of the Director movie. These are the files that Director refers to as *streaming sounds*.

Only Shockwave Audio (SWA) or MP3 files may be treated as streaming sounds.

To set a linked SWA or MP3 sound to stream:

1. In Director, choose Insert > Media Element > Shockwave Audio.

   The SWA Cast Member Properties dialog box opens (**Figure 13.35**).

2. Click Browse and select a local SWA or MP3 file.

   or

   Type a URL in the Link Address field (**Figure 13.36**).

3. Set the volume of the sound (a value between 0 and 15) with the Volume slider or the adjacent arrows.

4. From the Sound Channel pop-up menu, choose Any (**Figure 13.37**).

   The menu lists eight sound channels (including the six accessible only through Lingo), but choosing Any automatically prevents conflicts with other sounds.

Figure 13.35 The SWA Cast Member Properties dialog box. Despite its name, it applies to both SWA and MP3 cast members.

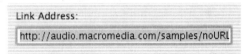

Figure 13.36 By default, the Link Address field contains the URL of a sample SWA file on Macromedia's Web site.

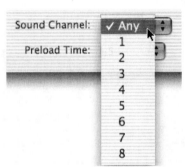

Figure 13.37 The Sound Channel pop-up menu lists eight channels, but pick Any for best results.

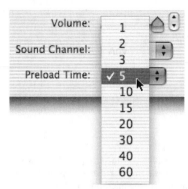

Figure 13.38 The numbers on the Preload Time pop-up menu represent the number of seconds of sound that Director will store in a buffer.

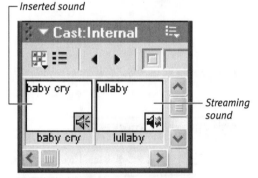

Figure 13.39 A streaming sound has a slightly different icon in the Cast window.

Inserted sound

Streaming sound

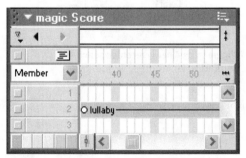

Figure 13.40 Streaming sounds go in the regular sprite channels of the Score, not the sound channels.

5. Use the Preload Time pop-up menu to specify how many seconds of sound Director should store in a buffer as it plays the sound file (**Figure 13.38**).

A longer preload time causes a longer delay before the sound begins to play but results in smoother playback of the sound.

6. If you wish, click Play to preview the linked sound file.

If the file is in a remote location, you must be connected to the Internet (or another network) to preview the file.

7. Click OK to close the dialog box.

The linked sound file appears in the Cast window (**Figure 13.39**).

To include a streaming sound in your movie:

◆ Drag the cast member to a sprite channel (not a sound channel) in the Score (**Figure 13.40**).

Recording Sounds in Director

On Macintosh computers only, Director can digitally record sound from a microphone connected to the computer. (How to connect the microphone varies according to your hardware: Some Macs have a built-in microphone, some have a standard mic input jack, others require a special Universal Serial Bus (USB) microphone, and still others require an external audio adapter.)

The sound-recording tool Director uses is actually part of the Mac operating system, not part of Director itself. It's a completely no-frills affair, without even a volume meter, but it can be handy in emergencies when more suitable sound-recording software isn't available.

To record a sound in Director (Mac only):

1. Make sure that you have a microphone attached to your computer, and that it's properly configured in System Preferences (**Figure 13.41**).

2. In Director, choose Insert > Media Element > Sound.

   The recording window opens (**Figure 13.42**).

3. Click Record and begin recording a sound with the attached microphone.

   The timer keeps track of the elapsed time.

4. If necessary, click Pause to pause the recording session; click Record again to resume.

5. When you're finished recording, click Stop.

6. If you want to listen to the sound, click Play.

7. Click Save to save the sound.

   The recording window closes, and the sound appears as an unnamed cast member in the Cast window (**Figure 13.43**).

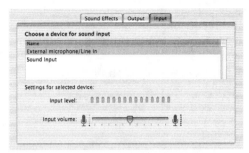

Figure 13.41 Check the Sound settings in Mac OS X's System Preferences panel to make sure your Mac recognizes input from the microphone.

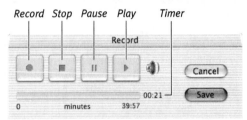

Figure 13.42 The no-frills sound-recording window.

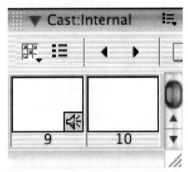

Figure 13.43 A newly recorded sound in the Cast window.

ADDING
BEHAVIORS

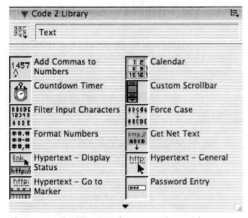

Figure 14.1 The Library palette contains ready-to-use behaviors grouped by category, such as Text, shown here.

You can add interactive features to movies without having to write or understand Lingo, Director's scripting language. You simply drag a *behavior* (a prefabricated Lingo script) onto a sprite or frame to make certain actions occur in response to events during your movie. Typical events include a click of a sprite or the entry of the playhead into a specific frame.

Director provides a Library palette of ready-to-use behaviors grouped by categories, including Animation, Internet, and Navigation (**Figure 14.1**).

In this chapter, you'll learn how to assign Director's drag-and-drop behaviors to sprites and frames, how to modify the supplied behaviors, and even how to create your own behaviors within the Behavior Inspector. A couple of specific examples will get you started building behavior interactivity into your movies.

Even if you plan to acquire Lingo scripting skills, it's a good idea to experiment with behaviors first to develop a feel for what Lingo can do.

Assigning Behaviors

You incorporate a behavior into your movie by dragging it from the Library palette. Depending on the behavior, you can drop it on a sprite in the Score or on the Stage (**Figure 14.2**) or on a frame in the script channel of the Score (**Figure 14.3**). You can assign multiple behaviors to a single sprite, but only one to a frame.

Certain behaviors can only be applied to sprites, and others can only be applied to frames. To find out which are which, you can use the Library palette's built-in "cheat sheet": If you hold the mouse pointer over a behavior's icon in the Library palette, a description of the behavior pops up, including a brief tip on how to use it (**Figure 14.4**).

For most behaviors, a Parameters dialog box appears when you drop the behavior on a sprite or frame. That dialog box allows you to choose settings that determine when the behavior will be triggered and how it will execute.

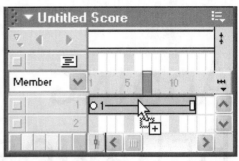

Figure 14.2 A behavior dragged to a sprite channel.

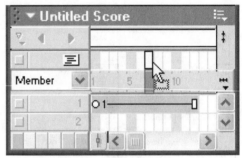

Figure 14.3 A behavior dragged to a frame in the script channel.

Figure 14.4 Hold the mouse pointer over a behavior icon in the Library palette to display a description of the behavior.

Behavior cast member

Figure 14.5 When you assign a behavior to a sprite or frame, the assigned behavior goes into the Cast window, like any other cast member.

After you assign a built-in behavior to a sprite or frame, that behavior goes into the Cast window (**Figure 14.5**), where you're free to modify it. You can't modify the original behaviors stored in the Library palette.

When you play the movie, any behavior assigned to a frame is triggered automatically when the playhead enters the frame. Some sprite behaviors—notably those in the Animation > Automatic category—also are triggered automatically, either when the movie begins to play or when the sprite first appears on the Stage. Most sprite behaviors, however, are triggered by a particular event, such as a mouse click. The Parameters dialog box allows you to specify the characteristics of the event that will trigger the behavior.

There are well over 100 behaviors in the Library palette—too many to describe individually in this chapter. (See the sidebar, "What's in the Library?" for an overview.) You're encouraged to look at them, read their pop-up descriptions, and most importantly, experiment with them. (It's only software; you can't break anything.)

What's in the Library?

The Library palette contains seven categories of behaviors. Here's a summary of what's in each category.

3D

These behaviors are used to animate and add interactivity to 3D objects. For more information, see Chapter 18, "Shockwave 3D."

Accessibility

These behaviors help make Director movies accessible to people with visual, hearing, or motor impairments. For more information, see Chapter 20, "Accessibility."

Animation

This category contains three groups of behaviors that may be assigned to sprites. The **Automatic** behaviors make sprites change in various ways (such as moving randomly or changing color) without any intervention from the user. The **Interactive** behaviors make sprites respond to the user's actions—for example, by making a sprite follow the mouse pointer or allowing a sprite to be "tossed" across the Stage. The **Sprite Transitions** behaviors create effects similar to scene transitions (see "Using Scene Transitions" in Chapter 5).

Controls

These behaviors allow you to create user-interface elements such as menus and several kinds of buttons.

Internet

This category contains two types of behaviors intended especially for Shockwave movies. The **Forms** behaviors enable you to create forms that can submit data to CGI scripts on a Web server. The **Streaming** behaviors, which allow you to configure a movie for effective streaming, will be explained in Chapter 17, "Making Movies for the Web."

Media

The three subcategories here—**Flash**, **QuickTime**, and **Sound**—contain behaviors that help you create control buttons for sprites of those three types.

Navigation

This category contains behaviors that can be assigned to frames. They control the action of the playhead in various ways—for example, making the playhead jump to a specific frame or loop between two frames.

Paintbox

This set of behaviors contains all the tools you need to create an interactive paint window on the Stage so that users can create their own images.

Text

These behaviors allow you to process and format text in a variety of ways—for example, as a scrolling ticker tape or a disguised password. There are also behaviors here that automatically create a timer and a calendar.

Library List

Figure 14.6 Choose a category of behaviors from the Library List pop-up menu.

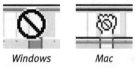

Windows   *Mac*

Figure 14.7 When you drag a behavior over areas where it can't be dropped, the mouse pointer becomes a "no" symbol (different for Windows and Mac).

Figure 14.8 Choose settings for the behavior—in this case, parameters for the Fade In/Out behavior.

To open the Library palette:

◆ Choose Window > Library Palette.

To assign a behavior from the Library palette to a sprite or frame:

1. Open the Library palette.

2. In the Library palette, choose a category—and, if necessary, a subcategory—from the Library List pop-up menu (**Figure 14.6**).

3. Drag a behavior from the Library palette to a sprite in the Score or on the Stage, or to a frame in the script channel of the Score.

   Director lets you know where it's OK to drop the behavior by displaying black rectangles around "legal" areas as you drag. If the behavior is meant to be dropped on a frame, only frames will display the black rectangle; if the behavior is meant to be dropped on a sprite, only sprites will display the black rectangle.

   When you drag over illegal areas, the mouse pointer becomes a "no" symbol (**Figure 14.7**).

4. Drop the behavior on the desired sprite or frame.

5. If a Parameters dialog box appears, provide the information requested to tailor how the behavior works.

   For example, if you drop the Fade In/Out behavior, you'll be asked to specify the kinds of settings shown in **Figure 14.8**.

   continues on next page

6. If necessary, click OK to close the dialog box.

Director assigns the behavior to the sprite or frame, and also places a copy of the behavior in the Cast window.

✔ Tips

■ If you drag the same behavior from the Library palette more than once per movie, additional copies of that behavior are added to the cast. To avoid cluttering the Cast window, drag a behavior from the Library only the first time you use it in a movie. Thereafter, drag it from the Cast window instead.

■ If you intend to use a particular behavior in your movie but you're not ready to use it yet, you can drag it from the Library palette to the Cast window. Later, you can drag it from the Cast window to a sprite or frame.

To assign a behavior from the cast to a sprite or frame:

1. Drag a behavior from the Cast window to a sprite in the Score or on the Stage, or to a frame in the script channel of the Score.

2. Drop the behavior on the desired sprite or frame.

3. If a Parameters dialog box appears, make the required settings.

Each time you reuse a behavior, you're prompted for a new set of parameters. The parameters you set for one frame or sprite are not carried over when you apply the behavior to another frame or sprite.

4. If necessary, click OK to close the dialog box.

Director assigns the behavior to the sprite or frame. The contents of the Cast window remain unchanged.

Modifying Assigned Behaviors

If you want to make changes in the behaviors you've assigned to sprites and frames, the place to do it is the Behavior Inspector (**Figure 14.9**). The Behavior Inspector permits you to change the order of behaviors assigned to a sprite or frame, change the parameters of an assigned behavior, delete one or more of the behaviors assigned to a sprite, and make other kinds of modifications. (As you'll see in the next section, you can also use it to create your own behaviors.)

continues on next page

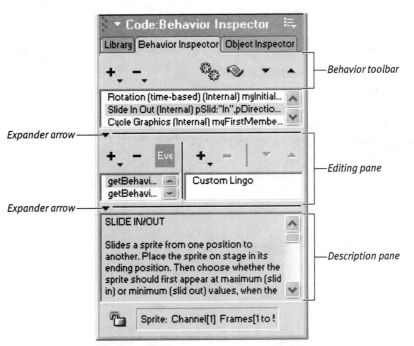

Figure 14.9 The Behavior Inspector is shown fully here so you can see all its parts, but its middle section (the editing pane) is normally closed.

Note: The Behavior tab of the Property Inspector contains the same toolbar as the Behavior Inspector (**Figure 14.10**). Of the tasks in this section, all but the first two can be accomplished in the Property Inspector as well as the Behavior Inspector.

To open the Behavior Inspector:

◆ Choose Window > Inspectors > Behavior.
   or
   Click the Behavior Inspector button in the Sprite toolbar (**Figure 14.11**).
   (If the Sprite toolbar isn't visible, you can open it by choosing View > Sprite Toolbar while the Score is the active window.)
   or
   Double-click a behavior in the Cast window.

To view the description of a behavior:

1. Open the Behavior Inspector.

2. In the Score, select a sprite or frame that has a behavior assigned to it.
   or
   Select a behavior in the Cast window.
   The name of the selected behavior (followed by its parameters) appears in the top pane of the Behavior Inspector. If you've selected a sprite that has more than one assigned behavior, their names appear as a list.

3. If the Behavior Inspector contains a list of behaviors, select one from the list (**Figure 14.12**).

4. Read the behavior's description in the description pane.
   All behaviors from the Library palette have a description. Behaviors created by you or other Director users may not.

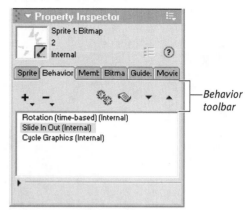

Figure 14.10 The Behavior tab of the Property Inspector has a toolbar identical to that in the Behavior Inspector.

Figure 14.11 The Behavior Inspector button in the Sprite toolbar.

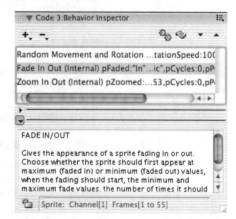

Figure 14.12 If the Behavior Inspector contains a list of behaviors, select one from the list to view its description.

Clear Behavior

Figure 14.13 The Clear Behavior pop-up menu allows you to delete a single behavior or all behaviors.

Behaviors

Figure 14.14 To delete all behaviors assigned to a sprite or frame without having to open the Behavior Inspector, choose Clear All Behaviors from the Behaviors pop-up menu in the Sprite toolbar.

To delete a behavior assigned to a sprite or frame:

1. Open the Behavior Inspector.

2. In the Score, select a sprite or frame that has a behavior assigned to it.

   One or more behaviors appear in the top pane of the Behavior Inspector.

3. If the Behavior Inspector contains more than one behavior, select the one that you want to delete.

4. Choose Remove Behavior from the Clear Behavior pop-up menu on the Behavior toolbar (**Figure 4.13**).

   or

   Press the Delete key.

To delete all behaviors assigned to a sprite or frame:

1. Open the Behavior Inspector.

2. In the Score, select a sprite or frame that has a behavior assigned to it.

   One or more behaviors appear in the top pane of the Behavior Inspector.

3. Choose Remove All Behaviors from the Clear Behavior pop-up menu on the Behavior toolbar.

   or

   Choose Clear All Behaviors from the Behaviors pop-up menu on the Sprite toolbar (**Figure 14.14**).

   (If the Sprite toolbar isn't visible, you can open it by choosing View > Sprite Toolbar while the Score is the active window.)

To change the order of behaviors assigned to a sprite:

1. Open the Behavior Inspector.

2. In the Score, select a sprite that has more than one behavior assigned to it.

3. Select a behavior from the list in the top pane of the Behavior Inspector.

4. Use the Shuffle Up and Shuffle Down buttons at the top of the window to move the selected behavior up or down in the list (**Figure 14.15**).

5. Repeat steps 3 and 4 if you want to change the position of other behaviors in the list.

To change the parameters of an assigned behavior:

1. Open the Behavior Inspector.

2. In the Score, select a sprite or frame that has a behavior assigned to it.

   One or more behaviors appear in the top pane of the Behavior Inspector.

3. If the Behavior Inspector contains more than one behavior, select the one whose parameters you want to change.

4. Click the Parameters button on the Behavior toolbar (**Figure 14.16**).

   The Parameters dialog box appears, displaying the parameters you set when you first assigned the behavior.

5. Change the parameters as desired.

6. Click OK to close the dialog box.

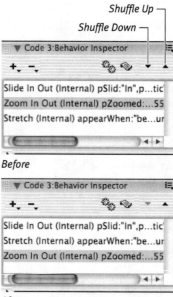

Shuffle Up
Shuffle Down

Before

After

Figure 14.15 The Shuffle Up and Shuffle Down buttons change the order of behaviors. Here, the Shuffle Down button is used to move the selected behavior down in the list.

Parameters

Figure 14.16 Click the Parameters button on the Behavior toolbar.

MODIFYING ASSIGNED BEHAVIORS

Figure 14.17 Open a behavior's script by clicking the Script Window button on the Behavior toolbar.

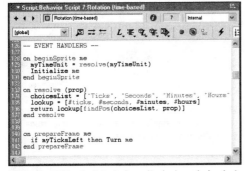

Figure 14.18 The Script window, displaying a behavior's Lingo script.

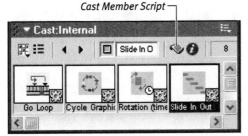

Figure 14.19 The Cast Member Script button in the Cast window can be used to open the Script window for a selected cast member.

To edit a behavior's Lingo script:

1. Open the Behavior Inspector.

2. In the Score, select a sprite or frame that has a behavior assigned to it.

   One or more behaviors appear in the top pane of the Behavior Inspector.

3. If the Behavior Inspector contains more than one behavior, select the one whose script you want to change.

4. Click the Script Window button on the Behavior toolbar (**Figure 14.17**).

   The Script window opens, displaying the Lingo script that underlies the behavior (**Figure 14.18**).

5. Edit the script as desired.

   To accomplish this step, you must be familiar with Lingo. (The following chapter, "Scripting Lingo," will give you an introduction.)

6. Close the Script window to make the changes take effect.

✔ Tip

- The Cast window has a button called the Cast Member Script button, which is identical to the Script Window button on the Behavior toolbar (**Figure 14.19**). It can be used to open the Script window for a behavior you've selected in the Cast window.

MODIFYING ASSIGNED BEHAVIORS

Creating and Modifying Behaviors

Although the behaviors in the Library palette were created by professional programmers using advanced Lingo, it's possible to create simple behaviors of your own using the tools available in the Behavior Inspector. This section shows you how to create a new behavior and how to modify it later.

To create a behavior:

1. Open the Behavior Inspector.

2. Choose New Behavior from the Behavior pop-up menu (**Figure 14.20**).

   The Name Behavior dialog box opens.

3. Type a name for the behavior and click OK (**Figure 14.21**).

   The dialog box closes. The newly named (but still empty) behavior is added to the Cast window (**Figure 4.22**), and its name is displayed in the upper pane of the Behavior Inspector.

4. If necessary, click the expander arrow to display the Behavior Inspector's editing pane.

5. From the Event pop-up menu, choose an event that will trigger your behavior (**Figure 14.23**).

   The selected event appears in the left column of the editing pane.

Behavior pop-up menu

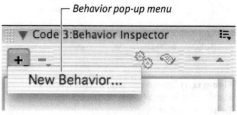

Figure 14.20 Choose New Behavior from the Behavior pop-up menu.

Figure 14.21 In this example, we'll create a behavior that beeps and sends the playhead back to frame 1 when the user clicks a sprite. Let's call it Rewind.

Figure 14.22 The new behavior appears in the Cast window as soon as it's named.

Event pop-up

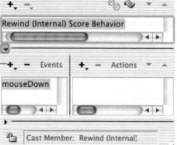

Figure 14.23 Choose an event that will trigger the behavior. For the Rewind behavior, we'll choose Mouse Down.

Figure 14.24 Choose an action that the event will trigger. For the Rewind behavior, we'll choose Navigation > Go to Frame.

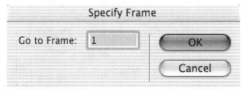

Figure 14.25 If a parameters box appears for the selected action, choose your settings and click OK.

Figure 14.26 An event may trigger multiple actions. In this case, the Sound > Beep action is added.

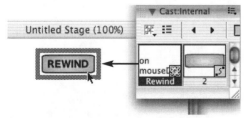

Figure 14.27 The Rewind behavior is dragged to a sprite (a rewind button) on the Stage.

6. From the Action Popup menu, choose a category of action and then a specific action that the event will trigger (**Figure 14.24**).

7. If a parameters dialog box appears, set parameters for the selected action and click OK (**Figure 14.25**).

   The selected action appears in the right column of the editing pane.

8. Repeat steps 5 through 7 as many times as necessary to add as many events and actions as you want (**Figure 14.26**).

   A behavior can have multiple events, and each event can trigger multiple actions. Actions for any event are executed in the order listed in the Actions list.

   When events and actions are selected, they automatically become part of the behavior. You don't have to do anything special to make them "stick."

9. Assign the behavior by dragging it from the Cast window to a sprite or frame (**Figure 14.27**).

✔ Tip

■ Always play back the movie to check the new behavior and then adjust the behavior settings, if necessary.

To modify a behavior:

1. Open the Behavior Inspector.

2. In the Score, select a sprite or frame that has a behavior assigned to it.

or

Choose a behavior from the Behavior Popup menu in the Behavior Inspector (**Figure 14.28**).

or

Select a behavior in the Cast window.

3. If the Behavior Inspector displays a list of behaviors, select the one you want to modify.

4. If necessary, click the expander arrow to display the Behavior Inspector's editing pane.

5. If you want to add events or actions, follow steps 5 through 7 in "To create a behavior," above.

6. If you want to delete an event or action, select the event or action you want to delete and do one of the following:

▲ Click the Clear Event or Clear Action button (**Figure 14.29**).

or

▲ Press the Delete key.

7. If you want to change the order of actions attached to a particular event, select the action you want to move and click the Shuffle Up or Shuffle Down button.

There's no need (and no way) to change the order of events in a behavior. Director will respond to any of the listed events when it occurs, regardless of its place in the list.

Any changes you make to a behavior take effect automatically.

✔ Tip

■ Any changes you make to a behavior affect all instances of that behavior that are already assigned to sprites or frames.

Figure 14.28 The Behavior Popup menu lists all behaviors in the cast that could potentially be applied to the currently selected sprite or frame.

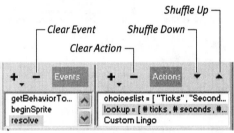

Figure 14.29 These buttons in the editing pane allow you to modify behaviors.

CREATING AND MODIFYING BEHAVIORS

SCRIPTING LINGO

Figure 15.1 Lingo allows users to communicate with a movie in a variety of ways, including typing text, clicking buttons, and dragging sprites.

Figure 15.2 Experienced Lingo programmers often control the animation, sounds, transitions, and other elements of their movies entirely by means of Lingo scripts. A movie constructed in this way may use only a single frame in the Score.

Lingo, Director's scripting language, adds an interactive dimension to Director movies. Through Lingo, you enable users to communicate with your movie: They can type text, drag sprites, and click on buttons, and the movie can respond to these inputs in limitless ways (**Figure 15.1**).

In the preceding chapter, "Adding Behaviors," you learned how to create behaviors with the tools supplied in the Behavior Inspector. Those tools, however, offer very limited control over just a few aspects of a movie. By contrast, Lingo scripts can control every aspect of a movie—sound, positions of sprites, text input and output, playback of digital video, and all the other features of Director that have been covered so far in this book (**Figure 15.2**).

To really use Lingo, you have to assimilate a lot more information than can be covered in this one chapter. Entire books have been written about Lingo, and if you want to get into Lingo scripting more deeply, you'll do well to get one of them. In the meantime, this chapter will introduce you to the basics of Lingo scripts and offer a few examples. The chapter covers types of scripts and how they differ, the basics of writing a script, ways to assign a script to a movie or one of its elements, and specific instructions for simple sprite and cast-member interactions.

SCRIPTING LINGO

Understanding Events and Handlers

A Director movie may be thought of as a series of *events*—things that happen on the Stage or in the Score. Some events are automatic, such as the playhead entering a new frame. Other events are user-initiated—for example, a click of the mouse button or the pressing of a key on the keyboard.

Whenever an event occurs, Director generates a one-word message acknowledging the event. (For example, when the mouse button is released, Director generates the message "mouseUp.") The user doesn't see these messages; they're solely for internal communication within Director. **Table 15.1** shows a list of common events that can occur while a movie is playing and the messages those events generate.

Table 15.1

Movie events and Lingo messages	
EVENT	MESSAGE AND HANDLER NAME
A window is activated	activateWindow
A window is closed	closeWindow
A window is deactivated	deactivateWindow
Playhead enters frame with a new sprite	beginSprite
Playhead leaves a sprite	endSprite
Playhead enters current frame	enterFrame
Playhead exits current frame	exitFrame
Playhead enters a frame but hasn't displayed it yet	prepareFrame
No event occurred	idle
A key is pressed	keyDown
A key is released	keyUp
Mouse button pressed	mouseDown
Mouse button released	mouseUp
Mouse pointer enters a sprite	mouseEnter
Mouse pointer leaves a sprite	mouseLeave
Mouse pointer stays within a sprite	mouseWithin
Movie starts playing	startMovie
Movie stops playing	stopMovie
Movie is about to start playing	prepareMovie

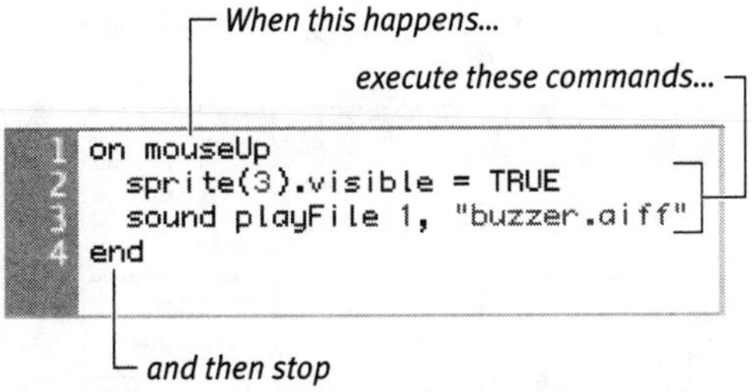

When this happens...

execute these commands...

```
1  on mouseUp
2     sprite(3).visible = TRUE
3     sound playFile 1, "buzzer.aiff"
4  end
```

and then stop

Figure 15.3 Every handler has three parts: The first line specifies the event that triggers the handler, the body lists commands that should be executed, and the last line concludes the handler.

You can give Director specific instructions about how you want it to *handle* (respond to) a particular message. That set of instructions is called a *handler*. Handlers are the building blocks of Lingo scripts.

Every handler has three parts (**Figure 15.3**):

◆ The first line always begins with the word on, followed by the message to which the handler should respond. (Handlers are referred to by the name of the message that triggers them. For example, the handler in **Figure 15.3** is called a mouseUp handler, because it responds to the message generated when a user releases the mouse button.)

◆ The body of the handler (the indented part) contains the commands that are executed when the handler is triggered. The commands are executed in the order in which they appear in the handler.

◆ The last line always consists of the word end. (This is so Director can know where one handler ends and the next one begins.)

(Note: For convenience, handlers are often described as responding to—or being triggered by—events in a movie. There's nothing wrong with using this informal shorthand, as long as you realize that handlers technically respond to the messages generated by events, not to the events themselves.)

Types of Lingo Scripts

A Lingo *script* is a series of one or more handlers. You can attach a script to any of the following elements of your Director movie:

◆ A sprite

◆ A frame

◆ A cast member

◆ The movie as a whole

A script attached to a sprite or frame is often referred to as a *behavior script,* or a *Score script.* A script attached to a cast member is a *cast-member script.* And a script attached to a movie is a *movie script.* (A more advanced type of script, called a *parent script,* is not covered in this book.) With the exception of cast-member scripts, every script appears as a cast member in the Cast window (**Figure 15.4**).

The element to which a script is attached determines when and where the script is executed, as described below.

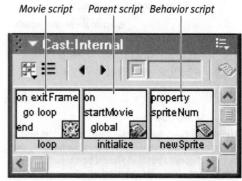

Movie script   Parent script Behavior script

Figure 15.4 The various kinds of script cast members as they appear in the Cast window.

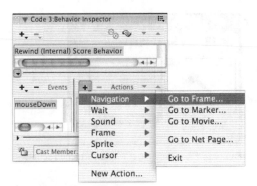

Figure 15.5 The Behavior Inspector offers a menu-driven approach to creating behaviors.

Figure 15.6 Writing behavior scripts gives you much more control than using the Behavior Inspector.

Behavior scripts

Behavior scripts are simply a different name for the behaviors you learned about in Chapter 14, "Adding Behaviors." As you saw in that chapter, you can create behaviors by using the Events and Actions pop-up menus in the Behavior Inspector (**Figure 15.5**). You can achieve much more flexibility, however, by writing behaviors as Lingo scripts in a Script window (**Figure 15.6**). In either case, once a behavior has been created, you use it by dragging it from the Cast window onto a sprite, or into a frame in the script channel of the Score.

You can attach multiple behavior scripts to one sprite, but you can attach only one script per frame in the script channel. If a sprite has multiple behaviors that respond to the same event, each of them is executed in the order in which you attached them. You can see which behaviors have been attached to a sprite—and their order—by selecting the sprite and opening the Behavior Inspector.

A behavior script attached to a sprite may be triggered by any of the following events:

♦ Movement of the mouse pointer relative to the sprite (for example, on mouseEnter or on mouseLeave).

♦ Pressing or releasing of the mouse button when the mouse pointer is positioned on the sprite (for example, on mouseUp or on mouseDown).

♦ Pressing or releasing of a key on the keyboard (for example, on keyUp or on keyDown).

♦ The playhead's entering or leaving the sprite in the Score (for example, on beginSprite or on endSprite).

A behavior script attached to a frame is generally triggered when the playhead prepares to enter, enters, or leaves the frame to which the script is attached (for example, on prepareFrame, on enterFrame, or on exitFrame).

TYPES OF LINGO SCRIPTS

Cast-member scripts

A cast member may have only one script attached to it, and a cast-member script may be attached to only one cast member. If a cast member has a script attached to it, the presence of that script is indicated by an icon in the lower-left corner of the cast member's thumbnail in the Cast window (**Figure 15.7**).

A cast-member script works the same way as a behavior script attached to a sprite. It can respond to any of the same mouse or keyboard events that a behavior script responds to. (It can't respond to movement of the playhead, however.)

A cast-member script remains attached to any sprite that's created from that cast member. So, for example, suppose you create a visual cast member and attach the following script to it:

on mouseDown

    go to frame 1

end

Any sprite based on that cast member will function as a button that returns the playhead to frame 1 when the user clicks it.

If you have a cast member that you want to use as a button, but you want the button to do different things at different points in the movie, don't attach a cast-member script to it. Instead, attach a behavior script to each sprite based on the cast member.

Script icon

Figure 15.7 A cast member with an attached script.

Movie scripts

A movie script is not explicitly attached to any object; instead, it's available to the entire movie. Two types of handlers are generally placed in movie scripts:

♦ Handlers that are triggered by the playing or stopping of the movie (for example, on `prepareMovie`, on `startMovie`, or on `stopMovie`).

♦ Handlers that are meant to be executed at any time during the movie, regardless of what sprites are on the Stage or where the playhead is. For example, if you want the backspace key to be available to rewind the movie at all times, you might include the following handler in a movie script:

```
on keyDown
    if the key = BACKSPACE then go to frame 1
end
```

A movie may contain any number of movie scripts. If a movie contains two movie scripts that respond to the same event (meaning they both use the same handler), only the first one that Director finds is executed. The other movie script is ignored.

Writing Scripts

Lingo scripts are written in Script windows. Unfortunately—the Script window being one of the less intuitive aspects of Director—*how* you open the Script window makes a difference. For example, if you double-click a frame in the script channel of the Score, you'll get a window that allows you to write a behavior script; but if instead you choose Window > Script, you'll get a window that allows you to write a movie script! Be sure to check the title bar of each Script window you open; it will tell you which type of script you're creating (**Figure 15.8**).

As you write a script, Director "looks over your shoulder" to make sure it understands what you're writing. Each time you start a new line, Director parses and color-codes the previous line. (For example, keywords such as on and end appear in blue; names of events appear in green.) Director also indents commands within handlers (and certain other lines as well) for readability. If these features bother you, you can turn them off by choosing Edit > Preferences > Script (Windows) or Director > Preferences > Script (Mac) and deselecting Auto Coloring and Auto Format. It's a good idea to leave them on, however, because they provide useful feedback: If Director fails to color-code your script properly, or if all the lines of the script appear flush against the left margin, you know you've made a scripting error (**Figure 15.9**).

Lingo isn't case-sensitive, so you don't necessarily have to adhere to the conventions you'll see in the sample scripts (for example, marking conjoined words by means of capital letters, as with the uppercase *U* in the middle of mouseUp). But if you plan to exchange your Director files with other developers, you should get accustomed to using this style of capitalization so your scripts will be easily understood.

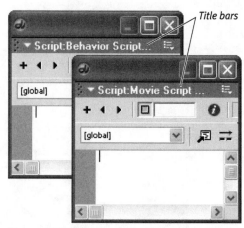

Title bars

Figure 15.8 The title bar of a Script window indicates the type of script that the window will create.

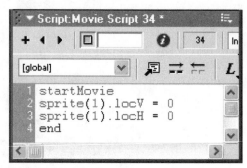

Figure 15.9 If all the lines of your script appear flush against the left margin, you know you've made an error. (In this case, the word on is missing from the first line.)

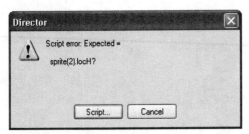

Figure 15.10 If Director finds an error in your script, it displays an alert box like this one when you close the Script window.

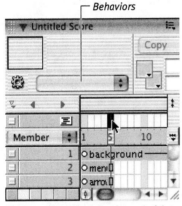

Figure 15.11 In the script channel of the Score, select the frame to which you want to attach a script. (In this example, frame 5 is selected.)

Figure 15.12 Choose New Behavior from the Behaviors pop-up menu on the Sprite toolbar.

When you finish writing a script, you must close the Script window. Doing so allows Director to *compile* the script—that is, to convert it into a format that it can use internally. If Director encounters an error when it tries to compile the script, it informs you of the error in an alert box (**Figure 15.10**). Click the Script button to reopen the Script window and correct the error.

To write a behavior script attached to a frame:

1. In the script channel of the Score, select the frame to which you want to attach a script (**Figure 15.11**).

2. Open a Script window by doing one of the following:

   ▲ Double-click the selected frame.

   or

   ▲ On the Sprite toolbar, choose New Behavior from the Behaviors pop-up menu (**Figure 15.12**).

   (If the Sprite toolbar isn't visible, you can open it by choosing View > Sprite Toolbar while the Score is the active window.)

continues on next page

A Script window opens, displaying the first and last lines of a handler (**Figure 15.13**).

3. *(optional)* If you want to change the first line of the handler from on exitFrame (which Director inserted automatically) to something else (such as on enterFrame), do so.

   The word me at the end of the first line is required only by certain handlers that use an advanced form of scripting. In most cases, you can leave it or delete it without making any difference in the way the script will execute.

4. Type one or more Lingo commands to form the body of the handler (**Figure 15.14**).

   Make sure that end (which Director inserted automatically) remains the last line.

5. Close the Script window.

   The finished, compiled script is now attached to the selected frame. (It's also available in the Cast window to be dragged to other frames if you wish.)

6. Rewind and test the movie.

   When the playhead reaches the frame to which the script is attached, Director executes the script.

Figure 15.13 When you open the Script window for a behavior script attached to a frame, these two lines appear by default.

Figure 15.14 Type the body of the handler. (In this example, the go to command is used to make the playhead jump back to frame 1. You'll learn more about this command in the next section.)

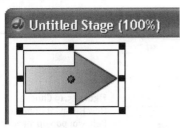

Figure 15.15 Select the sprite to which you want to attach a script.

Figure 15.16 When you open the Script window for a behavior script you're attaching to a sprite, these two lines appear by default.

Figure 15.17 Type the body of the handler. (In this example, the locH property is used to make the sprite move to the right. For more about sprite properties, see "Understanding Lingo Elements," later in this chapter.)

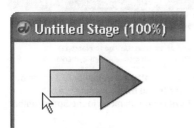

Figure 15.18 Each time you click this sprite, it moves 10 pixels to the right, thanks to the attached Lingo script.

To write a behavior script attached to a sprite:

1. Select a sprite in the Score or on the Stage (**Figure 15.15**).

2. Choose New Behavior from the Behaviors pop-up menu on the Sprite toolbar.

   (If the Sprite toolbar isn't visible, you can open it by choosing View > Sprite Toolbar while the Score is the active window.)

   A Script window opens, displaying the first and last lines of a handler (**Figure 15.16**).

3. *(optional)* If you want to change the first line of the script from on mouseUp (which Director inserted automatically) to something else (such as on mouseDown), do so.

   The word me at the end of the first line is required only by certain handlers that use an advanced form of scripting. In most cases, you can leave it or delete it without making any difference in the way the script will execute.

4. Type one or more Lingo commands to form the body of the handler (**Figure 15.17**).

   Make sure that end (which Director inserted automatically) remains the last line.

5. Close the Script window.

   The finished, compiled script is now attached to the selected sprite. (It's also available in the Cast window to be dragged to other sprites if you wish.)

6. Rewind and test the movie (**Figure 15.18**).

WRITING SCRIPTS

To write a behavior script that you can later attach to a sprite or frame:

1. Choose Window > Behavior Inspector to open the Behavior Inspector.

2. In the Behavior Inspector, choose New Behavior from the Behavior Popup menu (**Figure 15.19**).

   The Name Behavior dialog box opens.

3. Type a name for the behavior and click OK.

   The dialog box closes. The name of the new behavior is displayed in the upper pane of the Behavior Inspector.

4. Click the Script Window button in the Behavior Inspector (**Figure 15.20**).

   An empty Script window opens. (Since Director doesn't know whether this script will be attached to a frame or a sprite, it doesn't provide the first and last lines of a handler).

5. Type a script consisting of one or more handlers (**Figure 15.21**).

6. Close the Script window.

   The finished, compiled script is now available in the Cast window to be dragged to a frame or a sprite.

✔ Tips

- Another way to attach a behavior to a sprite is to select the sprite in the Score and choose the desired behavior from the Behaviors pop-up menu in the Sprite toolbar (**Figure 15.22**). You can repeat this procedure as often as you wish in order to attach multiple behaviors.

- To remove all behaviors attached to a sprite or frame, change the order of behaviors attached to a sprite, or do other sorts of "behavior housekeeping," see the tasks under "Modifying Assigned Behaviors" in Chapter 14.

Behavior pop-up menu

Figure 15.19 Choose New Behavior from the Behavior pop-up menu in the Behavior Inspector.

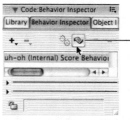

Script Window

Figure 15.20 Click the Script Window button to open a behavior Script window.

Figure 15.21 Type a script. (In this example, attaching this script to a sprite will cause an alert box saying "uh-oh!" to appear when the sprite is clicked.)

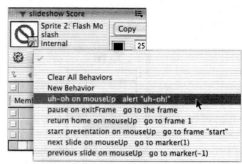

Figure 15.22 You can attach a behavior to a sprite by selecting the sprite and then choosing the behavior from the Behaviors pop-up menu in the Sprite toolbar.

Cast Member Script

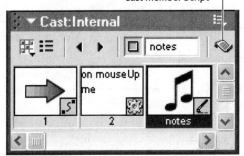

Figure 15.23 Select the cast member to which you want to attach a script (in this case, the musical notes), then click the Cast Member Script button.

Figure 15.24 Type the body of the handler. (The script in this example will cause all sprites based on this cast member to beep when they're clicked.)

Figure 15.25 Type a script in the Movie Script window. (The script in this example will set the background color of the Stage to black when the movie begins to play.)

To write a cast-member script:

1. Select a cast member in the Cast window.

2. Click the Cast Member Script button (**Figure 15.23**).

   A Script window opens, displaying the first and last lines of a handler (identical to those for a sprite behavior script).

3. *(optional)* If you want to change the first line of the script from on mouseUp (which Director inserted automatically) to something else (such as on mouseDown), do so.

4. Type one or more Lingo commands to form the body of the handler (**Figure 15.24**).

5. Close the Script window.

   The compiled script is attached to the cast member, but does *not* become a cast member itself.

6. Create a sprite by dragging the cast member to the Stage or Score.

7. Rewind and test the movie.

To write a movie script:

1. Select an empty position in the Cast window.

2. Choose Window > Script.

   An empty Script window opens.

3. Type a script consisting of one or more handlers (**Figure 15.25**).

4. Close the Script window.

   The finished, compiled script becomes a cast member.

5. Rewind and test the movie.

To change a behavior script to a movie script (or vice versa):

1. In the Cast window, select the script whose type you want to change.

2. Click the Script tab in the Property Inspector.

3. From the Type pop-up menu in the Property Inspector, choose the type of script you want (**Figure 15.26**).

   The script's icon changes in the Cast window.

Figure 15.26 Choose a script type from the Type menu on the Script tab of the Property Inspector.

✔ Tip

■ This technique is useful if you create the wrong type of script by mistake; but remember that certain handlers only work in certain types of scripts. For example, if a movie script starts with on startMovie, it won't work if you change it to a behavior script.

To edit an existing script:

1. In the Cast window, select the script you want to edit.

   or

   If the script you want to edit is a cast-member script, select the cast member to which it's attached.

2. Click the Cast Member Script button in the Cast window.

   The script opens in a Script window appropriate to the type of script.

3. Edit the script.

4. Close the Script window.

✔ Tips

■ Double-clicking a movie-script cast member opens the script in a Script window, as you would expect. But double-clicking a behavior script opens it in the Behavior Inspector. From there, you can access the script by clicking the Script Window button.

■ Editing a behavior script affects the behavior of all sprites and frames to which it is attached.

Understanding Lingo Elements

Now that you have a basic idea of how Lingo scripts are structured, you're probably curious about the Lingo language itself. Like any other language, Lingo is made up of words and symbols that play certain roles. These words and symbols are known as the *elements* of Lingo. All Lingo elements are defined and explained in Director's Lingo Dictionary, which you can open by choosing Help > Lingo Dictionary.

To get you started, here is a list of the types of elements you'll find in Lingo:

◆ **Commands** instruct your movie to do something. Here are some examples: beep produces a beep, go to moves the playback head to a specified frame, and updateStage makes Director redraw the Stage immediately instead of waiting for a new frame.

◆ **Functions** return a value. The time function, for example, tells you the current time that's set in the computer.

◆ **Keywords** are ordinary English words that have a special meaning in Lingo. Examples include on and the. Keywords are "reserved," meaning that they can't be used for other purposes (such as handler names or variable names).

◆ **Constants** are elements whose values never change. TRUE and FALSE are constants that always have the values 1 and 0, respectively.

◆ **Operators** are terms that compare, combine, or change values. Examples include +, >, and -.

◆ **Properties** are the attributes of an object. locH, for example, is a property of a sprite, indicating its horizontal position on the Stage. You can refer to a property in either of two ways: using dot syntax, as in sprite(1).locH; or using verbose syntax, as in the locH of sprite 1. (For more information about these two syntaxes, see the sidebar, "Flash Talk: Lingo vs. ActionScript.")

WRITING SCRIPTS

347

◆ **Variables** are storage containers to which you assign a name and a value. Typing $a = 0$ in your script, for example, creates a variable named a and assigns the value 0 to it.

◆ **Expressions** are parts of Lingo statements that generate values, such as $(3 * 5) + 10$.

To insert Lingo elements into a script without having to type them:

1. Open a Script window.

2. Click the script at the place where you want to insert a Lingo element.

3. Click one of the Lingo pop-up menus at the top of the Script window (**Figure 15.27**). The available menus are:

   ▲ **Alphabetical Lingo**, which lists Lingo elements (other than those pertaining to 3D) alphabetically.

   ▲ **Categorized Lingo**, which lists Lingo elements (other than those pertaining to 3D) by the type of task they are used to accomplish.

   ▲ **Alphabetical 3D Lingo**, which lists 3D Lingo elements alphabetically.

   ▲ **Categorized 3D Lingo**, which lists 3D Lingo elements by task.

   ▲ **Scripting Xtras**, which lists elements that are not part of standard Lingo but have been added to Lingo by means of specialized plug-ins. (See Chapter 19, "Using Xtras," for more information.)

4. Navigate to the desired submenu and choose the Lingo element you want (**Figure 15.28**).

   The selected element appears at the insertion point in the script.

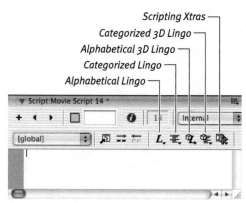

Scripting Xtras
Categorized 3D Lingo
Alphabetical 3D Lingo
Categorized Lingo
Alphabetical Lingo

Figure 15.27 These Lingo menus are on the toolbar at the top of the Script window.

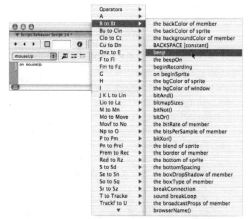

Figure 15.28 Navigate to the desired submenu and choose the Lingo element you want. (The menu shown here is Alphabetical Lingo.)

WRITING SCRIPTS

Flash Talk: Lingo vs. ActionScript

When Lingo was first developed, it was meant to be as easy as possible for beginners to learn. Therefore, it closely resembled other beginners' programming languages that were in use at the time, such as BASIC and HyperTalk. It consisted of a series of statements written in a simplified version of plain English, with each new statement beginning on a new line.

Now, a dozen or so years later, the environment has changed. BASIC is rarely used, and hardly anyone has even heard of HyperTalk. Most people's initial experiences with scripting come from adding JavaScript to their Web pages. Not surprisingly, then, when Macromedia developed the ActionScript language for Flash, the company modeled it closely on JavaScript. For people accustomed to JavaScript and ActionScript, the plain-English syntax of Lingo (which was supposed to be friendly and familiar) may seem hard to grasp.

Macromedia has developed an alternative syntax for Lingo based on the syntax used for JavaScript and ActionScript. The newer syntax is called *dot syntax;* the older is called *verbose syntax.* As an example of how they compare, here's a command that turns on the highlight (the check, *X,* or dot) in the middle of a check box or radio button:

Verbose syntax

```
set the hilite of member "myButton" to TRUE
```

Dot syntax

```
member("myButton").hilite = TRUE
```

Both syntaxes continue to work in Lingo; you can choose the one you feel more comfortable with (or even mix and match them in a single script).

If you choose to use the ActionScript-style dot syntax, you must still remember that the structure of the two languages is fundamentally different. In Lingo, line breaks are important: Director executes scripts line by line. In ActionScript, line breaks don't matter at all: The ends of commands are indicated by semicolons, and within those commands, the priority of tasks is indicated by the depth to which they're nested in a series of curly braces (**Figure 15.29**). An entire ActionScript script could theoretically be written on a single line; this is emphatically not true of Lingo.

```
1  on mouseUp
2     global gExpert
3     if gExpert = TRUE then
4        go to frame 10
5     else
6        go to frame 20
7     end if
8  end
```
Lingo

```
1  on (release) {
2     if (_global.expert == true) {
3        gotoAndPlay(10);
4     } else {
5        gotoAndPlay(20);
6     }
7  }
```
ActionScript

Figure 15.29 The same script as it would be written in Lingo (left) and in ActionScript (right).

WRITING SCRIPTS

Scripting Navigation

One of the most common uses for Lingo scripts is for setting up a movie's *navigation structure*—that is, a series of buttons or menus that permits them to view only the parts of the movie that they want to see, in the order that they want users to see them (**Figure 15.30**). A navigation structure consists of two equally important aspects: a user-interface design (or *front end*) that lets users know where there are and how to get to where they want to go; and a technical mechanism (or *back end*) that makes the user interface work. Designing a good front end is too big a topic to be covered in this book (and is, in fact, the subject of many books in its own right), but this section will show you a few scripting techniques you can use to set up the back end.

The first two tasks in this section will show you how to make a movie pause—either by making the playhead stop at a specific frame in the Score or by making the playhead loop continuously between two frames—until the user provides input by clicking a button. The remaining tasks will show you how to attach a script to a button that will make the playhead jump to a different frame in the Score.

These techniques will work best with a movie that has been designed as a collection of separate scenes. Each scene should have its own place in the Score, perhaps separated from the others by a few empty frames (**Figure 15.31**). For the greatest efficiency, label each scene with a marker (see "Setting Markers" in Chapter 3).

How you set up the front end is up to you, but you'll probably want to have the playhead stop or loop at the end of each scene, until the user can choose which scene he or she wants to go to next.

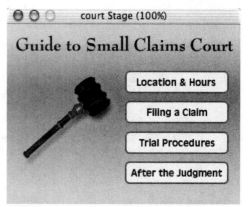

Figure 15.30 The buttons in this movie, with their attached Lingo scripts, allow users to decide which parts of the movie they want to see.

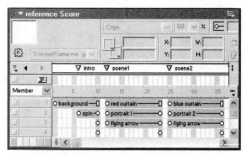

Figure 15.31 This Score is ideally set up for random access by users. Each scene occupies its own section of the Score and is identified by a marker.

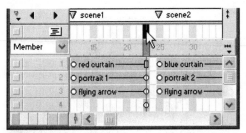

Figure 15.32 In the script channel, select the frame where you want the movie to pause.

Figure 15.33 This script causes a movie to pause by making the playhead play the same frame over and over.

To make the playhead pause at a frame:

1. In the script channel of the Score, select the frame at which you want the play-head to pause (**Figure 15.32**).

2. Double-click the selected frame.

   or

   Choose New Behavior from the Behaviors pop-up menu on the Sprite toolbar.

   A Script window opens, displaying the first and last lines of a handler.

3. In the Script window, type go to the frame as the middle line of the handler (**Figure 15.33**).

   The keyword the identifies the frame at which the playhead is located at the time Director executes the script. In other words, the frame means "the frame to which this script is attached."

4. Close the Script window.

5. Rewind and test the movie.

   When the playhead reaches the frame you selected in step 1, it goes no further.

✔ Tip

- Unlike Macromedia's Flash ActionScript, Director has no "stop" command. The playhead in a Director movie never stops. Instead, this script creates a one-frame loop, in which the playhead plays the same frame over and over again.

To make the playhead loop between two frames:

1. In the script channel of the Score, select the later of the two frames you want the playhead to loop between (**Figure 15.34**).

2. Double-click the selected frame.

   or

   Choose New Behavior from the Behaviors pop-up menu on the Sprite toolbar.

   A Script window opens, displaying the first and last lines of a handler.

3. If you want the playhead to loop back to a specific frame, type go to frame *X* as the middle line of the handler, with *X* identifying the frame you want the playhead to loop back to.

   Note that *X* may be either a frame number or the name of a marker. If it's the name of a marker, it must be enclosed in quotation marks (**Figure 15.35**). If it's a frame number, it must *not* be enclosed in quotation marks (**Figure 15.36**).

   or

   If you want the playhead to loop backward by a specific number of frames, type go to the frame - *X* as the middle line of the handler, with *X* being the number of frames. For example, if you want the playhead to loop back to the frame that's 4 frames before the current frame, you'd type go to the frame - 4 (**Figure 15.37**).

   or

   If you want the playhead to loop back to the closest previous marker, type go loop as the middle line of the handler (**Figure 15.38**).

4. Close the Script window.

5. Rewind and test the movie.

   When the playhead reaches the frame you selected in step 1, it loops back to the frame you identified in step 3 and repeats that pattern indefinitely.

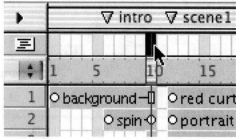

Figure 15.34 In the script channel of the Score, select the later of the two frames between which you want the playhead to loop. (In this example, we want the playhead to loop between frames 6 and 10, so frame 10 is selected.)

```
1  on exitFrame me
2     go to frame "intro"
3  end
```

Figure 15.35 This script causes the playhead to loop back to the marker called "intro."

```
1  on exitFrame me
2     go to frame 6
3  end
```

Figure 15.36 This script causes the playhead to loop back to frame 6.

```
1  on exitFrame me
2     go to the frame - 4
3  end
```

Figure 15.37 This script causes the playhead to loop back 4 frames.

```
1  on exitFrame me
2     go loop
3  end
```

Figure 15.38 This script causes the playhead to jump back to the closest previous marker.

SCRIPTING NAVIGATION

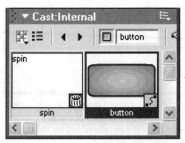

Figure 15.39 Select a cast member (as shown here) or a sprite that you want to use as a button.

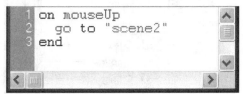

```
1  on mouseUp
2    go to "scene2"
3  end
```

Figure 15.40 This script causes the playhead to jump to the marker called "scene2."

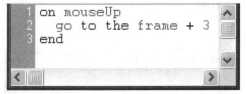

```
1  on mouseUp
2    go to the frame + 3
3  end
```

Figure 15.41 This script causes the playhead to jump ahead three frames.

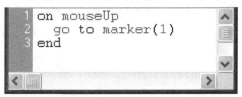

```
1  on mouseUp
2    go to marker(1)
3  end
```

Figure 15.42 This script causes the playhead to jump ahead to the next marker.

To script a button that makes the playhead jump to a new frame:

1. Select a cast member (in the Cast window) or a sprite (on the Stage or in the Score) that you want to use as a button (**Figure 15.39**).

2. If you selected a sprite, choose New Behavior from the Behaviors pop-up menu on the Sprite toolbar.

   or

   If you selected a cast member, click the Cast Member Script button in the Cast window.

   A Script window opens, displaying the first and last lines of a handler.

3. If you want the playhead to jump to a specific frame, type go to frame *X* as the middle line of the handler, with *X* identifying the frame to which you want the playhead to jump.

   Note that *X* may be either a frame number or the name of a marker. If it's the name of a marker, it must be enclosed in quotation marks (**Figure 15.40**). If it's a frame number, it must *not* be enclosed in quotation marks.

   or

   If you want the playhead to jump forward or backward by a specific number of frames, type either go to the frame + *X* or go to the frame - *X* as the middle line of the handler, with *X* being the number of frames. For example, if you want the playhead to jump to the frame that's three frames after the current frame, you'd type go to the frame + 3 (**Figure 15.41**).

   or

   If you want the playhead to jump forward or backward by a specific number of markers, type either go to marker(*X*) or go to marker(-*X*) as the middle line of the handler, with X being the number of markers. For example, if you want the playhead to jump to the next marker, you'd type go to marker(1) (**Figure 15.42**).

continues on next page

4. Close the Script window.

5. If you attached the script to a cast member, make sure there's a sprite on the Stage based on that cast member.

6. Rewind and test the movie.

When you click the button to which you attached the script, the playhead jumps to the frame you identified in step 3.

To script a button that makes the playhead jump to a new frame, and then return:

1. Follow the directions for the preceding task ("To script a button that makes the playhead jump to a new frame"), but in step 3 replace the phrase go to with the word play (**Figure 15.43**).

2. Select the final frame of the scene to which you made the playhead jump in step 1 (**Figure 15.44**).

3. Double-click the selected frame.

or

Choose New Behavior from the Behaviors pop-up menu on the Sprite toolbar.

A Script window opens, displaying the first and last lines of a handler.

4. In the Script window, type play done as the middle line of the handler (**Figure 15.45**).

5. Close the Script window.

6. Rewind and test the movie.

When you click the button to which you attached the script in step 1, the playhead jumps to the frame you specified in the script. When the playhead reaches the frame to which you attached the play done script in steps 3 and 4, it jumps back to the frame it was in when you clicked the button.

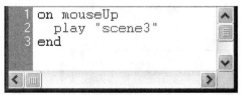

Figure 15.43 This script causes the playhead to jump to the marker called "scene3." The use of play rather than go to means that the playhead will be able to return to the frame it departed from.

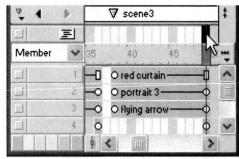

Figure 15.44 Select the final frame of the scene to which you made the playhead jump to (in this case, the final frame of Scene 3).

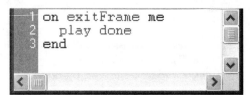

Figure 15.45 The play done command returns the playhead to the frame from which it departed.

✔ Tip

- The play command can also be used to play an entirely different movie. For an example, see "To create a stub projector with external movie files" in Chapter 16.

You type here

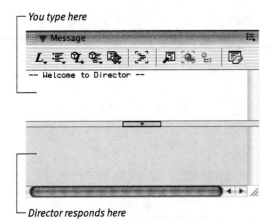

Director responds here

Figure 15.46 The Message window allows you to communicate with Director in real time.

Figure 15.47 Director instantly executes any command that you type in the Message window.

Using the Message Window

Director's Message window is a way for you to "talk" to Director, using the only language it understands: Lingo. When you type a Lingo command in the Message window, Director executes the command instantly. The Message window is therefore a very useful tool for testing and debugging scripts.

You can also use the Message window to keep an eye on what's happening behind the scenes while a movie is playing. When you turn on the Message window's Trace feature, it gives you a continuous, real-time report on the Lingo commands Director is executing. If your scripts aren't working as expected, this technique can help you uncover the problem.

To execute commands from the Message window:

1. Choose Window > Message to open the Message window (**Figure 15.46**).

2. Type a Lingo command in the upper pane of the Message window and press Enter (Windows) or Return (Mac).

   Director executes the command. For example, if you typed go to frame 15, Director would move the playhead to frame 15 (**Figure 15.47**).

✔ Tip

- If you want to enter commands automatically, the Message window offers the same Lingo pop-up menus that the Script window has. See "To insert Lingo elements into a script without having to type them," earlier in this chapter.

To get the value of expressions in the Message window:

1. Choose Window > Message to open the Message window.

2. In the upper pane of the Message window, type put, followed by an expression whose value you want to find out, and press Enter or Return.

   For example:

   ▲ If you wanted to know the product of 23 multiplied by 17, you'd type put 23 * 17.

   ▲ If you wanted to know the value of Director's time function (that is, if you wanted to know the current time), you'd type put the time.

   ▲ If you wanted to know the current value of the global variable named gMyVariable, you'd type put gMyVariable. (See the next section to learn about variables.)

   Director reports the result in the lower pane of the Message window (**Figure 15.48**).

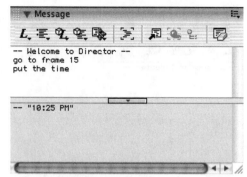

Figure 15.48 When you enter a command (such as the put command) that requires a response from Director, Director responds in the lower pane.

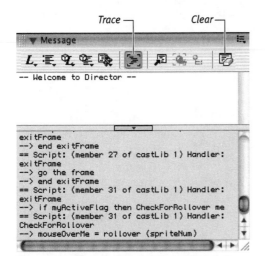

Trace — *Clear* —

```
▼ Message                          ≣,
  L, ≣, ℒ, ℒ, ℜ,  ▣  ▣ ▣ ℒ  ▣

-- Welcome to Director --


exitFrame
--> end exitFrame
== Script: (member 27 of castLib 1) Handler:
exitFrame
--> go the frame
--> end exitFrame
== Script: (member 31 of castLib 1) Handler:
exitFrame
--> if myActiveFlag then CheckForRollover me
== Script: (member 31 of castLib 1) Handler:
CheckForRollover
--> mouseOverMe = rollover (spriteNum)
```

Figure 15.49 When the Trace button is selected, the Message window displays information about each handler that Director executes.

To trace scripts while a movie is playing:

1. Choose Window > Message to open the Message window.

2. Click the Trace button to select it.

3. Play your movie.

   Director reports each Lingo command it executes in the lower pane of the Message window. In addition, it reports other information such as the name of the handler that contains the commands, and the frame that the playhead is in when the commands are executed (**Figure 15.49**).

✔ Tips

- The lower pane of the Message window can fill up quickly when Trace is turned on. In most cases, you won't be able to read the reports in real time. Instead, you can use the scroll bar to scroll through the contents of the window after the movie has finished playing.

- To clear the Message window, click the Clear button.

Using Variables

A *variable* is a container for storing information. The act of creating a variable is called *declaring* the variable. When you declare a variable, you must give it a name. Variable names in Lingo must consist of one or more alphanumeric characters, with no spaces. (They conventionally start with lowercase letters, though this is not technically required.)

The information stored in a variable is called its *value*. In most cases, you assign a value to a variable when you first declare it. (With global variables—which you'll read about in a moment—you declare the variable first and assign a value afterward.) Once a value has been assigned to a variable, it may be changed any number of times.

The value of a variable may be numeric, or it may be a series of alphanumeric characters called a *string*. In order for Lingo to tell the two kinds apart, string values must always be enclosed in quotation marks.

Lingo supports two kinds of variables: local and global. A *local* variable exists only within a single handler, and it ceases to exist after the handler has finished executing. A *global* variable, by contrast, persists throughout a movie: After the variable is created, every handler in the movie recognizes its name and its current value.

It's generally a good idea to use local variables unless you specifically need a variable to be global. That way, you avoid potential conflicts if you happen to give two variables the same name.

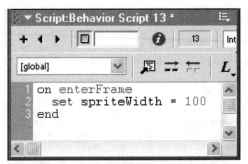

Figure 15.50 When the playhead enters the frame to which this script is attached, this script creates a local variable called spriteWidth with a value of 100.

Figure 15.51 When the movie begins, this script creates a global variable called gFirstName with a value of "Susan".

To declare a local variable:

◆ In any handler, type the line set *variable* = *value*, replacing *variable* with the actual name of the variable, and replacing *value* with the value that you want to assign to the variable.

For example, to create a variable called spriteWidth with a value of 100, type set spriteWidth = 100 (**Figure 15.50**).

✔ Tips

■ If you want to change the value of the local variable later in the handler, just type the same line again with the new value.

■ You can't declare local variables in the Message window. Any variable declared in the Message window is automatically set to be global.

To declare a global variable:

1. In any handler, type the line global *variable*, replacing *variable* with the actual name of the variable.

   Global variable names conventionally begin with the prefix g. So, for example, to create a global variable called gFirstName, type global gFirstName (**Figure 15.51**).

2. At any later point in the handler, type the line *variable* = *value*, replacing *variable* with the actual name of the global variable, and replacing *value* with the value that you want to assign to the variable.

   For example, to give the variable gFirstName a value of "Susan", type gFirstName = "Susan".

USING VARIABLES

359

✔ Tip

- If you want to change the value of the global variable later in the same handler, just type the line from step 2 again but with the new value. If you want to change the value of the global variable in a *different* handler, you must first re-declare the variable. See "To retrieve the value of a variable," below.

To retrieve the value of a variable:

1. If you want to retrieve the value of a global variable in a handler other than the one it was created in, re-declare the variable by typing global *variable* (where *variable* is the actual name of the variable) (**Figure 15.52**).

   If you forget to do this step, Lingo won't recognize the variable as global—it will assume you're using a local variable with the same name.

   (This step isn't necessary for local variables, since they only exist within the handler they were created in.)

2. Use the variable name in any Lingo command that would otherwise include a value.

   For example, to set the width of the cast member myMember, you'd ordinarily have to specify a numeric value, as in set the width of member "myMember" to 100. Instead, you can substitute the name of a variable that has a numeric value, as in set the width of member "myMember" to spriteWidth.

✔ Tip

- To retrieve the value of a variable in the Message window, use the **put** command. See "To get the value of expressions in the Message window," earlier in this chapter.

Figure 15.52 When the playhead enters the frame to which this script is attached, this script re-declares the global variable gFirstName, then puts its value ("Susan") into the text cast member called "Nametag".

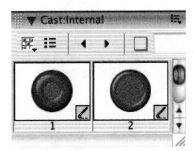

Figure 15.53 These two cast members will serve as the normal and rollover states of a button.

Making Sprites Interactive

This section offers several practical examples of ways in which you can make sprites interactive. Specifically, you'll learn to do the following:

◆ Create a *rollover effect,* in which the appearance of a sprite changes when the user moves the mouse pointer over it.

◆ Make a sprite rotate incrementally, one degree at a time, when it's clicked once.

◆ Make the words within a text sprite change each time it's clicked.

Even if you don't need to accomplish these exact tasks, it's worth experimenting with them anyway, because the scripting principles you'll use have wider applications. For example, the Lingo code that makes a sprite rotate 360 times can be adapted to make a sprite repeat *any* action a fixed number of times.

To create a rollover effect:

1. Create two visual cast members—one for the normal appearance of the sprite, and the other for the "rolled-over" appearance—and place them in adjacent positions in the Cast window.

You can place them anywhere, but for this example we'll assume that they're in positions 1 and 2 in the Cast window (**Figure 15.53**).

2. Drag the first cast member to the Score or the Stage to create a sprite.

The sprite can occupy any sprite channel in the Score, but for this example we'll assume it's in channel 1.

continues on next page

3. With the sprite still selected, choose New Behavior from the Behaviors pop-up menu on the Sprite toolbar.

A Script window opens.

4. Type the following handler in the Script window (**Figure 15.54**). (The last line is already provided by Director. You'll have to change the first line, which is on mouseUp by default):

```
on mouseWithin
    sprite(1).memberNum = 2
end
```

The event handler mouseWithin is activated whenever the mouse pointer is over the sprite to which the script is attached. (See **Table 15.1**, earlier in this chapter, for a list of event handlers.)

The sprite property memberNum specifies which cast member is associated with the sprite. Thus, the second line of this handler switches the cast member associated with sprite 1 to cast member 2. (If the sprite is in a channel other than 1, or if the rollover cast member is in a position in the Cast window other than 2, change the numbers accordingly.)

Continue the script by adding the following handler (**Figure 15.55**):

```
on mouseLeave
    sprite(1).memberNum = 1
end
```

The event handler mouseLeave is activated whenever the mouse pointer leaves the sprite to which the script is attached. (Again, if the sprite is in a channel other than 1, or if the "normal" cast member is in a position in the Cast window other than 1, change the numbers accordingly.)

5. Close the Script window.

Figure 15.54 This handler causes the rollover cast member to replace the normal cast member when the mouse pointer rolls over the button.

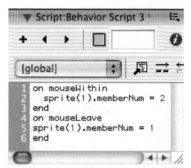

Figure 15.55 This handler causes the normal cast member to replace the rollover cast member when the mouse pointer rolls away from the button.

MAKING SPRITES INTERACTIVE

Normal   *Rollover*

Figure 15.56 The button in action.

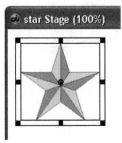

Figure 15.57 Select a sprite to which you want to attach a script that will cause it to rotate.

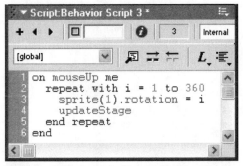

Figure 15.58 When attached to a sprite, this script causes the sprite to rotate 1 degree at a time (to a total of 360 degrees) when the sprite is clicked.

6. Rewind and test the movie.

The sprite's appearance changes whenever the mouse pointer moves onto or off of the sprite (**Figure 15.56**).

✔ Tip

- If you prefer verbose syntax, the lines containing the memberNum property can be written as set the memberNum of sprite 1 to *X* (where *X* is the number of the appropriate cast member).

To rotate a sprite 360 degrees, one degree at a time:

1. In the Score or on the Stage, select a rotatable sprite, such as a bitmap or a vector shape (**Figure 15.57**).

2. Choose New Behavior from the Behaviors pop-up menu on the Sprite toolbar.

A Script window opens.

3. Type the following handler in the Script window (**Figure 15.58**). (The first and last lines are already provided by Director. Director will also take care of the indentation automatically):

```
on mouseUp
    repeat with i = 1 to 360
        sprite(1).rotation = i
        updateStage
    end repeat
end
```

The body of this handler uses a technique called a *repeat loop*. The repeat with command declares a local variable, i, and gives it an initial value of 1. The rotation property of the sprite is set to the value of i, and the Stage is updated to show the 1-degree rotation. (The updateStage command is necessary because the playhead stays in the same frame until the loop completes. Normally, Director updates the Stage only when the playhead moves to a new frame.)

continues on next page

MAKING SPRITES INTERACTIVE

When Director gets to the line that says end repeat, it automatically returns to the repeat with line and increments the value of i by 1. It then sets the rotation of the sprite to the new value of i and updates the Stage again. This process continues until i reaches 360—the maximum value specified in the repeat with command—at which point the handler ends.

4. Rewind and test the movie.

When you click on the sprite, it rotates 360 degrees, one degree at a time, then stops.

✔ Tip

■ The letter i, which stands for *index*, is the traditional name for a local variable that's used as an incremental counter (as in this script).

To create a text cast member whose text changes when clicked:

1. Choose Window > Text to open the text window.

2. Type the word *YES* (**Figure 15.59**).

The font, size, and other text attributes may be set to whatever you like. (You may, of course, type something other than *YES*, but we'll be using *YES, NO,* and *MAYBE* in this example.)

3. In the Cast window, name the text cast member.

You can name it whatever you like, but in this example, it will be named "response."

4. Drag the text cast member to the Stage or Score to create a sprite.

5. Choose New Behavior from the Behaviors pop-up menu on the Sprite toolbar.

A Script window opens.

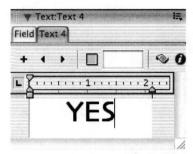

Figure 15.59 Create a text sprite (in this case, the word *YES*) in the Text window.

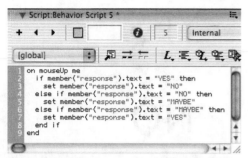

Figure 15.60 This script causes a text cast member's text to cycle among the words *YES*, *NO*, and *MAYBE* each time a sprite based on that cast member is clicked on the Stage.

6. Type the following handler in the Script window (**Figure 15.60**). (The first and last lines are already provided by Director):

```
on mouseUp
    if member("response").text = "YES"
    → then
        set member("response").text =
        → "NO"
    else if member("response").text =
    → "NO" then
        set member("response").text =
        → "MAYBE"
    else if member("response").text =
    → "MAYBE" then
        set member("response").text =
        → "YES"
    end if
end
```

(If you named the cast member something other than "response," or if the text within it is something other than "YES," change the script accordingly.)

The body of this handler is what's known as an *if-then* statement. Director tests the premise that follows the keyword if, and if it's true, it executes the command following the keyword then. If the premise isn't true, the if-then statement may offer additional premises for Director to test. Each of those additional premises is preceded by else if.

continues on next page

In this case, the original premise that Director tests is `member("response")` `.text` = "YES". In other words, Director looks at the `text` property of the cast member named "response" to see if its value is "YES". (The value of the `text` property is equivalent to the text that's in the cast member.) If so, Director changes the value of the cast member's `text` property to "NO" (and in doing so, changes the text contained in the cast member to *NO*). The remaining lines do pretty much the same thing: If the value of the cast member's `text` property is "NO", Director changes it to "MAYBE"; if it's "MAYBE", Director changes it to "YES".

A multiple-line if-then statement must always conclude with the line `end if`, so Director knows that the remainder of the handler is not part of the if-then statement.

7. Rewind and play the movie (**Figure 15.61**).

   Each time you click the text sprite, the text within it changes from *YES* to *NO* to *MAYBE*.

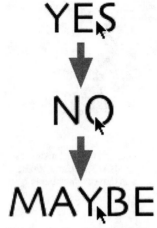

Figure 15.61 The results of clicking the text sprite.

Using Lingo for Animated Cursors

If you've created an animated cursor cast member (covered in Chapter 4, "Animating Sprites"), you can activate it by using the cursor command in a handler.

The following example assumes that you want an animated cursor to replace the normal cursor when the mouse pointer rolls over a particular sprite (which we'll call the *rollover target*), and that you want the normal cursor to return when the mouse pointer leaves the sprite. Once you see how the cursor command works, you can include it in other scripts that use different event handlers.

To activate an animated cursor on rollover:

1. Create an animated cursor.

   (For details, see "To create an animated cursor" in Chapter 4.)

2. In the Cast window, name the animated-cursor cast member.

   You can name it whatever you like, but in this example, it will be named myCursor. (Although a cast member name can be more than one word, it's a good idea to make it a single word if you're going to use the name in a Lingo script.)

3. In the Score or on the Stage, select a sprite to be the rollover target.

4. Choose New Behavior from the Behaviors pop-up menu on the Sprite toolbar.

   A Script window opens.

   continues on next page

USING LINGO FOR ANIMATED CURSORS

5. Type the following script—consisting of two handlers—in the Script window, changing Director's default text where necessary (**Figure 15.62**):

on mouseWithin

    cursor (member "myCursor")

end

on mouseLeave

    cursor –1

end

(If your cursor cast member is named something other than myCursor, change the script accordingly.) The command cursor -1 restores the default arrow cursor.

6. Close the Script window.

7. Rewind and test the movie.

Whenever the mouse pointer moves onto the rollover target, the animated cursor appears; when it leaves the rollover target, the normal cursor returns (**Figure 15.63**).

✔ Tip

■ The cursor command works with non-animated cursors as well. Any 1-bit cast member can be made into a cursor by means of the cursor command, so long as it's no larger than 16 pixels square.

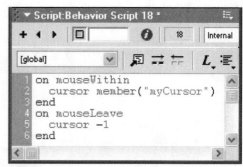

Figure 15.62 This script causes the normal cursor to be replaced by a cursor cast member when the mouse pointer rolls over the sprite to which the script is attached.

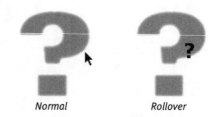

Normal   Rollover

Figure 15.63 The cursor changes when it rolls over the sprite.

CREATING A PROJECTOR

Projector

Figure 16.1 A projector file allows users to play your Director movies without having Director installed on their computers.

Up to this point, whenever you've created a movie in Director, you've played it back in Director. In the real world, however, you can't expect everybody to have Director installed on his or her computer, and you don't want to limit your audience to those who do.

For this reason, Director has the capability to create a *projector*, which is a stand-alone, self-running version of one or more Director movies (**Figure 16.1**). A projector reproduces the action on the Stage, including all interactive elements, just as it looks and sounds in Director. (Of course, the Score, Cast window, and other features of the authoring environment are not included in the projector.) The only serious drawback to using projectors is that the Macintosh version of Director can only create projectors that run on a Macintosh, and the Windows version of Director can only create projectors that run in Windows. (See the "Platform Politics" sidebar for more information.)

continues on next page

A projector can be distributed to users via any medium you choose: CDs, DVDs, Zip disks, email, or other means of file transfer. Projectors can even be distributed over the Web (but unlike Shockwave movies, which you'll learn about in the next chapter, they must be downloaded in their entirety before they can be played). All that's necessary to play a projector is to double-click its icon, just as you would with any Macintosh or Windows application.

This chapter covers setting projector options, creating projectors, packaging projectors and external files for distribution, and more. If you plan to include Xtras in a projector, see Chapter 19, "Using Xtras," for details.

Platform Politics

The fact that the Windows version of Director can only create Windows projectors, and the Macintosh version can only create Mac projectors, has long been a source of frustration among Director developers. Director is a relatively expensive application, and having to buy versions for both platforms makes cross-platform development unaffordable for many individuals and small businesses.

Macromedia has always claimed that the Mac-only/Windows-only restriction stems from fundamental differences between the platforms, and that it simply isn't technically feasible to allow both versions of Director to create projectors for both platforms. In response, many developers have claimed that Macromedia's motives are more mercenary than technical—that forcing cross-platform developers to buy two copies of Director is merely a handy way for Macromedia to increase its sales.

(Interestingly, Macromedia's more recent authoring product, Flash, *can* create projectors for both platforms on a single computer. This evidence weighs against the mercenary argument, since Macromedia could just as easily have increased Flash sales by placing the same platform restrictions on Flash that it did on Director.)

Director movies themselves work equally well on both platforms. Therefore, if you can't afford both Mac and Windows versions of Director, you can develop your movies on just one platform. Then find a friend who runs the other version of Director, and switch offices with him or her for a day or two. With any luck, that will be enough time for you to test your movies on the other platform, make any needed adjustments, and create a projector.

Making a Projector

You can create a projector using two different approaches. The first approach is to embed a Director movie (or multiple movies) inside the projector file, along with any external casts that the movie requires. The result is a single, self-contained file that includes everything necessary to play your movie. This is the easiest sort of projector to create, and it's especially suitable for a nontechnical audience that can't be relied on to handle multiple files.

The second approach is to place the movie (or movies), along with any external casts, *outside* the projector file. In this case, the projector can contain only a single, tiny movie containing a Lingo script that causes it to play the other movies. This sort of projector is called a *stub projector*, and it has several advantages over a self-contained projector:

◆ A stub projector starts playing more quickly than a self-contained projector.

◆ Because the movie files are stored outside the projector, you can easily modify them without having to re-create the projector file each time.

◆ If you're distributing a cross-platform CD-ROM or DVD-ROM, you can conserve disk space by including one stub projector for Windows, one stub projector for Mac, and a single movie (or set of movies) playable by both projectors.

Keep in mind that linked external cast members, unlike external casts, can't be embedded in a projector file. (For information about casts and cast members, both internal and external, see Chapter 2, "Assembling a Cast.") Therefore, if your movie makes use of cast members linked to external files, you'll need to distribute multiple files anyway—so you might consider using a stub projector instead of a self-contained projector.

To prepare movies for distribution in a projector:

1. If you plan to include multiple movies in your projector, copy all the original movie files (along with external casts, if any) into a single distribution folder (**Figure 16.2**).

   You can name the distribution folder whatever you like, but we'll call it Distribution Folder in this example.

2. If any of the movies that you plan to embed in the projector have cast members linked to external files, create a subfolder within the distribution folder, and copy the linked files into that subfolder (**Figure 16.3**).

   Note: If none of the movies has cast members linked to external files, you don't need to do anything else to prepare movies for distribution in a projector. You can skip this and all remaining steps in this task.

3. In Director, open one of the movies that has cast members linked to external files.

   Director attempts to load each external file. If it's unable to locate a file, it presents you with a Locate Replacement dialog box (**Figure 16.4**).

4. If the Locate Replacement dialog box appears, navigate to the proper file and click OK to reestablish the link.

5. In the Cast window, select any cast member that's linked to an external file.

6. Click the Member tab in the Property Inspector.

Figure 16.2 Copy all of the original movie files and external casts into a single folder.

Figure 16.3 Create a subfolder, and copy all linked external files into it.

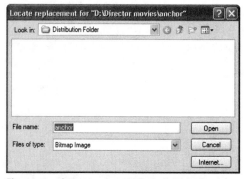

Figure 16.4 If Director doesn't find a linked external file in the expected location, it asks you to locate the file manually.

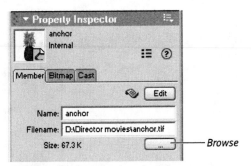

Browse

Figure 16.5 Check and update the link to an external file on the Member tab of the Property Inspector.

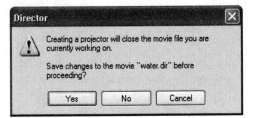

Figure 16.6 This alert box gives you the opportunity to save changes to an open movie before creating a projector. If you choose not to save them, the changes will be lost.

7. In the Filename field of the Property Inspector, check whether the cast member is linked to the proper file—the one that's in the subfolder you created in step 2 (**Figure 16.5**). If not—if it's linked to another copy of the file elsewhere on your hard drive—update the link.

   You can update the link by typing a new pathname directly into the Filename field, or you can click the Browse button (labeled with three dots) and navigate to the new file.

8. Repeat steps 5 through 7 for each remaining cast member that's linked to an external file.

9. Save your changes to the movie.

10. Repeat steps 3 through 9 for each remaining movie that has cast members linked to external files.

To create a self-contained projector:

1. Prepare the movie files as described in the preceding task, "To prepare movies for distribution in a projector."

2. In Director, choose File > Create Projector. If a movie is currently open with unsaved changes, an alert box asks whether you want to save the changes (**Figure 16.6**).

continues on next page

MAKING A PROJECTOR

3. If the alert box appears, click Yes (Windows) or Save (Mac) if you want to save the changes; or click No (Windows) or Don't Save (Mac) if you don't want to save the changes.

The Create Projector dialog box appears (**Figure 16.7**). (On the Mac, this dialog box is mistakenly titled Open.)

4. Click the Options button.

The Projector Options dialog box opens (**Figure 16.8**).

Choose from the following options:

▲ Check **Play Every Movie** if you plan to include several movies in the projector and want them all to play (**Figure 16.9**).

If you leave this option unselected, the projector plays only the first of the embedded movies. (However, the other movies will play if they're triggered by Lingo commands in the first movie.)

▲ Choose **Animate in Background** if you want the projector to continue playing when users switch to another application.

If you don't select this option, the projector pauses when a user switches to another program, and resumes playing when the projector once again becomes the active window.

Options ⌐

Figure 16.7 The Create Projector dialog box allows you to embed movies in a projector.

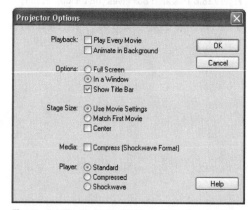

Figure 16.8 The Projector Options dialog box is where you specify how your movies will be displayed.

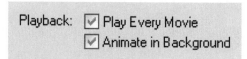

Figure 16.9 The Playback options.

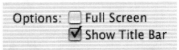

Windows

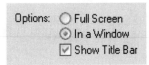

Mac

Figure 16.10 These projector-window options are displayed differently in Windows and Mac, but they accomplish the same thing.

Figure 16.11 A projector window, with and without a title bar.

▲ Select the **Full Screen** option if you want the movie to play in Full Screen mode (**Figure 16.10**). (For more information about Full Screen mode, see "To view the Stage in Full Screen mode" in Chapter 9.)

If you don't want the movie to play in Full Screen mode, select In a Window (Windows), or deselect the Full Screen check box (Mac). The projector will play in a window just large enough to hold the Stage, with the name of the projector displayed in its title bar (**Figure 16.11**).

▲ Deselect the **Show Title Bar** check box if you want the projector window to display without a title bar. (This option is unavailable if you selected Full Screen mode in the previous step.)

Without a title bar, the projector window can't be moved by the user.

continues on next page

▲ Select either **Use Movie Settings** or **Match First Movie** if you plan to include several movies in the projector (**Figure 16.12**).

If you choose Use Movie Settings, the projector window will resize itself to match the Stage dimensions of each movie (**Figure 16.13**). (See "To change the size, location, and background color of the Stage" in Chapter 9.)

If you choose Match First Movie, the projector window will match the Stage dimensions of the first movie in the projector, then remain at that size when it plays the other movies in the projector.

If the projector contains only one movie, it doesn't matter which option you choose.

▲ Select the **Center** check box if you want the projector window to be centered on the user's computer screen (**Figure 16.14**).

If you don't select this option, the projector uses the Stage location saved with each movie file. (See "To change the size, location, and background color of the Stage" in Chapter 9.)

▲ (Mac only) Select the **Reset Monitor to Match Movie's Color Depth** check box if your projector includes an old Director movie that has an 8-bit color depth and uses palette effects. (Since Director no longer supports the creation of 8-bit movies, you'll rarely have any reason to select this option.)

Figure 16.12 If you have multiple movies in a projector, choose a Stage Size setting.

Use Movie Settings

Match First Movie

Figure 16.13 If you choose Use Movie Settings, the size of the projector window changes for movies that have different stage sizes. If you choose Match First Movie, the window stays a constant size.

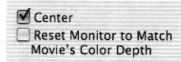

Figure 16.14 Select Center to place the stage at the center of the user's screen. The Reset Monitor option, found only on the Mac, is rarely used anymore.

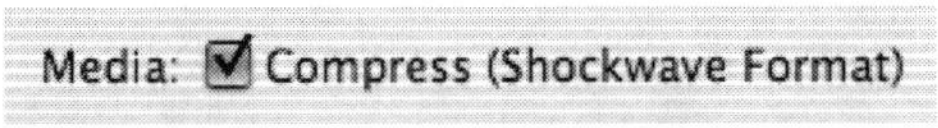

Media: ☑ Compress (Shockwave Format)

Figure 16.15 Select Compress (Shockwave Format) to compress the projector's embedded movies.

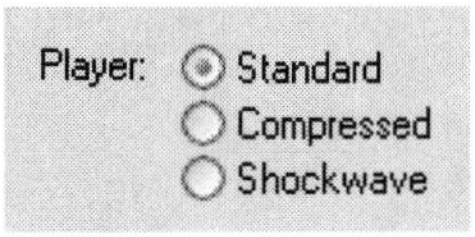

Player: ⦿ Standard
⦾ Compressed
⦾ Shockwave

Figure 16.16 Choose a player option for your projector.

▲ Select the **Compress (Shockwave Format)** check box if you want Director to compress each movie file when it's embedded in the projector (**Figure 16.15**).

This option reduces the projector's file size, but it could result in pauses during movie playback, because each movie file will need to be decompressed before it plays.

Despite the use of the phrase *Shockwave Format*, this option doesn't create a Shockwave movie, and—unlike the Shockwave Player option, which you'll encounter below—it doesn't require the user to have the Shockwave Player installed on his or her computer.

▲ Choose a Player option to determine what kind of mechanism will be loaded into the projector to play back the movies (**Figure 16.16**):

Standard embeds an uncompressed version of the Director player. This option produces a large projector file, but one that starts relatively quickly. **Compressed** embeds a compressed version of the player, which reduces projector size but adds a few seconds' delay before playback while the player is decompressed. **Shockwave** produces the smallest projector file by not embedding the player at all, relying instead on the Shockwave player installed on the user's system. If the player is not installed, the user is prompted to download it. This type of projector is called a *Shockwave projector* or *slim projector*. (Note: The Shockwave option is not available in the educational version of Director.)

continues on next page

MAKING A PROJECTOR

▲ *(Mac only)* Select the **MacOS X** option if you want to create a projector that will run in native mode under OS X, or select the **Classic MacOS** option if you want to create a projector that will run under Mac OS 9 and earlier (**Figure 16.17**).

A projector created with the Classic MacOS option will still run under OS X, but only in Classic mode.

If you select the Classic MacOS option, the **Use System Temporary Memory** option becomes available. This option allows the projector to use system memory when its own memory partition is full. It's selected by default, and there's generally no need to deselect it.

5. Click OK to close the Projector Options dialog box.

6. In the Create Projector dialog box, select the first movie that you want to include in the projector (**Figure 16.18**).

7. Click the Add button.

8. Repeat steps 6 and 7 as many times as necessary to add additional movies or external casts to the projector.

As noted in the introduction to this section, only Director movies and external casts can be embedded in a projector. All other types of linked external files (including digital video files) must remain outside the projector.

If your projector includes multiple movies, they will play in the order in which they appear in the File List (Windows) or Playback Order list (Mac) (**Figure 16.19**).

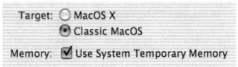

Figure 16.17 On the Macintosh, select the operating system on which you want the projector to play.

Figure 16.18 Select the first movie that you want the projector to play, and click Add.

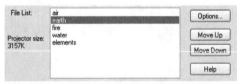

Figure 16.19 Movies in a projector play in the order in which they appear in the Playback Order list (called the File List in the Windows version, shown here).

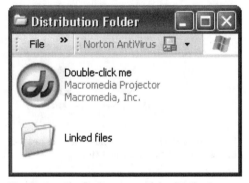

Figure 16.20 You can change the order of movies by clicking the Move Up and Move Down buttons. Here, the movie earth.dir has been moved up in the list.

Figure 16.21 After you double-check all the settings, click Create to create the projector.

Figure 16.22 The final contents of the distribution folder.

9. If necessary, change the order of movies in the list by selecting a movie and clicking Move Up or Move Down (**Figure 16.20**).

   If you need to remove a movie from the list, select it and click Remove.

10. Click Create (**Figure 16.21**).

    The Create Projector dialog box closes, and the Save dialog box appears.

11. Name the projector and click Save.

    If any of the movies in the projector has linked external cast members, be sure to save the projector to the same distribution folder that the original Director files are in, in order to preserve the file links.

12. Double-click the projector to test it.

13. Delete the original movie files from the distribution folder (assuming you have backup copies elsewhere).

    The contents of the distribution folder may now be copied to a CD, or to the distribution medium of your choice (**Figure 16.22**).

✔ Tips

- Whenever you click the Options button in the Create Projector dialog box, Director displays the same options you used the last time you created a projector.

- After a projector has been created, it can't be modified, so check all the settings carefully before you complete the process. The only way to make changes in a projector is to re-create it from scratch.

- Projectors made with the educational version of Director begin and end with a Macromedia splash screen that says "Not intended for commercial use or distribution." The only way to eliminate that splash screen is to create a projector with the full commercial version of Director.

MAKING A PROJECTOR

To create a stub projector with external movie files:

1. Prepare the movie files as described in "To prepare movies for distribution in a projector," earlier in this section, but place the movies in a subfolder within the distribution folder (**Figure 16.23**).

   The subfolder can be called whatever you want; we'll call it Movies in this example.

2. Create another subfolder within the distribution folder, and call it Xtras (**Figure 16.24**).

   The folder *must* be called Xtras, or else it won't be recognized. (To understand what you're doing in this and some of the following steps, you might want to skip ahead and read Chapter 19, "Using Xtras.")

3. Copy the following files from the Director MX application folder to the newly created Xtras folder:

   ▲ **Windows:** dirapi.dll, imi32.dll, proj.dll, msvcrt.dll

   ▲ **Mac:** DPLLib, IMLLib, ProjLib, MacromediaRuntimeLib

   The projector will need these resource files in order to run properly.

4. For each of the movie files in the Movies folder, follow the directions in "To distribute Xtras with a projector (without embedding them in a movie)" in Chapter 19, "Using Xtras."

   You can ignore step 9 of those directions, which tells you to create an Xtras folder, since you've already done so.

Figure 16.23 Place the movie files in a subfolder within the distribution folder.

Figure 16.24 The folder that holds resources needed by the projector must be called Xtras.

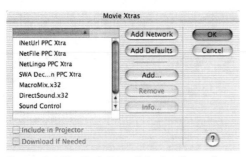

Figure 16.25 The Movie Xtras dialog box lists software plug-ins used by the movie. For more information, see Chapter 19, "Using Xtras."

Deselect

Figure 16.26 For each Xtra in the list, deselect Include in Projector.

5. If you want to keep users from opening your movie files, convert them to protected format. (See the next section, "Protecting Movie Files.")

   or

   If you want to protect your files and save disk space at the same time, compress them in Shockwave format. (See "Converting Multiple Movies" in Chapter 17)

   Of course, you're not required to do either of these things; you're free to leave the movie files as they are.

6. In Director, choose File > New > Movie to create a new, empty movie.

   This will be the *stub movie,* the only movie embedded in the stub projector.

7. If you wish, set the stub movie's Stage size and background color to match those of the first movie that the projector is intended to play.

   Doing so will "camouflage" the stub movie if it flashes on the screen when the projector first opens.

8. Choose Modify > Movie > Xtras.

   The Movie Xtras dialog box opens (**Figure 16.25**).

9. Select the first Xtra in the list.

10. Deselect the Include in Projector check box (**Figure 16.26**).

11. Repeat steps 9 and 10 for all the remaining Xtras in the list.

continues on next page

MAKING A PROJECTOR

12. Double-click the first frame in the Script channel of the Score (**Figure 16.27**).

A script window opens, containing the first and last lines of an exitFrame script (**Figure 16.28**). (For more information about frame scripts, see Chapter 15, "Scripting Lingo.")

13. In the Script window, type the following as the second line of the script (**Figure 16.29**):

`play movie "@:moviefolder:myMovie.dir"`

For `moviefolder`, substitute the name of the folder in which you placed the movies in step 1 (which, in this case, would be Movies). For `myMovie.dir`, substitute the name of the first movie you want the projector to play. (If the movie has been protected and has a .dxr extension, or has been converted to Shockwave format and has a .dcr extension, use those extensions instead of .dir.)

14. If you want the projector to play an additional movie, type the following as the third line of the script (**Figure 16.30**):

`play movie "moviefolder:myMovie.dir"`

(Make substitutions for `moviefolder` and `myMovie.dir` as described in step 13.) Note that there's no `@:` this time; the `@` character was necessary in the first `play` command, to tell Director to use a relative path; but it must be omitted in succeeding lines.)

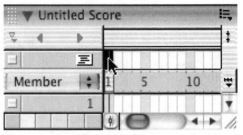

Figure 16.27 Double-click the first frame in the Script channel to create a new frame script.

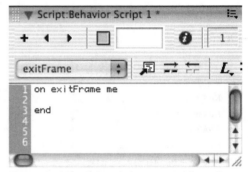

Figure 16.28 The Script window opens with two lines already written for you.

Figure 16.29 Enter this command to play the first movie.

Figure 16.30 The command to play additional movies doesn't need the @ character.

Figure 16.31 Add as many lines to the script as you need to play all the movies.

Figure 16.32 Click Add to embed the stub movie in the projector.

15. Repeat step 14 for all the movies you want the projector to play, in the sequence in which you want them played (**Figure 16.31**).

16. Choose File > Save to save the movie..

You can give it whatever name you like; in this example, we'll call it "stubmovie."

17. Choose File > Create Projector to open the Create Projector dialog box.

18. Set options for the projector, as described in step 4 of "To create a self-contained projector," earlier in this section.

19. In the file-selection pane of the Create Projector dialog box, select the stub movie.

20. Click the Add button to embed the stub movie in the projector (**Figure 16.32**).

21. Click Create.

The Create Projector dialog box closes, and the Save dialog box appears.

continues on next page

MAKING A PROJECTOR

22. Name the projector and click Save.

Be sure to save the projector to the highest level of the distribution folder (that is, not in any subfolders).

23. Double-click the projector to test it.

24. Drag the original stub movie file out of the distribution folder and place it elsewhere for safekeeping.

The contents of the distribution folder may now be copied to a CD, or to the distribution medium of your choice (**Figure 16.33**).

Figure 16.33 The final contents of the distribution folder.

Figure 16.34 The Update Movies dialog box, used here to protect movies, can also be used to update older movies or to convert movies to Shockwave format.

Figure 16.35 Select a folder in which to back up the original movie and cast files.

Protecting Movie Files

Projector files are permanent lockboxes. When you embed movie files and external casts in a self-contained projector, those files can no longer be opened or edited.

However, if you choose to distribute your movies using a stub projector rather than a self-contained projector, your movie files are *not* protected. They're sitting in an ordinary folder, where anyone who has Director can open them, edit them, and "borrow" your cast members or Lingo scripts.

If you don't want to give users that sort of access, you can convert your movie and cast files to a protected format. Protected files operate normally in a projector but can't be opened in Director.

Shockwave movies, which you'll learn about in the next chapter, offer the same level of security as protected files and have the additional advantage of being compressed to save disk space. However, using Shockwave movies may lead to a slight delay as the projector decompresses each one before it's played. By contrast, protected files can be played immediately.

To protect movie or cast files:

1. Choose Xtras > Update Movies.
   The Update Movies Options dialog box opens (**Figure 16.34**).

2. Choose the Protect option.

3. Choose the Back Up Into Folder option to copy the original files to a safe place.

4. Click Browse.
   The Select Folder for Original Files dialog box appears (**Figure 16.35**).

continues on next page

PROTECTING MOVIE FILES

5. Select a folder and click Select Folder (Windows) or Choose (Mac).

The Select Folder for Original Files dialog box closes, and the selected folder appears under Back Up Into Folder in the Update Movies dialog box.

6. Click OK.

The Choose Files dialog box appears (**Figure 16.36**).

7. Select a movie file that you want to protect.

8. Click Add.

9. Repeat steps 7 and 8 to add all the files you want to protect to the list at the bottom of the dialog box, or click Add All to add all the files in the current folder.

10. Click Proceed.

An alert box confirms that the selected files will be updated.

11. Click the Continue button in the alert box.

A progress bar shows you the filenames as they are converted. The resulting files have new file extensions: .dxr for protected movies and .cxt for protected casts (**Figure 6.37**).

✔ Tip

■ If you already have backups of the files you want to protect, you can select the Delete radio button in step 3, and then skip steps 4 and 5. You can't unprotect files once they're protected, though, so be absolutely sure you're not converting your only copies of the files.

File selection list   Proceed

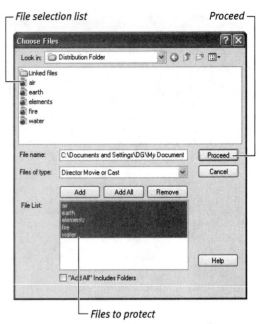

Files to protect

Figure 16.36 In the Choose Files dialog box, select the files that you want to protect.

earth.dir   elements.cst
Unprotected

earth.dxr   elements.cxt
Protected

Figure 16.37 Protected files have different file extensions and icons from unprotected files.

MAKING MOVIES FOR THE WEB

17

Sample.dir
399 KB
Macromedia Director Movie

Sample.exe
3,944 KB
Macromedia Projector

Sample.dcr
202 KB
Macromedia Director Shockwave

Figure 17.1 From the top: a Director movie, a projector file made from that movie, and a Shockwave file made from the same movie. Note the difference in file sizes.

In the previous chapter, you learned how to distribute Director movies by creating a projector. Like Director itself, projectors are self-contained programs that can run on any desktop computer, regardless of what other software is installed. But projectors have a major drawback: Their large file size makes them impractical to distribute over the Internet. Macromedia's response to this problem was to create an alternative distribution method called *Shockwave* (**Figure 17.1**).

Technically, Shockwave is just another file format for saving movies created in Director. What's special about Shockwave, however, is that it compresses Director movies down to a very small file size and enables those movies to be played in any Web browser that has the Shockwave Player installed. Also, unlike movies in projectors, Shockwave movies can be *streamed*—that is, the user can start watching the beginning of a movie while the rest of the movie continues to download. Because of these features, Shockwave is a great way to add multimedia and interactive capabilities to Web sites.

continues on next page

This chapter explains the basics of publishing a Director movie in Shockwave format. You'll learn how to create and organize supporting files, how to set the various browser display options, and how to set Shockwave movies to stream as they download. You'll also find tips for smoothing out streaming over low-bandwidth Internet connections.

Flash Talk: Shockwave vs. Flash

Director was being used by multimedia developers long before there was a World Wide Web. For years, Director movies were typically distributed on CD-ROM. When the Web began to eclipse CDs as a distribution source of multimedia content, Macromedia invented Shockwave as a way of keeping Director from becoming obsolete. In other words, Shockwave was an afterthought—a brilliantly designed afterthought, but an afterthought nonetheless.

Macromedia Flash came along a few years later, after the Web had already become popular. Though it has some similarities with Director, Flash was specifically designed as a tool for creating Web content. In addition to featuring data-efficient vector graphics, Flash includes specialized tools designed to test and refine streaming (such as the Bandwidth Profiler), which Director lacks.

Not surprisingly, then, Flash gradually surpassed Shockwave as the most common multimedia format on the Web. As Flash movies appeared in more and more Web pages, an increasing number of people installed the Flash Player on their computers. Today, about 98 percent of Web users in the United States have some version of the Flash Player installed. By contrast, only about 63 percent have some version of the Shockwave Player installed.

It's worth keeping these numbers in mind when you're developing a multimedia or interactive Web site. Naturally, if you want to include features that are unique to Director (such as real-time interactive 3D, described in the next chapter), it makes sense to use Director and Shockwave as your development environment. Similarly, if you plan to distribute your content via a variety of media (such as CD-ROM *and* the Web), Director has the edge in versatility. But if you're creating content specifically for the Web, it makes sense to ask yourself whether you might better off producing it in Flash rather than Director.

```
●●●          HTML: spinner
<!-- -->
<!-- -->
<HTML>
<HEAD>
<TITLE>spinner</TITLE>
<meta http-equiv="Content-Type" content="text/html; charset=i:
</HEAD>
<BODY bgColor="#000000">
<center>
<TABLE border=0 width=100% height=100%>
<TR><TD valign=middle align=center>
<OBJECT classid="clsid:166B1BCA-3F9C-11CF-8075-444553540000"
    codebase="http://download.macromedia.com/pub/shockwave/cabs/
    ID=spinner WIDTH=240 HEIGHT=240>
<param name=src value="spinner.dcr">
<PARAM NAME=swStretchStyle VALUE=none>
<param name=swRemote value="swSaveEnabled='true' swVolume='tr
<PARAM NAME=bgColor VALUE=#000000>
<EMBED SRC="spinner.dcr" bgColor=#000000  WIDTH=240 HEIGHT=24
    TYPE="application/x-director" PLUGINSPAGE="http://www.macrom
</OBJECT>
</TD>
</TR>
</TABLE>
</CENTER>
</BODY>
</HTML>
```

Figure 17.2 To be viewable in a browser, a Shockwave movie must be embedded in an HTML file. The necessary code can be generated by Director itself or by another Macromedia product, Dreamweaver.

Director file extensions

	MOVIES	EXTERNAL CASTS
Original	.dir	.cst
Protected	.dxr	.cxt
Shockwave	.dcr	.cct

Figure 17.1 Director changes the middle letter of each file extension to indicate what sort of file it is. The letter C—which indicates a Shockwave file—stands for "compressed." The letter X—which indicates a protected file—is used in its symbolic capacity to mean "off limits."

Creating a Shockwave Movie

Even with the Shockwave Player installed, a Web browser can't open a Shockwave movie directly. The browser can only open a Web page in which the Shockwave movie has been embedded (**Figure 17.2**). The HTML file for the Web page must contain a link to the embedded Shockwave movie, along with code that tells the browser how to display the movie.

If you use Dreamweaver—another Macromedia product—to construct your Web pages, you can import a Shockwave movie directly into Dreamweaver and embed it in a Web page, just as you would with an ordinary graphic image. Dreamweaver automatically adds all the necessary code to the HTML file.

If you don't use Dreamweaver, you can let Director create the HTML file for you. (See "To change the Formats tab settings," later in this chapter, for information on HTML templates.) This will be a relatively bare-bones HTML file, which you can then flesh out by adding additional code either by hand or in a Web-page editing application.

You convert a movie to Shockwave format by using Director's Publish command, which creates both the Shockwave file (which has a .dcr extension) and the accompanying HTML file. If your movie has any linked external casts, the Publish command creates Shockwave versions of those as well (and gives each one a .cct extension).

For a guide to Director file extensions, see Table **17.1**.

To prepare a movie for conversion to Shockwave format:

1. Create a distribution folder on your hard drive and copy the original Director movie into it.

   If the movie contains Lingo scripts that cause it to play other movies, copy those movies into the folder as well.

2. If the movie has any linked external casts or cast members linked to external files, create a subfolder called dswmedia within the distribution folder, and copy the linked files into that subfolder (**Figure 17.3**).

   The subfolder *must* be called dswmedia, or else the Shockwave movie won't be able to use the linked files.

3. Open the movie in Director.

   Director attempts to load each external file. If it's unable to locate a file, it presents you with a Locate Replacement dialog box (**Figure 17.4**).

4. If the Locate Replacement dialog box appears, navigate to the proper file and click OK to reestablish the link.

5. In the Cast window, select any cast member that's linked to an external file.

   If your movie contains no cast members that are linked to external files, you can skip ahead to step 9.

6. Click the Member tab in the Property Inspector.

7. In the Filename field of the Property Inspector, check whether the cast member is linked to the proper file—the one that's in the dswmedia folder you created in step 2 (**Figure 17.5**). If not—if it's linked to another copy of the file elsewhere on your hard drive—update the link.

Figure 17.3 Create a subfolder called dswmedia, and copy all linked external files into it.

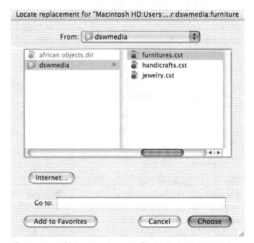

Figure 17.4 If Director doesn't find a linked external file in the expected location, it asks you to locate the file manually.

Figure 17.5 Check and update the link to an external file on the Member tab of the Property Inspector.

CREATING A SHOCKWAVE MOVIE

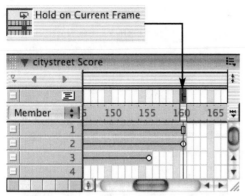

Figure 17.6 Drag the Hold on Current Frame behavior to the last frame of your movie in the script channel.

You can update the link by typing a new pathname directly into the Filename field, or you can click the Browse button (labeled with three dots) and navigate to the new file.

8. Repeat steps 5 through 7 for each remaining cast member that's linked to an external file.

9. If your movie uses any nonstandard Xtras, follow the directions in the section called "Using Xtras with Shockwave Movies" in Chapter 19.

   If you're not sure whether your movie contains nonstandard Xtras, you might want to read Chapter 19 now to get some background on Xtras.

10. Shockwave movies loop by default, regardless of whether the Loop Playback button is selected in the Control Panel. If you want your movie *not* to loop—that is, if you want it to play once and then stop—do the following:

    ▲ Choose Window > Library Palette to open the Library palette.

    ▲ In the Library palette, choose Navigation from the Library List pop-up menu.

    ▲ Drag the Hold on Current Frame behavior from the Library palette to the Score, and drop it in the script channel of the last frame of your movie (**Figure 17.6**).

11. Choose File > Save to save your changes to the movie.

12. Repeat steps 2 through 11 for any additional movies that you copied into the distribution folder in step 1.

To convert a movie to Shockwave format:

1. Follow the instructions in the previous task, "To prepare a movie for conversion to Shockwave format."

2. Open the movie in Director (if it's not open already).

3. If you wish, adjust Director's Publish settings to suit your needs. (See "Working with Publish Settings" later in this chapter for instructions.).

    If you don't change the Publish settings, Director will use the default settings, which are suitable for most purposes.

4. Choose File > Publish.

    If you've changed the Publish Settings, or made any other changes to the movie that haven't been saved, a dialog box appears asking if you want to save the changes (**Figure 17.7**).

    You must choose Save in order to continue the publishing process. If you choose Don't Save, Director won't create a Shockwave movie.

5. Click Save to close the dialog box.

    Director creates several files: a Shockwave version of the movie, the HTML file needed to play the movie in a browser, and Shockwave versions of any external casts used by the movie. By default, all these files are placed in the same folder as the original Director movie—that is, in the distribution folder you created in step 1 (**Figure 17.8**).

    Director launches your default browser and plays the Shockwave movie in the browser (**Figure 17.9**).

Figure 17.7 If this dialog box appears, you must click Save in order to continue the publishing process.

Figure 17.8 All Shockwave-related files— the Shockwave movie, the HTML file, and any external casts—are placed in the same folder as your Director movie.

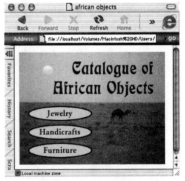

Figure 17.9 Director launches your default browser and plays the Shockwave movie.

CREATING A SHOCKWAVE MOVIE

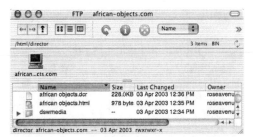

Figure 17.10 This FTP program has been used to upload the contents of the distribution folder to a Web server.

6. Repeat steps 1 through 5 for any additional movies in the distribution folder.

7. If Director has placed Shockwave cast files (with a .cct extension) in the root level of the distribution folder, drag them into the dswmedia folder.

8. Remove the original Director movies from the distribution folder, and remove original external cast files (if any) from the dswmedia folder.

   (Shockwave movies and casts can't be edited or changed, so make sure not to delete the original Director movies and casts unless you have backup copies somewhere.)

   Everything in the distribution folder—including the Shockwave movies, the HTML files, and the dswmedia folder and its contents—may now be uploaded to a Web server, using the FTP application of your choice (**Figure 17.10**).

✔ Tip

- If you want a Shockwave movie or cast to be saved to a folder other than that where the original movie or cast is located, hold down the Alt key (Windows) or Option key (Mac) while you choose File > Publish. Director will give you a standard Save As–style dialog box that allows you to choose a new name or location for each file.

Playing a Shockwave Movie

If you don't already have the latest version of the Shockwave Player installed, go to Macromedia's Web site, at www.macromedia.com/software/shockwaveplayer/download/, and download it before proceeding. (Director MX is designed to work with version 8.5 of the Shockwave Player, the same version that was used with Director 8.5. There's no MX-specific Shockwave Player.) The Shockwave Player can play Shockwave movies created by Director 6 or later.

The Shockwave Player is designed to work with Netscape Navigator 4.0 or later and AOL 4.0 or later on both Mac and Windows computers. Shockwave Player also works with Microsoft Internet Explorer 4.0 or later (Windows) or Internet Explorer 4.5 or later (Mac). In general, however, it works with any current browser that accepts standard browser plug-ins.

To play a Shockwave movie that's on a drive in your computer:

1. Launch your Web browser.

2. From the Web browser, choose File > Open File, and select the HTML file to which the Shockwave movie is linked.

3. Click Open.

    The HTML page opens and plays the embedded Shockwave movie (**Figure 17.11**).

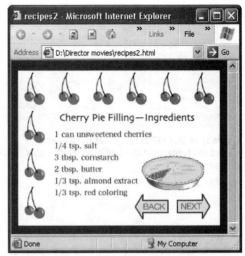

Figure 17.11 The Shockwave movie displayed in this browser window is located on the computer's hard drive. It was opened by choosing File > Open File and navigating to the HTML file associated with the movie.

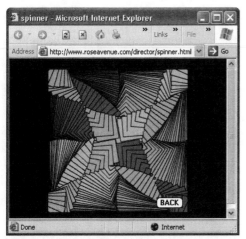

Figure 17.12 This Shockwave movie is on the Web. It was opened in the browser by entering the URL of the HTML file associated with the movie.

To play a Shockwave movie that's on the Web:

1. Connect to the Internet and launch your Web browser.

2. In the Web browser, enter the URL of the HTML document to which the Shockwave movie you want to view is linked.

   The HTML page opens and plays the embedded Shockwave movie (**Figure 17.12**).

To preview a Shockwave movie from within Director:

1. Open the Director movie that you want to preview in a browser.

2. Choose File > Preview in Browser.

   Director launches your default browser and plays the Shockwave movie. (Certain features, such as the ability to resize the Shockwave movie window, may not work when you preview a Shockwave movie using the Preview in Browser command.)

✔ Tip

■ If you want Director to preview the movie in a browser other than your computer's default browser, follow the directions in the following task, "To specify a browser for previewing a movie."

To specify a browser for previewing a movie:

1. In Director, choose Edit > Preferences > Network (Windows) or Director > Preferences > Network (Mac) to display the Network Preferences dialog box (**Figure 17.13**).

2. Click Browse.

   The Select Browser dialog box appears (**Figure 17.14**).

3. Choose the browser application that you want Director to use for previewing your movie.

4. Click Open (Windows) or Choose (Mac).

5. Click OK to close the Network Preferences dialog box.

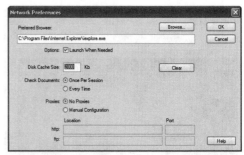

Figure 17.13 Use the Network Preferences dialog box to select the browser that Director will use to preview your Shockwave movie.

Figure 17.14 Navigate to your preferred browser in the Select Browser dialog box.

PLAYING A SHOCKWAVE MOVIE

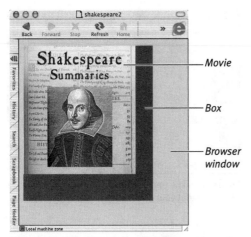

Movie

Box

Browser window

Figure 17.15 The dimensions of these three elements interact with each other in ways that affect the Shockwave movie's appearance in the browser.

Controlling the Size of a Shockwave Movie

Director gives you control over how your Shockwave movie will behave when a user resizes a browser window. For example, you can set the Shockwave movie to resize dynamically along with the browser window, or to remain the same size regardless of the size of the browser window.

To set these resizing options, you use Director's Publish settings. You'll find out more about the Publish settings in the next section, "Working with Publish Settings."

Controlling the size of a Shockwave movie involves relationships among three different elements, each of which may be resized independently of the others (**Figure 17.15**):

◆ The browser window, whose size is determined by the user.

◆ The rectangle within which the Shockwave movie appears on the HTML page. Macromedia has no official name for this rectangle; we'll just call it "the box." You change the size of the box using the Dimensions menu on the General tab in the Publish Settings dialog box.

◆ The Shockwave movie itself. You change the size of the movie using the Stretch Style menu on the Shockwave tab in the Publish Settings dialog box.

Some of the relationships among these elements may be counterintuitive at first, but will become clear after some experimentation.

To set Shockwave movie resizing options:

1. Choose File > Publish Settings to display the Publish Settings dialog box.

2. Select the General tab (**Figure 17.16**).

3. Make a choice from the Dimensions pop-up menu (**Figure 17.17**):

   The choices on this menu affect the size of the box (the rectangle within which the Shockwave movie is displayed), which isn't necessarily the same as the size of the Shockwave movie.

   ▲ Choose **Match Movie** (the default setting) to make the box match the exact dimensions of the Stage in your Director movie. The box will remain at this size regardless of how the user resizes the browser window. If the user makes the browser window smaller than the box, the box (and the movie within it) will be cropped.

   ▲ Choose **Pixels** to set fixed rectangular dimensions for the box by using the Width and Height fields below the menu (**Figure 17.18**). As with Match Movie, the box will remain at the size you specify regardless of how the user resizes the browser window.

   ▲ Choose **Percentage of Browser Window** to make the box change size dynamically along with the browser window. Set percentages in the Width and Height fields below the menu (**Figure 17.19**) to determine the size of the box relative to the browser window. If you set both of these to 50 percent, for example, then the box will always be half the size of the browser window. The width and height default to 100 percent each.

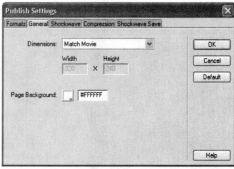

Figure 17.16 The General tab allows you to set the size of the box that your Shockwave movie is displayed in.

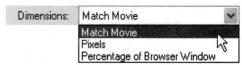

Figure 17.17 Choose a sizing option from the Dimensions pop-up menu.

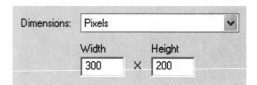

Figure 17.18 Set fixed rectangular dimensions for the box by filling in the Width and Height fields when you choose Pixels from the Dimensions pop-up menu.

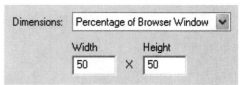

Figure 17.19 Set percentages for the size of the box relative to the browser window by filling in the Width and Height fields when you choose Percentage of Browser Window.

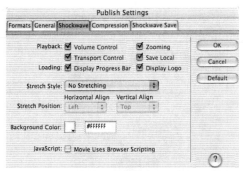

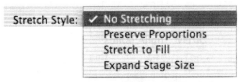

Figure 17.20 The Shockwave tab lets you determine the display characteristics of your Shockwave move, including its size and position.

Figure 17.21 Make a selection from the Stretch Style pop-up menu, which determines the size of your Shockwave movie in relation to the box it's displayed in.

Figure 17.22 A Shockwave movie as it looks in a browser when published with the default settings of Match Movie (on the Dimensions menu on the General tab) and No Stretching (on the Stretch Style menu on the Shockwave tab).

4. Select the Shockwave tab (**Figure 17.20**).

5. Make a choice from the Stretch Style pop-up menu (**Figure 17.21**):

The choices on this menu affect the size of the Shockwave movie itself, which isn't necessarily the same as the size of the box you set on the General tab.

▲ Choose **No Stretching** (the default setting) to make the movie play at the same size at which it was created in Director, regardless of the size of the box that it's displayed in (**Figure 17.22**). If the box is smaller or larger than the movie, Director aligns the movie at the upper left corner of the box, as shown earlier in **Figure 17.15**. If the box is larger than the movie, Director fills in the unused portions of the box with the color that you'll specify in step 8.

continues on next page

▲ Choose **Preserve Proportions** if you want the movie to grow or shrink to fit the size of the box and you also want it to retain its original *aspect ratio* (that is, its ratio of width to height). If the box is smaller or larger than the movie, Director aligns the movie within the box according to the alignment settings that you'll specify in step 6. If the aspect ratio of the box is different from the aspect ratio of the movie, Director fills in the unused portions of the box with the color that you'll specify in step 8 (**Figure 17.23**).

▲ Choose **Stretch to Fill** if you want the movie to grow or shrink to fit the size of the box, without retaining its original aspect ratio. This option is rarely used, since it allows the movie to be distorted (**Figure 17.24**).

▲ Choose **Expand Stage Size** if you want the Stage in the Shockwave movie to grow or shrink to fit the size of the box. Only the Stage changes size; the sprites remain the same (**Figure 17.25**). If the Stage becomes smaller or larger than the Stage in the original movie, Director aligns the sprites in relation to the Stage according to the alignment settings that you'll specify in step 6.

Figure 17.23 If you choose Preserve Proportions, the movie grows or shrinks to fit the size of the box, but it always retains its aspect ratio.

Figure 17.24 If you choose Stretch to Fill, the sprites in a movie may appear distorted if the browser window is resized.

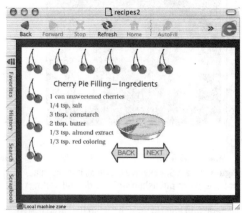

Figure 17.25 If you choose Expand Stage Size, the Shockwave movie's Stage grows and shrinks as the browser window is resized, but the sprites remain the same size. (This movie's original Stage size can be seen in Figure 17.11.)

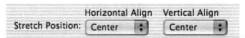

Figure 17.26 Align your movie in the browser window by making choices from the Horizontal Align and Vertical Align pop-up menus.

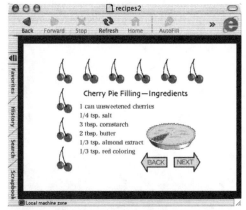

Figure 17.27 The same movie as in Figure 17.25, with Expand Stage Size still selected, but with the Horizontal Align and Vertical Align pop-up menus set to Center.

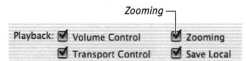

Figure 17.28 Choose the Zooming option to allow your movie to resize along with the browser window.

6. Use the Horizontal Align and Vertical Align pop-up menus (**Figure 17.26**) to specify how the Shockwave movie is aligned with the box it's displayed in (**Figure 17.27**).

(These menus may or may not be available, depending on the previous selections you've made.)

7. If you chose anything other than No Stretching from the Stretch Style menu, make sure the Zooming check box is selected (**Figure 17.28**).

If the Zooming check box (which is selected by default) is deselected, the Shockwave movie will always remain at its original size, regardless of what's chosen on the Stretch Style menu.

8. Choose a color from the Background Color menu to specify the color that Director uses to fill unused portions of the box. (This color also fills the entire box when the Shockwave movie is loading.)

By default, Director sets this color to be the same as the background color of the Stage.

9. Click OK to close the Publish Settings dialog box.

Working with Publish Settings

Choose File > Publish Settings to change the settings used by the Publish command when you create your Shockwave movie. These settings are saved when you save your Director movie.

While the purposes of many of the Publish settings are self-explanatory, a few require some background information:

◆ **Contextual menu:** When a Shockwave movie is displayed in a Web browser, users can right-click (Windows) or Control+click (Mac) the browser window to display a contextual menu that contains various playback commands (**Figure 17.29**). You can determine what commands are available on the contextual menu by making choices on the Shockwave tab in the Publish Settings dialog box.

◆ **Image compression:** Because bitmapped images often have large file sizes, it's highly desirable to compress them when they're intended for downloading from the Web. Director allows you to specify compression settings for each bitmapped cast member individually or to set global compression settings on the Compression tab in the Publish Settings dialog box. For more about image compression, see the "Compressing Bitmapped Images" sidebar later in this section.

Figure 17.29
This contextual menu becomes available when a Shockwave movie is playing in a browser.

WORKING WITH PUBLISH SETTINGS

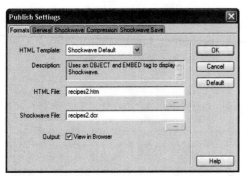

Figure 17.30 The Formats tab is where you choose the type of HTML file you'd like to associate with your Shockwave movie. It also allows you to rename the movie file and associated files.

◆ **Shockmachine:** Macromedia used to market a product called Shockmachine that would allow users to download Shockwave movies from the Web, save the movies on their computer, and play them whenever they wanted. (It was mostly used as a games console.) Though Shockmachine is no longer developed or supported, it's still available on a few software-download Web sites. The Shockwave Save tab in the Publish Settings dialog box is intended strictly for movies that are designed for use with Shockmachine. Unless you have reason to believe that your movie will be saved by users of Shockmachine, you can ignore this tab entirely.

The Publish Settings dialog box contains up to six tabs, depending on which HTML template you select. This section serves as a reference for these settings.

To change the Formats tab settings:

1. Choose File > Publish Settings to open the Publish Settings dialog box (if it's not open already).

2. Select the Formats tab (**Figure 17.30**).

continues on next page

3. Choose a template from the HTML Template pop-up menu (**Figure 17.31**) to determine what sort of HTML file will be created along with the Shockwave movie:

▲ Choose **No HTML Template** to create only the Shockwave movie, without an accompanying HTML file. You might choose this option if you plan to distribute the Shockwave movie with a stub projector (see "To create a stub projector with external movie files" in Chapter16) or if you plan to create an HTML page in Dreamweaver (see "Creating a Shockwave Movie" at the beginning of this chapter).

▲ The **3D Content Loader** template creates an HTML file identical to that created by Shockwave Default (below), except that it includes a fancier progress bar advertising that the movie includes 3D content. Director selects this as the default template if your movie has any 3D sprites, but there's never any technical need for you to use it.

▲ Choose **Shockwave Default** to create an HTML file that simply plays your Shockwave movie, with no "bells and whistles" other than a progress bar and Shockwave logo that appear while the movie loads (**Figure 17.32**).

▲ Choose **Detect Shockwave** to create an HTML file that includes code to detect whether users have the correct version of the Shockwave Player installed. If they don't, they receive a message to update their Player; otherwise, the Shockwave movie plays normally. (Note that, due to the many possible combinations of browser versions and operating system versions, this code isn't 100 percent reliable; it can produce false positives and false negatives.)

Figure 17.31 Choose a template from the HTML Template pop-up menu.

Figure 17.32 If you select the Shockwave Default template, this logo and progress bar appear while the Shockwave movie loads.

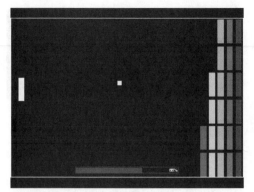

Figure 17.33 If you select the Loader Game template, the user can play a game while the Shockwave movie loads.

▲ Choose **Fill Browser Window** to expand the Shockwave movie so that it fills the entire browser window. Choosing this option is equivalent to selecting the Shockwave Default template, selecting Percentage of Browser Window (with 100 percent specified for both dimensions) from the Dimensions menu on the General tab, and selecting Stretch to Fill from the Stretch Style menu on the Shockwave tab. (See "To set Shockwave movie resizing options," earlier in this chapter.)

▲ Choose **Loader Game** to create an HTML file that displays a game with a progress bar while your Shockwave movie loads (**Figure 17.33**). When the Shockwave movie is fully loaded, the game disappears (in mid-play!) and the movie plays.

▲ Choose **Progress Bar with Image** to create an HTML file that displays a progress bar and an image while your Shockwave movie loads. (The image is, by default, the first frame of the Shockwave movie, but this can be changed on the Image tab.) When the Shockwave movie is fully loaded, the image disappears and the movie plays.

continues on next page

WORKING WITH PUBLISH SETTINGS

▲ The **Shockwave with Image** template includes code that automatically installs the Windows version of the Shockwave Player if the user doesn't already have it installed. For Mac users who don't have the Shockwave Player installed, the HTML page displays a still image instead of the Shockwave movie. (The image is, by default, the first frame of the Shockwave movie, but it can be changed on the Image tab.) For users on either platform who already have the Player installed, this template behaves identically to the Progress Bar with Image template (above).

▲ The **Simple Progress Bar** template is similar to the Shockwave Default template, but it displays a larger, 3D-style progress bar (without the Shockwave logo) while the Shockwave movie loads **(Figure 17.34)**.

▲ The **Center Shockwave** template is similar to the Shockwave Default template, but it uses an HTML table to center the Shockwave movie on the Web page.

4. By default, Director saves the Shockwave, HTML, and image files to the same folder (and with the same name) as the original Director movie. If you want to change the name or location of any of these files, do so in the fields at the bottom of the dialog box **(Figure 17.35)**.

Figure 17.34 If you select the Simple Progress Bar template, this 3D-style progress bar appears while the Shockwave movie loads.

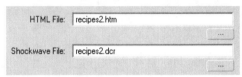

Figure 17.35 Specify the names and locations of the HTML and Shockwave files by using the HTML File and Shockwave File fields.

Output: ☑ View in Browser

Figure 17.36 Leave the View in Browser option selected if you want Director to launch the default browser and play your Shockwave movie when you use the Publish command.

5. The View in Browser check box (**Figure 17.36**), selected by default, instructs Director to launch the default browser and play your Shockwave movie when you choose the Publish command. If you don't want Director to do these things, deselect the check box.

6. If you don't wish to change any more settings, click OK to close the Publish Settings dialog box.

✔ Tip

■ If you choose an HTML template that displays additional material before the beginning of the Shockwave movie, Director may create additional Shockwave files when you publish the movie. (For example, if you choose the Loader Game template, Director will place a file called loader_game.dcr in the same folder in which it places your Shockwave movie.) Be sure to upload these files to the Web server along with the rest of the contents of your distribution folder.

WORKING WITH PUBLISH SETTINGS

407

To change the General tab settings:

1. Choose File > Publish Settings to open the Publish Settings dialog box (if it's not open already).

2. Select the General tab.

3. Set the size of the box in which your Shockwave movie will be displayed by making a selection from the Dimensions pop-up menu.

   (For information about this menu and its choices, see "To set Shockwave movie resizing options," earlier in this chapter.)

4. Choose a background color for the Web page by making a selection from the Page Background menu (**Figure 17.37**) or by entering a hexadecimal value in the adjacent field.

   By default, Director sets this color to be the same as the background color of the Stage.

5. If you don't wish to change any more settings, click OK to close the Publish Settings dialog box.

To change the Shockwave tab settings:

1. Choose File > Publish Settings to open the Publish Settings dialog box (if it's not open already).

2. Select the Shockwave tab.

3. Set the Playback options to determine which choices will be available to your users from the contextual menu when your movie is played in a browser (**Figure 17.38**).

Figure 17.37 Use the Page Background color menu to choose a background color for your HTML page.

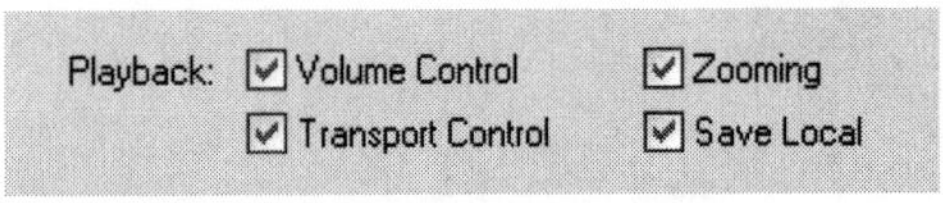

Figure 17.38 The Playback options determine which menu choices are available from a Shockwave movie's contextual menu during playback.

Figure 17.39 The Loading options determine whether the user will see a progress bar or a Shockwave logo while the Shockwave movie loads.

All of these choices are selected by default. (Note that the contextual menu isn't displayed automatically, so most users won't know that these choices are available.)

▲ Select **Volume Control** to allow your users to adjust the volume of your movie.

▲ Select **Transport Control** to give your users controls for restarting, pausing, playing, and fast-forwarding your movie.

▲ Select **Zooming** to allow the Shockwave movie to resize dynamically when the user resizes the browser window (This option has no effect if No Stretching is selected on the Stretch Style menu. See "To set Shockwave movie resizing options," earlier in this chapter.)

▲ Select **Save Local** to allow your users to save the movie in Shockmachine. (This option is, for the most part, obsolete. See the introduction to this section.)

4. Set the Loading options to determine what the user will see while the Shockwave movie is being loaded in the browser (**Figure 17.39**).

(These options have no effect unless you've chosen Shockwave Default from the HTML Templates menu on the Formats tab. See "To change the Formats tab settings," earlier in this section.)

5. Make a choice from the Stretch Style pop-up menu to determine the size of your Shockwave movie in relation to the box it's displayed in.

(For information about this menu and its choices, see "To set Shockwave movie resizing options," earlier in this chapter.)

continues on next page

WORKING WITH PUBLISH SETTINGS

6. Make choices from the Horizontal Align and Vertical Align pop-up menus to determine how the Shockwave movie is aligned with the box it's displayed in.

(For information about these menus, see "To set Shockwave movie resizing options," earlier in this chapter.)

7. Choose a color from the Background Color menu to specify the color of the box in which the Shockwave movie is displayed. (For more information, see "To set Shockwave movie resizing options," earlier in this chapter.)

8. If your movie includes any Lingo scripts that communicate with the browser via JavaScript, select the Movie Uses Browser Scripting check box (**Figure 17.40**).

9. If you don't wish to change any more settings, click OK to close the Publish Settings dialog box.

✔ Tip

■ If you don't want viewers of your Shockwave movie to have access to a contextual menu, you can deselect the Display Context Menu in Shockwave check box on the Shockwave Save tab in the Publish Settings dialog box. If you do so, any changes you made to the menu in step 3 become irrelevant.

Figure 17.40 Select the Movie Uses Browser Scripting option if your movie includes any Lingo scripts that communicate with the browser via JavaScript.

Compressing Bitmapped Images

Director offers two types of compression for bitmapped images: Standard and JPEG. Standard compression is *lossless* compression, meaning that Director uses sophisticated algorithms to squeeze all the image data into a smaller space for storage. When the movie is played back, Director decompresses the data in order to display the image. The advantage of lossless compression is that the final image looks identical to the original one. However, this form of compression offers relatively little savings in file size, and it causes some delay in playing the movie while the compressed images are being decompressed.

If you want to greatly reduce the file size, you can choose JPEG compression. JPEG is a *lossy* form of compression, meaning that Director throws away information when it stores the image. JPEG compression offers you an image-quality slider that controls how much information will be thrown away, and thus how much the compressed image will differ in quality from the original. There's no "correct" setting for JPEG quality—results vary from image to image, and the best way to find the optimal setting for a particular movie is trial and error. (Note that JPEG compression doesn't work on images with a bit depth of 8 bits or less.)

To get the best results with image compression, you can specify compression settings for each individual bitmapped cast member. Doing so allows you to decide which form of compression (Standard or JPEG) is preferable for each cast member, and—if you decide to use JPEG—what level of quality works best for that particular image. To specify compression settings for a particular cast member, do the following:

1. Select the cast member in the Cast window.

2. Select the Bitmap tab in the Property Inspector (**Figure 17.41**).

continues on next page

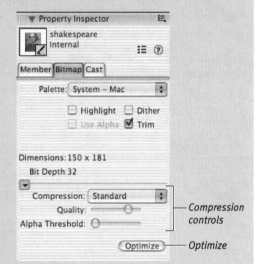

Figure 17.41 The Bitmap tab of the Property Inspector includes compression controls in its lower pane.

Compressing Bitmapped Images *continued*

3. Make a choice from the Compression pop-up menu in the lower pane of the Property Inspector (**Figure 17.42**).

- ▲ Choose **Movie Setting** if you want to apply the movie's global compression settings to this cast member (see below). This is the default choice for all bitmapped cast members.

- ▲ Choose **Standard** if you want to apply standard (lossless) compression.

- ▲ Choose **JPEG** if you want to apply JPEG compression; then choose a quality level on the Quality slider beneath the menu.

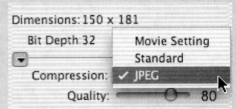

Figure 17.42 The Compression pop-up menu.

If you have Fireworks MX installed, you can skip these steps and click the Optimize button instead. Fireworks will launch automatically, the cast member will open in Fireworks, and you can use Fireworks' optimization features to find the best compression settings for the cast member.

If you don't want to take the time to specify compression settings for each cast member, you can specify global compression settings on the Compression tab in the Publish Settings dialog box (see "To change the Compression tab settings" on the next page). The choices you set there will affect every bitmapped cast member for which individual compression settings haven't been specified. .

Keep in mind that these compression settings—whether individual or global—take effect only when a movie is converted to Shockwave format. They have no effect on movies that are saved in a projector, unless the Compress (Shockwave format) option is selected in the Projector Options dialog box. (See Chapter 16, "Creating a Projector.")

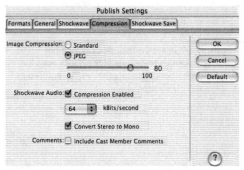

Figure 17.43 Use the Compression tab to compress all bitmapped cast members and sounds used in your movie.

Figure 17.44 Specify JPEG image quality by using this slider.

Figure 17.45 The sound compression controls affect all sounds in the movie that aren't already compressed.

To change the Compression tab settings:

1. Choose File > Publish Settings to open the Publish Settings dialog box (if it's not open already).

2. Select the Compression tab (**Figure 17.43**).

3. Choose either Standard or JPEG image compression (See the sidebar "Compressing Bitmapped Images" for more information.)

   If you choose JPEG compression, choose a quality level on the Quality slider (**Figure 17.44**). The lower the quality, the more each image will be compressed.

4. By default, sounds in your movie will be compressed in Shockwave Audio (SWA) format. If you don't want them to be compressed, deselect the Compression Enabled check box (**Figure 17.45**).

   (This option does not affect MP3 cast members or other sounds that were already compressed when you imported them into your movie. For more information, see "Compressing Sounds" in Chapter 13.)

   continues on next page

5. If Compression Enabled is selected, choose a bit rate from the pop-up menu.

A lower bit rate means more compression but poorer sound quality.

6. If you've selected a bit rate of 48 or higher, you have the option to deselect Convert Stereo to Mono.

This option, which is selected by default, halves the amount of data in a stereo sound file.

7. If you've appended comments to any of your cast members (see "To view and set asset-management fields for a cast member" in Chapter 2) and you want those comments to be included in the Shockwave movie file, select the Include Cast Member Comments check box (**Figure 17.46**).

The comments don't appear in the movie, but they're accessible by Lingo.

8. If you don't wish to change any more settings, click OK to close the Publish Settings dialog box.

Figure 17.46 Select the Include Cast Member Comments option to include in the Shockwave file any cast-member comments that you've entered in the Property Inspector.

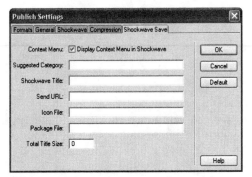

Figure 17.47 In most cases, you can disregard the Shockwave Save tab. It contains controls that allow your movie to work with a discontinued product called Shockmachine.

To change the Shockwave Save tab settings:

1. Choose File > Publish Settings to open the Publish Settings dialog box (if it's not open already).

2. Select the Shockwave Save tab (**Figure 17.47**).

3. If you don't want viewers of your Shockwave movie to have access to a contextual menu, deselect the Display Context Menu in Shockwave check box.

   (For more information about the contextual menu, see the introduction to this section.)

4. If you specifically need your Shockwave movie to work with Shockmachine—an obsolete product—fill in the following fields (otherwise, you can just leave them blank):

   ▲ In the Suggested Category field, type a category under which the movie will be filed in Shockmachine.

   ▲ In the Shockwave Title field, type a movie title that will appear in Shockmachine.

   ▲ In the Send URL field, type the URL of the Web page that contains the Shockwave movie.

   ▲ In the Icon File field, specify a path to a .bmp file to be used as the icon for the movie in Shockmachine.

   ▲ In the Package File field, type the URL of an XML file containing a list of URLs for supporting files (if any) that must be downloaded in addition to the current movie.

   ▲ If you entered a URL in the Package File field, use the Total Title Size field to indicate the total size (in bytes) of the files that must be downloaded.

5. If you don't wish to change any more settings, click OK to close the Publish Settings dialog box.

To change the Image tab settings:

1. Choose File > Publish Settings to open the Publish Settings dialog box (if it's not open already).

2. Select the Image tab (**Figure 17.48**).

   The Image tab becomes visible only when you choose Progress Bar with Image or Shockwave with Image from the HTML Template menu on the Formats tab. (See "To change the Formats tab settings," earlier in this section.)

3. In the Poster Frame field, type a frame number from your movie.

   The specified frame will be displayed as a JPEG image for users who are waiting to view (or cannot view) your Shockwave movie.

4. Specify a quality level for the image by using the Quality slider.

   The lower the quality, the more the image is compressed.

5. By default, the image is created as a *progressive* JPEG file, which means that it will initially display at a low resolution but increase in quality as it downloads. If you want the image to be created as a normal JPEG file (which has a smaller file size but requires a longer delay before it appears), deselect the Progressive check box.

6. If you don't wish to change any more settings, click OK to close the Publish Settings dialog box.

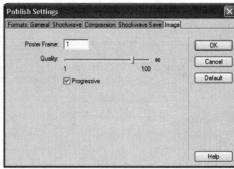

Figure 17.48 Use the Image tab to determine which frame of your movie will be displayed as a still image.

Original movie (in Director)

Streaming Shockwave movie (in browser)

Figure 17.49 If the cast members needed for a frame haven't been downloaded by the time the Shockwave Player arrives at the frame, the movie gets played without them.

Making Streaming Shockwave Movies

Streaming is the process that allows users to view the beginning of a movie (or hear the beginning of a sound) while the rest of it downloads from the Web. Streaming greatly improves the viewing/listening experience by engaging the user right from the start. Unfortunately, though any Shockwave movie can technically be made to stream, not every Shockwave movie works *well* as a streaming movie.

A streaming Shockwave movie downloads in two stages. The Score and Lingo scripts, which comprise a relatively small amount of data, are downloaded first. Then the cast members are downloaded, one by one, in the order in which their sprites appear in the Score.

Here's where the problems come in: Unless you specify otherwise, a streaming movie begins to play as soon as the Score and Lingo information has been downloaded. The Shockwave Player then plays every frame of the movie, regardless of whether the necessary cast members have had a chance to download. If a sprite is supposed to appear on the Stage, but its cast member hasn't been downloaded yet, users see a big empty space where the sprite should have been (**Figure 17.49**).

One way to make sure the necessary cast members are present is to use the "Download __ Frames Before Playing" feature in the Movie Playback Properties dialog box. (See "To convert a movie into a streaming Shockwave movie," later in this section.) This feature causes the movie to delay playing until the specified number of frames—including their cast members—is downloaded. For example, if all of the cast members for the first part of the movie appear in the first 10 frames, you might set the number of frames to 10.

The drawback to this option is that the user is stuck looking at an empty screen and a progress bar while he or she waits for the specified number of frames to download. (Depending on the size of the cast and the speed of the Internet connection, this wait might be anywhere from a few seconds to a few minutes.)

Therefore, many Shockwave movie authors use a different strategy: They construct their movie so that the introductory portion is relatively simple, requiring only a few very small (primarily vector or text) cast members. These cast members can be downloaded very quickly—perhaps in the first frame— and can hold the viewer's attention while the cast members for the remainder of the movie are being downloaded (**Figure 17.50**).

Figure 17.50 Many Shockwave movies begin with a short, quickly downloadable scene called a *preloader* that lets the user know that the main part of the movie is about to begin. The preloader loops continuously while other cast members are being downloaded.

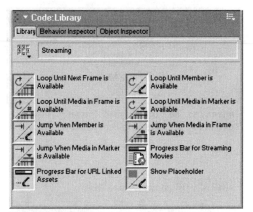

Figure 17.51 These behaviors are available in the Library palette to control the loading of cast members in a streaming movie.

To make this strategy work, Director's Library palette offers an assortment of behaviors to control the loading of cast members in a streaming movie (**Figure 17.51**). These behaviors are of two types:

◆ **Loop:** These behaviors cause the Shockwave movie to loop back to a particular frame (the current frame, the first frame of the movie, or anything in between) until a specified condition is met. That condition could be that a certain cast member has been downloaded, or that all the cast members for a particular frame have been downloaded. You can attach one of these behaviors to the last frame of your introductory sequence, allowing the sequence to repeat as many times as necessary until the next portion of the movie is ready to be seen.

◆ **Jump:** These behaviors cause the Shockwave movie to jump to a particular frame when a specified condition is met. (The conditions are similar to those used with the "loop" behaviors.) If you attach a "jump" behavior to the last frame of your introductory sequence, the movie will pause at that frame until the next portion of the movie is ready to be played.

Of course, it's also possible to write your own behaviors that will detect when certain cast members are downloaded and direct the movie accordingly. Analyze the Lingo in the supplied behaviors and use that as your starting point.

MAKING STREAMING SHOCKWAVE MOVIES

To convert a movie into a streaming Shockwave movie:

1. Open the movie in Director.

2. Choose Modify > Movie > Playback. The Movie Playback Properties dialog box opens (**Figure 17.52**).

3. Select the Play While Downloading Movie check box.

   This check box is essentially the on/off switch for streaming. When it's selected, streaming is turned on for the movie.

4. Type a value in the Download __ Frames Before Playing field to specify the number of complete frames to download before starting to play the movie (**Figure 17.53**).

   If you enter 5, for example, your movie starts playing after all the cast-member media—both internal and linked—used in the first five frames of the score have completely downloaded. By default, this value is set to 1 frame. You'll have to experiment to find the best value for each movie. (See the "Tips for Effective Streaming" sidebar.)

5. Choose the Show Placeholders option if you want rectangular placeholders to appear in place of cast members that have not yet been downloaded (**Figure 17.54**).

   These placeholders are useful for testing streaming movies, but you probably don't want them to show up in a movie that anyone will actually see.

6. Save the movie.

7. Follow the steps in "To convert a movie to Shockwave format," earlier in this chapter, to publish the Shockwave movie.

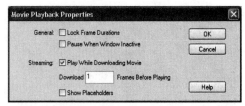

Figure 17.52 The Movie Playback Properties dialog box is where you set streaming options for a movie.

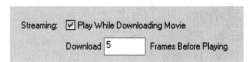

Figure 17.53 Type the number of frames that you want the Shockwave Player to download before the movie starts to play.

Figure 17.54 If you choose the Show Placeholders option, placeholders like this one appear in place of cast members that have not yet been downloaded.

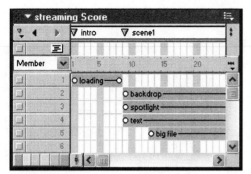

Figure 17.55 In this example, we want the playhead to loop between frames 1 and 8 until the large cast member in frame12 is loaded, then we want it to begin playing Scene 1.

To loop or pause a movie until specific cast members have been downloaded:

1. Open the movie in Director (**Figure 17.55**).

2. Choose Window > Library Palette to display the Library palette.

3. Choose Internet > Streaming from the Library List pop-up menu.

4. Decide which of the streaming behaviors is most appropriate for the situation:

   ▲ **Loop Until Next Frame is Available** causes the playhead to loop back repeatedly to a specified frame until all cast members required for the next frame—that is, the frame following the one to which the behavior has been assigned—have been downloaded.

   ▲ **Loop Until Member is Available** causes the playhead to loop back repeatedly to a specified frame until a cast member you specify has been downloaded.

   ▲ **Loop Until Media in Frame is Available** causes the playhead to loop back repeatedly to a specified frame until all cast members required for another specified frame have downloaded.

   ▲ **Loop Until Media in Marker is Available** causes the playhead to loop back repeatedly to a specified frame until all cast members required by frames between the marker you specify and the next marker have been downloaded.

   ▲ **Jump When Member is Available** causes the playhead to pause at a specified frame until a cast member you specify has been downloaded.

   continues on next page

▲ **Jump When Media in Frame is Available** causes the playhead to pause at a specified frame until all cast members required for another specified frame have downloaded.

▲ **Jump When Media in Marker is Available** causes the playhead to pause at a specified frame until all cast members required by frames between the marker you specify and the next marker have been downloaded.

5. Drag the desired behavior from the Library palette to the Score, and drop it in the appropriate frame in the script channel.

   If you're using a "loop" behavior, drop it in the later of the two frames between which you want the playhead to loop (**Figure 17.56**).

   If you're using a "jump" behavior, drop it in the frame at which you want the playhead to pause.

   A Parameters dialog box appears.

6. Set the parameters for the behavior (**Figure 17.57**).

7. Click OK to close the dialog box.

8. If you haven't already done so, follow the steps in the preceding task, "To convert a movie into a streaming Shockwave movie."

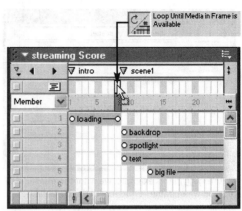

Figure 17.56 The Loop Until Media in Frame is Available behavior is dropped into the script channel in frame 8 (the last frame in the looping sequence).

Figure 17.57 These parameters will cause the playhead to loop back to frame 1 repeatedly until the cast members for frame 12 are loaded, and then continue playing the movie.

Tips for Effective Streaming

If you're creating a streaming Shockwave movie, careful planning can increase its chances of streaming smoothly:

◆ Try to prevent users from jumping far ahead in a movie. If you're using scripts or behaviors to jump around in the score—because you're offering navigational controls to the user, for example—restrict the user to short hops. Because Director downloads cast-member data in frame order, a sudden jump over many frames means waiting for *all* intervening cast members to load, even if the users never see those cast members.

◆ Don't waste pixels. Make sure the dimensions of your bitmapped cast members are no larger than they'll be when the bitmap appears on the Stage. If possible, scale and crop each image in Photoshop before importing it into Director.

◆ Avoid using large sound files—loop small ones instead.

◆ Where possible, create motion by means of tweening rather than frame-by-frame animation, to limit the number of cast members that must be downloaded.

◆ "Recycle" cast members to reduce file size. For example, if your movie includes several buttons, use one cast member for all the button sprites and superimpose different text on each sprite. If your movie includes a cloudy sky, make multiple sprites from a single cloud cast member, and rotate and skew each one to make them look different.

◆ If your movie requires large, memory-hungry cast members, such as QuickTime movies or 32-bit bitmaps, start the movie with a simple scene that uses compact cast members; then use one of Director's streaming behaviors to loop the scene until the bigger media have downloaded fully. The looping scene can entertain the user immediately while the movie continues to load in the background.

◆ Instead of looping, you can try to time animations using the tempo channel to allow the process of downloading media to stay ahead of the end of the animation sequence. Estimating the time required is guesswork, but you can safely assume that a 56K modem—which is the slowest Internet connection that members of your audience are likely to have—downloads at an average rate of at least 4 kilobytes per second. This means that if you have 40 kilobytes' worth of compressed cast-member media to download for the next scene, you try to make the current animated sequence about 10 seconds long.

◆ Experiment with the Download __ Frames Before Playing value in the Movie Playback Properties dialog box to find a reasonable compromise between streaming and letting the user wait for downloading. If the value is too low, too many sprites will be missing from your movie. If the value is too high, the user may give up and surf elsewhere.

Converting Multiple Movies

If you have multiple Director movies and casts to save as Shockwave files, you can batch-process them instead of opening and saving each one individually. Because this procedure doesn't create HTML files, it's best used for movies that you want to compress and protect for distribution with a stub projector. (See "To create a stub projector with external movie files" in Chapter 16.) If you plan to use the Shockwave movies on the Web, you're still better off using Director's Publish command.

To batch-convert movie or cast files to Shockwave format:

1. Choose Xtras > Update Movies.

   The Update Movies dialog box opens (**Figure 17.58**).

2. Choose the Convert to Shockwave Movie(s) option.

3. Choose the Back Up into Folder option to copy the original files to a safe place.

4. Click Browse.

   The Select Folder for Original Files dialog box appears (**Figure 17.59**).

5. Select a folder and click Select Folder (Windows) or Choose (Mac).

   The Select Folder for Original Files dialog box closes, and the selected folder appears under Back Up into Folder in the Update Movies dialog box.

Figure 17.58 The Update Movies dialog box can be used to convert multiple movies and casts to Shockwave format

Figure 17.59 Select a folder in which to back up the original movie and cast files.

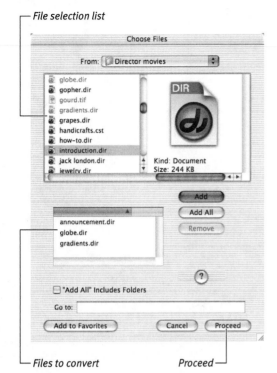

File selection list

Files to convert   *Proceed*

Figure 17.60 In the Choose Files dialog box, select the files that you want to convert to Shockwave format.

6. Click OK.

The Choose Files dialog box appears (**Figure 17.60**).

7. Select a movie or cast file that you want to convert to Shockwave format.

8. Click Add.

9. Repeat steps 7 and 8 to add additional files to the list at the bottom of the dialog box, or click the Add All button to add all the files in the current folder.

10. Click Proceed.

An alert box confirms that the selected files will be converted to Shockwave format.

11. Click Continue.

A progress bar shows you the filenames as they are converted.

✔ Tip

■ If you already have backups of the files you want to convert to Shockwave format, you can select the Delete radio button in step 3, and then skip steps 4 and 5.

CONVERTING MULTIPLE MOVIES

SHOCKWAVE 3D

Figure 18.1 You can include 3D cast members in your movies and give users the opportunity to click, drag, and rotate them on the Stage.

One of Director's newer features is the ability to include 3D cast members in Director movies. At the time this feature was introduced (in Director 8.5, the version preceding Director MX), it was considered revolutionary, and it remains cutting-edge even now. It's rare to find 3D of any sort on the Web, and by making it a component of Shockwave, Macromedia has taken a big step toward bringing 3D into the mainstream. More important, Director's implementation of 3D is fully interactive, allowing users to move and control 3D objects in ways that were formerly found chiefly in sophisticated video games (**Figure 18.1**).

continues on next page

You can include 3D objects in your Director movies three different ways:

◆ You can create 3D text sprites, using simple tools built into Director.

◆ You can export files from 3D modeling programs—such as Discreet's 3ds max, SoftImage's XSI, and Alias/Wavefront's Maya—and import them into Director.

◆ You can create primitive 3D shapes—such as boxes, spheres, and cylinders—using Lingo. (These don't exist as cast members; Director creates them on the fly when it executes the Lingo script in which they're defined.) Because this technique requires advanced Lingo skills and is of limited usefulness, it won't be covered in this chapter.

The major drawback to using 3D in Director movies is that Director's implementation of 3D is not especially intuitive. Hardly any of the 3D features can be accessed through Director's usual interface; apart from a limited selection of prewritten behaviors, nearly all 3D manipulation requires you to write complex Lingo scripts. For this reason, this book covers only a limited number of Director's 3D capabilities.

Fortunately, Director still offers a few 3D features that are accessible to beginners without the use of sophisticated Lingo. We'll be looking at those features in this chapter.

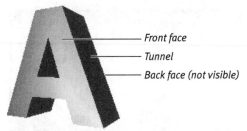

Front face

Tunnel

Back face (not visible)

Figure 18.2 The anatomy of extruded text. Extruded text takes on a 3D effect courtesy of a *tunnel* that connects the front and back face of the text.

Front   Side

Figure 18.3 A 3D text object, viewed by an imaginary camera, from the front and the side.

Creating and Modifying 3D Text

The easiest way to add 3D to a Director movie is by using 3D text. Text is the only kind of 3D cast member that can be created entirely within Director without the use of Lingo.

Director creates 3D text by *extruding* ordinary two-dimensional text—that is, expanding it along the z-axis. (When you studied geometry in high school, you may have stopped at the x- and y-axes; in that case, think of the z-axis as the one that connects your eye with this page.) An extruded object has identical, flat front and back faces, connected by what Director calls a *tunnel* (**Figure 18.2**).

Keep in mind that 3D objects in Director— or in any 3D program, for that matter—don't really have three dimensions. The software provides the *illusion* that an object is three-dimensional, despite the fact that it exists only on a two-dimensional computer screen. A 3D program does this in two ways: first, by using tricks of perspective drawing; and second, by simulating the play of light and shadow on the surface of the object. Both of these techniques require that the 3D object be seen from a specific point of view, which is defined through the position of an imaginary camera (**Figure 18.3**).

If you're new to 3D, you may be surprised at the number of issues you'll have to think about. The actual process of converting text from 2D to 3D can be accomplished instantly, through a simple menu choice. Thereafter, the majority of your time is spent modifying the positions of lights and the camera in the imaginary space that Director calls a *3D world*. You can make these adjustments in two different places: the Shockwave 3D window (**Figure 18.4**) and the 3D Extruder tab of the Property Inspector (**Figure 18.5**).

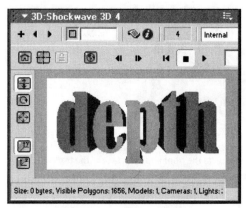

Figure 18.4 The Shockwave 3D window lets you modify camera positions visually.

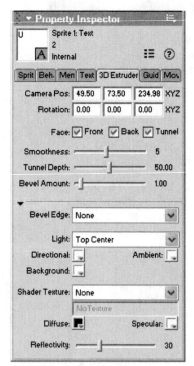

Figure 18.5 Use the 3D Extruder tab to change the properties of 3D text.

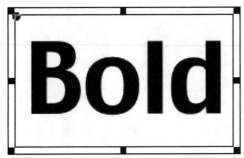

Figure 18.6 Large, bold text like this works best for converting to 3D.

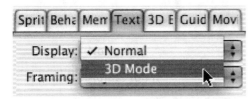

Figure 18.7 Choose 3D Mode from the Display menu.

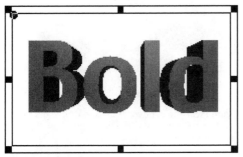

Figure 18.8 The same text, now in 3D mode.

To convert 2D text to 3D text:

1. Select a regular text sprite (not field text) in the Score or on the Stage.

   For best results, use text that's big and bold (**Figure 18.6**).

2. Click the Text tab in the Property Inspector.

3. From the Display pop-up menu, choose 3D Mode (**Figure 18.7**).

   The selected text sprite takes on a 3D appearance on the Stage (**Figure 18.8**).

To change the structural properties of 3D text:

1. Select a 3D text sprite in the Score or on the Stage.

2. Click the 3D Extruder tab in the Property Inspector.

3. If you want to make the front, back, or sides of the 3D text disappear, deselect the Front, Back, or Tunnel check box in the Face row (**Figure 18.9**).

   All three check boxes are initially selected when you create 3D text.

   continues on next page

Front, back, and tunnel   Tunnel only

Figure 18.9 You can create a striking effect by deselecting the Front and Back check boxes, leaving only the tunnel.

4. To make curved areas of the text more or less jagged (**Figure 18.10**), drag the Smoothness slider to the left or right.

    Increasing the smoothness greatly increases the amount of processing power required to display the 3D text. In most cases, it's recommended that you keep the smoothness setting at the default value or below.

5. To change the text's extrusion depth (**Figure 18.11**), drag the Tunnel Depth slider to the left or right.

6. To give the edges of the text an angled or rounded appearance (**Figure 18.12**), choose Miter or Round from the Bevel Edge pop-up menu.

7. If you chose Miter or Round in step 6, set the degree of beveling (**Figure 18.13**) by dragging the Bevel Amount slider.

Less smoothness   *More smoothness*

Figure 18.10 Use the Smoothness slider to increase or decrease the jaggedness of the text.

Less depth   *More depth*

Figure 18.11 Use the Tunnel Depth slider to increase or decrease the extrusion depth of the 3D text.

Miter bevel   *Round bevel*

Figure 18.12 The differences between miter and round beveling are very subtle; round beveling has slightly richer shadows.

Less beveling   *More beveling*

Figure 18.13 You can use the Bevel Amount slider to set the degree to which the edges of 3D text are angled or rounded.

Size: 0 bytes, Visible Polygons: 244, Models: 1,

Figure 18.14 The Shockwave 3D window opens.

To change the position of the camera relative to 3D text:

1. Select a 3D text sprite in the Score or on the Stage.

2. Choose Window > Shockwave 3D.

   The Shockwave 3D window opens (**Figure 18.14**) displaying the 3D world from the camera's point of view.

3. Click one of the buttons along the left side of the window (**Figure 18.15**) to determine how the camera will move when you drag the mouse.

   The **Dolly Camera** button causes the camera to move toward and away from the 3D text is if it were on a wheeled base (a *dolly*) (**Figure 18.16**).

continues on next page

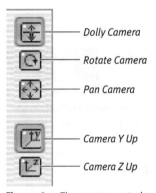

— Dolly Camera

— Rotate Camera

— Pan Camera

— Camera Y Up

— Camera Z Up

Figure 18.15 The camera control buttons in the Shockwave 3D window.

Dolly in   *Dolly out*

Figure 18.16 Use the Dolly button to move toward and away from the 3D text.

CREATING AND MODIFYING 3D TEXT

433

The **Rotate Camera** button causes the camera to move in a circular manner around the 3D text. Dragging the mouse vertically causes the camera to rotate around the x-axis, while dragging horizontally causes the camera to rotate about one additional axis. Select the Camera Y Up button for y-axis rotation, or the Camera Z Up button for z-axis rotation (**Figure 18.17**).

The **Pan Camera** button causes the camera to remain at a fixed location (as if it were on a tripod), but to swivel left, right, up, and down (**Figure 18.18**).

4. Drag the mouse within the 3D world to move the camera as desired.

At any time, you can return the camera to its original position by clicking the Reset Camera Transform button (**Figure 18.19**).

5. Repeat steps 3 and 4 as many times as necessary to get the results you want.

For example, you might want to dolly the camera out to increase its distance from the 3D text, then rotate it along the x-axis to get above it.

6. To make the new camera position "stick," click the Set Camera Transform button.

The 3D sprite on the Stage changes to match the new view of the 3D world in the Shockwave 3D window.

If the 3D Extruder tab is visible in the Property Inspector, the values in the Camera Position and Rotation fields update to match the new position of the camera (**Figure 18.20**).

✔ Tip

■ If you prefer to work numerically rather than visually, you can change the position of the camera by entering values directly in the Camera Position and Rotation fields on the 3D Extruder tab of the Property Inspector.

Rotate around x-axis

Rotate around y-axis

Rotate around z-axis

Figure 18.17 Click the Rotate Camera button to rotate completely around the 3D text.

Pan left

Pan up

Figure 18.18 The Pan button keeps the camera in one place, but lets you swivel the camera view.

Figure 18.19 The camera transform buttons in the Shockwave 3D window.

Camera Pos:	166.14	109.63	204.16	XYZ
Rotation:	-8.00	27.00	0.00	XYZ

Figure 18.20 These values change automatically in the Property Inspector when you set the position or rotation of the camera in the Shockwave 3D window.

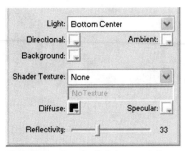

Figure 18.21 Use the lighting controls on the 3D Extruder tab to create different kinds of lighting for your 3D text.

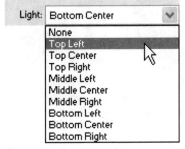

Figure 18.22 From the Light pop-up menu, choose the location from which the directional light should shine.

To change the way 3D text is lit:

1. Select a 3D text sprite in the Score or on the Stage.

2. Click the 3D Extruder tab in the Property Inspector.

3. Use the Directional, Ambient, and Background color menus to set the colors of the three kinds of light that illuminate the 3D world (**Figure 18.21**).

   Directional light is the equivalent of a spotlight: It aims a concentrated beam of light at the 3D text from a particular direction, creating conspicuous areas of light and shadow.

   Ambient light illuminates the entire 3D world evenly. It comes from no particular direction and creates no shadows.

   The interplay of directional and ambient light, particularly when they use contrasting colors, can have significant and unpredictable effects on the appearance of 3D text. Getting the look you want requires experimentation.

   Background light illuminates only the background of the 3D world, with no effect on the 3D text. Changing its color is equivalent to changing the background color of 2D text.

4. From the Light pop-up menu, choose the location from which the directional light should originate (**Figure 18.22**).

To change the surface characteristics of 3D text:

1. Select a 3D text sprite in the Score or on the Stage.

2. Click the 3D Extruder tab in the Property Inspector.

3. To change the surface color of the 3D text, use the Diffuse color menu.

   Changing the Diffuse color (**Figure 18.23**) is equivalent to changing the foreground color of 2D text.

4. To change the degree of reflectivity (glossiness) of the text's surface (**Figure 18.24**), drag the Reflectivity slider.

5. To change the color of the text's *specular highlights*—the areas in which directional light is reflected most brightly—use the Specular color menu.

   The specular color is initially set to white. If you change it to a darker color, you reduce the tonal range of the image, and other colors in the image may get darker as a result.

✔ Tip

■ In 3D terminology, the surface of an object is known as its *shader*. Though the word *shader* doesn't appear in the names of these particular controls, you'll see it used in Director's interface and documentation, and in this chapter as well.

Figure 18.23 Use the Diffuse color menu to change the color of 3D text.

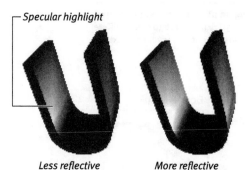

Specular highlight

Less reflective   *More reflective*

Figure 18.24 You can use the Reflectivity slider to adjust the degree of gloss on your 3D text.

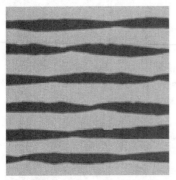

Figure 18.25 A 128-by-128-pixel texture.

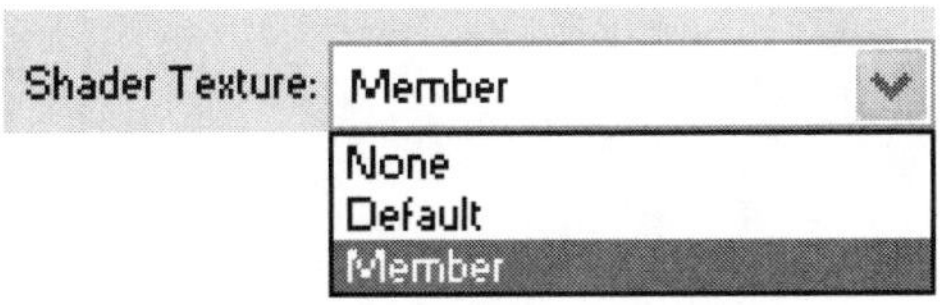

Shader Texture: Member
None
Default
Member

Figure 18.26 The Shader Texture pop-up menu.

To "paint" the surface of 3D text:

1. Create or import a texture.

(In 3D terminology, a *texture* is a 2D image intended to be painted onto the surface of a 3D object.)

The texture may be any bitmapped image, vector shape, or Flash movie. (If a Flash movie has multiple frames, only the first frame will be used.)

For best results, the texture should be square, with pixel dimensions that are powers of 2 (for example, 64 by 64, 128 by 128, or 256 by 256) (**Figure 18.25**). Textures that don't meet these guidelines can still be used, but they'll put an unusually heavy load on the computer's processor.

2. If the texture cast member doesn't have a name, give it one. (See "To name a cast member" in Chapter 2.)

3. On the Stage or in the Score, select the 3D text sprite to which you want to apply the texture.

4. Click the 3D Extruder tab in the Property Inspector.

5. From the Shader Texture pop-up menu, choose Member (**Figure 18.26**).

continues on next page

CREATING AND MODIFYING 3D TEXT

6. In the text field directly below the Shader Texture pop-up menu, type the name of the cast member that you want to use as a texture and press Enter (**Figure 18.27**).

On the Stage, the surface of the selected 3D text sprite displays the texture (**Figure 18.28**).

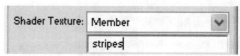

Figure 18.27 Type the name of the cast member that you want to use as a texture.

✔ Tips

- Displaying textures is highly processor-intensive, so use them sparingly. When you do use textures, try to keep their dimensions small and their color depth low.

- Director gives you no control over which parts of a texture are mapped onto which parts of a 3D text sprite. You may have to redraw the texture several times, rotating and repositioning its elements as necessary, to get the results you want.

- Choosing Default from the Shader Texture pop-up menu gives you a red-and-white test pattern that's useful for previewing lighting effects and camera positions.

Figure 18.28 Here is 3D text with a texture.

Text in Disguise

We generally use the word *text* to refer only to alphanumeric characters. From Director's point of view, however, anything that can be found in a font is text. Common fonts such as Wingdings and Webdings contain a variety of shapes and symbols that can instantly be turned into 3D sprites in Director (**Figure 18.29**). If you search the Web, you'll find many free fonts that contain images of all sorts.

If you want to create a custom 3D object to use in a Director movie but you don't have access to 3D image-creation software (see "Using Imported 3D Files,") you can "cheat" by creating your object as a character in a font. Use a font-editing program such as FontLab Limited's FontLab or Macromedia's Fontographer to create the 2D character and export it as part of a font (**Figure 18.30**). Then import the customized font into Director, embed the character in your movie (see "To embed a font" in Chapter 12), and use it as the basis for a 3D text sprite (**Figure 18.31**).

Figure 18.29 With the exception of the ball and spindle, everything shown on the Stage is 3D text. The card suits are characters in the Zapf Dingbats font. The roulette wheel and coins are made from a text bullet (•). The roulette wheel has a texture applied, and its camera has been rotated around the *x*-axis.

Figure 18.30 You can create a custom 3D object by first creating it as a font character in a font-creation program. Here, this logo is being created as a text character in FontLab.

Figure 18.31 The logo as a 3D text sprite in Director.

Using Imported 3D Files

If you want to use full-featured 3D cast members in your Director movies, you have to create them in a 3D modeling program and import them into Director. Director can import 3D files in only one format: the Web 3D format, whose file extension is W3D. Many popular 3D modeling programs, such as 3ds max and Maya, can export W3D files.

There are two notable differences between imported 3D files and the 3D text cast members you worked with earlier in this chapter. First, an imported file may contain any number of separate 3D models, lights, and cameras, each of which can be manipulated individually within the 3D world. In this regard, a 3D cast member is fundamentally different from an ordinary Director cast member, which is a single entity that can only be manipulated as a whole.

Second, a 3D file may have movement or animation built into it by the 3D program in which it was created. A 3D cast member containing animation may be handled like a digital video or Flash cast member, which has its own time-based content. (See "Working with Video Sprites" in Chapter 10.)

Keep in mind that 3D is a high-bandwidth format. Most 3D modeling programs tend to create large, processor-intensive files, which may be fine for disk-based applications but are often not suitable for streaming over the Web. For this reason, be careful to keep your 3D cast members as simple as possible. Otherwise, the users who download your Shockwave movies will need a fast computer and either a broadband Internet connection or a good amount of patience.

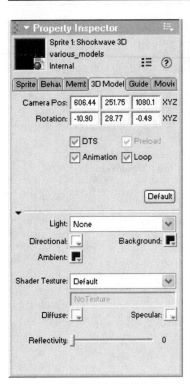

Figure 18.32 The 3D Model tab in the Property Inspector.

You can view and change the properties of imported 3D files in the 3D Model tab of the Property Inspector (**Figure 18.32**). This tab has many of the same controls as the 3D Extruder tab described earlier in the chapter, but not all of them are useful. The shader and texture controls (Shader Texture, Diffuse, Specular, and Reflectivity) work only if the imported file contains a single 3D object that doesn't already have a shader applied. Otherwise, the controls do nothing. The directional lighting controls (the Light pop-up menu and the Directional color menu) can be used to add a directional light to the 3D world, but they have no effect on any existing directional light. In general, if you want to change internal characteristics of the 3D world, the best place to do it is in the 3D program that produced the file.

To import a W3D file:

◆ Follow the same procedure that you use to import other kinds of cast members. (See "Importing Cast Members" in Chapter 2.)

To preview an imported 3D cast member:

1. Double-click the 3D cast member in the Cast window.

   The Shockwave 3D window opens, displaying the 3D world contained in the file (**Figure 18.33**). If the file contains more than one camera, Director uses the first camera it finds.

continues on next page

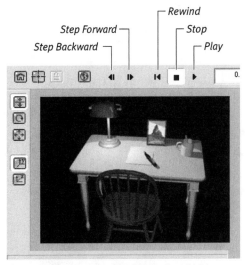

Figure 18.33 An imported 3D file displayed in the Shockwave 3D window.

USING IMPORTED 3D FILES

2. If you want to view the 3D objects from different angles, use the mouse and the camera-movement buttons (described in "To change the position of the camera relative to 3D text," earlier in this chapter) to move the camera around the 3D world.

3. If the 3D file contains animation, use the playback controls at the top of the Shockwave 3D window to preview the animation.

To change the position of the camera within an imported 3D cast member:

◆ Follow the procedure described in "To change the position of the camera relative to 3D text," earlier in this chapter.

To restore the original position of the camera:

1. In Cast window, select the 3D cast member whose camera position you want to restore.

2. Click the 3D Model tab in the Property Inspector.

3. Click the Default button in the Property Inspector (**Figure 18.34**).

The camera reverts to its original position and rotation.

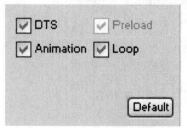

Figure 18.34 Click the Default button to revert a camera to its original settings.

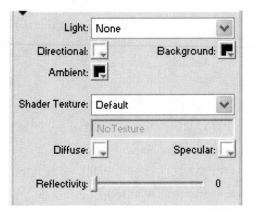

Figure 18.35 Of the lighting and shader controls on the 3D Model tab, only the Background and Ambient color menus are generally useful.

To change the properties of an imported 3D cast member:

1. Select a 3D text sprite in the Score or on the Stage.

2. Click the 3D Model tab in the Property Inspector.

3. Change properties as desired.

   DTS: This option is selected by default. DTS stands for Direct to Stage. When this option is selected, the 3D sprite is placed in front of the Stage instead of interacting with other sprites on the Stage, thus improving the playback performance of your Director movie.

   Animation: If the 3D cast member contains animation, this option allows the animation to be played. Otherwise, only the first frame of the 3D cast member will be seen.

   Loop: This option is available only if the Animation option is selected. It causes the animation to play repeatedly for as long as the 3D sprite is on the Stage.

4. If you want to change the color of the background or ambient light, use the Background and Ambient color menus (**Figure 18.35**). They work the same way as the ones described in "To change the way 3D text is lit," earlier in this chapter.

✔ Tip

■ The remaining controls on the 3D Model tab—the directional lighting, shader, and texture controls—don't work as you'd expect. See the introduction to this section, "Using Imported 3D Files."

To see the internal structure of an imported 3D cast member:

1. Choose Window > Object Inspector. The Object Inspector opens (**Figure 18.36**).

2. Drag a 3D cast member from the Cast window to the Object Inspector.

   The name of the 3D cast member appears in the left column of the Object Inspector (**Figure 18.37**).

3. Click the plus sign (Windows) or expander arrow (Mac) to the left of the cast member's name.

   A list appears, showing 3D models, lights, shaders, textures, and all other components of the 3D file.

4. Click other plus signs or expander arrows as necessary to find the specific elements or values that you want to look at (**Figure 18.38**).

✔ Tip

- Like the Property Inspector, the Object Inspector is interactive: You can edit values in the Object Inspector and see the changes reflected on the Stage. However, changes made in the Object Inspector *are not saved with the movie file.* Therefore, editing values in the Object Inspector is useful only for testing. If you want to make permanent changes in a 3D cast member, you'll need to edit the original file in a 3D modeling program.

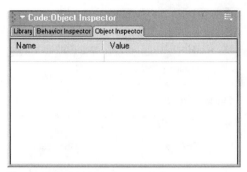

Figure 18.36 The Object Inspector always opens empty, regardless of what may be selected in the Score or Cast windows.

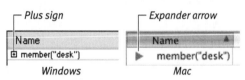

Figure 18.37 Click the plus sign or expander arrow to see the components of the 3D file.

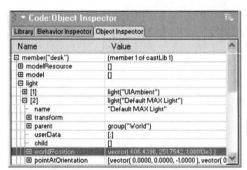

Figure 18.38 Every element and every setting in the 3D file is nested somewhere in the Object Inspector.

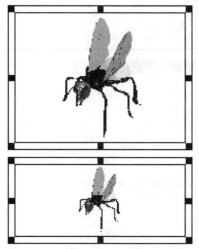

Figure 18.39 All 3D objects within a sprite retain their proportions when the sprite is resized.

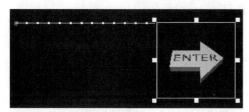

Figure 18.40 This 3D sprite has been tweened across the Stage like any ordinary sprite.

Working with 3D Sprites

A 3D cast member, like any other visual cast member, can be made into a sprite by dragging it to the Stage or Score.

A 3D sprite can be tweened and resized, but it can't be rotated or skewed. When you resize a 3D sprite, you can change its bounding box in any way you like, but the 3D objects within the sprite always maintain their proportions (**Figure 18.39**).

When talking about 3D sprites, it's important to distinguish between the 3D sprite itself—an ordinary object on the Director Stage—and the 3D world contained within the 3D sprite. You can use tweening to animate a 3D sprite, but in doing so you're only moving the sprite around on the Stage; you're not animating the models, lights, cameras, and other objects that populate the 3D world (**Figure 18.40**). If you want to create animation *within* the 3D world, the best place to do so is in the 3D program that originally created the file.

If you don't have access to 3D software (or if you want to animate 3D text that was created in Director), you can use Lingo to animate the contents of a 3D world. The required Lingo is too advanced for this book, but as a starting point Director provides a behavior in the Library palette that can place a 3D object in motion. It's described in "To rotate a 3D object" on the next page.

To turn a 3D cast member into a sprite:

◆ Drag it to the Stage or Score. (See "Working with Sprites" in Chapter 3.)

To make the background of a 3D sprite invisible:

1. Select a 3D sprite on the Stage or in the Score.

2. Select the Sprite tab in the Property Inspector.

3. Choose Background Transparent, Transparent, or Blend from the Ink menu.

   The background of the 3D sprite disappears, irrespective of which background colors are set in the Property Inspector or on the Tool palette.

✔ Tip

- The Background Transparent, Transparent, and Blend ink effects are the only ink effects that work with a 3D sprite. Their only effect is to make the background disappear; they don't change the appearance of the 3D sprite in any other way.

To rotate a 3D object:

1. Choose Window > Palette to open the Library palette.

2. Choose 3D > Actions from the Library List pop-up menu (**Figure 18.41**).

   The list of 3D actions appears. (To learn more about these actions, see the next section, "Making 3D Sprites Interactive.")

3. Find the Automatic Model Rotation behavior and drag it from the Library palette (**Figure 18.42**).

4. On the Stage or in the Score, drop the behavior on a 3D sprite containing an object that you want to rotate.

   The Parameters dialog box appears (**Figure 18.43**).

Figure 18.41 From the Library List pop-up menu, choose 3D > Actions.

Figure 18.42 The Automatic Model Rotation behavior in the Library palette.

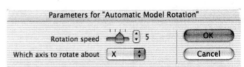

Figure 18.43 When you drop the behavior on a 3D sprite that contains an object you want to rotate, the Parameters dialog box appears, prompting you to adjust settings for that object.

Figure 18.44 A 3D sprite with the Automatic Model Rotation behavior applied.

5. In the Parameters dialog box, use the "Rotation speed" slider to select a speed at which you want the object to rotate.

The available speeds range from -20 to 20. Rotation at a negative speed goes in the opposite direction from rotation at a positive speed. The numbers are arbitrary (they don't refer to rotations per minute or anything similarly measurable), so you'll have to experiment to find the speed you want.

6. If the 3D world contains more than one object, choose the one you want to rotate from the "Which model?" pop-up menu.

If you want to rotate all the objects, select Rotate All.

7. Use the "Which axis to rotate about" pop-up menu to select the x-, y-, or z-axis.

8. Click OK to close the dialog box.

9. If you want a single object to rotate in more than one direction, or if you want more than one object within the 3D world to rotate, repeat steps 3 through 8 (but drag the behavior from the Cast window instead of the Library palette).

You can apply an unlimited number of instances of this behavior to a sprite, specifying different parameters for each instance.

10. Play the movie.

Within the 3D sprite, the specified object or objects rotate in the specified manner (**Figure 18.44**).

Making 3D Sprites Interactive

The Automatic Model Rotation behavior, described in the previous task, is an unusual 3D behavior in that it operates independently: The 3D object rotates on its own, regardless of what else happens on the Stage.

By contrast, most 3D behaviors are meant to be *interactive*—that is, to respond to the user's mouse and keyboard input. For example, the person viewing the movie might use his or her mouse to rotate a 3D object, or press a key to play back the 3D object's animation. This sort of interactivity is achieved by combining two different behaviors from the Library palette: an action and a trigger.

An *action* is a change that happens on the Stage, most often a movement of either a model or the camera. A *trigger* is the user input that causes the action to happen. An action is connected to its trigger by placing them in a named relationship, called a *group*.

There are three kinds of actions. *Independent actions*, such as Automatic Model Rotation, don't require a trigger. (There are very few of these.) *Local actions*, such as Drag Model, require a trigger to be attached to the same 3D object that the action is attached to. *Public actions*, such as Reset Camera, also require a trigger, but the trigger can be attached to any object within the 3D sprite.

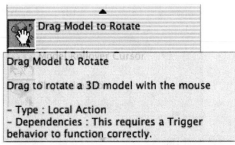

Drag Model to Rotate

Drag to rotate a 3D model with the mouse

- Type : Local Action
- Dependencies : This requires a Trigger behavior to function correctly.

Figure 18.45 Pop-up descriptions give you additional information about a specific behavior. Here, the pop-up description for the Drag Model to Rotate behavior indicates that it requires a trigger—that is, it requires mouse or keyboard input from the user.

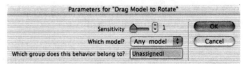

Figure 18.46 Parameters for the Drag Model to Rotate behavior. (The settings on the Sensitivity slider, like many settings in 3D behaviors, are arbitrary numbers, so you have to experiment to get the results you want.)

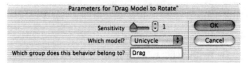

Figure 18.47 Type in a group name that you'll recognize later.

To add interactivity to a 3D sprite:

1. Choose Window > Library Palette to open the Library palette.

2. Choose 3D > Actions from the Library List pop-up menu.
   The list of action behaviors appears.

3. Choose an action behavior and drag it from the Library palette.
   The pop-up description for each behavior tells you what it does, which category of actions it falls into (independent, local, or public), and whether it requires a trigger (**Figure 18.45**).

4. On the Stage or in the Score, drop the behavior on the 3D sprite to which you want to apply the action.
   The Parameters dialog box appears (**Figure 18.46**).

5. Fill in the parameters as desired.

6. For all actions (except independent actions), the last parameter is "Which group does this behavior belong to?" Fill in a descriptive group name that you'll be able to recognize later (**Figure 18.47**).

7. Click OK to close the dialog box.

continues on next page

8. In the Library palette, Choose 3D > Triggers from the Library List pop-up menu.

The list of trigger behaviors appears (**Figure 18.48**).

9. Choose a trigger behavior and drag it from the Library palette.

The pop-up description for each behavior tells you what it does (**Figure 18.49**).

10. On the Stage or in the Score, drop the behavior on the 3D sprite to which you previously applied an action.

The Parameters dialog box appears (**Figure 18.50**).

11. Fill in the parameters as desired.

If you use the Mouse Left or Mouse Right behavior, you're given the opportunity to specify a modifier key that must be held down while the mouse button is pressed. The options—which are available on a pop-up menu—are Shift, Control, or Shift+Control Other common modifier keys, such as Alt (Windows), Option (Mac), and Command (Mac), can't be used. If you don't want to use a modifier key, choose the "No modifier key" option. (**Figure 18.51**).

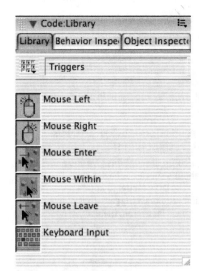

Figure 18.48 Choose from the list of trigger behaviors.

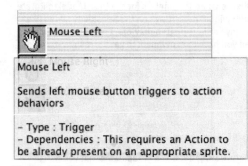

Figure 18.49 The pop-up description for the Mouse Left behavior.

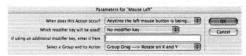

Figure 18.50 Parameters for the Mouse Left behavior.

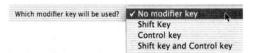

Figure 18.51 Only a few modifier keys can be used with the Mouse Left and Mouse Right behaviors. If you prefer, you can choose not to use a modifier key.

Figure 18.52 If you want to use a secondary modifier key, it must be a standard alphanumeric character.

Figure 18.53 Parameters for the Keyboard Input behavior.

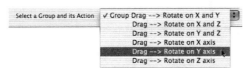

Figure 18.54 You can choose an arrow key from the pop-up menu.

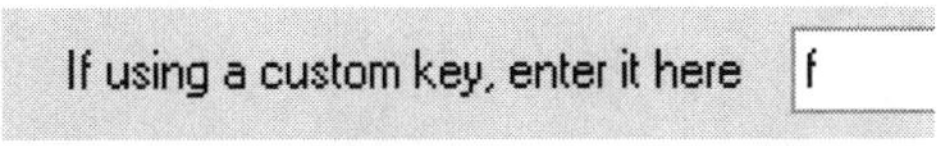

If using a custom key, enter it here [f]

Figure 18.55 Any alphanumeric key can be used with the Keyboard Input behavior. (For example, you might want the user to press B to move the camera back or F to move it forward.)

Select a Group and its Action
✓ Group Drag --> Rotate on X and Y
Drag --> Rotate on X and Z
Drag --> Rotate on Y and Z
Drag --> Rotate on X axis
Drag --> Rotate on Y axis
Drag --> Rotate on Z axis

Figure 18.56 Choose the specific action that you want to trigger.

You're also given the opportunity to specify a secondary modifier key. This must be a standard alphanumeric key (**Figure 18.52**). Other kinds of keys, such as Tab or Backspace, won't work here. If you don't want to use a secondary modifier key, leave this field blank.

If you use the Keyboard Input behavior, you're asked to specify the key that must be pressed to trigger that action (**Figure 18.53**). Your options are Left Arrow, Right Arrow, Up Arrow, Down Arrow, or the alphanumeric key of your choice. If you want one of the arrow keys, choose it from the pop-up menu (**Figure 18.54**). Otherwise, choose "The custom key I've entered below" from the menu, and enter an alphanumeric key in the field below the menu (**Figure 18.55**).

12. For the last parameter, associate the trigger with an action by making a selection from the "Select a Group and its Action" pop-up menu. Look for the group name you assigned in step 6, and specify exactly what you want the sprite to do when the trigger is activated (**Figure 18.56**).

13. Click OK to close the dialog box.

continues on next page

14. If you wish, repeat steps 8 through 13 to apply additional triggers to the same action. (For example, you may want a particular action to be triggered by either a mouse click or a key press.)

15. Play the movie.

16. Test the interaction by doing whatever is necessary to activate the trigger, such as dragging the mouse or pressing a key (**Figure 18.57**).

✔ Tip

■ Remember that Mac users have only one mouse button. If you associate the Mouse Right trigger with an action, it will work when Windows users press the right mouse button, but it won't work on the Macintosh at all. Be sure to repeat steps 8 through 13 to add an additional trigger (such as Mouse Left with the Control key as a modifier) that will work for Mac users.

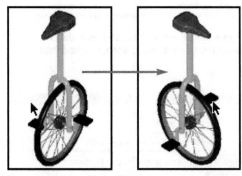

Figure 18.57 The Mouse Left trigger, combined with the Drag Model to Rotate action, allows you to rotate the 3D object with your mouse.

USING XTRAS

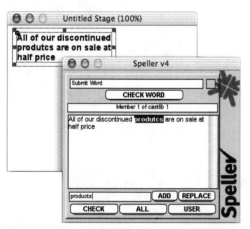

Figure 19.1 Spell checking in Director? A third-party Xtra (in this case, Speller4 from Design Lynx Ltd.) makes it possible.

Like one of those kitchen gadgets advertised on late-night TV—"It's a grinder! It's a grater! It's a slicer!"—Director can be made to do nearly anything, depending on what add-ons you attach to it (**Figure 9.1**). In Director's case, the add-ons come in the form of software modules called *Xtras*.

Xtras allow Director to import diverse cast-member types, link to networks and external files, expand its scripting vocabulary, add special effects, and handle a variety of other tasks. (See the sidebar "Types of Xtras" on the following page.) Xtras are integral to Director's design—so much so that when Macromedia developers add features to Director, they often don't tinker with the program's code; they simply add another Xtra.

continues on next page

Dozens of Xtras were copied to your hard drive when you installed Director. Every time you create a vector shape, embed a font, format text, or perform many other seemingly basic tasks, it's not Director itself doing the work, but an Xtra. These Macromedia-supplied Xtras function behind the scenes, without your necessarily even knowing they exist.

But the writing of Xtras isn't confined to Macromedia developers. Lots of third-party developers also create Xtras, which you can download from the Web and install in Director. If you have programming skills, you can even write Xtras yourself.

This chapter will show you how to install and work with Xtras, and how to make sure the people to whom you distribute your movies have the Xtras they need to view the movies properly.

Types of Xtras

Xtras can be classified into six general categories:

- **Cast-member Xtras,** which allow Director to handle nonstandard types of cast members (such as Flash movies and digital video files).

- **Importing Xtras,** which allow Director to link to various kinds of external files.

- **Transition Xtras,** which add transition effects that are not built in to Director (see Chapter 5, "Playing and Refining Movies").

- **Lingo Xtras,** which add new commands and functions to Director's scripting language.

- **Network Xtras,** which allow Director movies to access the Internet or other external networks.

- **Tool Xtras,** which are designed to help you with authoring. (An example is the Xtra that allows the Windows version of Director to convert WAV audio files to Shockwave Audio files.)

In general, if you use any of these Xtras in creating a movie, your audience must have the same Xtras in order to play the movie. (See "Including Xtras with Projectors" and "Using Xtras with Shockwave Movies," later in this chapter.) The only exceptions are the tool Xtras, which need only to be present in Director, not in the viewing environment.

Acquiring, Installing, and Using Xtras

The Xtras that are integral to Director's operation are installed automatically when you install Director. You don't have to do anything further with them.

If you're like many Director users, however, you'll want to expand Director's capabilities by adding Xtras that didn't come with the program. In most cases, you'll find these Xtras through the Xtras page of Macromedia's Web site. (You can reach the Xtras page via a link on the main Director support page, www.macromedia.com/support/director.) On the Xtras page, you'll find links to the following resources:

◆ A list of Xtras from third-party developers, with links to the developers' Web sites. (In most cases, you can download the Xtras from the developers' sites. Some are free; most are for purchase.)

◆ A list of Xtra-related tech notes, including links to updated versions of Macromedia-supplied Xtras.

◆ The Director Exchange (part of a site-within-a-site called Macromedia Exchange), where users can upload and download tips, hints, sample files, templates, and—yes—Xtras. Some of the Xtras you'll find here were created by Macromedia developers, some by third-party developers, and some by amateurs. Some are free; some are not.

Any time you acquire a new Xtra, you have to install it manually. You must do this using the file-management features of your computer's operating system; you can't do it from within Director. (Some Xtra developers supply an automated installer file that allows you to install an Xtra in the same way you'd install an application.)

Many Xtras, once they are installed, will operate transparently—that is, you don't have to do anything special to use them. For example, if you install a Lingo Xtra, the new commands or functions will automatically be available in Lingo; if you install a transition Xtra, the new transition will automatically be available in the Transition dialog box. (For descriptions of the various types of Xtras, see the "Types of Xtras" sidebar, earlier in this chapter.)

Using tool Xtras and cast-member Xtras may require extra steps, as described below. In general, it's a good idea to read the documentation file that comes with an Xtra to see how its developers intended it to be used.

If you use any non-Macromedia Xtras (other than tool Xtras) in the course of creating a movie, make note of the ones you used, because you'll have to supply those Xtras to users when you distribute the movie. (See "Including Xtras with Projectors" and "Using Xtras with Shockwave Movies," later in this chapter.)

To install an Xtra:

1. If Director is running, choose File > Exit (Windows) or Director > Quit Director (Mac) to quit the program.

2. Find and open the Director MX application folder on your hard drive.

3. Drag the new Xtra into the Xtras folder inside the Director MX application folder (**Figure 19.2**).

   If the Xtra is already in a folder (along with other Xtras or supporting files), you can drag the entire folder into the Xtras folder. Director will recognize Xtras in folders-within-folders so long as they're not nested more than five levels deep.

4. Restart Director.

   The Xtra is installed and ready for you to use.

Figure 19.2 You install Xtras—either individually or in folders—by dragging them into the Xtras folder.

Figure 19.3 The Xtras menu shows installed tool Xtras.

Figure 19.4 Each tool Xtra has its own unique dialog box. (Shown here is Macromedia's 3D SpeedPort Xtra, which converts 3D files in OBJ format to Director's native W3D format.)

Figure 19.5 Cast-member Xtras such as this one (PDF Xtra from Integration New Media, which allows Director to import PDF files) are listed under Media Element on the Insert menu.

To use a tool Xtra:

1. Choose Xtras > *Xtra name* (**Figure 19.3**).

   A custom dialog box appears (**Figure 19.4**).

2. Perform any desired tasks in the dialog box. (See the documentation that came with the Xtra for details.)

3. Click OK (or whatever the equivalent is in this particular Xtra) to close the dialog box.

To import a cast member by means of a cast-member Xtra:

1. Choose Insert > Media Element > *Xtra name* (**Figure 19.5**).

   An options dialog box appears (**Figure 19.6**).

2. Set the properties for the cast member you're importing.

continues on next page

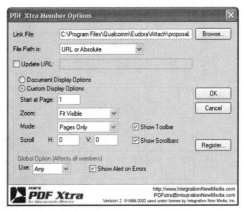

Figure 19.6 A dialog box allows you to set properties for the cast member you're about to import.

3. Click OK to close the dialog box.

The newly imported cast member appears in the Cast window (**Figure 19.7**). You can use it in your movie just as you would use any other cast member.

✔ Tips

■ The imported cast member may have additional properties you can set. To see them, select the cast member in the Cast window, then click the Cast Member Properties button. The properties will be displayed on a custom tab in the Property Inspector (**Figure 19.8**).

■ Double-clicking the cast member in the Cast window will have different effects depending on the Xtra that was used to import the cast member. In some cases, a media editor will open; in others, the properties dialog box (which you used in step 2, before the cast member was imported) will reopen.

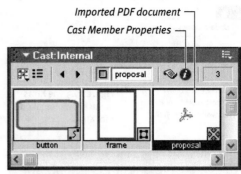

Imported PDF document ⌐
Cast Member Properties ⌐

Figure 19.7 A cast member imported via an Xtra appears in the Cast window, just like ordinary cast members.

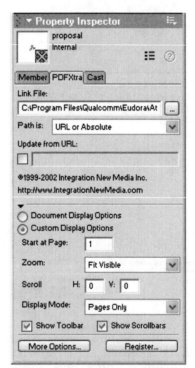

Figure 19.8 Properties for a cast member imported via an Xtra will usually appear on a custom tab in the Property Inspector.

Including Xtras with Projectors

If you use Xtras (other than tool Xtras) to create a movie, the members of your audience must have the same Xtras available on their computer in order to view the movie. Therefore, if you distribute your movie by means of a projector file, you must include not only the movie itself, but also all the Xtras needed to view the movie. (See Chapter 16, "Creating a Projector.")

There are two approaches to including Xtras with a projector: You can embed the Xtras directly into the movie that will be contained in the projector, or you can include a separate Xtras folder alongside the projector. The advantage of embedding Xtras into your movie is that the user gets one, self-sufficient file, which makes things easier. The advantage of including a separate Xtras folder alongside the projector is that the movie starts more quickly, because the projector file doesn't have to unpack the Xtras before playing the movie.

If a projector contains several movies that use the same Xtras, you don't have to embed those Xtras in all the movies. The Xtras stay in memory for as long as the projector is running, so you only have to embed the necessary Xtras in the first movie, and the succeeding movies will still have access to them.

Become an Xtras Developer

After you've had some experience working with Xtras, you may decide you want to write your own. Be aware that writing an Xtra is not a trivial task; it requires professional-level programming experience. Most Xtras developers work in the C++ programming language, but some use Lingo.

If you're interested in creating Xtras, look on Macromedia's Web site for information for Xtra developers. (You can get there from the main Director support page at www.macromedia.com/support/director.) In addition to explaining the basics of Xtra development, Macromedia offers the Xtras Developer Kit (XDK) as a free download.

To embed Xtras in a movie:

1. Choose Modify > Movie > Xtras.

   The Movie Xtras dialog box opens (**Figure 19.9**). The list in this dialog box shows the Xtras that are currently embedded in your movie. Those include:

   ▲ The default Xtras that are automatically embedded in every movie.

   ▲ Xtras that were embedded "behind the scenes" as you created your movie. For example, if you use text in a movie, Director embeds several text-related Xtras at the moment the first text cast member is created (**Figure 9.10**).

   The list may not include all the Xtras that have been used in the movie. Some Macromedia Xtras, and many third-party Xtras, are not embedded automatically by Director. (An example is the Speech Xtra required for the text-to-speech feature. See Chapter 20, "Accessibility," for more information the Speech Xtra.)

   If you've used any Xtras in creating this movie that are not on the list, you'll need to add them manually.

2. If you need to add an Xtra, click the Add button.

   The Add Xtras dialog box appears (**Figure 19.11**).

3. Select the Xtra that you want to add.

4. Click OK to close the Add Xtras dialog box.

5. Repeat steps 2 through 4 as many times as necessary for additional Xtras.

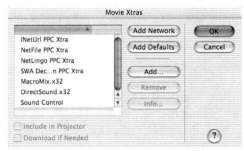

Figure 19.9 The Movie Xtras dialog box lists the Xtras that are embedded in a movie.

Text Xtras

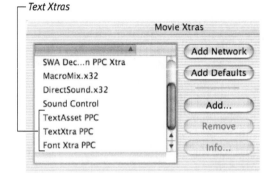

Figure 19.10 When you create or import a cast member, Director automatically embeds the Xtras needed to display that type of cast member (in this case, text).

Figure 19.11 The Add Xtras dialog box allows you to select an Xtra that you want to embed.

INCLUDING XTRAS WITH PROJECTORS

6. If your movie is intended to connect to the Internet, click the Add Network button in the Movie Xtras dialog box.

The necessary network Xtras are added to the list, if they're not there already.

7. Click OK to close the Movie Xtras dialog box.

The movie is now ready to be included in a projector file. (See Chapter 16, "Creating a Projector.")

✔ Tips

- Some Xtras are so commonly used in Director movies that they're automatically embedded in every movie, as noted in step 1. That doesn't mean, however, that they're necessarily required by *your* movie. If you're sure that a particular Xtra isn't necessary, you can reduce the movie's file size by deleting that Xtra. (See "To remove embedded Xtras from a movie," on the following page.)

- As described in step 1, when you create or import certain types of cast members, Director automatically embeds the necessary Xtras in your movie. If you later delete those cast members, the Xtras remain embedded. To reduce your movie's file size, you should manually remove the embedded Xtras for cast-member types that are no longer in your movie. (Again, see "To remove embedded Xtras from a movie" on the following page.)

To remove embedded Xtras from a movie:

1. Choose Modify > Movie > Xtras.

   The Movie Xtras dialog box opens.

2. In the list, select the Xtra that you want to remove (**Figure 19.12**).

   Removing unneeded Xtras is a good way to reduce your movie's file size, but you should remove an Xtra only if you're absolutely certain that your movie doesn't require it. If in doubt, leave it alone.

3. Click the Remove button.

   The selected Xtra disappears from the list.

4. Repeat steps 2 and 3 as many times as necessary to remove other Xtras.

5. Click OK to close the Movie Xtras dialog box.

✔ Tips

- If you want more information about what an Xtra does before you delete it, select it in the Movie Xtras dialog box and click the Info button. (The Info button is dimmed for some Xtras.) Assuming your computer is connected to the Internet, Director will download a description of the Xtra and display it in your browser.

- If you accidentally delete one of the default Xtras, click the Add Defaults button to restore the full default set.

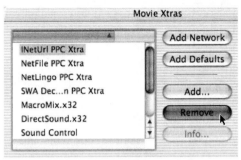

Figure 19.12 If you're certain that a particular Xtra isn't needed in your movie, you can remove it by selecting it and clicking Remove.

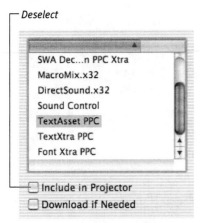

Deselect

Figure 19.13 If you want to distribute Xtras in an external folder, deselect Include in Projector in the Movie Xtras dialog box.

To distribute Xtras with a projector (without embedding them in a movie):

1. Open a movie that you plan to include in a projector.

2. Choose Modify > Movie > Xtras.

   The Movie Xtras dialog box opens.

3. Select the first Xtra in the list.

4. Deselect the Include in Projector check box (**Figure 19.13**).

5. Repeat steps 3 and 4 for all the remaining Xtras in the list.

6. Write down the names of all the Xtras in the list.

   These are the Xtras you'll have to distribute along with the projector.

   If you intend to create a Shockwave projector (also known as a *slim projector*)— a projector that uses the resources of the Shockwave Player to play movies—you can omit the Xtras that are installed with the Shockwave Player. For more information, see step 3 of "To make a movie's Xtras downloadable by the Shockwave Player," later in this chapter.

7. Repeat steps 1 through 6 for any additional movies that you plan to include in the projector.

   In step 6, you need only add the names of Xtras that you haven't already written down.

8. Create the projector (see Chapter 16, "Creating a Projector").

continues on next page

INCLUDING XTRAS WITH PROJECTORS

9. Create a folder called Xtras in the same folder where the projector file resides (**Figure 19.14**).

10. Locate the Xtra files whose names you wrote down in step 6. (All are in the Xtras folder inside the Director MX application folder, but some may be in subfolders.)

11. Copy each of the Xtra files you located in step 10 into the folder you created in step 9.

12. If any of the movies in the projector use Xtras that aren't on your list, copy them into the new folder as well. (See step 1 of "To embed Xtras in a movie," earlier in this section.)

13. When you distribute your projector file, make sure the new Xtras folder accompanies it.

Figure 19.14 The folder in which you distribute your Xtras must be called "Xtras," and it must be in the same folder that contains your projector.

Using Xtras with Shockwave Movies

Because Shockwave movies are designed to be as small as possible for quick downloading, Xtras can't be embedded in Shockwave movies. Instead, any necessary Xtras must be installed in the Shockwave Player on the user's computer.

The most commonly used Xtras are included in the initial installation of the Shockwave Player. These include the Xtras that support text; vector shapes; Flash movies; PICT, BMP, GIF, and JPEG images; sound; and Shockwave Audio. (For a complete list of the Xtras included with the Shockwave Player, see **Table 19.1**.)

Table 19.1

Xtras installed with the Shockwave MX Player		
WINDOWS ONLY	**MAC ONLY**	**BOTH WINDOWS AND MAC***
DirectSound	Animated GIF Asset	CBrowser
MacroMix	Havoc	Flash Asset
Shockwave Updater	LRG Import Export	Font Asset
SWADCmpr	Mix Services	Font Xtra
SWAstrm	MPEG 3 Import Export	INetURL
	PNG Import Export	Multiusr
	QT6 Asset	NetFile
	Sound Import Export	NetLingo
	Sun AU Import Export	Shockwave 3D Asset
	SWA Decompression PPC	Sound Control
	SWA Import Export	Speech
	SWA Streaming PPC	Text Asset
	Targa Import Export	Text Xtra
	TIFF Import Export	
	XmlParser PPC Xtra	

Filenames may vary slightly between platforms.

When the Shockwave Player plays a movie, one of the first things it does is check whether the movie requires any Xtras that aren't already present on the user's computer. If so—assuming you've set up the movie as described on the next page in "To make a movie's Xtras downloadable by the Shockwave Player"— it automatically downloads those Xtras from the Internet. (For security reasons, some Xtras aren't downloadable. This fact will be clearly noted in the Xtra's documentation, in which case you shouldn't use that Xtra in a Director movie that you intend to distribute via Shockwave.) Once a particular Xtra has been downloaded to a user's computer, it remains installed, so it won't have to be downloaded again for future movies that use that Xtra.

In order for the Shockwave Player to be able to download the Xtras it needs, Director must embed the URLs for those Xtras in the Shockwave movie. Director gets those Web addresses from a text file on your computer called xtrainfo.txt, which contains the URLs for all Macromedia-supplied Xtras. If you use non-Macromedia Xtras in your movie, you'll need to add their URLs manually to xtrainfo.txt. (If you install an Xtra by means of an install program provided by the developer, that program may automatically add the Xtra's URL to the file.)

To edit the xtrainfo.txt file:

1. Double-click the xtrainfo.txt file (**Figure 19.15**). The file is located in the Director MX application folder on your computer's hard drive.

   The file opens in your computer's default text-editing program.

2. Follow the directions at the beginning of the file to add to or change the data in the file (**Figure 19.16**).

3. Save the file. (Be sure to keep the same filename and location.)

xtrainfo.txt

Figure 19.15 The xtrainfo.txt file contains the URLs for Xtras that are downloadable by the Shockwave Player.

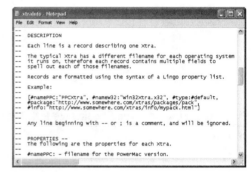

Figure 19.16 Directions for editing the xtrainfo.txt file are contained within the file.

To make a movie's Xtras downloadable by the Shockwave Player:

1. Follow steps 1 through 5 of "To embed Xtras in a movie," earlier in this chapter.

   This brings the information in the Movie Xtras dialog box up to date. (Though no Xtras will be embedded in the Shockwave version of the movie, Director needs to know which Xtras to make available for download.)

2. If your computer doesn't have an active connection to the Internet, initiate the connection.

3. From the list in the Movie Xtras dialog box, select an Xtra that you want to make downloadable.

   The Xtras listed in **Table 19.1** are included in the default installation of the Shockwave Player, so you don't have to make them downloadable. Note, however, that the Windows and Mac versions of the player have different default Xtras. If your audience includes both Mac and Windows users, and your movie includes Xtras that are in the Mac-only or Windows-only column, you should make those Xtras downloadable as well.

continues on next page

USING XTRAS WITH SHOCKWAVE MOVIES

4. Check the Download if Needed checkbox (**Figure 19.17**).

The movie gets the URL for the selected Xtra from the xtrainfo.txt file and does a trial download of the Xtra, shown by a progress bar on the screen (**Figure 19.18**).

If the download is successful, the progress bar disappears and you can continue. If the download is unsuccessful, Director informs you via an alert box (**Figure 19.19**), in which case you should check xtrainfo.txt to make sure the listed URL is correct and current.

5. Repeat steps 3 and 4 for all other Xtras that you want to make downloadable.

6. Click OK to close the Movie Xtras dialog box.

Your movie is now ready to be published as a Shockwave movie. (See Chapter 17, "Making Movies for the Web.")

Select

Figure 19.17 To make an Xtra downloadable, select the Download if Needed check box in the Movie Xtras dialog box.

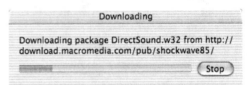

Figure 19.18 Director performs a trial download of the Xtra that you want to make downloadable by the Shockwave Player.

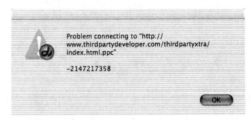

Figure 19.19 If the download is unsuccessful, Director shows you this alert box.

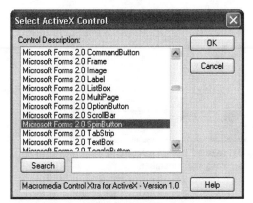

Figure 19.20 The Select ActiveX Control dialog box displays all the ActiveX controls available on your computer.

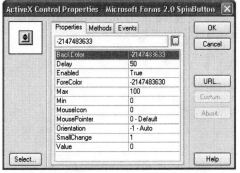

Figure 19.21 The Properties dialog box for an ActiveX control allows you to modify the control's properties, methods, and events.

Using ActiveX Controls

ActiveX controls are similar to Xtras in that they can expand the capabilities of Director movies. You can use them to add interface elements (such as menus and sliders), to import a variety of file types, and to interact with other programs from within a Director movie.

Many ActiveX controls come installed on PCs as part of the Windows operating system. Others are available for purchase from third-party developers. Unlike Xtras, ActiveX controls are neither developed by nor supported by Macromedia.

ActiveX controls have several restrictions that may limit their usefulness:

◆ ActiveX controls can be used only in the Windows version of Director.

◆ Movies containing ActiveX controls can be played only on Windows computers.

◆ Movies containing ActiveX controls can be distributed only in projectors; they can't be published as Shockwave movies.

To add an ActiveX control to a movie (Windows only):

1. Choose Insert > Control > ActiveX.

   The Select ActiveX Control dialog box opens, displaying all the ActiveX controls available on your computer (**Figure 19.20**).

2. Select the ActiveX control that you want to import.

3. Click OK.

   The ActiveX Control Properties dialog box opens (**Figure 19.21**).

continues on next page

4. Change the settings in the dialog box as desired.

There are three tabs—Properties, Methods, and Events—that allow you to customize the ActiveX control.

5. Click OK to close the dialog box.

The ActiveX control appears in the Cast window (**Figure 19.22**). You can incorporate it into your movie by dragging it to the Stage or Score; thereafter, it can be repositioned or resized on the Stage like any other sprite (**Figure 19.23**).

Figure 19.22 The ActiveX control becomes a cast member.

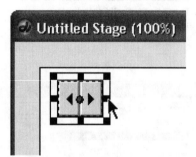

Figure 19.23 An ActiveX control can be repositioned or resized like any other sprite.

20

ACCESSIBILITY

Back when computers were entirely text-based, people with physical disabilities could use them without much difficulty. Blind people could use screen-reading software that translated the text on the screen into a synthesized voice; then they could simply type their response on the keyboard. People with motor impairments could use alternative input devices to type characters. And for the hearing-impaired, a text-based interface presented no barrier at all.

Ironically, many so-called user-friendly computer technology advances in the 1980s and 1990s made computers *less* accessible to people with disabilities. The mouse-based, point-and-click interface proved useless for visually impaired people who couldn't see what they were supposed to click, and many motor-impaired people found that they couldn't maneuver a mouse with the necessary precision. The introduction of streaming sound and video meant that a significant fraction of the audience was cut off from multimedia content: Blind people couldn't see the video portion, and deaf people couldn't hear the soundtrack.

continues on next page

Even text was no longer the common denominator it once had been. Many Web sites and CDs used bitmapped text, which screen-reading software didn't recognize. Macromedia's Shockwave and Flash players were impervious to screen-reading software, so even regular text in a Director or Flash movie was inaccessible to visually-impaired users.

In recent years, hardware and software designers have been working to rectify these problems. In 1998, the U.S. Congress passed Section 508 of the Rehabilitation Act, which requires that all Web sites maintained by the federal government be accessible to people with disabilities. An increasing number of states and private organizations have also chosen to adhere to the guidelines established by Section 508.

Macromedia has responded to the challenge by including powerful, easy-to-use accessibility features in Director MX. You'll find separate sets of features available for making Director movies accessible to people with visual, hearing, and motor impairments. After learning how to use these features in this chapter, perhaps you'll be inspired to make your own Director movies accessible to a larger audience.

ACCESSIBILITY

Figure 20.1 A scene is suitable for keyboard navigation if it stays still and waits for the user to choose a button.

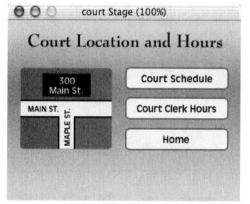

Figure 20.2 Buttons in another part of the movie would constitute a different accessibility group.

About Keyboard Navigation

Keyboard navigation—an alternative to the point-and-click style of user interface—makes Director movies accessible to users with motor and visual impairments. If there are buttons on the Stage that the user would ordinarily click with the mouse, he or she has the option of using the Tab key to move from button to button, then pressing the Enter or Return key to "click" the currently selected button. (For blind users, keyboard navigation must be accompanied by an audible means of identifying each button. See "Adding Text-to-Speech Capability," later in this chapter.)

In order for keyboard navigation to work properly, all the available buttons must be on the screen at the same time, and the movie must be designed to pause or loop until the user has clicked a button that will make the movie continue (**Figure 20.1**). (For instructions on designing this type of interaction, see "Scripting Navigation" in Chapter 15.) The buttons and other objects that the user may navigate at any given time constitute an *accessibility group*. A movie may contain any number of accessibility groups, each of which appears on the Stage at a different time (**Figure 20.2**).

To implement keyboard navigation, you apply behaviors from the Library palette to the sprites you want to make accessible from the keyboard. If you're not familiar with using the behaviors in the Library palette, see Chapter 14, "Adding Behaviors."

While many of the tasks in this chapter may seem rather lengthy, don't be intimidated by the number of steps involved in adding accessibility features to your Director movie. You'll find that the steps described in each task are simple and straightforward.

To add keyboard navigation to a Director movie:

1. In an empty channel of the Score, select the frame where you want the keyboard navigation to begin.

   All of the buttons that will be accessible to the user should be visible on the Stage.

2. Click the Rectangle, Rounded Rectangle, or Ellipse tool on the Tool palette (**Figure 20.3**).

   You'll be using this tool to create a *focus ring*—an outline that surrounds the currently selected button each time the user presses the Tab key (**Figure 20.4**).

3. Select a line thickness from the Tool palette.

   For best results, choose the heaviest line (**Figure 20.5**).

4. Select a color from the Foreground Color menu on the Tool palette.

   This will be the color of the focus ring.

5. Drag the mouse anywhere on the Stage to create a shape.

   The shape's size and proportions don't matter—Director will resize it on the fly when the movie is played—so for convenience, you'll probably want to keep it relatively small.

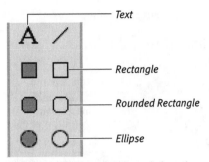

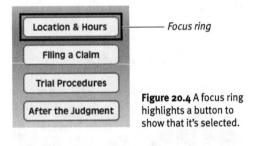

Figure 20.3 You'll need these tools from the Tool palette to set up keyboard navigation.

Figure 20.4 A focus ring highlights a button to show that it's selected.

Figure 20.5 The Tool palette offers very few options for line thickness; the heaviest line works best for a focus ring.

ABOUT KEYBOARD NAVIGATION

Figure 20.6 Drag the shape into the gray area that surrounds the Stage.

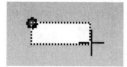

Figure 20.7 The size of the text box doesn't matter, but a smaller box is usually more convenient.

Figure 20.8 Drag the text sprite into the offstage area.

Figure 20.9 The Text tab of the Property Inspector, showing appropriate settings for the text sprite.

6. Drag the shape off the Stage into the gray offstage area (**Figure 20.6**).

    Its exact position doesn't matter.

7. Click the Text tool on the Tool palette.

    You'll be creating an editable text sprite that will eventually intercept the user's keystrokes when he or she presses the Tab or Enter keys.

8. Drag the mouse anywhere on the Stage to create a text-entry box.

    Its size doesn't matter (**Figure 20.7**).

9. Without entering any text in the box, click outside its boundaries to take it out of editing mode.

10. Drag the newly created text sprite off the Stage into the gray offstage area (**Figure 20.8**).

    Its exact position doesn't matter.

11. With the text sprite still selected, click the Text tab in the Property Inspector.

12. Make the following selections in the Property Inspector (**Figure 20.9**):

    ▲ From the Framing menu, choose Fixed.

    ▲ Select the Editable check box.

    ▲ Make sure the Tab check box is not selected.

13. Choose Window > Library Palette to open the Library palette.

continues on next page

ABOUT KEYBOARD NAVIGATION

14. Choose Accessibility from the Library List pop-up menu.

The list of accessibility behaviors appears (**Figure 20.10**).

15. Drag the Accessibility Target behavior from the Library palette to the Stage, and drop it on the shape you created in step 5.

(For these purposes, the Stage includes the gray offstage area, where you dragged the shape.)

A Parameters dialog box appears (**Figure 20.11**).

16. In the "Name of this Accessibility Group?" field, type a group name (**Figure 20.12**).

This name will be used to identify the current set of buttons that can be accessed from the keyboard. (If you set up keyboard navigation for another set of buttons later in the movie, you'll need to give that group a different name.)

Deselect the "Speech initially enabled?" check box if you want to disable the text-to-speech feature (it's enabled by default).

If you disable text-to-speech, you can allow the user to enable it later by means of a button. See "To create an on/off switch for speech-to-text," later in this chapter.

17. Click OK to close the dialog box.

18. Drag the Accessibility Keyboard Controller behavior from the Library palette to the Stage, and drop it on the empty text sprite you created in steps 8 and 9.

A Parameters dialog box appears (**Figure 20.13**).

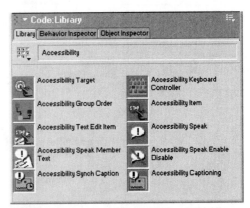

Figure 20.10 The accessibility behaviors in the Library palette let you add keyboard navigation, captioning, and text-to-speech capabilities to your movie.

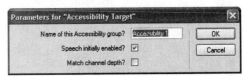

Figure 20.11 Parameters for the Accessibility Target behavior, which is used to create a focus ring.

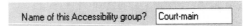

Figure 20.12 Type an easily identifiable name for the accessibility group.

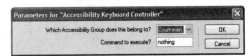

Figure 20.13 Shown here are the parameters for the Accessibility Keyboard Controller behavior, which allows a user's keystrokes to be intercepted from the keyboard and used to navigate sprites on the Stage.

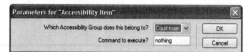

Figure 20.14 Parameters for the Accessibility Item behavior, which make a sprite navigable from the keyboard.

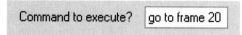

Figure 20.15 This Lingo command makes the playhead jump to frame 20 when this button is highlighted and the user presses the Enter key.

19. From the "Which Accessibility Group does this belong to?" pop-up menu, choose the group name that you entered in step 16. (In most cases, that will be the only name on the menu.)

20. Click OK to close the dialog box.

21. Drag the Accessibility Item behavior from the Library palette to the Stage, and drop it on one of the buttons that you want to make keyboard-accessible.

A Parameters dialog box appears (**Figure 20.14**).

22. From the "Which Accessibility Group does this belong to?" pop-up menu, choose the group name that you entered in step 16. (In most cases, that will be the only name on the menu.)

In compiling this menu, Director looks at the group names of all focus-ring sprites—that is, all sprites with the Accessibility Target behavior applied to them—that are currently on the Stage. (The "Stage," for this purpose, includes the offstage area.) Since there should be only one focus-ring sprite on the Stage at any given time, there will generally be only one group name on the menu.

Type a command in the "Command to execute?" field if you want a Lingo command to be executed when the button is "clicked" (that is, when the user navigates to this button and presses the Enter key). Most often, this will be a simple go to command (**Figure 20.15**),

For information on writing Lingo commands and handlers, see Chapter 15, "Scripting Lingo."

23. Click OK to close the dialog box.

continues on next page

ABOUT KEYBOARD NAVIGATION

24. Repeat steps 21 through 23 for each of the remaining buttons that you want to make keyboard-accessible.

25. Drag the Accessibility Group Order behavior from the Library palette to the Stage, and drop it on one of the buttons to which you've applied the Accessibility Item behavior.

A Parameters dialog box appears (**Figure 20.16**).

26. From the "Which Accessibility Group does this belong to?" pop-up menu, choose the group name you entered in step 16. (In most cases, that will be the only name on the menu.)

27. In the "Tab order?" field, type a number corresponding to the order in which you want the buttons to be highlighted by the Tab key.

For example, if this is the first button that you want to be highlighted, type 1; if this is the second button, type 2; and so on.

28. Click OK to close the dialog box.

29. Repeat steps 25 through 28 for each of the remaining buttons. Be sure that the buttons are numbered in consecutive order, and that no numbers are skipped or repeated.

30. Click on the Stage to make it the active window.

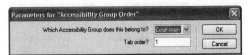

Figure 20.16 Parameters for the Accessibility Group Order behavior, which determines the sequence in which sprites will be highlighted by pressing the Tab key.

Focus ring

Figure 20.17 Now that keyboard navigation has been added to this movie, pressing the Tab key makes the focus ring move from button to button.

31. Test the movie.

When the buttons appear on the Stage, the first button (the one you numbered "1" in step 27) is highlighted by the focus ring you created in step 5. When you press the Tab key, the focus ring moves to the next button (**Figure 20.17**)—and so on, until it returns to the first button.

✔ Tips

■ You can use the same cast member in more than one accessibility group, but you can't use the same *sprite* in more than one accessibility group. If you want to include a particular cast member in multiple accessibility groups, drag it anew to the Stage or Score each time you use it.

■ As you'll see in the next section, keyboard navigation can be used with any kind of sprite—not just buttons. The preceding steps will work with all kinds of sprites except editable text fields. To make editable text fields navigable from the keyboard, follow the same directions, but use the Accessibility Text Field Item behavior in steps 21 through 23 instead of the Accessibility Item behavior.

ABOUT KEYBOARD NAVIGATION

Adding Text-to-Speech Capability

Text-to-speech builds on Director's keyboard navigation capability to make your Director movies accessible to people with visual impairments. Each time the user presses the Tab key to highlight an object on the Stage, Director uses a synthesized voice to speak the text associated with that object. The text may be anything from a short label to a long description.

While keyboard navigation by itself is generally used only for sprites that the user would ordinarily need to click on—that is, buttons or editable text fields—keyboard navigation in conjunction with text-to-speech can be used to present the entire contents of a movie aurally. Therefore, when using text-to-speech, you may want to implement keyboard navigation for sprites that the user wouldn't ordinarily click on—such as pictures and noneditable text sprites—so that the user can navigate to each item in turn and hear a spoken description (**Figure 20.18**).

Director uses the Speech Xtra to implement text-to-speech. (For information on Xtras, see Chapter 19, "Using Xtras.") This Xtra isn't installed with the Shockwave Player, but the player automatically downloads the Xtra from Macromedia's server the first time it plays a movie that includes text-to-speech behaviors. If you distribute a movie as a projector file, you must manually add the Speech Xtra to the movie before you create the projector. To do so, see "To add the Speech Xtra to a movie," later in this section.

Unlike Flash MX—which requires a third-party, Windows-only screen-reading program to implement its text-to-speech feature—Director MX has no requirements for text-to-speech other than that the speech component of the operating system be properly installed.

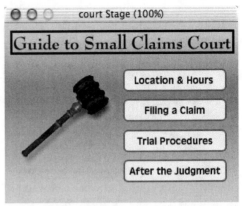

Figure 20.18 Since a visually impaired user can't see the title or the picture in this scene, you might want to make these elements navigable from the keyboard so that the user can hear a spoken description of each.

Every Mac operating system since OS 7 includes speech capability. Windows 2000 and Windows XP also come with built-in speech capability. Users with earlier versions of Windows must manually install the speech component, which can be downloaded from the Microsoft Agents page of Microsoft's Web site at `www.microsoft.com/msagent/`. (If your movie depends on text-to-speech, it's a good idea to include a Lingo script that tests for the presence of the necessary operating-system software. See "To test for text-to-speech system support," below.)

To test for text-to-speech system support:

◆ Include a Lingo script that uses the `voiceInitialize()` function. This function returns **1** if the computer is equipped for text-to-speech and **0** if it isn't.

For example, you might write a movie script that includes the following handler. (For information on movie scripts, see "To write a movie script" in Chapter 15.)

```
on startMovie
    if voiceInitialize() = 0 then
        go to frame X
    end if
end
```

(The *X* in `frame X` should be replaced by the frame number of your choice.) This handler checks for the necessary text-to-speech system software when the movie starts. If the software is not present, the playhead jumps to another section of the Score—perhaps containing an alternate version of the movie that doesn't use text-to-speech, or perhaps containing a sound file advising the user to download the software. If the text-to-speech software is present, the handler does nothing, and the movie plays normally from frame 1.

To give a movie text-to-speech capability:

1. Open a movie in which keyboard navigation has been implemented. (See "About Keyboard Navigation," earlier in this chapter.)

2. If necessary, follow steps 21 through 29 of "To add keyboard navigation to a Director movie" to make additional sprites—such as images, text, or Flash movies—accessible from the keyboard.

3. Choose Window > Library Palette to open the Library palette.

4. Choose Accessibility from the Library List pop-up menu.
The list of accessibility behaviors appears.

5. Drag the Accessibility Speak behavior from the Library palette to the Stage, and drop it on a sprite that requires only a few words or less of spoken text. (Sprites that require larger amounts of text will be dealt with later.)
The sprite must already have the Accessibility Item behavior and the Accessibility Group Order behavior applied to it (from when you added keyboard navigation).
When you drop the behavior on the sprite, a Parameters dialog box appears (**Figure 20.19**).

6. From the "Which Accessibility Group does this belong to?" pop-up menu, choose the name of the sprite's accessibility group. (In most cases, there will be only one name on the menu.)

7. In the "Text to speak?" field, type the text that you want to be spoken when the sprite is highlighted (**Figure 20.20**).

8. Click OK to close the dialog box.

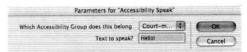

Figure 20.19 Parameters for the Accessibility Speak behavior, which is used to implement spoken text of a few words or less. (Director automatically inserts "Hello!" as the default text.)

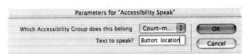

Figure 20.20 Enter a few words of text that you want Director to speak.

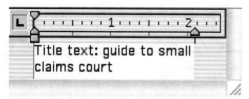

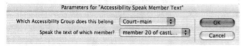

Figure 20.21 When you create a spoken-text cast member, you can include as much text as you like.

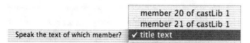

Figure 20.22 Parameters for the Accessibility Speak Member Text behavior, which allows you to associate a spoken-text cast member with a keyboard-navigable sprite.

| member 20 of castLib 1 |
| member 21 of castLib 1 |
| ✓ title text |

Figure 20.23 The pop-up menu lists all text cast members that are in the movie's Cast. Choose the one that you want Director to speak.

9. Repeat steps 5 through 8 for each sprite that requires only a small amount of spoken text.

10. If the movie contains a sprite that requires *more* than a few words of spoken text, do the following:

   ▲ Choose Window > Text to open the Text window.

   ▲ Click the New Cast Member button in the Text window.

   ▲ Type the text that you want to be spoken when the sprite is highlighted (**Figure 20.21**). (The font, size, and other attributes don't matter.)

   ▲ *(optional)* Select the newly created text cast member in the Cast window and give it a name. (See "To name a cast member" in Chapter 2.)

11. Drag the Accessibility Speak Member Text behavior from the Library palette to the Stage, and drop it on the sprite for which you prepared the text in step 10.

   The sprite must already have the Accessibility Item behavior and the Accessibility Group Order behavior applied to it (from when you added keyboard navigation).

   When you drop the behavior on the sprite, a Parameters dialog box appears (**Figure 20.22**).

12. From the "Which Accessibility Group does this belong to?" pop-up menu, choose the name of the sprite's accessibility group. (In most cases, there will be only one name on the menu.)

13. From the "Speak the text of which member?" pop-up menu, choose the name or number of the text cast member you created in step 10 (**Figure 20.23**).

continues on next page

ADDING TEXT-TO-SPEECH CAPABILITY

483

14. Click OK to close the dialog box.

15. Repeat steps 10 through 14 for each sprite that requires more than a few words of spoken text.

16. Click on the Stage to make it the active window.

17. Test the movie.

As you press the Tab key to move from sprite to sprite, the computer speaks the text associated with each sprite.

✔ Tip

■ When you write the text that accompanies each sprite, it's customary (and useful) to precede it with a function-oriented word—such as *picture* or *button*—to let the user know what kind of object he or she has selected.

To create an on/off switch for text-to-speech:

1. Create a cast member (bitmapped, vector, Flash, or whatever you like) that will be used as a button to turn text-to-speech on and off.

or

Create two cast members—one to serve as a Speech On button and the other to serve as a Speech Off button.

2. In an empty channel of the Score, click the frame where you want the button(s) to appear (**Figure 20.24**).

3. Drag the cast member(s) to the Stage to create a sprite or sprites (**Figure 20.25**).

4. In the Score, drag the endpoint(s) of the sprite(s) to the frame where you want the button(s) to disappear.

5. Choose Window > Library Palette to open the Library palette.

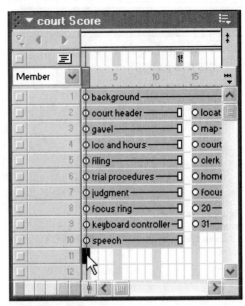

Figure 20.24 Click the frame where you want the on/off switch to make its first appearance on the Stage.

Figure 20.25 This bitmapped sprite will be used as an on/off switch for text-to-speech.

ADDING TEXT-TO-SPEECH CAPABILITY

Figure 20.26 Parameters for the Accessibility Speak Enable Disable behavior, which allows you to create an on/off switch for text-to-speech.

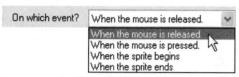

Figure 20.27 The "When the mouse is released" event is most appropriate for use with an on/off switch.

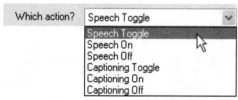

Figure 20.28 Choose an event from the "Which action?" menu to determine what the button does when it's clicked.

6. Choose Accessibility from the Library List pop-up menu.

The list of accessibility behaviors appears.

7. Follow steps 21 through 29 of "To add keyboard navigation to a Director movie" to implement keyboard navigation for the new sprite(s).

Add them to the same accessibility group that the other buttons on the Stage belong to.

8. Follow steps 5 through 9 of "To give a movie text-to-speech capability" to add spoken text to the sprite(s).

9. Drag the Accessibility Speak Enable Disable behavior from the Library palette to the Stage, and drop it on the sprite (or on the first of the two sprites).

A Parameters dialog box appears (**Figure 20.26**).

10. From the "Which Accessibility Group does this belong to?" pop-up menu, choose the name of the sprite's accessibility group. (In most cases, there will be only one name on the menu.)

11. From the "On which event?" pop-up menu, choose the event that you want to trigger the enabling or disabling of text-to-speech (**Figure 20.27**).

Choose "When the mouse is released" if you want to follow standard user-interface conventions.

12. From the "Which action?" pop-up menu, choose the action that you want the button to accomplish (**Figure 20.28**).

If you're using only one sprite for the switch, choose Speech Toggle. If you're using two sprites, choose Speech On.

continues on next page

13. In the "Speak these words when enabling" and "Speak these words when disabling" fields, type the words that you want spoken to let the user know that text-to-speech is being turned on or off.

If you don't want any words to be spoken, delete the default "Speech On" and "Speech Off" (**Figure 20.29**).

14. Click OK to close the dialog box.

15. If you're using two sprites for the switch, repeat steps 9 through 14 for the second sprite, but choose Speech Off in step 12.

16. Test the movie.

To add the Speech Xtra to a movie:

1. Open a movie that uses text-to-speech.

2. Choose Modify > Movie > Xtras.
The Movie Xtras dialog box opens (**Figure 20.30**).

3. Click Add.
The Add Xtras dialog box opens (**Figure 20.31**).

4. Select Speech.x32 (Windows) or Speech (Mac).

5. Click OK to close the Add Xtras dialog box.

6. Click OK to close the Movie Xtras dialog box.

If you make a projector file from this movie, the Speech Xtra will now be included in the file. (For more information, see Chapter 16, "Creating a Projector.")

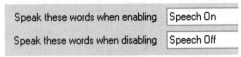

Figure 20.29 By default, Director inserts the words "Speech On" and "Speech Off" in these fields.

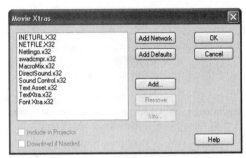

Figure 20.30 The Movie Xtras dialog box lists the Xtras that are currently included in a movie.

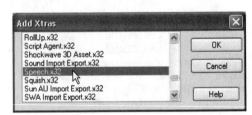

Figure 20.31 The Xtras on this list are available for inclusion in a movie. Select the Speech Xtra.

Adding Captions

Director allows you to provide text captioning for hearing-impaired users. Although this feature was most likely added to meet Section 508 guidelines, its implementation in Director is of extremely limited use.

Director's text captioning works only with sprites for which text-to-speech has been implemented. When the user selects a sprite—either with the mouse or from the keyboard—and the accompanying text is spoken, the text also appears in a caption box on the Stage, where hearing-impaired users can read it. Since the purpose of text-to-speech is to describe visual sprites to visually impaired users, it's hard to imagine why hearing-impaired users would need to read the descriptions (since they can presumably see the sprites that are being described).

A legitimately useful implementation of text captioning would allow captions to be synchronized with sound or digital video files, similar to the closed captioning used on TV. Though this can't be done in Director, it can be done with Apple's QuickTime Pro, by adding a text track to a QuickTime file. The resulting captioned file can then be imported into Director. (Techniques for implementing captioning in QuickTime are outside the scope of this book, but you can find much information on the subject by searching for *QuickTime captioning* on the Web.)

To add text captioning to a Director movie:

1. Open a movie in which keyboard navigation and text-to-speech have been implemented. (See "About Keyboard Navigation" and "Adding Text-to-Speech Capability," earlier in this chapter.)

2. Choose Window > Text Inspector to open the Text Inspector.

3. In the Score, select the cell where you want the caption box to appear.

4. Click the Text tool in the Tool palette. You'll use this tool to create the caption box.

5. On the Stage, position the mouse pointer at the place where you want the upper-left corner of the caption box to be.

6. Press the mouse button and drag horizontally.

   A rectangle appears on the Stage.

7. When you reach the desired width of the caption box, release the mouse button.

   The border of the rectangle widens, and a flashing insertion point appears inside (**Figure 20.32**).

8. In the Text Inspector, set the font, size, style, and other attributes of the caption text. (If you wish, you can type some text in the rectangle to use as a reference; see **Figure 20.33**)

   You may want to set the background color of the text to be different from the background color of the Stage, so that the caption box is easily visible.

9. If you typed any text in the rectangle, delete it.

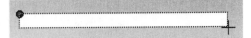

Figure 20.32 When you first create the caption box, you can set its width, but not its height.

Figure 20.33 You may want to type some temporary text in the rectangle so you can see the effects of the settings you've made in the Text Inspector.

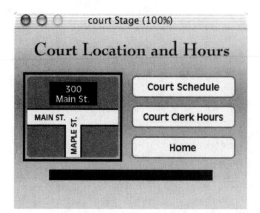

Figure 20.34 The empty caption box on the Stage.

Figure 20.35 Parameters for the Accessibility Captioning behavior, which turns a regular text sprite into a caption box.

10. Click anywhere on the Stage outside the rectangle.

The rectangle disappears, but the empty caption box remains on the Stage (**Figure 20.34**).

11. Select the caption box sprite on the Stage or in the Score.

12. Click the Text tab in the Property Inspector.

13. From the Framing menu in the Property Inspector, choose Fixed.

14. On the Stage, drag the lower-right corner of the caption box until it reaches the desired depth.

15. Choose Window > Library Palette to open the Library palette.

16. Choose Accessibility from the Library List pop-up menu.

The list of accessibility behaviors appears.

17. Drag the Accessibility Captioning behavior from the Library palette to the Stage, and drop it on the caption-box sprite.

A Parameters dialog box appears (**Figure 20.35**).

18. From the "Which Accessibility Group does this belong to?" pop-up menu, choose the name of the accessibility group of the other sprites currently on the Stage. (In most cases, there will be only one name on the menu.)

19. Click OK to close the dialog box.

continues on next page

ADDING CAPTIONS

20. Drag the Accessibility Sync Caption behavior from the Library palette to the Stage, and drop it on a sprite for which you want captioning to be enabled.

The sprite must already have the Accessibility Item behavior and the Accessibility Group Order behavior applied to it (from when you added keyboard navigation), as well as the Accessibility Speak or Accessibility Speak Member Text behavior (from when you added text-to-speech).

When you drop the behavior on the sprite, a Parameters dialog box appears (**Figure 20.36**).

21. From the "Which Accessibility Group does this belong to?" pop-up menu, choose the name of the accessibility group of the other sprites currently on the Stage. (In most cases, there will be only one name on the menu.)

22. If you want the text caption to remain visible in the box after the speech is finished, deselect the "Clear when done?" check box. Otherwise, leave it selected.

23. In the first "At word" field, enter the number of the word at which you want captioning to begin.

For example, if you want the caption to start displaying when the first word is spoken, enter 1. If you want the first word to be omitted from the caption (which you might, if the first word is *Picture:* or *Button:*), enter 2.

24. In the "Display how many of the words that follow?" field, enter the total number of words that you want to be displayed at the same time the first word is displayed. For example, if you want the caption box to hold ten words at a time, enter 10.

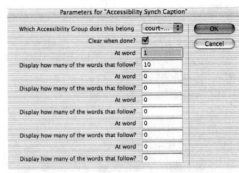

Figure 20.36 Parameters for the Accessibility Sync Caption behavior, which allows you to determine the rate at which a text caption is displayed.

At word	2
Display how many of the words that follow?	8
At word	10
Display how many of the words that follow?	8
At word	17
Display how many of the words that follow?	5

Figure 20.37 Here's how the parameters might be filled in for a 21-word caption.

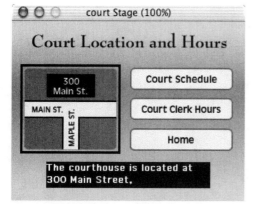

Figure 20.38 As each sprite is highlighted in turn, its spoken text appears in the caption box.

25. In the next "At word" field, enter the number of the word at which you want the next chunk of captioning to begin.

At most, this should be 1 plus the total number of words that have been displayed so far. If you want portions of the captions to overlap, you might enter a lower number.

26. In the next "Display how many of the words that follow?" field, enter the total number of words that you want to be displayed in the second chunk of the caption. This may or may not be the same number you entered in the previous "Display how many of the words that follow?" field.

27. Repeat steps 25 and 26 until you've accounted for all the words in the spoken text that accompanies the sprite (**Figure 20.37**).

28. Click OK to close the dialog box.

29. Repeat steps 20 through 28 for each sprite on the Stage to which you want to apply text captioning.

30. Click on the Stage to make it the active window.

31. Test the movie.

As you press the Tab key to move from sprite to sprite, the computer speaks the text associated with each sprite, and the spoken text is displayed visually in the caption box (**Figure 20.38**).

To create an on/off switch for text captioning:

◆ Follow the directions for "To create an on/off switch for speech-to-text" (earlier in this chapter), but choose Captioning On and/or Captioning Off in step 12.

NUMERIC KEYPAD SHORTCUTS

A

Several frequently used Director commands—chiefly those involving playback of a movie—can be executed quickly and conveniently by pressing keys on the numeric keypad. If you can memorize these numeric-keypad shortcuts, they may speed up the process of editing a Director movie. If you can't easily memorize them—or if you're using Director on a notebook computer that doesn't have a numeric keypad—don't be concerned: the same command are available by means of standard keyboard shortcuts (listed in Appendix B) or menu choices (described in their appropriate places throughout the book, chiefly in Chapter 5).

If you're testing your Director movies on dual platforms, keep in mind that some of the Windows (**Figure A.1**) and Macintosh (**Figure A.2**) numeric keypad shortcuts are located in different positions on the keypad.

✔ Tip

■ To use the numeric keypad shortcuts, Num Lock must be turned off.

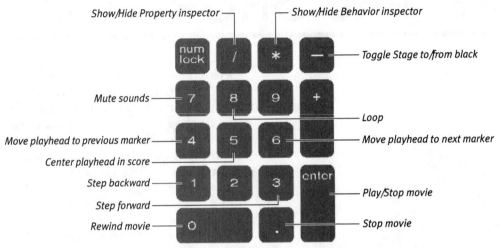

Figure A.1 The Windows numeric keypad shortcuts make it easy to quickly navigate through a Director movie without having to constantly click the mouse.

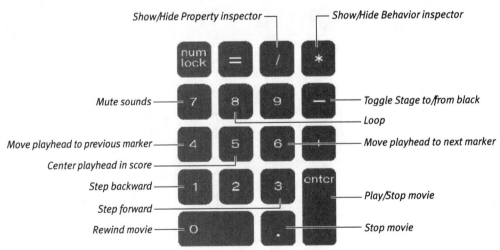

Figure A.2 The Macintosh numeric keypad shortcuts are identical to the Windows shortcuts, but the layout of the actual keypad is a little different.

KEYBOARD
SHORTCUTS

File Menu	Windows	Mac
New Movie	Ctrl N	⌘ N
New Cast	Ctrl Alt N	⌘ Option N
Open	Ctrl O	⌘ O
Close	Ctrl F4	⌘ F4
Save	Ctrl S	⌘ S
Import	Ctrl R	⌘ R
Export	Ctrl Shift R	⌘ Shift R
Publish as a Shockwave movie	Ctrl Shift S	⌘ Shift S
Preview Shockwave movie in Browser	F12	F12
Page Setup	Ctrl Shift P	⌘ Shift P
Exit/Quit	Alt F4	See Director Menu

Edit Menu	Windows	Mac
Undo	Ctrl Z	⌘ Z
Repeat	Ctrl Y	⌘ Y
Cut	Ctrl X	⌘ X
Copy	Ctrl C	⌘ C
Paste	Ctrl V	⌘ V
Clear	Del	Del
Duplicate	Ctrl D	⌘ D
Select All	Ctrl A	⌘ A

Edit Menu (cont.)	**Windows**	**Mac**
Find Text	Ctrl F	⌘ F
Find Handler	Ctrl Shift ;	⌘ Shift ;
Find Cast Member	Ctrl ;	⌘ ;
Find Selection	Ctrl / (forward slash)	⌘ / (forward slash
Find Again	Ctrl Alt F	⌘ Option F
Replace Again	Ctrl Alt E	⌘ Option E
Edit Sprite Frames	Ctrl Alt]	⌘ Option]
Edit Entire Sprite	Ctrl Alt [	⌘ Option [
Exchange Cast Members	Ctrl E	⌘ E
Launch External Editor	Ctrl ,	⌘ ,
Preferences	Ctrl U	See Director Menu

View Menu	**Windows**	**Mac**
Next Marker	Ctrl right arrow	⌘ right arrow
Previous Marker	Ctrl left arrow	⌘ left arrow
Zoom in	Ctrl +	⌘ +
Zoom out	Ctrl - (minus)	⌘ - (minus)
Show Grid	Ctrl Shift Alt G	⌘ Shift Option G
Snap to Grid	Ctrl Alt G	⌘ Option G
Show Guides	Ctrl Shift Alt D	⌘ Shift Option D
Snap to Guides	Ctrl Shift G	⌘ Shift G
Show Info	Ctrl Shift Alt O	⌘ Shift Option O
Show Paths	Ctrl Shift Alt H	⌘ Shift Option H
Sprite Toolbar (Score must be selected)	Ctrl Shift H	⌘ Shift H
Control Toolbar (Stage must be selected)	Ctrl Shift H	⌘ Shift H
Keyframes	Ctrl Shift Alt K	⌘ Shift Option K
Full Screen	Ctrl Alt 1	⌘ Option 1

Insert Menu	Windows	Mac
Keyframe	Ctrl Alt K	⌘ Option K
Insert Frame	Ctrl Shift]	⌘ Shift]
Remove Frame	Ctrl [	⌘ [

Modify Menu	Windows	Mac
Cast Member Properties	Ctrl I	⌘ I
Cast Member Script	Ctrl ' (apostrophe)	⌘ ' (apostrophe)
Sprite Properties	Ctrl Shift I	⌘ Shift I
Sprite Script	Ctrl Shift ' (apostrophe)	⌘ Shift ' (apostrophe)
Tweening	Ctrl Shift B	⌘ Shift B
Movie Properties	Ctrl Shift D	⌘ Shift D
Movie Casts	Ctrl Shift C	⌘ Shift C
Font	Ctrl Shift T	⌘ Shift T
Paragraph	Ctrl Shift Alt T	⌘ Shift Option T
Lock Sprite	Ctrl L	⌘ L
Unlock Sprite	Ctrl Shift L	⌘ Shift L
Join Sprites	Ctrl J	⌘ J
Split Sprite	Ctrl Shift J	⌘ Shift J
Extend Sprite	Ctrl B	⌘ B
Bring to Front	Ctrl Shift up arrow	⌘ Shift up arrow
Move Forward	Ctrl up arrow	⌘ up arrow
Move Backward	Ctrl down arrow	⌘ down arrow
Send to Back	Ctrl Shift down arrow	⌘ Shift down arrow
Tweak	Ctrl Shift K	⌘ Shift K

Control Menu	Windows	Mac
Play	Ctrl Alt P	⌘ Option P
Stop	Ctrl Alt . (period)	⌘ Option . (period)
Rewind	Ctrl Alt R	⌘ Option R
Step Forward	Ctrl Alt right arrow	⌘ Option right arrow
Step Backward	Ctrl Alt left arrow	⌘ Option left arrow

Control Menu (cont.)	**Windows**	**Mac**
Loop Playback	Ctrl Alt L	⌘ Option L
Volume: Mute	Ctrl Alt M	⌘ Option M
Toggle Breakpoint	F9	⌘ Shift Option K
Watch Expression	Shift F9	⌘ Shift Option W
Ignore Breakpoints	Alt F9	⌘ Shift Option I
Step Script	F10	⌘ Shift Option down arrow
Step into Script	F8	⌘ Shift Option right arrow
Run Script	F5	⌘ Shift Option up arrow
Recompile All Scripts	Shift F8	⌘ Shift Option C

Window Menu	**Windows**	**Mac**
Toolbar	Ctrl Shift Alt B	⌘ Shift Option B
Tool Palette	Ctrl 7	⌘ 7
Behavior Inspector	Ctrl Alt ;	⌘ Option ;
Property Inspector	Ctrl Alt S	⌘ Option S
Text Inspector	Ctrl T	⌘ T
Align	Ctrl K	⌘ K
Stage	Ctrl 1	⌘ 1
Control Panel	Ctrl 2	⌘ 2
Markers	Ctrl Shift M	⌘ Shift M
Score	Ctrl 4	⌘ 4
Cast	Ctrl 3	⌘ 3
Paint	Ctrl 5	⌘ 5
Vector Shape	Ctrl Shift V	⌘ Shift V
Text	Ctrl 6	⌘ 6
Field	Ctrl 8	⌘ 8
Shockwave 3D	Ctrl Shift W	⌘ Shift W
RealMedia	Ctrl Shift Y	⌘ Shift Y
Color Palettes	Ctrl Alt 7	⌘ Option 7
Video Panel Group (with QuickTime tab selected)	Ctrl 9	⌘ 9

Window Menu (cont.) **Windows**   **Mac**

Script	Ctrl 0 (zero)	⌘ 0 (zero)
Message	Ctrl M	⌘ M
Object Inspector	Ctrl Shift ` (back single quote)	⌘ Shift ` (back single quote)

Director Menu (Mac only)   **Mac**

Hide Director	⌘ H
Hide Others	⌘ Shift H
Quit Director	⌘ Q
Preferences	⌘ U

Help Menu   **Windows**   **Mac**

Director Help	F1	F1

INDEX

INDEX

INDEX

INDEX

W

X

Macromedia Press...helping you learn what the Web can be

Training from the Source

Macromedia's Training from the Source series is the only series on the market that was created by insiders at Macromedia and modeled after Macromedia's own training courses. This series offers you a unique training approach that introduces you to the major features of the software you are working with and guides you step by step through the development of real-world projects.

Each book is divided into a series of lessons. Each lesson begins with an overview of the lesson's content and learning objectives and is divided into short tasks that break the skills into bite-size units. All the files you need for the lessons are included on the CD that comes with the book.

Macromedia Authorware 6:
Training from the Source
By Orson Kellogg and Veera Bhatnagar
ISBN 0-201-77426-7 • 568 pages • $49.99

Macromedia ColdFusion MX:
Training from the Source
By Kevin Schmidt
ISBN 0-321-16224-2 • 304 pages • $44.99

Macromedia Director 8.5 Shockwave
Studio 3D: Training from the Source
By Phil Gross and Mike Gross
ISBN 0-201-74164-4 • 800 pages • $44.99

Macromedia Dreamweaver MX:
Training from the Source
By Khristine Annwn Page
ISBN 0-201-79929-4 • 560 pages • $44.99

Macromedia MX eLearning Advanced:
Training from the Source
By Jeffrey Bardzell
ISBN 0-201-79536-1 • 488 pages • $44.99

Macromedia Fireworks MX:
Training from the Source
By Patti Schulz
ISBN 0-201-79928-6 • 312 pages • $44.99

Macromedia Flash MX ActionScripting:
Advanced Training from the Source
By Derek Franklin and Jobe Makar
ISBN 0-201-77022-9 • 616 • $44.99

Macromedia Flash MX:
Training from the Source
By Chrissy Rey
ISBN 0-201-79482-9 • 472 pages • $44.99

Macromedia Flash MX FreeHand 10
Studio: Training from the Source
By Brad Kozak
ISBN 0-201-77502-6 • 304 pages • $44.99

Macromedia FreeHand 10: Training
from the Source
By Tony Roame and Subir Choudhury
ISBN 0-201-75042-2 • 472 pages • $44.99

Other Macromedia Press Titles

Advanced ColdFusion MX
Application Development
By Ben Forta
ISBN 0-321-12710-2 • 1200 pages • $49.99

Macromedia Flash MX Creative Web
Animation and Interactivity
By Derek Franklin
ISBN 0-321-11785-9 • 952 pages • $44.99

Macromedia Flash MX: Creating
Dynamic Applications
By Michael Grundvig, et al
ISBN 0-321-11548-1 • 504 pages • $44.99

Macromedia Showcase:
Flash Interface Design
By Darci DiNucci
ISBN 0-0-321-12399-9 • 304 pages • $34.99

www.peachpit.com

WWW.PEACHPIT.COM

Quality How-to Computer Books

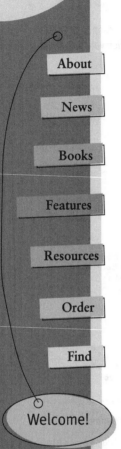

About

News

Books

Features

Resources

Order

Find

Welcome!

Visit Peachpit Press on the Web at www.peachpit.com

- Check out new feature articles each Monday: excerpts, interviews, tips, and plenty of how-tos

- Find any Peachpit book by title, series, author, or topic on the Books page

- See what our authors are up to on the News page: signings, chats, appearances, and more

- Meet the Peachpit staff and authors in the About section: bios, profiles, and candid shots

- Use Resources to reach our academic, sales, customer service, and tech support areas and find out how to become a Peachpit author

Peachpit.com is also the place to:

- Chat with our authors online
- Take advantage of special Web-only offers
- Get the latest info on new books